SHREDDING

the TAPESTRY

of MEANING

Harvard
East
Asian
Monographs
178

SHREDDING

the TAPESTRY

of MEANING

the poetry

and poetics of

Kitasono Katue (1902–1978)

John Solt

Published by the Harvard University Asia Center
and distributed by Harvard University Press
Cambridge, Massachusetts, and London 1999

The Harvard University Asia Center publishes a monograph series and, in coordination with the Fairbank Center for East Asian Research, the Korea Institute, the Reischauer Institute of Japanese Studies, and other faculties and institutes, administers research projects designed to further scholarly understanding of China, Japan, Vietnam, Korea, and other Asian countries. The Center also sponsors projects addressing multidisciplinary and regional issues in Asia.

Printed in the United States of America

Library of Congress Cataloging-in-Publication Data
Solt, John, 1949–
    Shredding the tapestry of meaning : the poetry and poetics of
  Kitasono Katue (1902–1978) / John Solt.
       p.   cm.
  Includes bibliographic references and index.
  ISBN 0-674-80733-2 (alk. paper)
    1. Kitasono, Katsue, 1902---Criticism and interpretation.
  2. Experimental poetry--History and criticism.   I. Title.
  PL832.I85Z87   1999
  895.6'144--dc21   98-45848
                                     CIP

Index by Sallie W. Steele

♾ Printed on acid-free paper

Last number below indicates year of this printing
08 07 06 05 04 03 02 01 00 99

for my father and mother

ACKNOWLEDGMENTS

This book is the product of a long time and the help of many people.

First, I acknowledge my continuing debt to three professors who have given freely of their knowledge and time and without whom this project would never have been completed. I thank Howard Hibbett (Harvard University), my dissertation advisor, for being a model mentor and for his encouragement to study Japanese avant-garde poetry. I am also fortunate to have profited from the immense learning of Stephen Owen (Harvard University), whose comments and direction, especially on theoretical matters, forced me to rethink many crucial points. My debt to Masao Miyoshi (University of California at San Diego) is immeasurable; he introduced me to concepts and issues which became the basis for many of the questions that this study aims to answer, and because he has provided me with the most engaging paradigm of the contemporary intellectual.

I also profited immensely from friends and colleagues who were kind enough to read the book and offer suggestions. They include Professors Sumie Jones (Indiana University), William Johnston (Wesleyan University), and Donald Stone, Jr. (Harvard University); poets Morgan Gibson, Uri Hertz, and Jeff Gold; and the anonymous referees.

I gratefully acknowledge the following organizations for their support: the United States Department of Education for a Fulbright-Hays Fellowship, which enabled me to live in Japan and conduct the research for the dissertation that eventually became this book; the Edwin O. Reischauer Institute of Japanese Studies at Harvard University for a grant to continue work on the project in Japan; and Amherst College for a Faculty Research Award that allowed me to return to Japan and update and revise the manuscript.

I thank the staffs of the following libraries who graciously helped me find materials relevant to the book: (United States) Harvard-Yenching Library, Beinecke Library at Yale University, and Robert Frost Library at Amherst College; (Japan) Nihon Kindai Bungakukan, Kokkai Toshokan, Chūō

Toshokan, Shōwa Joshi Daigaku Kindai Bunko, Keiō Daigaku, Tokyo Daigaku, and Musashino Bijutsu Daigaku. Unfortunately, many of the primary and secondary materials on Japanese avant-garde poetry published before and during the war are not in any public collections.

My research was immeasurably enhanced and simplified after I met Torii Shōzō, poet and VOU member, and Fusako, his wife, and gained access to their renowned collection. Shōzō's deep affection for Katue was an inspiration. Likewise, it was a great pleasure to interview Katue's wife of 44 years, Hashimoto Ei (Eiko), a number of times before she passed away in November 1987. Since then, their only child, Akio, has been equally cooperative.

I thank John Ziemer for his editorial skills and his patience. Any errors in the book are, of course, my responsibility alone.

I thank the following institutions and individuals for granting permission to reproduce objects for which they hold the copyright (the numbers in parentheses refer to the figures in this book):

Eishōji Temple, Asama (5)
Uji-Yamada Shiritsu Shōgyō Kōtō Gakkō archives (6)
Torii Fusako (8)
Haruyama Yukio (12)
Chiba Sen'ichi (20)
Yamamoto Toshio (32)

I especially wish to thank Hashimoto Akio for giving me permission to reproduce all the images for which he holds the copyright or other ownership rights.

I also thank Sachiko Sekine and our children, Ken and George, for their patience during the research and writing of this book.

List of people interviewed, in alphabetical order:
(abbreviations used)

KK   Kitasono Katue
MB   poet in Katue's Arcueil Club of 1932–34; published in *Madame Blanche*.
VOU   poet in Katue's VOU Club (1935–40; 1946–47; 1949–78); published in *VOU*.
WW2   poet published by Katue during the Pacific War (1941–45) in *Shin gijutsu*, *Shin shiron*, or *Mugi tsūshin*.

(* = interview conducted in the United States; all others took place in Japan)

Aida Tsunao (poet); Andō Kazuo (VOU); Arima Akihiko (WW2); Atake Yoshio (junior high school classmate of KK); Chiba Sen'ichi (professor; wrote encyclopedia entries on KK); Claus Clüver (concrete poetry expert, professor); Robert Creeley (published KK's *Black Rain* in 1954)*; Ema Shōko (MB; VOU); Fujita Akira (scholar; journalist); Fujitomi Yasuo (wrote book on KK; edited KK's posthumous works); Fukuda Kazuhiko (VOU); Allen Ginsberg (poet)*; Gonokuchi Reiji (historian of KK's hometown, Asama; distant relative); Haruyama Yukio (wrote preface and published KK's first book in 1929; poet); Hashimoto Akio (KK's son; economist); Hashimoto Chiyo (KK's sister-in-law); Hashimoto Ei (KK's wife); Hashimoto Teruko (KK's daughter-in-law); Hattori Shinroku (author, artist); Hishinuma Nobuhiko (artist); Horiuchi Reiko (VOU); Ikeda Tatsuo (artist; first heard of Dali in KK's art criticism); Irie Kiyoshi (editor, journalist); Ishida Ichirō (VOU; composed music for KK poems); Itasaka Gen (professor of Japanese literature); Itō Isao (VOU); Itō Motoyuki (VOU); Jō Naoe (MB); Jōkō Midori (editor of art journals for which KK wrote criticism); Kagiya Yukinobu (scholar, critic); Kambayashi Michio (poet); Kamijō Takejirō (VOU); Katagiri Yuzuru (poet); Katō Kōjirō (junior high school classmate of KK); Kawabe Gen (poet); Kikushima Tsuneji (MB); Kiyohara Etsushi (VOU); Kobayashi Yoshio (MB, VOU, WW2); Kodaira Yoshio (VOU); Kodama Sanehide (scholar; edited Ezra Pound–KK letters); Kondō Azuma (MB); Kuroda Iri (VOU); James Laughlin (published KK in New Directions from 1938)*; Matsuoka Seigō (interviewed KK with Sugiura Kōhei); Matsushita Isao (composed music for KK poems); Miyoshi Toyo'ichirō (poet); Mori Fumiko (poet, singer); Morihara Tomoko (VOU); Morimoto Hidekazu (VOU); Morisaki Masuo (mathematics professor; work colleague of KK); Muroga Motoichi (wrote B.A. thesis at Tokyo University on KK); Nagayasu Shūichi (VOU, WW2; KK's closest friend for many years); Nakada Yoshie (artist; painted KK's only oil portraits, 1940 and 1958); Nakahara Sen (son and successor to Nakahara Minoru, KK's employer, 1935–78); Nakano Ka'ichi (poet, doctor, scholar of Japanese avant-garde poetry); Nakayama Yō (poet); Nishi Taku (VOU); Nishimatsu Fuei (shamisen musician who arranges and sings KK poems); Oda Kurō (publisher of KK's selected poems); Ogihara Toshitsugu (composed music to KK poems); Ohie Toshio (designed special edition of two KK posthumous poem books); Okada Tadashi (colleague of KK; traveled abroad with him in 1964); Okazaki Katsuhiko (VOU); Okunari Tatsu (VOU); Onchi Kunio (son of Onchi Kōshirō, artist who designed two KK books); Ōnishi Takashi (mayor of Asama, KK's hometown); Ōno (also, Ohno) Kazuo (founder of butō dance; acquaintance of KK); Ōno Susumu (professor of Japanese literature and linguistics); Ōnuki Banyō (professional haiku teacher); Ōshima Hakkō (MB, VOU); Mary de Rachewiltz (Ezra Pound's daughter); Kenneth Rexroth (poet, critic); Sakaki Nanao (poet)*; Sakuramoto Tomio (educator; leading critic of war poetry); Sasaki Kikyō (bibliophile; published two KK books); Satō Saku (scholar; introduced surrealism with KK in late 1920s); Seki Shirō (VOU); Shibata Minao (composed music for KK's poems); Shimamura Sakutarō (junior high school classmate of KK); Shimizu Masato (VOU); Shimizu Toshihiko (VOU; jazz critic); Shiraishi Kazuko (VOU); Sō Takahiko (poet, KK acquaintance in early 1930s); Sugiura Kōhei (designer; interviewed KK with Matsuoka Seigō); Suzuki Masafumi (photographer, critic, poet); Suwa Yū (VOU); Suzuki Takashi (VOU, theorist with KK for Nikaten avant-garde artists); Taguchi Tetsuya (professor); Takahashi Shōhachirō (VOU); Tanno Sei (MB, VOU); Carol Tinker (poet); Torii Ryōzen (VOU, WW2); Torii Shōzō (VOU; published two of KK's posthumous books; bibliophile); Tsuji Setsuko (VOU); Tsukatani Akihiro (VOU; composed music for KK poems); Tsuruoka Yoshihisa (scholar; edited KK's posthumous work); Uchihori Hiroshi (author); Ueda Osamu (MB); Yamada Arikatsu (VOU, WW2); Yamaguchi Kenjirō (gallery owner; exhibited KK's work); Yamaguchi Yasuhiro (curator, Mie Prefectural Art Museum); Yamamoto Kansuke (VOU, WW2); Yamamoto Toshio (artist); Yatate Takeo (publisher); Yoshihara Sachiko (poet; critical of KK's poetry); Yoshimasu Gōzō (poet); L. C. Vinholes (Concrete poet; link between Brazilian poets and KK); and Watanabe Masaya (first introduced KK poems in a high school textbook).

J.S.

CONTENTS

ILLUSTRATIONS

SHREDDING

the TAPESTRY

of MEANING

INTRODUCTION

Where will the people of the twenty-first century look to discover the most creative impulses in twentieth-century Japanese poetry? Certainly not in rehashes of four centuries of *haikai*. Rather, they will have to look at those Japanese who were themselves cosmopolitan, who had the audacity to ignore the expectations of *Japonisme* that so many Westerners, in their cultural Orientalism, imposed upon the Japanese. This book examines the life, poetry, and poetics of Japan's flamboyant and controversial avant-garde leader, Kitasono Katue (1902–78),[1] whose activity spanned the middle fifty years of the twentieth century and left an indelible mark on poetry written in the international idiom.

In spite of numerous volumes in English on twentieth-century Japanese poetry, it is surprising that so little has been written about the most vital antitraditional current, that mishmash of -isms collectively referred to as the "avant-garde" (*zen'ei*)—futurism, dadaism, constructivism, and surrealism before the Pacific War, and abstract expressionism, minimalism, pop, op, and concrete poetry after the war.[2]

To clarify my general approach, a few words should be said about my choice of vocabulary. I have opted to use the word "avant-garde" to mean those movements influenced by the West both before and after the Pacific War. Not only was the word "modernism" not current in Japan until after the war, but "modernism" and "postmodernism" tend to create an artificial division that is more accurately depicted in the Japanese context simply as "prewar" and "postwar." Moreover, the way "postmodern" has been defined in the West—as, for example, a mix of styles without hierarchical ordering—applies in Japan equally well to prewar "modernism" and even in many respects to premodern (Edo period) literature.[3] Imported Western movements were uprooted and transplanted and then interacted with the vibrant Japanese tradition, which stretched back over a millennium. This special mix needs to be understood on its own terms.

A story often told by Japanese poets active in the prewar period is that André Breton, founder of the surrealist movement, was shocked to learn in 1936 from a Japanese artist in Paris that 500 poets and painters in Tokyo considered themselves "surrealists."[4] Most books on surrealism in the West, however, continue to treat the movement as if it had never existed in Asia. The reasons for this neglect are themselves worthy of consideration. Despite an active history of exchanges between Western and Japanese avant-garde poets since the early 1930s—which made their work quite accessible to one another—scholars in the West have for the most part been introducing more traditionalist Japanese poets, not those associated with the avant-garde West. Given a choice between Japan as the "exotic Other" and Japan as a creative amalgam of traditional Japan and the West, Westerners have been attracted to the former. This curiosity is understandable, but it has come at a price—namely, the distortion by neglect of a series of imported literary movements and the story they relate of intercultural activity.

Westerners teaching dadaism and surrealism invariably register surprise and amusement when told about the movements that thrived in Japan in the two decades preceding the Pacific War, claiming that books on the subject omit mention of Japan. This book was written partially to dispel the widespread misconception that futurism, dadaism, surrealism, and other avant-garde movements spread only in the West. Much groundwork still needs to be done.

I have chosen to concentrate on one poet, Kitasono Katue, and trace his life, poetry, and poetics. I could have focused on any of a dozen fine poets active before the war—such as Takiguchi Shūzō (1903–79), Nishiwaki Junzaburō (1894–1982), Kondō Azuma (1904–88), Haruyama Yukio (1902–94), Sagawa Chika (1911–36), or Yamanaka Sansei (Chiruu or Tiroux; 1905–77)—I found Kitasono Katue, however, to be the most original poet among them, especially because of the esthetic thread that wove through his poems, essays, book designs, and photographs; his poetics, which were strict and yet allowed for perceptive playfulness; and most of all the sheer quality of his poetry. In this book, I examine Katue's work in terms of the societal context in which he functioned and the constraints under which he worked. These include not only the obvious pressure of the war, which especially impinged between 1939 and 1945, but also the on-and-off neglect by the poetry establishment, which forced him to publish almost exclusively through the coteries he led. Though focusing on Katue, I use him as a window to look at the literary activity of his colleagues and their poetry circles. Especially in Chapter 6 on the wartime years, I stress that Katue's case is not unusual, since almost every Japanese poet responded similarly to that oppressive situation.

Katue is relatively understudied in Japan, perhaps because his literary activity abroad has been either inaccessible or alien to critics at home. The neglect, however, gave me added incentive to view his domestic and foreign production in relation to one another. Now that his generation has mostly departed, interest in writers of the prewar era has steadily been growing.

Generally speaking, literary studies in Japan focus more on the presentation than on the interpretation of data. This is partly because of restricted access to most archival holdings. University libraries, for example, are rarely open to the public or even to scholars from other institutions. Therefore, scholars tend to regard the possession of a private library as a key source of legitimacy. Some zealously guard texts from those whom they consider rivals. This atmosphere takes on added significance in the subfield of prewar avant-garde literary studies, because many literary magazines were published in small print runs and seldom circulated outside Tokyo (the center of almost all the movements). Few personal libraries in Tokyo survived the wartime firebombing. Therefore, even such an act as publishing the tables of contents from a few rare magazines of the 1920s and 1930s has been considered a valuable scholarly enterprise.

The presentation of data is also highly regarded because interpretation and evaluation tend to be held in low esteem as too subjective and conjectural. Western studies usually take a bird's-eye view of a subject and search for an overriding theory with universal applicability. This study of Kitasono Katue takes a methodological approach between the two sides, presenting data from a microscopic viewpoint, while also raising pertinent, macroscopic questions about the particular nature of intercultural transmissions.

I never met Katue, but to trace his roots I visited his birthplace several times, and to gain a deeper understanding of his life, poetry, and poetics, I interviewed over 100 people who had known him personally or who had had a connection with his literary activities. Because the subject of this book is a poet who lived until 1978 and not a figure of remote antiquity, it seemed advisable to meet the many poets, artists, photographers, musicians, and others who had worked with Katue from the 1920s until his death. This study therefore draws to a large extent on information of an oral-biographic nature. One of the benefits of interviewing people from three generations was that I glimpsed how Katue changed over time. For example, colleagues from the 1920s and 1930s told me that Katue would get into lengthy, heated discussions about poetry, whereas younger poets who worked with him only after the war or near the end of his life said he never engaged in such discussions at their monthly meetings. If I had started this project a decade later, when many of those who knew him before the war would have been dead, I am sure that a quite different portrait of Katue would have emerged.

I was fortunate in receiving the cooperation of his family and friends, as well as the critics of his poetry. The Japanese poetry world (*shidan*) is every bit as factionalized as the political world it often appears to ignore. As a foreigner, I took advantage of my marginal status and talked to people who refuse to talk to each other. Although I became close to my subject and praise Katue at times, as do others moved by his work, on occasion I am as critical of him as his harshest opponents. Katue's writing tends to polarize readers, and I attempt to evaluate him in terms of what he was writing at a given time, and not in an absolute manner.

Immersing myself in his life and works, I decided to read not only his important poetry and essays, which were available in print, but also to cull out-of-print writings and drawings for a broader picture of his activities. It is often with the more ephemeral and obscure publications that one glimpses the extremes of a writer and gains insight into the way he or she ticks. I was fortunate in being the only person outside Katue's nuclear family allowed to read his wartime diaries (analyzed in Chapter 6).

The hardest part of the research was locating Katue's patriotic poetry, which had been written with prompting from the government during World War II. When I began this study, I believed that Katue had resisted penning patriotic poetry, as he and others had insisted in print. It was only after meeting many people and discussing a multitude of issues that I ascertained the breadth of his involvement. Ferreting out Katue's seven patriotic poems from public and private collections was a laborious process.[5]

Having accumulated material about Katue from before, during, and after the war, I decided to analyze his poems in light of his entire production. Dissatisfied for the most part with the literary histories written in Japan on the avant-garde in general and on Katue in particular, I have re-evaluated the arguments of scholars, especially regarding key aspects of dadaism, surrealism, and patriotic poetry.

I have not used the book as a framework to legitimize the universality of any currently popular trend of literary theory, using Katue as the Japanese model. A theory evolves or devolves into the next one, and interest in an author's work seen only through one lens tends to recede with the demise of the theory. Some readers may find my unwillingness to pull everything into one neat theoretical package to be a weakness of the book. My goal, however, is to establish a firmer understanding of the life, times, and work of Kitasono Katue. As opposed to an overarching theory, I deal with a series of issues relevant to specific contexts. In the final chapter I do relate Katue's poetics to theorizing by Michael Riffaterre, Roland Barthes, and Marjorie Perloff to suggest Western strategies that have been devised for interpreting modernist and postmodernist abstract poetry like Katue's, but on the whole I am not aiming to interpret his work through the lens of other critics.

In any case, innovative theorizing is necessary to better account for what it means to import literary methods from one culture, in this case the prewar West, into another culture, in this case Japan. Until recently, the power and prestige of the hegemonic West have dictated the terms of discourse on matters literary, political, economic, and military. But literary theorizing has not adequately taken into account the particular ambivalences encountered by those importing and adapting literary movements on the neglected margins, as opposed to those holding the reins at the centers of origination.

For example, dadaism and surrealism originated in the West; hence the measure or standard of what is Dada or surreal becomes a construct of the West. But to judge someone an authentic dadaist or surrealist in Tokyo (or in Eastern Europe, South America, Africa, and elsewhere), one would need to define the measure further in terms of the degree of deviation from the norm developed at the movement's place of origin. Otherwise, a poet's originality paradoxically would be acknowledged only when it was imitative, and even composition in one's native language would be simply a "translation" of method. Japanese adaptation or deviation from the Western norm is the most reliable measure of originality, but it has often been perceived as misunderstanding or inept copying. There are numerous other theoretical concerns peculiar to the process of importation; for example, importers have to establish not only a foreign movement but also their claims to legitimacy in introducing it—their licenses to advocate, so to speak—whereas for the originators their manifestos and genealogies are ample proof. Conversely, the complexities—both positive and negative—involved in importing were rarely accessible to the West, the dominant culture. I believe that the foundation laid in this book raises questions pertinent to a comprehensive theory that would adequately encompass the experience of the Japanese avant-garde. That theory would take into account the societal constraints imposed at home, such as the emperor system, and the paradoxical bind of double alienation—from mainstream Japanese poetry and from the Western movements that so influenced these poets.

I envision two main audiences for this book—readers with an interest in Japan and those with an interest in poetry—and I have not addressed myself exclusively to one group or the other. Japan specialists may have preferred more information than I provide in certain cases about literary developments in the West. Although I try to make the point that the avant-garde is of vital importance to twentieth-century culture, having been the fountainhead for many styles and motifs that later became popular, I do not dwell in detail on the significance of figures such as Ezra Pound, William Carlos Williams, Charles Olson, and Kenneth Rexroth, all of whom at one time or another lavished praise on Katue's poetry. I take it for granted that the reader is fairly well informed about them; if not, information on them is easily available elsewhere.[6] In a similar vein, readers of poetry and criticism who know little of Japan may occasionally feel at a loss, but I have tried to rectify that situation by adding a few, brief background sections on historical and cultural trends.

The book is organized chronologically and thematically, with an eclectic structure that gives it a multidimensional focus. I conceptualized it metaphorically as a wheel: Katue is the hub, and each chapter, which treats a separate set of issues, functions as a spoke. My chapter arrangements intentionally mimic the cubist experiment in trying to create a third dimension with the illusionistic tools of only two. By viewing Katue from various angles and not glossing over the contradictions, we discover a complex poet whose existence and work raise many questions.

In Chapter 1, I present Katue's roots, based on trips I took to his hometown and meetings I had with his relatives and boyhood friends. I was also fortunate to have access to his school records. Katue did not return to his hometown for the last forty years of his life, but an understanding of his family background and childhood provides a starting point for this study.

In Chapters 2 and 3, I discuss Katue's role at the forefront of introducing and writing Dada and surreal verse. I place the narrative about him within the larger context of the history of the literary movements in Japan during the 1920s and compare them to the Western versions.

Chapter 4 focuses on Katue's activity in the early 1930s and the three different styles of poetry he developed simultaneously. I examine his leadership of the Alcueil Club of poets and reveal for the first time one of his pen names, Kasuga Shinkurō. Katue's creation of Kasuga has a bearing on the persona we find in his wartime poetry.

Chapter 5 continues the chronological presentation and deals with Katue from the mid-1930s until the Pacific War. I focus on his thirty-year correspondence with Ezra Pound, who enthusiastically introduced Katue's work along with that of his newly formed VOU Club to the West. Ezra Pound the American—a citizen of Japan's declared enemy from 1941 to 1945—lived in Italy before and during the war and was supportive of fascist Italy, Japan's ally. I begin with Katue's letter of self-introduction in 1936. Ezra Pound's subsequent praise of Katue's poetry (in English translation) opened the way for the Japanese poet's reception by other top writers in the West. Pound and "Kit Kat," as he affectionately called Katue, never met in person, but their relationship as revealed through their correspondence provides interesting clues on the two authors and the state of East-West cultural communications in the interwar period. Because of Pound's favorable introduction, Katue became the most highly respected Japanese poet of his generation among avant-garde literati in Europe and North and South America, and he was repeatedly invited to publish with them.[7]

In Chapter 6, I take a close look at Katue's controversial wartime activity and offer a comprehensive analysis of his patriotic poetry. This chapter is even more rigidly chronological than the others in its attempt to gauge what literature was written and what literature could be written as the government's grip tightened on all artistic expression from 1939 to 1945. We also glimpse Katue as revealed in his 1944–45 diary and juxtapose that view with the persona found in his poems. I trace the trajectory of his ideological zigzags from liberal to conservative and, after the war, back to liberal again, not to judge his culpability or complicity, but to demonstrate his responses to the shifting political situations in their complexity.

In Chapter 7, I turn to Katue's life in the postwar period, but turn away from politics to take an in-depth look at his poetic experiments during what

is widely considered his peak period, the early 1950s. I also discuss his appro-
priation of the particle *no* (の), with which Katue fragmented the Japanese
language to an unprecedented degree. Finally, in Chapter 8 I review his role
at the forefront of the international concrete poetry movement from the
1950s through the 1970s. The movement was an attempt to demolish lan-
guage barriers in the new technological age, defined by Marshall McLuhan
as the "global village." Concrete poetry was as vital to this goal as were read-
ings and sound poetry in the cultural renaissance of the late 1960s. Kitasono
caused a mini-incident by declaring the movement dead while it was in full
swing. In retrospect, his pronouncement was prescient. His response was to
start a new genre, "plastic poetry," which were photographed constructions.
His plastic poems were published as book covers and magazine graphics in
over a dozen countries. I trace the development of his photographic activity
from cover layout designs to plastic poems and focus on the relationship of
the photographs to his word poems.

My aim in writing this book has been to inform the general reader unac-
quainted with Kitasono Katue's literary experiments, as well as to satisfy the
expectations of specialists well acquainted with his work in the original.
While disavowing the authorial fallacy (taking at face value what the author
says his poem means), I am nevertheless interested in presenting what the
author thought he was attempting—his poetics—as well as how his work
has been interpreted by others. Although it is fashionable these days to treat
a text as a wholly unique event that transcends what the author knew or
could know about it, I believe that my contextualization approach, based on
literary history, is valid in introducing a relatively unknown poet such as
Kitasono Katue. My time will have been well spent if this book lays a foun-
dation for further study of Japanese avant-garde poetry, and helps later gen-
erations transcend my readings and contribute new interpretations of
Katue's poetry.

1 FROM ASAMA

to

TOKYO

Kitasono Katue was born Hashimoto Kenkichi, the third of five children of Hashimoto Yasukichi (1865–1932) and Hashimoto Ei (1874–1928), on October 29, 1902 (Meiji 35), in Asama village in Mie prefecture. Asama lies in a narrow valley at the confluence of the Isuzu and Asama rivers, which drain into Ise Bay, and is located about three miles from the Ise Shrine, one of the three most sacred Shinto shrines in Japan. The villagers considered themselves *shinryōmin* (people of the gods) and prospered during the nineteenth century when thousands of people made pilgrimages to Ise.[1]

Katue's ancestors were probably low-ranking samurai (*gōshi*).[2] When feudal stipends were eliminated in 1876, his maternal grandfather invested the settlement money in a profitable sake venture. Casks of liquor were delivered by the family's private boat up the Asama River to the pier near their house. Late in life, Katue would recall an oar in his family's backyard that remained from this time.[3]

Katue's grandfathers were brothers, and his parents were first cousins. Katue's father, Yasukichi, one of the better-educated men in Asama, attended the Kōgakukan (now Kōgakukan University). After graduating, he married Hashimoto Ei and was subsequently adopted into her—the richer—side of the family. Yasukichi took over the sake business, run from the house, and expanded sales to include more general necessities such as comestibles and fabrics. Yet, in spite of his efforts, the family fortune declined in comparison to what it had been in Katue's grandfather's time.

Kitasono only wrote about his parents once, in a short article for a Mie prefecture journal. He recalled his father as active in many areas:

In his spare time father made a windmill and a waterwheel to hull the rice he sold. He was a bit of a dilettante who tried his hand at everything. For example, he made an orchard and sold the pears and peaches at the market in Yamada. More interesting were the Bunsen's battery cell he made and the darkroom he set up to develop photos taken with his camera. I also remember that he invented a machine to coat wire and even started work on a telephone. But nothing came of any of them. He was more adept at making potted roses and chrysanthemums; in fact, he was as good as a professional.[4]

Yasukichi was born at the end of the Edo period, and he embodied both the fading Edo-period traditions and the exciting new frontiers of Meiji modernization. Katue took after his father in finding pleasure in that which has no purpose and in being fond of novelties (Yasukichi was the first in Asama to own a bicycle and a wristwatch).[5] Katue respected Yasukichi's technological innovativeness but did not have a high regard for his poetic ability: "[My father] would go around delightfully humming *kyōka* [mad verse] that his friends had composed. He was always making up *Shin-kokinshū*-style waka poems,[6] but they were dreadful. He liked the poem 'Hinkōkō' and would chant it in a muttering voice."[7] Even though Katue was unimpressed with his father's old-fashioned poetry, early and constant exposure to the art gave the young boy a solid foundation in traditional verse. He seemed more interested in taking his father's inventive attitude toward technology and applying it to modern poetry.[8]

Katue's mother, Ei, was eleven years younger than Yasukichi. Skilled at household activities, she could embroider, dye clothes, weave, and cook Western as well as Japanese food.[9] Katue later recalled: "My mother studied English and math and didn't seem like the country woman she was. Her textbooks from then remain. I still have a manuscript of the *Shin-kokinshū* style poems she wrote."[10]

Although they owned a camera,[11] there are no extant family photos besides the one taken, without Yasukichi, at a studio in Ise City around 1905 (Fig. 1). The oldest son, Heihachi (1897–1935), who became one of the founders of modern sculpture in Japan and a member of the Nihon Bijutsuin (Japan Fine Arts Academy), did individual sketches of his parents and Katue in 1925–26. All of them are dressed in kimono; Yasukichi and Katue have bowls of Japanese tea in front of them, whereas Ei has a Western coffee cup and saucer (Figs. 2–4). Katue had one older sister and one older brother and

Fig. 1   Earliest extant photo (ca. 1905) of Kitasono Katue. From left to right: Katue's paternal grandmother; sister Fumi (twelve years old); Katue (Hashimoto Kenkichi; two years old); mother Ei (twenty-nine); brother Heihachi (seven).

one younger brother and one younger sister.[12] He was closest to Heihachi, his elder brother by five years. In old age, Katue credited Heihachi with being the person who interested him in the arts. Heihachi, an outstanding student in grammar school and agricultural school, started to sculpt after seeing pictures of Egyptian classical carvings and Auguste Rodin's work (introduced in the journal *Shirakaba*) and being exposed to wooden Buddhist figures from the Japanese past.

Heihachi had a reputation for being strict with himself and courteous to outsiders. Although physically frail, he pushed himself relentlessly. According to Katue, "At home Heihachi was reckless. For example, he fasted, he swam until he almost drowned, he got zealous about jogging, and he even used to jump into the river in freezing weather. For him it was all an ascetic ritual."[13]

In Heihachi's short lifetime, he sculpted only about one hundred, mostly small, wooden figures; many have unusually compelling and vital expressions and are of villagers, animals, and sages from Taoist and Zen lore (Fig. 5).[14] Heihachi often visited the Zen temple Eishōji in Asama and soon proclaimed himself enlightened, a proclamation that is uncommon even among accomplished monks.[15] Heihachi continued to sculpt energetically until one day in 1935 when he was seized by a brain hemorrhage while being interviewed by a journalist in his Asama studio. His death, at the age of thirty-eight, was a great blow to Katue.

Katue went to Shigō Sonritsu Jinjō Kōtō Shōgakkō (Shigō Village Normal Elementary School) in Asama for six years. Both boys and girls attended the school, but it was not coeducational; they studied in separate classrooms. Katue was bright, ranking third of forty-four students. He took courses in ethics, Japanese, arithmetic, Japanese history, geography, science, library, singing, physical education, and crafts. Katue at one time or another received at least a grade of 9 (of a possible 10) in each subject, and he had an overall average of 8.61 for the six years. The students' conduct was also evaluated. Contrasting with his strong academic performance is his consistently low score for conduct. Other students who did well in their coursework had high marks for conduct. We can infer that Katue was academically sharp, displaying a capacity to achieve in all subjects, but was unruly in his behavior.[16]

Yasukichi had hoped Katue would become a merchant. Heihachi, before deciding to become a sculptor, had spent three years in agricultural school.

Figs. 2–4   Ink drawings by Hashimoto
Heihachi, 1925–26. (*upper left*) mother, Ei;
(*upper right*) father, Yasukichi; (*lower left*)
brother, Katue

Rather than following in his footsteps, however, Katue went to Uji-Yamada Shiritsu Shōgyō Gakkō (Uji-Yamada Municipal School of Commerce; abbreviated Yama-shō), a three-year technical school. Katue received a conventional education in a rural area and wore kimono to school along with the other children (Fig. 6)—years later, he would become known among the avant-garde in Tokyo for always being impeccably dressed in the latest Western attire. According to the recollections of three Yama-shō classmates, Katue was quiet and neither had many friends nor was conspicuous in class.[17] He was skillful at *kendō*, in which he displayed fine posture. Katue also participated in tennis and track (baseball was not introduced until six years after he graduated).

Katue's performance at Yama-shō differed dramatically from that at Shigō Elementary School. He slipped from being a first-rate student to being slightly below average and was not outstanding in any subject.[18] The curriculum consisted of courses in ethics, reading, composition, calligraphy, arithmetic, algebra, use of the abacus, geometry, bookkeeping, merchandising, commerce, law and economics, English, and physical education. His conduct was consistently average.

Katue seems to have had no early aptitude for English as he encountered it in the textbooks geared for business.[19] Ironically, two decades later some of the world's leading poets would read his poems and essays in his own English translations. Katue's performance did improve in reading and composition, two other courses that had a close bearing on his future career as a writer. By the time he graduated, they were his strongest subjects, and he received a grade of 80 percent in each. In the more business-oriented classes such as arithmetic, abacus use, merchandising, bookkeeping, and commerce, however, Katue's performance ranged from fair to poor. This was perhaps a result of incompetence or of rebellion against his father.[20] Katue's grade of 27 percent in abacus use his final year should have dashed Yasukichi's hope that his son was material for the business world.

But his father seems not to have heeded the warning signal. After Katue graduated in 1918, the fifteen-year-old boy went to work in Osaka for a company that sold hospital machinery.[21] He hated the job and returned to Asama after a few months. Taniguchi Eizō, a visitor to Katue's house at this period, gives this description of him: "Unlike the other village boys working outside in farm clothes, Katue would study seated indoors and wearing a

Fig. 5   Hashimoto
Heihachi, sculpture
of Boddhidharma
(first Zen patriarch).
Ca. 1930, wood, about
16 inches tall. Eishōji,
Asama.

formal kimono. Even as a teenager he exuded a cultural air and had a reputation in the village for being quite knowledgeable, but he never impressed me as someone who would later become famous."[22]

In 1919 Katue secured a minimal allowance from his parents and set out for Tokyo to attend college and become a newspaper reporter.[23] Once in the capital, he went to live with Heihachi in Kanda. He passed the entrance examination to Chūō Daigaku Senmonbu Keizai Gakka, the three-year program in the Economics Department of the Technical College affiliated with Chūō University. Student files containing records of grades went up in flames during the Great Kantō Earthquake of 1923, and no evidence survives of Katue's performance. The only surviving pre-1923 records for Chūō University are class lists, which were kept in a fireproof safe. Hashimoto Kenkichi (Kitasono Katue) is listed for 1919 and 1920, but not for 1921. It cannot be determined if he attended more than one year and a day, but he dropped out before graduating. Altogether Katue spent nine to ten years in school; beyond that, he was self-educated. He was only the second person from Asama to attend college.[24]

Once Katue found his bearings in the city and began college, he left Heihachi and moved in with two roommates. At this time, he was reading the poetry of Satō Haruo (1892–1964), Murō Saisei (1889–1962), Hagiwara Sakutarō (1886–1942), and Senge Motomaro (1888–1948), who were among the leading poets aiming to forge a new poetics for the age, and even started composing some short poems himself. He was still, however, far from seriously considering becoming a poet.[25] In the next few years, Katue changed his Tokyo residence a half-dozen times. While attending school, he temporarily boarded in the house of haiku poet Hara Sekitei (1886–1951), but he had no interest in haiku at the time and did not become his disciple. He occasionally visited the sentimental poet Ikuta Shungetsu (1892–1930), but did not become his disciple either. Although Katue was to learn from and be influenced by many poets in the course of his career, he never had a mentor (*sensei*) in the traditional Japanese manner. Disapproval of Heihachi's subservience to his sculptor-master, Satō Chōzan (1888–1963), possibly influenced Katue in this regard, because Satō had made Heihachi dissect a cat before sculpting one. The result was a masterpiece that earned Heihachi a prize, but Katue condemned Satō's method and deplored his brother's willingness to comply.[26]

吉健本橋

Fig. 6   Katue (Hashimoto Kenkichi), fifiteen years old. Yama-shō graduation album, 1917.

In 1922 Katue sent four poems from Tokyo to *Kōyū*, the student magazine of his alma mater Yama-shō. They are his earliest surviving poems and all in a similar style. The following can serve as an example.

> *Hill*
>
> oh hill!
> yet it's sad
> oh hill growing still,
>
> in tranquil antiquity
> concealing
> those gold tiles
> in your breast
>
> oh hill
> in eternal sleep,
>
> you speak not
> you sing not
>
> because it is
> this pitiful
> present life's
> curse,
>
> it's
> the shape
> of eternity,
>
> it's
> the form
> of a fierce being
> pitiful because it's
> a song of extinction.
>
> August 18, 1922[27]

Typical of the romantic groping found in much Taishō-period verse, the language, tone, and metaphorical treatment of the subject, "hill," are conventional. By using the Buddhist words *gense* (this life) and *yōgō* (eternity), Katue invokes a traditional worldview. The emotionally charged words— *kanashiku* (sadness), *shohei no mukashi* (tranquil antiquity), *mune ni hime* (buried in breast), *itamashiki* (pathetic), and *aware* (pitiful)—overload the poem. Katue does not create an effect in the reader but names what should be felt. The poem's main value is to mark the starting point from which he would deviate. When he later attacked poets who wrote such orthodox verse, he must also have been belittling the sentimental poet of "Hill."

It is not unusual for a nineteen-year-old to write a conventional poem, especially when sending it to his alma mater. By the 1920s in Japan, there had already been a slow penetration of Western literary and art movements that openly denounced tradition, but they had not yet caught Katue's attention. When they did, he would change his style and discard all traces of old-fashioned rhetoric.

Katue never acknowledged sending these four poems to *Kōyū*. He considered his appearance in the prestigious journal *Bunshō kurabu* (Writing club) to be his literary debut. Forty years later he recalled:

> I wrote to kill time. They were stupid and infantile poems, but one day I selected fifty from my notebook. I don't know why, but I took them to Ikuta Shungetsu, even though I didn't have a letter of introduction. Ikuta was about ten years older than I was and already a well-known poet. He leafed through the poems, told me I should show them to Saijō Yaso [1892–1970], and wrote a letter of introduction for me. A few days later I went to Saijō's house and showed him the poems. He said, "You are very talented," and I was elated on the way home. Years later I found out that was Saijō's standard line to any visitor who went bearing poems.[28]

At the time Katue probably respected Ikuta's maudlin verse, although it must have embarrassed him later; hence his evasiveness about the reasons he knocked on Ikuta's door.[29] In any case, Katue returned to him and reported what Saijō, a well-known lyrical poet, had said. Ikuta was generous and offered to contact Katō Takeo (1888–1956), novelist and editor of *Bunshō kurabu*, which had been in existence for eight years; past contributors included the poets Hagiwara Sakutarō, Kaneko Mitsuharu (1895–1975), and Miki Rofū (1889–1964) and the novelists Tokuda Shūsei (1871–1943) and Kawabata Yasunari (1899–1972), as well as two mysterious authors named ABC and XYZ. One poem by Hashimoto Kenkichi (Katue) appeared in the September 1924 issue in a section titled "Four Poems by Four Up-and-Coming Poets."[30] Twenty-one-year-old Katue initially appeared on the Tokyo literary scene as the writer of fresh, new-style poetry, laying the foundations of his avant-garde identity.

Night Mechanist

the café girl
is completely transparent
continuing her pink breathing

> she makes her expensive finger shine
> and hides mint-colored talk
> in a lobelia leaf
> while playing the table's piano
> dreamer of chairs and curtains
> bohemian of a pitiful city.

———————

> from the shadow of curaçao
> and peppermint
> she flashes a seven-colored heart
> seducer with stunning matches
> on stove chimneys
> ties passion ribbons
> and dissolves her lovers
> into cash register buttons—
> mechanist of splendid night[31]

The "café girl," a bohemian stereotype of the new woman in the Roaring Twenties of Japan, was a bar hostess, not a waitress, and the café was the forerunner of today's cabaret. Katue conveys the impression of a woman who is enticing but dangerous. He endows her with ethereal, romantic qualities—she is "transparent" and "pink breathing"—while simultaneously seeing her as a femme fatale who "dissolves her lovers / into cash register buttons."

"Night Mechanist" stands out from the other new poems featured in the same issue of *Bunshō kurabu* because of a conspicuous typographical feature—his use of ten words in the katakana script (the common convention for writing foreign loanwords in Japanese) within the poems eighteen lines. The English word *mechanist* (written in *katakana* メカニスト) appears both in the title and at the end of the poem. From this time on, Katue mixed English and French words in his verse, even though his usages were occasionally stilted or in error.

The line "dreamer of chairs and curtains" may sound odd today, but for most Japanese in 1924, chairs and curtains were still rare and glamorous articles from the West.[32] The mention of other exotic items such as "table," "piano," "curaçao," "peppermint," "stove," "ribbons," and "cash register" in describing the café setting demonstrates the poet's familiarity with the bohemian subculture and fashionable life (or at least a claim of familiarity).

The use of *lobelia*, a rather uncommon plant in both Japan and the West, is noteworthy because its conspicuousness foreshadows Katue's *shuchishugi* (intellectualism); he was not adverse to mystifying and confusing the reader. A sense of playfulness and "putting one over the reader" with such obscurities is evident in "Night Mechanist." Writing without the desire to be completely understood, Katue was demonstrating the avant-gardist's characteristic "antagonistic stance."[33]

This tendency of Katue to obfuscate becomes more pronounced in his poems of a few years later in which he strings together dissimilar images, each clear by itself but unclear in its relation to any previous or subsequent image. The poems of this period, however, demonstrate a unified relationship among the elements contained in the subject matter, often identifiable by the title. Here, "Night Mechanist" refers to "the café girl" of the first line who is described throughout the poem. Katue's flexibility in choosing words and arranging them would subsequently become a cornerstone of his poetry. Indeterminacy focuses attention on the word, imbues it with immediacy, and retrieves the poetic function from the reservoir of ordinary language used as a communicative tool by everyone.

The ideology in "Night Mechanist" is ambivalent: we can see it either as a critique of capitalism with its consumer products and creatures—the café girl as alienated seductress who "dissolves her lovers / into cash register buttons"—or simply as the expression of an adolescent's fascination with a Westernized woman and the objects that surround her. The first, ironic reading is made possible by the loose relationship between the words and their arrangement into lines, on the one hand, and meaning, on the other. Similar to the ambiguous point of view expressed in the poem, the imagery wavers between appearing conscious and unconscious, between being pregnant with meaning or being simply meaningless, such as the seemingly phallic images, "seducer with wonderful *matches*" and "she ties passion *ribbons* / on stove *chimneys*."

Even though "Night Mechanist" is by no means outstanding, the short piece does have admirable features, especially its lucid imagery. "Pink" and "mint-colored" add freshness and immediacy to the poem. Colors are also evoked in the unspecified hues of "seven-colored heart" and "peppermint" (green), "curaçao" (orange), "cash register" (metallic silver or bronze). At this period Katue opted for rare colors; this contrasts with his stubborn adherence to primary colors in his post–World War II poetry.

Katue's poem is a conflation of "Japanese self" and "Western other," a pattern that he would repeat time and again in different poetry experiments. "Night Mechanist" is marked as foreign because of the ten words written in the katakana script. Katue was already aware of "concretism," how the design on the page strikes the reader's eye. Twenty years later the government would ban katakana in an attempt to eradicate the influence of foreign thinking (see Chapter 6). Forty years later Katue would find himself at the forefront of the international avant-garde's concrete poetry movement (see Chapter 8).

2 DADAISM and

GE.GJMGJGAM.PRRR.GJMGEM

The search for an absolute point of origin is as endless as it is fruitless, yet there are relative turning-points that help demarcate the transition from one attitude or movement to another. F. T. Marinetti's "Initial Manifesto of Futurism" is often cited as a starting point for what later snowballed into dadaism, surrealism, and subsequent movements.[1] A French translation was published on the front page of the February 20, 1909, issue of *Le Figaro*. The news traveled rapidly to Japan; a full translation, by an unnamed translator, appeared in the May 1909 issue of the literary journal *Subaru*.[2] Among other proclamations, Marinetti's manifesto glorifies war and calls for the destruction of museums and libraries. At the end of the Japanese version, the translator commented: "How tame the members of *Subaru* are. Ha ha ha ha." *Subaru*'s docility contrasted with this wild news from the West in another respect: whereas the European version aimed at embarrassing the bourgeoisie, the Japanese translation was intended to embarrass the local literati. However speedy the introduction of futurism to Japan may have been, the rate of absorption was understandably much slower.[3]

Twelve years after the article in *Subaru*, Hirato Renkichi (1893–1922) issued his "Nihon miraiha undō dai ikkai no sengen" (First manifesto of Japanese futurism; 1921) and passed it out on the streets of Tokyo. Dadaism had already been introduced a year earlier in the newspaper *Yorozuchōhō*. Shortly thereafter, Tsuji Jun (1884–1944), a poet with anarchist leanings, published *Dada no hanashi* (Dada talk; 1922) and also edited *Dadaisuto Shinkichi no shi* (Poems of dadaist Shinkichi; 1923) by Takahashi Shinkichi (1901–87). Dadaism's arrival in Japan and the emergence in print of self-proclaimed dadaists took only two years. News was now traveling quickly from the West and having a near-immediate effect in winning converts.

Hirato, Tsuji, and Takahashi follow a pattern: each takes the name of a Western movement, whether futurism or dadaism, and embeds it in the title of a work. By doing so, the writer becomes the Japanese authority on the subject. This unconcealed tendency to appropriate what was going on in Western poetry can also be noticed in the titles of magazines dealing with surrealism and other avant-garde currents both before and after the Pacific War.[4] The introducers of these innovative trends gained prestige, but they had less at stake than did the Western originators. For example, Takahashi soon abandoned dadaism for traditional Zen Buddhism. And, in the late 1930s, the militarist government's crackdown on the avant-garde halted its exploratory activity altogether.

Dadaism arose in Europe in 1916 partly as a reaction to the barbarism of World War I. Intellectuals realized that the technological spurt since the Renaissance with its promise of a better future was, on the contrary, culminating in a nightmare of unparalleled proportions, and they blamed all social institutions including *art* for giving a false sense of "civilization."

Japan did not participate in the carnage of World War I; rather, it prospered economically by taking over the Asian markets of the embattled European nations. It was only after the war, with the 1918 rice riots, the recession, and the Great Kantō Earthquake of September 1, 1923, that major economic, political, and social ills surfaced and pushed the nation toward the brink of chaos. Following the immense earthquake in the Tokyo area, which left over 100,000 people dead and 63 percent of the houses in the capital razed by fire, the dadaist wave inundated Japan with great force. The remains of the Edo past disappeared with the earthquake.[5] By early the next year, rebuilding was occurring on a massive scale, and the city took on a new face. To fill the vacuum of the cultural past that had been swept away with the earthquake rubble, contemporary Western art, architecture, design, and literature were imported on a wide scale. Thus dadaism, "destructive" of the tradition, spread easily in the atmosphere of constructing the new.

The Japanese dadaists were reacting essentially to a natural disaster rather than to a man-made one, and this obviated the need for much of the confrontational politics found in Western dadaism. Whereas the Europeans wanted to insult and overturn the bourgeoisie, the Japanese did not zero in on a target; they were more inclined to bemoan the human predicament in general, philosophical terms.[6] The Japanese dadaists also did not provoke the physical skirmishes with the audience or one another found in Western dadaism.[7]

Dadaism in Japan was not completely removed from politics, however. The instability resulting from the post–World War I recession, the rice riots, and the earthquake combined to create a volatile situation that gave impetus to anarchists and socialists. Several of the dadaist poets were left-wingers, or at least associated with radicals. For example, Tsuji Jun, poet and editor, was a close friend of the well-known Taishō (1912–26) anarchist Ōsugi Sakae (1885–1923), until Tsuji's wife, Itō Noe (1895–1923), left him for Ōsugi. Later Itō and Ōsugi paid for their political beliefs—they were tracked down and murdered by the police in the aftermath of the earthquake.[8] Tsuji sensed the danger and left the country the following year, having accepted an invitation to advise a group of young Korean anarchists.[9]

Although Katue later claimed that he had not been a socialist at this time, he did admit that he had been making socialist pamphlets on the second floor of a makeshift publishing house when the earthquake struck. In 1977, the year before he died, he briefly recalled that day:

I wore high *geta* [wooden clogs], took an umbrella, and left my house for Ginza. Looking up, I could tell there would be thundershowers. I remember enormous columns of clouds in the sky over Tokyo Bay. The earthquake scattered those of us who were gathered in a clandestine house, practicing drawing and making pamphlets. I located my brother [Heihachi] who used to commute between the atelier of his mentor, Satō Chōzan, and the Fine Arts Academy, and we evacuated to the countryside.[10]

The Tōkaidō train line, which they would normally have taken to Asama, was not in service because of damage to the tracks, and they made their way to Asama by the roundabout Shin'etsu line. After a short stay with their parents and siblings, the two brothers moved to the outskirts of Nara. Heihachi wanted to spend time researching wooden Buddhist sculptures (Nara has the oldest surviving examples in the world), and Katue accompanied him.

While there, Katue started painting.[11] He also wrote poetry and was published in a local magazine, *Kumo* (Clouds), although he had never met the editor and was not a member of the Kumo group.[12] One of the poems, "Tokai no koi" (City love), is personal and romantic, with echoes of the ancient *Man'yōshū* in the grammar and vocabulary.[13] The poem is similar in tone and diction to "Hill," and Katue was again demonstrating his ability as a traditional poet, without being original or experimental. His proximity to ancient historical sites may have contributed to his adoption of archaic mannerisms. Both "City Love" and "Night Mechanist" were published in 1924, yet decades separate them in language and sensibility. The dissimilarity can be attributed to differences in the stimulations provided by the unchanged lifestyle of the countryside and the fever of modernization in the city. Katue was able to write with facility in both styles.

Tokyo was actively undergoing reconstruction when Katue and Heihachi returned in early 1924 (Fig. 7). They renewed contacts with old friends and settled back into city life. Katue visited the painter and writer Tamamura Zennosuke (dates unknown), whom he had met a few months before the earthquake:

Tamamura made a living painting chrysanthemums and other objects in Japanese style (*Nihon-ga*). He had been in the Fine Arts Academy but, after quitting, was considered a heretic. He was rich and would buy books about new art trends in the West. My first encounter with the Bauhaus was when Tamamura bought all the volumes in the Bauhaus series and showed them to me.[14] He published *Takahara* (Plateau), but gave it up and issued a new art magazine, *Epokku* (Epoch), in which expressionism and cubism were presented with examples of the works.[15]

Besides exposing Katue to new ideas in the arts, Tamamura also introduced him to the Nogawa brothers, Hajime (dates unknown) and Takashi (popularly known as Ryū; 1901–44).[16] Hajime was a few years older than Katue and fond of Russian literature. The Nomura brothers and Katue spent many hours talking about the state of the arts in Japan and abroad, and shortly thereafter moved in together in a European-style house with huge rooms. Katue recalled, "I liked Nogawa Hajime's personality and his knowledge of literature. Soon we became close friends. He played an influential role in exciting me about the world of letters and, consequently, in my becoming a writer instead of a painter."[17]

Hajime mentioned that Ryū had agreed to edit a literary magazine, published with Tamamura's financial backing. A few months later, the magazine *Ge.Gjmgjgam.Prrr.Gjmgem* (abbreviated GGPG) arrived in Katue's mailbox. Ryū's editorial statement was a kind of manifesto:

We want to publish *Epokku* again soon. In the meantime we have decided to issue *Ge.Gjmgjgam.Prrr.Gjmgem* as a way of notifying you. In *Epokku* we put our efforts

Fig. 7　A rare photograph of the two artists-brothers, Hashimoto Heihachi (standing) and Kitasono Katue (seated), ca. 1924

into introducing the latest artistic trends from abroad, but here we won't do that; instead, we will only present our original writing.

Ge.Gjmgjgam.Prrr.Gjmgem is being sent to all the former readers of *Epokku*. It is not for sale. If anyone wants a copy, please let us know. Since it is published irregularly, there will probably be times when it appears three times a month, or only once in three months.

Even if *Epokku* is revived,[18] we are still planning to issue *Ge.Gjmgjgam.Prrr. Gjmgem*. There are people who are interested in asking about the name, but that is unnecessary. (At least according to my interpretation) it is sufficient to understand it with a musical sensitivity. "To add feet to a snake,"[19] for the machine-made, human-like animal dolls who move the quarters within the city, the oscillation frequency and the wave shape of G are appealing.[20]

Nogawa's last sentence uses earthquake and *tsunami* imagery: "move the city . . . oscillation frequency . . . wave shape." Whatever GGPG meant to Nogawa, the name signaled a complete break with literary tradition and the notion that a title should embody meaning. The European dadaists, who had playfully selected an "empty" name for their movement, were at the same time experimenting at their poetry readings with phonic poems dislodged from meaning. Nogawa followed in their footsteps with his chosen string of letters.

Sound poems (syllables without meaning) and soundless poems (poems without letters) had been composed since the late nineteenth century,[21] and Hugo Ball, one of the main dadaists in Zürich, helped popularize them in his live performances.[22] So as not to alienate the audience entirely, Ball gave a brief explanation before reading his work:

With these sound poems we should renounce the language devastated and made impossible by journalism.

We should withdraw into the innermost alchemy of the world, and even surrender the word, in this way conserving for poetry its most sacred domain. We should stop making poems secondhand; we should no longer take over words (not even to speak of sentences) which we did not invent absolutely anew, for our own use.[23]

The fact that the Dada movement originated in neutral Switzerland, and consisted of foreigners from countries on both sides of the conflict—Romania, Italy, France, Hungary, and Germany—may have been a factor in making the Japanese feel they could easily belong. Richard Huelsenbeck, one of the collaborators, expressed the aim of the Zürich dadaists, "Above everything, our art had to be international, for we believed in an Internationale of the Spirit and not in different national concepts."[24]

Huelsenbeck and the others probably conceived of this Internationale of the Spirit as extending as far as Russia. There is no indication that the movement encouraged diversity; for example, a photograph of the "constructivist-dadaist congress in Weimar, 1922" shows a group of all Caucasian men and women.[25] The dadaists were, however, sympathetic to and influenced by the poetry and art of what would later be called the "Third World." According to Hugo Ball, "On March 30th [1916] we put on a magnificent performance of Negro music on the initiative of M. Tristan Tzara."[26] Also, at the June 1922 art show entitled Dada Salon, the dadaist "Philippe Soupault, disguised as a Negro, was a magnificent President of Liberia, visiting the exhibition."[27] Unlike the dadaists who performed Negro music or played the *role* of the President of Liberia, the surrealists a decade later would directly engage Third World poets and artists, including Aimé Césaire, cofounder of the Négritude movement.[28]

The first issue of GGPG, which came out in June 1924, had several distinguishing characteristics besides the long and unpronounceable name written in roman letters on the front cover and in katakana ゲエ・ギムギガム・プルルル・ギムゲム on the back cover. Next to the name of the magazine is written in Esperanto, "La Unua Volumo" (Volume 1). The fourteen pages of text (not counting the cover) are unpaginated and contain short stories, poems, and a one-scene play. This play, "One Cigar," written by Ryū, is the first piece the reader encounters after the table of contents. It begins:

> Characters:
>   A naked human
>   3 persons who show only their heads
> Scenery:
>   A broken-down hut
> On the hut's wall is one window; like an idiot, someone looks up.[29]

Even in these few lines we can see dadaist traits in the absurdity of someone by "a broken-down hut" looking up "like an idiot," and the constructivist possibilities of organizing into dance "a naked human" and "3 persons who show only their heads."

A poem by Kondō Masaji (dates unknown), "For Mr. A's Self-Introduction" ("A-shi no jiko shōkai ni"), is noteworthy because the author spontaneously presents a surrealistic line before the movement had even been introduced to Japan, "From idle tongue's tip, hair grew out."[30] One result of the freedom of imagination let loose by dadaism was the outpouring of such surrealist imagery, an area where the two movements naturally overlap. There is no visual material in the first issue of *GGPG* unless we count the partially concrete poem by Hiraiwa Konji (dates unknown) in which he repeats some of the characters up to seven times, embedding these identical graphs within an arrangement of mixed signs.[31]

Nogawa Ryū kept his promise to publish irregularly; the second issue of *GGPG* came out seven months later, this time with Nogawa as contributor and Hashimoto Kenkichi (Katue) as editor-publisher. Katue was living on a meager allowance sent by his father from Asama, and *GGPG* was the main activity in his life.[32] The delegation of the responsibility to edit *GGPG* indicates that Tamamura Zennosuke, the sponsor, trusted Katue's ability. Or, perhaps, Katue was the only one in the group with enough time to devote to the magazine. With Katue at the helm, the magazine began to appear regularly—*GGPG* was issued monthly for several issues starting with no. 2. From no. 5 on, Nogawa Ryū returned to co-edit with Katue until the magazine folded with the tenth issue on New Year's Day, 1926, because of a lack of funds.[33] No notice that it was the final issue was given.

The *GGPG* poets showed their visual stylishness not only in the typography and arrangement of words and syllables—often upside down and sideways—but also in the color of print and type of paper used: nos. 4, 6, 7, and 8 are printed in cinnabar instead of the customary black ink, and the final two issues, printed on paper containing sulfuric acid, have decomposed to a large extent, as if dramatically embodying the dadaist message on impermanence.

Katue's first contribution to *GGPG* (Fig. 8) was a poem showing him in his city mode:

> Excerpt
>
> CONCEPT *999*
>
> > let everything be a symbol of ruin
> > let everything decay in the realm of cursed existence
>
> so———I put on a tinplate cap
> then walked toward the city
> neither night nor day, behind pale lightrays

with dullness of a slapped-down instant, I walked on

"really boring"
I whispered, and from my enamel-coated belt pulled out a plunger
gripped it tightly and
an ozone smell wafted to my nose

 "ah it's summer"
then I tore to shreds my silver-paper necktie[34]

Traditional vocabulary and sentiment are conspicuously absent from "Concept 999." The first two lines, indented, serve as a motto and summarize Katue's nihilistic philosophy at the time. The negative, world-bedamned indictment emerges with "ruin" (*botsuraku*), "decay" (*kusarete iru*), and "realm of cursed existence" (*norowareta seizonken*), setting the tone for later phrases such as "pale lightrays" (*aojiroi kōsen*), "dullness of a slapped-down instant" (*harareta setsuna no donkansa*), and "really boring" (*jitsu ni taikutsu da*). These sentiments evoke a gloomy psychological state, yet a positive, dynamic vitality also winds through the poem. Katue's use of several action verbs ("put on," "walked," "whispered," "pulled out," "gripped," "wafted," "tore") and his use of colorful, almost science-fiction gear ("tinplate cap," "silver-paper necktie") add an energetic, youthful exuberance to the poem that offsets the nihilistic tone. Present existence is condemned with a few strokes, but what stands in contrast to the ennui is ultimately only flashy clothes, semi-violent gestures, and this new poem.[35]

In "Concept 999" Kitasono is probably not describing his own experiences, but there is enough of a narrative thread to interpret the content as a fantasized scenario of a young person's life in Tokyo. The balance of despondency and enthusiasm creates a tense elasticity that makes the poem one of his most successful of this period. It still retains a vividness and vitality that seem to speak for all disgruntled youth.

Katue's poetry from 1925 to 1929, when he was most influenced by dadaism, often contains a phrase or line that acts as a critical aside and undercuts the poem. It is as if a timed fuse runs through the lines and, at a certain place, detonates the poem in an attempt to destroy the traces of its own creation. These self-critical phrases in Katue's early work are ambiguous and can be interpreted as outwardly directed, general statements about life or as an introspective criticism of the poem itself. In "Concept 999," for example, the line "really boring" doubles in this capacity.

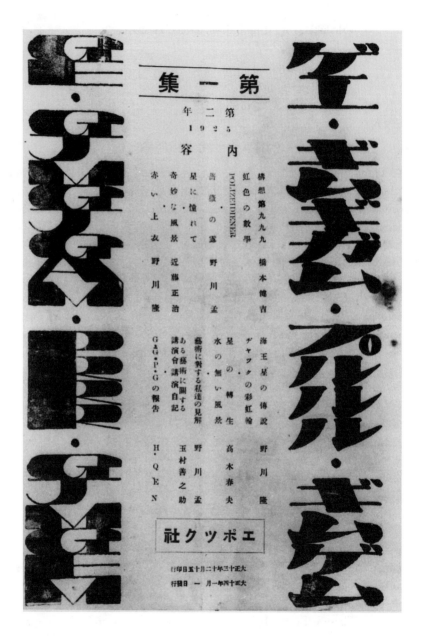

Fig. 8   Cover of *Ge.Gjmgjgam.Prrr.Gjmgem*, no. 2 (2, no. 1: Jan. 1925)

Katue's undermining of the poem fits the dadaist impulse to destroy. European dadaists believed that not only the poem but also the very notion of art itself had to be smashed. Instead of making artifacts that simply attacked the surrounding world but remained precious in themselves, a genuine dadaist would also shine the spotlight of negativity on himself and his creation. This impulse was succinctly summarized by Tristan Tzara when he wrote in reminiscence, "The true Dadaists were against Dada."[36] The Japanese dadaists, although distant from the Western movement in space and culture, were not free of the characteristically European move to separate the authentic ("true" dadaists) from the retrograde and false. Both Western and Japanese dadaists can be seen in this regard as elite groups with a fear of pollution.

Katue had just turned twenty two when "Concept 999" was published, and we can sense that his writing had taken a fresh direction. Katue started publishing poems with a semiotic orientation beginning with the third issue of *GGPG*. In the following example the "(a)" and "(b)" and other letters in parentheses at the end of lines appear to be characters carrying on a half-intelligible conversation amid a flurry of numerical and lexical signifiers:

Electrical Enunciation

JAG·JOT
JAG·JOT
now————on top of the kuppelhorizont
V frequency red light rays and
X frequency violet rays and
Q frequency yellow rays and
P frequency silver light————turned by a steering wheel
TORONTO
TORONTE
TORONTA
————what is the speed of light? (a)
————of course it is 186,000 miles per second (b)
————it's really an excellent situation (a)
————shut up (b)
TORONTO
TORONTA
TORONTE
————is a wavelength 30,907,053? (a)
————shut up (b)

. . . .

if a triangle, it has 3 sides

if a pentagon, 5 sides

. . . .

————if a heptagon, 8 sides————if an octagon, 73 sides (a)

————shut up (b)

S·O·S

T·O·S

Krupphood anti-aircraft guns (100)

Hotchkiss cannons (310)

Vickers rapid-fire guns (500)

automatic battleships (Schuba Dreadnought model) (73,000)

SPAD airplane bombers (9,700)

shiny bullets (786,321)

explodable bullets (50,000)

————are you saying those are necessary supplies for

       Weimar-style fire-rope warfare? (a)

————shut up (b)

piston size: 5,000,000

length of pierce: 77,000

number of explosive collisions: 900,000,000

————it seems something is missing (a)

————P=G (b)

————33,000 (b)

can you ride it? (a)

it's not for riding (b)

X00010,000 horse power (a)

E·&·O·E

E·&·O·E

————that's it (S)

    *0   1   2   3   4   b   O

   *↑ ↓ ↓ ↓ ↑ ↓ ↑ ↑ ↑

    *9 8 7 6 5   a   C

RIRO·RIRA

RORO·OROO

TANKA·TANZ

TATTO·TO·TE·TOTE

~~~~~~~~~~~~~~~~~~~~~~~~~~~~~~~~~

~~~~~~~~~~~~~~~~~~~~~~~~~~~~~~~~~

00,033 (million.grams.is)

~~~~~~

VAN·VAN·VAN·····
·URU·URU·RE
it's getting worse and worse (P)
RUTO·RUTO·FURUUTO
PRINN → RR.RRRRROOO
————I suppose it's a gaseous substance (O)
————I am a lens (B)[37]

Katue's poem is baffling (intentionally so) even when understood in the context of European developments in the arts and the advent of sound poetry. Literary historian Annabelle Melzer sums up the situation in the West around 1916, "The image of the human form was gradually disappearing from the painted canvas. The next step was for poetry to do away with language."[38] Painters turned their attention to nonfigural, abstract subjects and to the processes and materials of the medium itself, partially because of the wide use of the camera with its superior ability to mimic reality. In poetry, the move "to do away with language" came not from any specific technological development, but from a series of frustrations—with the state of the world, with the inability of languages to cross cultural boundaries without translation, and with the ineffectiveness of traditional poetry to reflect adequately the complexity and absurdity of modern life.

Originally, Katue was interested more in becoming a painter than a poet. In "Electrical Enunciation" he paints with language, using signs for their outward shape and sound as much as for their inner content (excluding the enumerated list of armaments, which is laden with judgments, semantics, and value). Katue sprinkles an assortment of scripts and signs into the poem—*kanji*, *hiragana*, *katakana*, roman letters, arabic numerals, arrows, dots, and straight and wiggly lines. As the logical connection between words, phrases, and lines dissolves and meaning recedes, what remains is a swarming field of visual and auditory signifiers. The dadaists encouraged the spontaneous collision of random stimuli to produce a state of simultaneity. The poem is no longer a vehicle for conveying quotidian emotions but an attempt to shake up the psyche of the reader as a symbolic critique of the society.

"Electrical Enunciation" is full of scientific jargon as well as bruitist noise and may initially give one the impression of having stumbled upon an adolescent's notebook of doodles spliced together from school lessons. The words can be perceived as meaningful or meaningless, a state that is achieved

by the rapid and continuous alternation between everyday language and ab-
surdity. As soon as the obvious is grasped—a triangle has three sides and a
pentagon five sides—Katue throws a monkey wrench into normal logic with
a heptagon that has eight sides and an octagon that has seventy-three sides.
In a similarly illogical vein, "TORONTO / TORONTE / TORONTA" is
a pseudo-declension in which Toronto (signifying a city in Canada) is a fixed
name while the word Toronto is mutable, transforming into meaningless
syllables of sound. This doubling technique recalls the *kakekotoba* (pivot
word) of ancient *waka* poetry. Katue had also learned from the dadaists
about privileging chance; "Electrical Enunciation" is his adaptation of the
method using his own peculiar blend of seemingly random signs.

In spite of the fairly compelling audio-visual material in the poem, it is a
mixture of numerous incoherent strands that scatter in various directions
and then fizzle out in isolation. As in "Concept 999," a one-line statement
embedded in the poem—in this case, when the character "(a)" utters, "it
seems something is missing"—can be construed as an introspective, self-
critical comment on the poem itself.

In his old age, Katue acknowledged that these had been his formative
years.[39] About GGPG, he said, "To tell the truth, I didn't have any guiding
principle that I was attached to; I just wrote with abandon. But I guess we
continued because it was fun."[40]

European movements were imported rapidly one after another—fauvism,
cubism, futurism, constructivism, and dadaism. The main message received
by Japanese avant-garde poets of the mid-1920s was that the visual and
auditory aspects of poetry now took precedence over the cognitive function
and sentimental affectivity that had predominated for centuries. Young
Japanese writers were being pulled in several directions. Should a poet limit
himself or herself to copying exclusively from one European movement? Or
would it be preferable to weave several strands together into one style?
Would that not be just as imitative as copying a single -ism? The solution
would lie in the originality of the synthesis.

Hirato Renkichi, who typifies the impulse to absorb and transcend, was
acutely aware of being at the forefront of a shifting situation in which his
work was essentially a reshuffling of cards dealt by literary movements in
Europe: "What modern poets want to sing about is complicated. Some feel-
ings incline toward futurism, others toward cubism, imagism, expressionism,
or analogism. It goes without saying, I am the inventor of analogism."[41]

Hirato died in 1922, and analogism, a name without a movement, died with him. One frustration Japanese poets must have felt, especially during the 1920s, was that whereas the practices of Western poets had altered Japanese poetry dramatically, they had had no effect on Western poets. Japanese were enthusiastically translating and introducing the work of Western literati, yet almost no one outside Japan was aware of what the Japanese were composing, much less introducing them in print. The transmittable commodity "art" was traveling in one direction only—from West to East—making the claim of European movements to be international hollow.[42] Japanese poets, even more so than their European counterparts, found themselves writing in a near-vacuum for a small in-group. Because of the language barrier and the lack of translations, their Western colleagues could not read the output of contemporary Japanese poets and were familiar, at best, only with the traditional Japanese poets whom the avant-garde purposely ignored.

Tamamura, Nogawa, and Kitasono occasionally published programmatic essays in *GGPG* describing their goals for that journal, although for the most part they let the new works speak for themselves. Tamamura Zennosuke, aware of the typographical revolution led by futurism and dadaism and carried on by the Bauhaus, seemingly had prescience of the concrete poetry movement of the 1950s and 1960s when he claimed, "The present moment is the beginning of the purely visual triumph of the sign."[43]

Nogawa Ryū advocated absolute freedom: "People are completely free to use whatever method, material, and form they want, without any restrictions."[44] Ryū, in an attempt to give his commonsensical proclamation a scientific twist, referred to it as "the axiom of unfixed method, material, and form." On the surface he was calling for tolerance toward all approaches to creative writing, but in actuality he promoted innovation, emphatically championing the heretofore unseen and unknown—the future.

Katue, for his part, called for *richi no jiyū* (intellectual freedom), a vague concept that echoed Ryū's stance.[45] Intellectuality would come under fire as elitist and bourgeois by sympathizers with the proletariat and nationalists alike in the years ahead, but Katue would hold to the belief that poetry should be a repository for intellectual meanderings generated without preconceptions, independent of other spheres such as state politics and organized religion. His ideas on poetry were unsophisticated at this stage, but they would develop and sharpen as his experiments proliferated. Nevertheless, the seeds of his lifelong concerns—visual poetry, method, material, and form—were planted by Tamamura and Nogawa during the GGPG years.

Despite their seeming attraction to dadaism, Ryū and Katue were ambivalent about, if not outright hostile to, the movement. Readers labeled the magazine Dada, and the poets felt they had to fight their way out of the shadow of the imposed image. In GGPG no. 4, Ryū stated: "Dada is one of the products of contemporary people's intellectual freedom, but dadaists, without realizing it, have imprisoned themselves in their dadaist concept."[46] Ryū was mistaken: Tzara and the European dadaists did realize they had painted themselves into a corner. Only surrealism promised genuinely dialectical and non-self-destructing foundations.

Reminiscent of Buddhism's apophatic approach, Katue managed to affirm what GGPG was only by explaining what it was not: "People that I encounter take it for granted that GGPG is a dadaist magazine, but it isn't. Of course, it also is not cubism, not futurism, not symbolism, and not constructivism. And, of course, it is neither 'new sensationalism' nor so-called estheticism."[47] Again, in the editorial column of the following number, a tongue-in-cheek Katue announced: "We have inserted a dadaist element in this issue. It is not that we have retreated to Dada. What we have printed up until now seems to have been incomprehensible, and so we are experimenting with reconstruction."[48]

This willingness to criticize dadaism also carried over to indictment of individual artists. One of the earliest abstract painters, Wassily Kandinsky, was singled out for reproach by Ryū, who wanted to demystify the intangible. He contended that Kandinsky's *Concerning the Spiritual in Art* should be renamed *Concerning the Material in Art*. Katue, probably out of loyalty to Ryū, showed the adolescent insensitivity that he was capable of at this time: "Hey, Kandinsky! You should die coiled in rope!"[49] Ironically, the future development of Katue's poetry toward abstraction was parallel to Kandinsky's course as an artist.

Editorial commentary in GGPG could get quite polemical. In a similar vein, some of the fiction and poetry overturned traditional literary norms of content and style. Perhaps the most outlandish piece was Nogawa Hajime's short story "Rinja rokku no seirisui" (Rinja rock's menstrual fluids), which featured him and his girlfriend discussing the previous issue of GGPG and giving themselves ten-minute-long intravenous injections of menstrual juices between their breasts.[50]

Hiraiwa Konji (dates unknown) contributed a bizarre poem—"Three Circumcisions"—to GGPG, which contains the following segment:

> let's feed the head of 18th-century Romanticism to a cow!
> If he won't eat it, let's stuff it in his mouth!
> Ah beef's blood's dripping circumcision![51]

Hiraiwa stands alongside European dadaists in mocking Judeo-Christian civilization, symbolized by the practice of circumcision. Takagi Haruo (dates unknown), in his poem "The Empty Sounds of Dada," similarly makes light of the Western tradition by blaspheming Christ: "crimson liquid of finger of suicided Jesus Christ / reflected in late-night glass window."[52] The GGPG poets, in reacting to art developments in the West, joined the Dada bandwagon and denounced post-Renaissance poetry and Western religious icons. More significant, however, is the fact that none of the poets attacked sacred Japanese institutions, for example, the emperor system, Shintoism, Buddhism, or even ancient superstitions such as fox possession. To poke fun at Western values in a magazine written in Japanese with hardly any circulation was safe and at a great distance from the European battleground of ideas. This should have struck even the poets themselves as hypocritical—their imitating the anti-Western behavior of Western poets had an oddly sympathetic resonance with the anti-Westernism of Japanese nationalists.

After GGPG ceased publication, Nogawa Ryū turned his critical eye on Japan, joined the Communist party, and visited Moscow. He died in 1944, but sources differ as to whether it was in a Korean jail or in a Manchurian hospital.[53] Katue, for his part, opted not to entangle himself in partisan politics. In one of his rambling editorial statements for GGPG, he expressed his personal attitude: "It is not that I have ennui; rather, it's that I don't like to fight."[54]

The eighteen GGPG poets, all male, were not the only avant-gardists on the scene.[55] Nakano Ka'ichi (1907–98), who has best documented the era, estimates that about forty to fifty avant-garde poets were writing in the mid-1920s.[56] Most of them knew each other, and they frequently contributed to one another's literary magazines.

Of them, only the versatile artist Murayama Tomoyoshi (1901–77) had firsthand experience of European dadaism.[57] After being admitted to Tokyo University, he immediately dropped out and, in 1921, went to Berlin to research early Christianity. There he visited art exhibits and was exposed to the work of Kandinsky, Paul Klee, and the dadaists. Murayama returned to Japan when he was twenty-one years old and began artistic activity on several fronts. After a highly acclaimed one-man show of paintings, he went on to found MAVO, a literary and theater group. One month after GGPG first appeared, Murayama published the first issue of *MAVO*. Katue, a contributor to later issues, explained the derivation of the acronym *MAVO*: "They took the first letter of each member's name, threw them in the air, and they came down arranged as MAVO; at least that is what they have been saying since then. The V stands for Bubnova [Varvara], a Russian woman who was a woodblock artist in the MAVO group."[58]

Unlike GGPG, *MAVO* included artwork as well as text. Each copy was handmade, with illustrations and poems attached to a background of newspaper pages. The *MAVO* artwork and the information printed on the newspaper contrast sharply, yet both echo the mid-1920s in their separate ways. Consonant with the fascination of Picasso and the dadaists for found objects and collage, hair and other sundry items were glued onto the covers of *MAVO*.[59]

Katue and Murayama were on good terms; each published in the other's magazine, and GGPG and *MAVO* exchanged advertisements. There was much overlap between the two groups; they differed in that MAVO openly championed dadaism, constructivism, and anarchism, whereas GGPG aimed at continual absorption of Western techniques and methods without aligning itself with any specific -ism.

Every issue of *MAVO* listed the leading avant-garde magazines in Europe along with their addresses. The desire to weave Japan into a European network is evident in Murayama's strategy. The seventh issue of *MAVO* notes nineteen foreign magazines, including *L'Esprit nouveau* (Paris), *Stauba* (Prague), *MA* (Vienna), *De Stijl* (Leiden), *Der Sturm* (Berlin), *Integral* (Bucharest), and *Blok* (Warsaw). Murayama played a pivotal role in connecting Japanese with a network of contemporary European artists. Years later when Katue was asked, "Who was the Marcel Duchamp of Japan?" he responded, "Murayama and his group."[60] Such questions are delightfully painful because they seem to strike a core issue—who led the movement—even as they unmask the ambivalent Japanese position of being able to attain leadership status only as an imitator.

Katue contributed to another new-style, dadaist-influenced magazine of the time, *Neo donachi kometo* (Neo-donachi comet) edited by Miyazaki Tomoo (1901–?; popularly known as Don Zakki).[61] The second issue included a humorous collection of eight "Human Dismantlement Poems" by Katue. In 1922 Tristan Tzara had written a successful dadaist play, *Le Coeur à gaz* (The gas heart), which was first staged at the Galerie Montaigne in Paris. The characters were Ear, Eye, Eyebrow, Nose, Mouth, and Neck gathered around a gas-heated Heart. Katue, who most probably got the idea for his poem from Tzara's play, presented Head, Nose, Ear, Mouth, Forehead, Hand, Torso, and Leg. Here he reveals an earthier side that is not apparent in most later experiments.

> *Nose*
>
> tinplate nose
> twist it
> stuff a brush inside
> and drag that spiral out from the rear!
>
> *Ear*
>
> when I see an ear
> I want to eat it
> it's a serious toy
> a spoon with a hole
> ouch!
>
> *Mouth*
>
> biting sound waves
> licking red socks
> with a triangular oval, one straight line
> at the manhole of appetite, a sewer hole
> a plunger for kissing
>
> *Hand*
>
> fingertips
> face the wind
> and spin
>
> *Leg*
>
> the top is erotic
> the middle grotesque
> warm

hairy spiral
legs![62]

Katue also appeared on stage occasionally. When Don Zakki started the periodical *Sekai shijin* (World poets) in 1925, he held a poetry reading at the Tsukiji Little Theater. Katue and Nogawa Ryū, contributors to the magazine, were invited to read. Katue presented some short poems, but he was unimpressed with his own performance and wrote about it metaphorically: "I loaded six bullets in my pistol, left the house, and was going to get one good shot off. I don't know why, but they all ended up misfiring."[63]

Katue was also writing and performing in his own avant-garde plays. Murayama enlisted him in his newly formed theater group, Tan'i sanka (Third wave unit). Previously, Murayama had organized Sanka (Third wave), but when anarchists crashed a Sanka event, a brawl ensued that made the newspapers, and the group was forced to disband. The new group, after a few successful Tokyo appearances, took to the road. During an Osaka appearance, an electrical short caused a curtain fire, and the theater burned down, putting an end to the Tan'i sanka.[64] Katue's time on stage was short-lived, and no records remain to cast light on what exactly he did, but the experience brought a new dimension to his poetry—directly in that he started composing verse dramas[65] and indirectly in that his acute awareness of the interplay between stasis and movement was to underlie much of his later experimental writing.

In October 1926, Hashimoto Heihachi moved back to Asama and gave Katue his rented house on the outskirts of Tokyo. For the next three years, Katue lived alone, surrounded by wheat and potato fields, with only one other house in view. He was close enough to the center of the city to meet friends and be a part of the art scene, and at the same time far enough removed to read, write, and paint without distraction. His parents sustained him with an allowance from Asama. Although low on money, he had an abundance of free time to enjoy the atmosphere, if not all the fruits, of Tokyo life. Katue recalled: "In that house I was poor and cooked for myself. I experienced, like other young poets and painters of the time, 'the pinnacle of art, the abyss of survival.'"[66]

The end of GGPG signaled a new beginning for Katue. Little magazines for non-traditional poetry were still in their post-earthquake infancy, yet new titles were cropping up every month. Several editors requested contributions from Katue, for he could be counted on to provide original writing.

His work appeared in, for example, *Bungei jidai* (Literary age) and *Hakuchi no yume* (Idiot's dream), and was reviewed in *Mokusha* (Wooden car).[67]

Katue continued to paint and beginning in 1926 exhibited his oil paintings at the Sanka keishiki geijutsu ten (Third wave form-art exhibit). Although few of his oil paintings are extant, those that have survived tend to resemble his numerous drawings and book covers in the use of geometrical shapes and primary colors. Katue's interests fanned out in several directions at once: poetry, theater, and painting. But he approached the various arts as extensions of a fundamentally new spirit of the age based on the latest avant-garde methodology emanating from the West.

Hagiwara Kyōjirō (1899–1938) was another prominent literatus of the mid-1920s. Initially published as a waka poet, Kyōjirō absorbed futurism, dadaism, and the other modern art and literary movements entering Japan. A self-proclaimed anarchist, he became one of the driving forces behind *Aka to kuro* (Red and black)[68] and, later, *MAVO*. His mix of poetry and anarchism is summed up best in the manifesto of *Aka to kuro*: "What is poetry? What are poets? Discarding all concepts of the past, we boldly proclaim, 'Poetry is a bomb! Poets are dark criminals hurling bombs at the hard walls and doors of prisons!'"[69]

Hagiwara's first book of poems, *Shikei senkoku* (Death sentence; 1925), was a visual feast and caused an immediate sensation. Various sizes and shapes of type are used, giving a messy but dynamic impression. The last poem in the collection, "Roshitsu yori shoka gaijō o miru" (Looking at the city below from a balcony in early summer), combines symmetry and asymmetry, giving the viewer the sensation of observing the crowded urban landscape from above (Fig. 9).[70] Some of the signs have decipherable meanings, others are just letters, dots, and lines. The words with meanings are names of objects that one might encounter on a city street: "cars," "shoes," "charcoal," "a horse's eye," "water," and so on. The only abstract item is the final word (in the lower left corner): "hopeless."

Kyōjirō's known affiliation with anarchist politics seeps into the content and choice of images in several of the poems. For example, flags are invariably colored communist red or anarchist black. Forced to read Hagiwara's signs in terms of political referents, one can grow weary of fixed and facile correspondences between image and ideology. Nevertheless, *Shikei senkoku* was a milestone in Taishō poetry, combining typographical innovation with

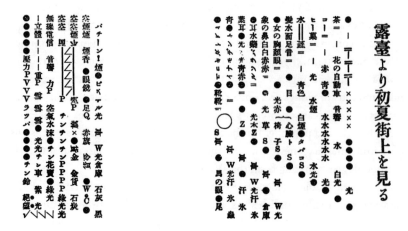

Fig. 9   Hagiwara Kyōjirō's visual poem "Looking at the City from a Balcony in Early Summer," in *Shikei senkoku* (Chōryūsha, 1925), pp. 160–61.

a firm political stance. Kyōjirō typified the new breed of poet—anarchist in spirit and experimental in writing approach.

Artistic trends that had developed over the first two decades of the twentieth century in Europe spread in Tokyo at a rapid rate after the Kantō earthquake of 1923. Nihilism and anarchism sank roots in the relatively liberal atmosphere. These were the years of Taishō democracy in Japan and the Roaring Twenties in the United States.

Avant-garde poetry sprouted on a modest scale in Japan. Kitasono Katue (Fig. 10), Nogawa Ryū, Murayama Tomoyoshi, and Hagiwara Kyōjirō were among the main actors. If Katue's career had ended here, he would be remembered only as a curiosity for the historical reason of being active at the dawn of the avant-garde movement. Although the bulk of his poetic achievement lay in the future, the GGPG years represent his baptism into the modern arts. In 1923 Katue was writing classical poems in Nara. A short year later he was at the forefront of those writing in the latest style, an indication of how uncharted the frontier still was.

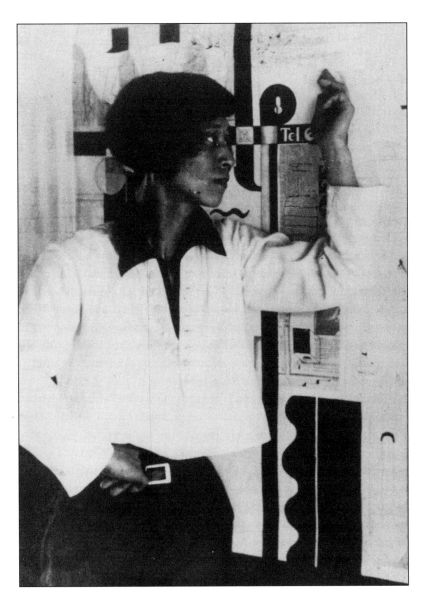

Fig. 10 Kitasono Katue during his neo-dadaist phase at GGPG (mid-1920s), striking a pose reminiscent of a flamenco dancer, with a constructivist poster in the background

3   LITERARY
SURREALISM

Surrealism was born in France in late 1919. As the twentieth century nears its end, it is apparent that the movement has had a more enduring impact in Japan than anywhere else, even its birthplace. Founder André Breton was aware that in a capitalist society surrealism would probably end up as just another trick in the arsenal of advertisers, rather than fulfilling the ideal of self-liberation of the psyche that he and the other writers and artists in the movement had envisaged. Present-day Japanese consumerism is perhaps proof of Breton's realism. Whatever the gap between surrealism's goals and its achievements, the phenomenon of its existence and spread in Japan is worthy of closer attention than it has received.

The movements in France and Japan, although called by the same name, had obvious differences from the outset. For example, French surrealism was at once a rupture of the European logo-centric tradition and a flowering from the soil of that same tradition. In Japan, on the other hand, it was an imported idea with all that connoted about its being secondhand, uprooted, fragmentary, and elusive. Whereas the movement in Europe started in literature and then shifted its emphasis to painting, Japanese surrealists were from the start as influenced by painting as by writing.[1] The political situations in the two countries were also quite different. Ironically, just as French surrealists were signing on with the Communist party in 1927, Japanese surrealists were cutting their ties to the local proletarian poetry movement. Another key to understanding prewar Japanese surrealism is that the artists and writers who joined the movement did so without a base in psychology. Sigmund Freud's theories were hardly known in Japan; consequently, psychoanalysis was not being practiced. In this chapter, I briefly survey the introduction of literary surrealism into Japan in the late 1920s and the role played by Kitasono Katue in its dissemination.[2]

The introduction of the poetry of French surrealists to Japan can be traced to the massive volume of translations by Horiguchi Daigaku (1892–1981), *Gekka no ichigun* (A moonlit gathering; 1925), which includes work by Philippe Soupault, Ivan Goll, and sixty-six other poets.[3] Horiguchi introduced the surrealists as part of his larger aim to present an anthology of French poetry.

Ueda Toshio (1900–1982), the first self-proclaimed surrealist in Japan, read a short story by Katue in the journal *Ningen* (Human) and was reminded of Théophile Gautier. He wrote Katue, who was flattered to be compared to a major Western thinker. Japanese poets would time and again resort to the same strategy to praise each other. Katue invited Toshio to visit, and the two discussed future directions for poetry. The meeting proved fortuitous for Katue, because it exposed him to surrealism.

Tokuda Jōji (1898–1974), editor of *Bungei tanbi* (Literary esthetics; another publication to which Kitasono contributed), was also excited by the latest agitation from Europe and decided to print a selection of the works of the French surrealists. The May 1927 issue of *Bungei tanbi* contains poems by Paul Eluard and Louis Aragon translated by Ueda Toshio and his younger brother, Tamotsu (1906–73), as well as poetry criticism by the two brothers. Toshio contributed the essay "Pōru Eruaru ni tsuite" (On Paul Eluard), and Tamotsu wrote "Furansu gendai shi no keikō" (Trends in contemporary French poetry).

Ueda Toshio's two-page article on Eluard is mysterious in that the French poet is never mentioned, directly or indirectly, in the body of the essay. Was Ueda practicing a form of *réclame* in imitation of the 1919 vow taken by André Breton and Louis Aragon to use literature not to gain fame but only to signal kindred spirits? If so, Eluard became a password for the initiated. Less likely, Toshio (or Tokuda) was trying to evade the censors, who usually only glanced at the table of contents. Although proletarian writers occasionally practiced the tactic of burying an inflammatory message under an innocuous title, little magazines devoted to experimental poetry were not victims of government pressure at this time. Toshio's article is a stinging indictment of the state of the arts in Japan:

Take a look at [modern] Japanese music, painting, and poetry. They show how easily people can exist without participating in the arts. . . . Like barbarians showing off their wealth.

There is no naturalist movement of the novel as there is in France, and no symbolist movement as in French poetry. There are only imitations of naturalism and symbolism.

We want to create art that fits the times. If not, existence is unrewarding and painful. *And to forget the custom of love.* It would be gratifying if also in our country the birth and happiness of natural art were to begin their rightful development.[4] (Italics added)

Toshio's manifesto-like tone encouraged poets to participate in making a new future and abandon the writing of traditional Japanese and imitation foreign verse, while paradoxically setting up France as the standard of what was "natural" and "rightful." Ueda's injunction "to forget the custom of love" was diametrically opposed to the French surrealist concept of spotlighting "the couple" and promoting loss of self-identity by total absorption in "mad love" for one's partner.[5]

Ueda Tamotsu's essay is more even-tempered than his brother's. He explains in Hegelian terms how surrealism presented itself as the most viable direction out of the impasse of dadaism's chaotic negativity: "[Dadaist] negation set in motion easily gains momentum. Stretched to its natural conclusion, don't we arrive at the negation of valuelessness? The departure toward surrealism is an intellectual negation at the border of the absolute."[6]

Kitasono's contribution to this issue of *Bungei tanbi* was "Hakushoku shishū" (Collection of white poems), a series of eleven short poems. Two years later, he reordered the poems, added others, and changed the title to "Kigō setsu" (Semiotic theory). Kitasono was always proud of "Kigō setsu," believing that he had succeeded in writing a "purely original poem."[7] Although in organization, tension, and effect "Kigō setsu" is arguably a more satisfying series of poems than "Hakushoku shishū," the earlier version illustrates in simpler terms Katue's new method.[8]

> *Collection of White Poems*
>
> *1*
>
> white residence
> white table
> pink noblelady
> white distant view
> blue sky
>
> 2
>
> bright port
> white steamship

red flag
white hotel
decolorized boy
flowers and food

    3
glove holding parasol
white outfit
candy
white porcelain and white socks
French language

    4
flat red disk
white dancer doll
lady's white shoes
red curtain

    5
flower and mirror
white room
white couch
silver boy
cherry

    6
pink toys
world map
saber
balloon

    7
cup and water
one white carnation
white table
cup and water

    8
red hat
black jacket
white socks
black shoes
modern noblelady's equipment
1 2 3 10
white hat

red jacket
white socks
white shoes

9
white tableware
flower
spoon
spring, 3 pm
white
white
red

10
prism architecture
white animal
space

11
wet paint
blue flag
apple and noblelady
white landscape
hands off

"Hakushoku shishū" resembles a set director's list for a minimalist production. Nothing happens in a sequential, narrative sense, and what remains—colors and objects layered collage style upon the reader's mind—gives the impression of time stopped. Grammatically, the list contains no verbs, only adjectives and nouns.[9] By eliminating verbs, Kitasono has also removed the dynamic aspect of the remaining words; the poem displays three-dimensional objects in two dimensions the same way a photograph does. The adjectives and nouns are robbed of a certain energy, and in spite or because of this, they come alive in an elemental state of vibrant potentiality. The poem draws attention to the function and possibilities of language and to the graphic role of *kanji* and the alien orthography of English.

As with Kitasono's avoidance of one part of speech in favor of an unbalanced concentration on others, the poem is also noteworthy for the absence of imagery that is unpleasant or Japanese. Most objects are implicitly Western and sparkling white. The key to the poem is the word *furansugo* (French language), for it specifically pinpoints France as the utopia. Perhaps because he felt hypocritical for being unable to speak French (he was teaching him-self how to read) or embarrassed by the implied francophilism, Kitasono erased the clear path to Paris and cut the word from the later version of the poem.

By repeating *shiro* (white) so that it modified almost everything on his list, Kitasono makes the word synonymous with "pure, unsullied."[10] The color white was a fetish among self-styled European surrealists in particular and the avant-garde in general. It was associated with abstraction and the abso-lute.

The hometown of Asama that he knew and the Paris that he did not know both pulled on Katue in Tokyo. He could approach Asama by train or memory. Without the funds to visit Paris, his only access was through books and Ginza shopwindows. Katue, enjoying the relatively libertine years of the early Shōwa era (1926–89), lived as Western a lifestyle as he could manage. He wore up-to-date European clothes, sporting a beret, walking stick, and monocle. He had the long hairdo popular among avant-garde painters—with curled bobs on each side like earmuffs. His appearance, coupled with po-ems like "Hakushoku shishū," was a form of rebellion, a questioning of Japa-nese traditional values.

Katue's work was slowly becoming known. One day in 1927 the young poets Fujiwara Sei'ichi (1908–died in World War II) and Yamada Kazuhiko (dates unknown) approached him with a proposition. They wanted to over-haul their small magazine, *Retsu* (Rows), hand over artistic control to Kita-sono, and have him retitle it and update the contents. Katue agreed to be editor and renamed the magazine *Shōbi.Majutsu.Gakusetsu* (Rose.magic. theory; hereafter *SMG*).[11] Fujiwara remained the publisher and sponsor.

Katue enlisted the Ueda brothers to contribute translations and original poetry. Watching the dizzying rate of change in the arts of mid-1920s Europe and America, they were aware of the futility of working under out-dated premises. Before engaging in their own creative writing, they required as much familiarity as possible with the shifting trends of Western art and literature. *SMG* was launched to promote original Japanese compositions based on surrealism. A few years earlier, Katue had done the same with neo-dadaism as co-editor of *GGPG*. He was at the forefront of not only intro-ducing the avant-garde movements but also urging Japanese to try writing in the new styles and, eventually, to transcend -isms altogether.

In 1977, on the fiftieth anniversary of the first issue of *SMG*, all four numbers were reprinted with a three-page article by Kitasono in which he reflects on the magazine and its place in Japanese surrealism:

I don't recall this very clearly, but the reason Inagaki Taruho [1900–1977] and his group left is probably that they harbored doubts about the future of *surrealism*. In any case, *SMG* was edited as a purely *surrealist* organ from the second issue of Vol. 1.

The *surrealist* movement at this time was divided into our *SMG* group and the *Fukuiku taru kafu yo* [O fragrant firemen] group. Both started with a connection to Professor Nishiwaki Junzaburō at Keiō University. Among the *Fukuiku taru kafu yo* group, some were loyal to Breton's doctrine, but the *SMG* group was more enthusiastic about opening up a world of specifically Japanese *surrealism*.

And so, the movement of *surrealists* . . . was first published in Japan in the magazine *SMG*.[12]

Reading this article, one gets the impression that, despite their differences from Breton, Kitasono and the others at *SMG* considered themselves surrealists. Curiously, no such direct commitment to the surrealist cause is apparent in the four issues of *SMG*. The word *surrealism* appears five times in the few sentences quoted above, but only four times in the hundred-plus pages of *SMG*, and never on the cover or as part of a policy statement in the editorial column (in contrast, the word *Dada* appears thirteen times). Katue's later comments notwithstanding, there was no indication to the reader in 1927 and 1928 that it was a surrealist magazine (except for the separatist manifesto inserted in *SMG* 2, no. 3; discussed below). Occasionally, a poem by Eluard and Aragon appears, or the name Joan Miró, but if Japanese readers were acquainted with them at this time, it was only through imported books, *Bungei tanbi*, or by word of mouth. Complicating matters, *SMG* had no notes on contributors to shed light on who these people might be.

In 1977, when surrealism's place as a leading twentieth-century art movement was unshakable, Katue's willingness to have his name associated with it is understandable, but how about in 1927? If the *SMG* group considered themselves surrealists, why the hesitation to admit it publicly? Fear of persecution by the Thought Police (Shisō keisatsu) may have been on Katue's mind.[13] To declare himself, at twenty-four and without gainful employment, as a follower of a movement based in a foreign country could have invited danger. Why subject himself to liability for changes in direction on which he would never be consulted? If the reluctance to announce *SMG* as openly surrealist was calculated and a matter of political caution, time would prove it not unjustified.

On the other hand, the *SMG* group, although excited about surrealism, was not yet well enough informed about the movement to pose confidently as advocates. We cannot be sure they were even familiar with Breton's "Surrealist Manifesto of 1924," in which he logically explains the need to use illogic as a tool to probe dreams and subconscious terrain for the "blueprint of thought." A partial translation of the manifesto did not appear until 1929.[14] The intellectual framework supporting Breton's ideas (especially Freud's theory of the unconscious) would have been hazy or new to Japanese surrealists. Therefore, even if they had surmounted the language barrier, they still would have encountered difficulties in puzzling out some of Breton's text. In any case, there was no logical exposition of surrealist policy in *SMG*, only illogical poetry and prose. If Katue and the others were surrealists at this time, it was their secret recipe. Readers could enjoy the meal, but no hints were forthcoming on the ingredients.

SMG was published monthly. The first issue included work by eight poets and featured a cover illustration by Inagaki Taruho, who had also contributed to issues 6 through 8 of *GGPG*. After Taruho and his group dropped out, Katue put one of his own drawings on the cover of *SMG* (1, no. 2). His editorial tone was a throwback to the *GGPG* days—incisive, humorous, and combative—as in his explanation of the magazine's name.

Locus of Judgment (a)

At this point it is really superfluous to repeat—and to have to explain is such a hassle.

Rose, magic, theory—all were here in the Middle Ages.[15] Aren't they absolutely not new?—Who said they weren't around in the Middle Ages? Who said they were new? Clocks that want to slide only on the type's surface. If the concepts of old and new aren't one step outside history textbooks, then you, rather than we, will commit suicide in hopelessness. In any case, don't you realize that your philosophy is not a step outside the academy?

How can we make colorfully effective conditions for a different reflex when facing the concept of ROSE? How far have we been able to actualize a fundamental shift in esthetics and formalism regarding a rearranged introduction of the concept of MAGIC? Are you sneering? And for THEORY, how can we emphasize, with logical purity and refinement, what doing literature is all about?—Dumbheaded pigeon clocks we request to get the hell away. ROSE. You say you don't like the ideograms?[16]—Then rewrite it as "chimney," or "factory," or whatever you fancy. Still, for the fad of a 24-hour volume, there is a problem in that we are discolored and abused to the degree of being neither journalists nor weaklings toward life.

Altering direction.[17]

If the meaningless sounds *ge.gjmgjgam.prrr.gjmgem* somehow symbolize the rebellious abandonment of tradition in favor of dadaism's incoherence, the name *Rose.Magic.Theory* signals the new direction of drawing esthetic order out of chaos. Kitasono strings together words that are common in themselves but usually not considered elements of the same set (such as "rose," "magic," and "theory"). Rather than pointing to one meaning or denying meaning altogether by substituting empty letters, the elements of Kitasono's odd set bounce back and forth in the reader's mind to suggest multiple meanings. In his postwar poetry he continually expanded this tendency in new ways, and his essential strategy was to line up multiple signifiers in which possibilities of meaning ricochet without privileging any one meaning, thus jamming the code of communication. For Kitasono, poetry is found in breaking down the process of cognition and paralyzing efficient communication. This breakdown, in turn, gives way to new significations. Language ultimately cannot be empty in an absolute sense, because even "nonsense" is a form of signification. This kind of writing, by implication, becomes a metaphorical critique of society's fragmentation and alienation.

In "Locus of Judgment (a)" Katue supports a turning away from romanticism and symbolism and calls for a "different reflex when facing the concept of ROSE." Under MAGIC, he arrives at his key point: "how to actualize a fundamental shift in esthetics and formalism." Estheticism was also implied in Fujiwara Sei'ichi's English-language message on the back cover of the second issue of *SMG*: "Art for rose / Rose for art / Atr [sic] for magic / Magic for art / Art for theory / Theory for art." Unlike French surrealism, with its basis in psychology (and later, politics), the *SMG* group's primary concern was artistic and esthetic: how to use language to conjure up new beauty distinct from that of the receding past. Breton's definition of surrealism excludes the Kitasono and Fujiwara emphasis on "the dictation of thought . . . outside all esthetic or moral preoccupations." Katue believed that he had a firm grounding in the theory crucial for opening new poetic terrain, and he urged weak minds to stay away. However, there were no theoretical essays in any of the issues of *SMG*.

While the members of the *SMG* group were at their branch office busily writing what they considered surrealist poetry, Breton and his inner circle at the home office were dividing over political issues. Disturbed by the French government's colonial policy of teaming up with Spain to suppress the Rif tribesmen in Morocco and fearing that surrealism was being perceived as a powerless, strictly esthetic movement, five of the most active members joined the Communist party in April 1927.[18] The news quickly reached Japan. Later that year Kitasono (signing himself as Asaka Kenkichi) and the Uedas issued "A Note" in Japanese and English,[19] and mailed it to the subscribers of *SMG* as well as to "communist-surrealists Louis Aragon, Paul Eluard, and André Breton; and non-communist surrealist Antonin Artaud."[20]

A Note December 1927

We hailed surrealism's development of artistic desire or the development of perceptive ability. Our baptized intellect, accepting no limits, received a technique that uses material which has passed through the intellect.

We, by our fated poetic operation, are constructing a condition removed from the human. This condition reminds us of something similar to the indifference of technique. We feel our condition resembles that of a poetic scientist measuring the boundaries of objectivity. We are neither depressed nor happy. The perceptions of humans who do not take being human as necessary are moderately rigorous and level-headed. While undergoing our poetic operation, we feel the appropriate excitement. We will continue surrealism. We praise the virtue of saturation.

Asaka Kenkichi
Ueda Toshio
Ueda Tamotsu[21]

This brief document, which has earned itself a distinguished place in literary history as "the first surrealist manifesto in Japan," shows that surrealism was for its authors a literary method, a way of freeing the imagination to create artistic works with greater perception. Scientific vocabulary abounds—"poetic operation," "scientist measuring objectivity," "saturation"—but there is nothing even hinting of Freud, the subconscious, or automatic writing. The manifesto's second paragraph can be interpreted as a broad attack on what its authors perceived as the overemotionalism of the quarreling French surrealists, or as a veiled criticism of the factional drift into communism. The trio was essentially encouraging poets to write from a dispassionate and imaginative viewpoint, rather than from the narrow confines dictated by a party line.[22]

Years later, Kitasono gave two conflicting motives for the manifesto:

To show that our surrealism was new and completely different from the French, we sent the manifesto.[23]

and

Aragon, Eluard, and others became communists, while Breton [sic; it was actually Artaud who did not join] etc., did not join, and surrealism was on the brink of splitting apart. In response to that, we sent our manifesto.[24]

It is unclear whether the manifesto was meant to admonish the French in hopes of sealing the rift in the movement or to declare independence from both sides in the feud. As for the French reaction, no records remain to shed light on whether they interpreted the manifesto as a sign of solidarity or separatism. Incidentally, Japan itself was not highly regarded by the French surrealists, who excluded it from their "Surrealist Map of the World, 1929."[25]

While Kitasono and his friends were starting *SMG*, another hub of surrealist activity was forming around Nishiwaki Junzaburō, a poet and professor of English literature at Keiō University.[26] Although not an outspoken enthusiast of surrealism, Nishiwaki did nevertheless play a pivotal role in disseminating the ideas of the movement. Sent to England in 1922 by Keiō to further his literary studies, he lived there for three years and was one of only two surrealist poets in Japan to have had firsthand experience of the West before World War II.[27] Junzaburō arrived at an exciting time: both T. S. Eliot's *The Wasteland* and James Joyce's *Ulysses* were published in 1922. After living in London for a year, he enrolled in an honors course of English literature at Oxford University. Nishiwaki, who had written his senior thesis in Latin, published a book of his English poems, *Spectrum*, while in the country.

In 1924 Junzaburō married an English woman, Marjorie Bittle, and the following year they sailed back to Japan. On the way, they briefly visited Paris, where he tried unsuccessfully to publish a volume of his French poems (*Une Montre sentimentale*). Nishiwaki's vast learning and ability to write in several foreign languages were to impress the Japanese. Many promising students gathered around him, including the Ueda brothers, Takiguchi Shūzō, Miura Kōnosuke (1903–1964), and Satō Saku (1905–96).[28] The first books on surrealism to be found in Japan had been brought back by Nishiwaki,[29] and that is probably where Ueda Toshio got the information he passed on to Katue. Only about ten years older than his students, Junzaburō frequently invited them over to his house, where they would burn the midnight oil excitedly discussing the new literature from the West. Katue occasionally met with the Keiō group, although irregularly since he lived quite far away. Junzaburō recognized Katue's talent, however, and directed his students to call on the aspiring poet.

Two months after the first issue of *SMG* (dated Nov. 1, 1927), the Keiō group issued an anthology of surrealist verse titled *Fukuiku taru kafu yo* (O fragrant firemen), with a preface by Nishiwaki. For him, poets were "fragrant firemen," igniting the boredom of everyday reality to create a more splendid world of the imagination. (*Kafu* means fireman in the sense of a stoker or caretaker of a fire as on a steam locomotive and not one who extinguishes flames.) Nishiwaki's preface, while containing the leaps of logic characteristic of surrealism, seems to derive from a more conscious base than the subconscious utterings of automatism. Nevertheless, to abandon the normal form and write a preface in a style approximating a poem was a novelty that would be copied by other Japanese surrealists in the following years.

Cerebrum ad acerram recidit. The world of reality is nothing more than the brain. To destroy this brain is the goal of surrealist art. The forms of noble art are all surrealistic. Therefore, a noble poem is also a surrealist poem. Poems construct a vacuous desert inside the brain and, by beating down all sensations, sentiments, and ideas connected to the experience of reality, are one method by which to squeeze the brain purely. Here is pure poetry. The brain becomes something like ultra-pink glass. Poems destroy the brain in this way. The destroyed brain is extremely fragrant like a destroyed perfume tank. Here perfume has a trading company's honor. We are already unlike animals eating dusty grapes. Yet we crush them and drink the juice. Therefore, the value of forming poetry is none other than the value of champagne. Also, poetry is something to burn the brain. Here are poems as sparks and heating power. For us, reality is only fuel, but not in the way natural people enjoy fuel in and of itself. We burn this fuel of the world of reality and from within absorb only light and heat. Make it pure you warmly fragrant firemen!
The brain from its tower faces chicken cutlets and perpetually shudders.[30]

Nishiwaki defined reality as intrinsically negative—the boredom and drudgery of everyday life—and posited surrealism as its antidote, transcendence into a superior world of creativity. His statement that "reality . . . is the brain" has an affinity with the Yogachara (Mind Only) School of Buddhist philosophy. Since the world is how we perceive it, passing into a higher state (whether Buddhahood or surreality) requires that we destroy our tired perceptions and replace them with vivid new ones. Although Nishiwaki's interpretation of the word *surreal* was valid in itself, there was virtually no overlap with Breton's goal of uncovering for self-revelation the repressed and discredited domain of the subconscious.[31] All Japanese surrealists (with the exception of Takiguchi Shūzō who tried to adhere to Breton's line),[32] followed the same way of thinking as Nishiwaki, whether directly influenced by him or not. For them, surrealist poetry could not be ugly, since that would be realistic and of this world. Yet for Breton the point was not to screen thoughts at all, because in the irrational disarray that emerged could be found clues to the automatic (that is, true) functioning of the mind.

The Keiō group, unlike *SMG* with its covert surrealism, clearly announced their commitment by putting the French words *Collection Surréaliste* on the cover. Nishiwaki's high-prestige job at Keiō University provided any security the students might have needed against possible police harassment.

Of the *SMG* group, only Ueda Tamotsu was published in *Fukuiku taru kafu yo*. At Ueda Toshio's urging, the *SMG* and Keiō groups decided to merge as a united front and publish a monthly review of their surrealist writing. Toshio titled the magazine *Ishō no taiyō* (The costume's sun), and Katue drew the cover illustration.[33] Editorial tasks were rotated among the eleven members, who represented all the Japanese literary surrealists living in Tokyo at that time.[34] Each issue consisted of about thirty pages. On the cover of issues 1–4 was written "L'évolution Surréaliste" in French, and on issues 5–6, "Chōgenjitsu shugi kikan zasshi" (Surrealist periodical).

Unlike the French surrealists, who were splitting into factions, the Japanese were emphasizing unity, like many movements in their early stages when unity against outsiders helps paper over differences. However, this unity never had the same force as in France, where not only magazines and books but several long manifestos, a list of recommended reading, a map of the world, subversive decals, and other paraphernalia were issued to emphasize the momentum of the movement. Not only that, but (in the early phase at least) French poets went to séances, underwent hypnosis, took drugs, and wrote poetry en masse. One of the intentions of the French surrealists, who came from a culture that prized individualism, was to nullify the importance attached to individual creation. After all, if the subconscious is a matter of self-discovery for the author and archetypes of the subconscious are universal in any case (Carl Jung), then of what consequence could it be whose pen actually touched the paper? On the other hand, for the Japanese, whose literature had a long tradition of group participation in poetry writing[35] and who were using literature not as a means to the end of self-discovery but as an end in itself, the idea of group composition simply did not have the same appeal. Japanese surrealists published *Ishō no taiyō* as a demonstration of their solidarity, but not too much should be made of their banding together: they did not write as a group nor explore together the mutual psychic space that so fascinated the French.

Although mostly of historical value, *Ishō no taiyō* does contain some literary curiosities, especially writing by Nishiwaki, Takiguchi, Kitasono, and the Uedas. Since *Ishō no taiyō* was an openly surrealist periodical, we can safely assume that Kitasono contributed what he considered to be his most surrealistic poems at that time. Here are two examples:

> *Vin du Masque*
>
> the Queen of imagination who wears the sun's hat is the imagined
>   sun's Queen
> the King is watching a movie theater
> the King should ride an airship
> climbing glass chimney glass airship climbs
> the Kiiiiing of eternity
> the Queeeen of eternity
> but, oh wandering mailman I wonder where you carried your
>   love letters and mother
> King of eternity worship on sand dune throne the Queen of eternity
>   worship her the worshiped Queen of eternity has trombone hips
>   and a circular head
> she is the Queen of sadness[36]

> *Portrait of a Moonlit Night and a Poet's Tale*
> *à Jacobus Phillipus [Nishiwaki Junzaburō] et Ueda Tamotsu*
>
> the crystal poet closes his eyes the crystal poet opens his eyes
> the crystal poet talks to the desert's park
> he looks at a pure lady cutting
> sublimely celestial vegetables
> the pure lady is riding on a sublimely crystal
> boat her lofty parasol is opening above her lofty pupils
> she also was a majestic lady
> the crystal poet closes his eyes the crystal poet
> opens his eyes
> the crystal poet is on a crystal balcony
> there he saw a wise magician manipulating
> with moonlight and seawater

the pinnacle's sublime lady wearing crystal glasses
the purely wise magician is a purely tranquil
crystal poet
have you all seen the crystal poet?
on his cheeks are an autumn's bride's smile
and mystery
he sits on a harbor chair in extreme luxury
like a street vendor
he is perfect like the pope in Rome gone broke
you are all idiots[37]

One of Kitasono's methods for creating his surreal cosmos is to take or-
dinary objects and make them transparent. The images—"glass airship,"
"glass chimney," "crystal boat," "crystal glasses," "crystal balcony," and "crystal
poet"—transport the reader into a precious world of fragile beauty. As we
are already used to finding in Katue's poetry, all the objects are Western and
lofty. He chooses to present a "Kiiiiing" and "Queeeen" instead of an em-
peror and empress, and all the attributes of the "pure and majestic lady" of
the second poem are elevated (parasol, pupils) and "sublime." The world
close at hand is rejected in favor of a Europe of the imagination.[38] Even the
landscapes with "sand dune" and "desert" are clearly outside Japan.

A new element in Katue's poetry (and therefore what he must have un-
derstood as surrealistic) is the use of ambiguity to surprise and disorient the
reader. This technique, a variation of the "pivot word" (*kakekotoba*) of Heian-
period (794–1185) poetry, is now used for surrealist ends. A simple example
is how the throne suddenly gains double occupancy in the first poem: "King .
. . on sand dune throne . . . the Queen." We imagine the King sitting and
then realize that the throne also refers to the Queen. In a similar way, Kita-
sono plays with the possibilities in Japanese grammar and dangles adjectival
phrases that seem to, but ultimately do not, modify the nouns that directly
follow them. We first read, "head with trombone hips" ("toronbon no koshi
o motte iru *atama*") until we continue and make the natural correction to
"Queen . . . with trombone hips and circular head" ("toronbon no koshi o
motte iru atama no marui *Queen* de aru").

Somewhat more complicated is the bifurcated thinking engendered by
ambiguities in "the King should ride an airship / climbing glass chimney glass
airship climbs" ("Vin du Masque," ll. 4–5). The subjective, authorial intru-
sion of "the King *should* ride an airship" jars because what precedes this is
purely descriptive. Then, while we are still unsure whether the King indeed

boards the airship, we are confronted with "climbing glass chimney," which can be taken to mean "the King *climbing* the glass chimney," "the glass *chimney climbing* [the sky]," or "the King inside the *airship climbing* the glass chimney." If we opt for the last, then the following phrase, "glass airship climbs," becomes redundant except for adding the fact that the airship is constructed of glass. These shifts in perception, often impossible for the translator to reproduce faithfully in the original word order with corresponding syntax, can be rejected as a case of muddled writing, or, on the other hand, they can be a source of delight to the unsuspecting reader. Part of what surrealism implied for Kitasono and the other *Ishō no taiyō* poets was the freedom to be unreadable. On the cover of the final issue, as if wearing its incoherence as a medal, is the anonymous quote, "A magazine that does not transcend the level of nobody being able to read it."

The humor in Katue's dadaist poetry was always far-fetched and at the expense of the reader, whereas his surrealist humor is less antagonistic,[39] ranging from the wordplays above to outright one-line jokes. For example, the King watches the movie theater, not the movie. And the mailman is questioned as to where he carried "love letters and mother." Katue's mother, Hashimoto Ei, had died in August 1928, a few months before the poem was written. The word *mother* also appears in another poem of his from around this time: "1928 was a dark year kind lovers kind mothers how often I lost the chest's tower! / How very light and limitlessly transparent I am!"[40] In spite of Katue's aim to write "objective and impersonal poetry," his subconscious preoccupations did occasionally seem to surface in his verse. Uncovering this kind of Freudian signal was an integral part of Breton's automatism, but it was tangential if not accidental to Kitasono's brand of surrealism.

Ishō no taiyō and other small magazines of the time were suddenly pushed into obscurity when the publishing house Kōseikaku hired poet and literary theorist Haruyama Yukio to take over the editorship of its new quarterly, *Shi to shiron* (Poetry and poetics; 1928–31) as well as their multivolume *Gendai no geijutsu to hihyō sōsho* (Series on modern art and criticism).[41] Gambling on Haruyama's editorial talent and on the marketability of the new poetry among the nation's youth, Kōseikaku sponsored the venture and printed 1,000 copies of *Shi to shiron*, of which 650–700 were sold.[42] As originally conceived, the magazine contained 200 pages, but it soon grew to a hefty 400 pages.

Shi to shiron had eleven regular members (*dōnin*), but Haruyama's policy from the beginning was purposely inclusive, and he sought contributions from outside the group.[43] His popularization of the phrase *l'esprit nouveau*—the intangible "new spirit" of the age—allowed Japanese poets and readers to feel up-to-date without having to commit themselves to any particular literary persuasion. He was aware of surrealism's emerging role in modern poetry and solicited work from Nishiwaki, Kitasono, the Uedas, Takiguchi, and the others at *Ishō no taiyō*.[44] But he also gathered poetry, essays, and translations from practically everyone knowledgeable about twentieth-century Western trends. He was uninterested, however, in printing politically inspired poetry such as proletarian verse.

The impact of *Shi to shiron* over its three years and fourteen issues[45] was much larger than the circulation data suggest.[46] Until then, news about topics of interest to young literati had trickled in from the West, but now they were dealt with systematically and in depth. There were special issues on André Breton, James Joyce, T. S. Eliot, André Gide, Paul Valéry, and other writers, along with hundreds of pages of essays, poems, and manifestos in translation. The word *modernism* to refer to this period did not gain currency in Japan until after the Pacific War, but we can date the concept of modernism from *Shi to shiron*, which was itself part of a larger trend—a quantum leap in the West's influence throughout the arts. Art deco patterns adorning everything from buildings to dresses to ashtrays were ubiquitous signs of the spreading cultural inroads made by the West.

When interviewed a half century later, Haruyama Yukio recalled the barren state of Japanese poetics in the 1920s:

Hinatsu Kōnosuke [1890–1971] wrote that the essence of poetry is "to move demons to tears." He was about ten years older than I was, and that was the only [poetics] discussion going on at the time. Hinatsu Kōnosuke criticized all those who did not agree. I certainly don't write poems to move a demon—something that makes no sense—to tears.[47]

"Moving demons to tears" was an allusion to the expressionist poetics of Ki no Tsurayuki, author of the *Kokinshū* preface (written in 905). Haruyama, along with Kitasono and the other avant-gardists, thought that the only way for Japanese to sweep away the cobwebs of tradition was to study the flow of ideas from Europe and America and create original work based on them. Already in the first issue of *Shi to shiron*, Haruyama, using "theory" as a weapon, made a scathing attack on the star of the poetry world, Hagiwara Sakutarō, denouncing the older poet as "byō teki na ego-shimuborisuto" (a morbid ego-symbolist).[48] Sakutarō was somewhat of an unfair target; he had, after all, been the first to write successfully in the modern colloquial idiom.[49] But Sakutarō's poetics, valuing nostalgia and sentimentality, were an easy and appealing target for Haruyama.[50]

With *Shi to shiron*, the poetry establishment could no longer ignore the collective force *l'esprit nouveau* represented. One consequence of the new breed of poets having propelled themselves onto center stage behind the shield of "theory" was that their own poetry started to come under scrutiny and attack. That experience made them clarify their positions in order to counterattack. Numerous debates ensued over the following decade, occasionally of substance but often merely personal and petty. Haruyama can be credited with being one of the first to light the polemical brushfires.

Unlike the situation in Paris, there was no pope of surrealism in Tokyo. Only Nishiwaki was qualified to play André Breton's role, but he was occupied with teaching and writing and was not particularly committed to surrealism. Takiguchi Shūzō would emerge as the main spokesman for surrealism in Japan and even gain recognition from Breton, but he was still a newcomer on the poetry scene and was grappling with French. Kitasono had been around long enough to take the helm, but both his language ability and his knowledge about the movement were inadequate. The result was a power vacuum enabling the poets to meet as equals yet denying them much of the organizational and ideological momentum that a leader could have provided.

Breton wrote several essays about surrealism. The concept changed over time and according to the imagination of individual painters and poets. The word *surrealism* had been coined by Guillaume Apollinaire in 1917, but Breton traced the idea to the writings of Isidore Ducasse (pen name, Comte de Lautréamont, 1846–70) and Arthur Rimbaud (1854–91). For instance, surrealists rallied around Lautréamont's illogical and evocative image of "the encounter between an umbrella and a sewing machine on a dissecting table." Breton also had great respect at that time for Pablo Picasso, calling him a "searchlight" and his work surrealistic. Ferdinand Cheval (1836–1924), the French postman who collected stones and for thirty-three years singlehandedly constructed "Le Palais idéal" in his backyard, was also praisingly dubbed a surrealist.[51] For Breton, whose main aim was to spread surrealism, it was natural to reach back in time and across space for examples of the kind of art and literature he was hoping the new movement would produce. He did not use the word *surreal* in a strict and limited historical sense; rather, he applied it widely to whatever he felt supported his notion of a state of mind transcending the oppositional relationship of dreams and everyday life.

None of the literary surrealists in Japan before World War II took this approach.[52] The literature and art of the Japanese past were considered bankrupt and unworthy of being exhumed. French surrealism appealed to Japanese youth as a complete cultural Other—a counterweight to the claustrophobic pressure of their own tradition. Unwilling to see the surrealist gems in Japan's cultural past, they lost the opportunity to formulate aspects of the movement in terms that their audience would have easily understood. They put more effort into proving themselves authentic surrealists with their poetry, essays, and translations than into theorizing on how best to spread the movement. To be fair to them, the movement in France, as it emerged from dadaism, was still quite amorphous and defined itself only gradually. The Japanese, given their lack of grounding in Freudian psychology, may have had difficulty with the concept of surrealism, but at least two essential characteristics should have been clear to them: the method of automatism and "the incongruous image."

If the Japanese had probed their cultural past, what examples of these characteristics of surrealism could they have found? If André Breton had been Japanese, who might he have cited in place of Lautréamont, Cheval, de Chirico, Picasso, Jarry, and others to provide cultural ammunition for the expanding movement?

As one example of "automatic writing," Japanese surrealists could have pointed to the late-seventeenth-century pastime of *yakazu haikai* (literally, "counting arrow poems") in which the poet orally recited as many original verses as possible in a given period, usually twenty-four hours. The all-time champion, Ihara Saikaku (1642–93), supposedly recited 23,500 poems in a single day and night in 1684, at the Sumiyoshi Shrine in Osaka. With his phenomenal average of one poem every 3.7 seconds, the scribes could record only the number of poems, not the individual words. Japanese surrealists could have found in Saikaku's works traces of the same high-speed, spontaneous approach to language, and they would have discovered abundant leaps of logic and passages of free association.

As for the "incongruous image," Pierre Reverdy had already set forth in 1918 a position close to what the French surrealists would adopt (although Reverdy was not in Breton's circle): "The image is a pure creation of the spirit. It cannot be born of a comparison but of the bringing together of two realities which are more or less remote. The more distant and just the relationship of these conjoined realities, the stronger the image—the more emotive power and poetic reality it will have."[53] Reverdy's "bringing together of two remote realities" and Breton's "absence of all control exercised by reason" ("First Surrealist Manifesto"; 1924) were revolutionary statements to the logo-centric West. The Japanese tradition, on the other hand, has for several centuries accommodated "illogic" and "remote realities." For instance, in the Nara period when Chinese culture was grafted onto the Japanese way of life, and again in the Meiji period when Western artifacts and styles were superimposed on native modes, we see the combining of two remote worlds. The clash in everything from religious outlook to clothing and food can be considered a surrealistic encounter. One example is the Taishō-period men's fashion of wearing Derby hats and kimono. The relative ease with which Japanese juxtapose foreign and native cultural elements has been a source of both pride (Japan the adaptable) and derision (Japan the imitator). As a result of successfully "civilizing" itself in the Nara period and "modernizing" in the Meiji, Japan could be said to crave remote realities in order to bring them closer and eventually assimilate them.

Incongruity has been tolerated, if not highly appreciated, as an integral part of Japanese esthetics since the Heian period (794–1185). Courtiers partook of parlor games, such as putting together (*awase*) objects like shells (*kai-awase*) and poems (*uta-awase*). Similarly, layering (*kasane*), familiar in both the joining of steps in classical dance and the twelve-color arrangement of formal kimono sleeves, allowed for striking combinations that often ran counter to expectations. The group pastime of linked poetry (*renga*), in which each poet took the stanza of the previous participant as the first component of his own poem, led to some wild leaps of imagination. For instance, a given stanza may have a man as the assumed but unstated subject, yet when another poet adds a subsequent verse, the context now demands the reader reconsider the previous subject as having been a woman. French surrealists invented their own literary game, "The Exquisite Corpse," in which a new line was added to the unseen lines of other poets.[54] Japanese surrealists, however, failed to point out the similarity between renga and this practice.

Haikai sequences, the successor to renga, shared similar conventions and rules. In addition to the gap in a single *haiku* (or the opening verse *hokku* of a sequence) formed by the juxtaposition of two separate and seemingly irreconcilable realities, there is the gap between any two verses in a linked sequence. A variation occurs when two apparently close realities are merged in an illogical way, as in the following haiku by Matsuo Bashō (1644–94):

shizukasa ya	stillness—
iwa ni shimiiru	a cicada's voice
semi no koe	seeps into the rocks[55]

The cicada's voice seeps into the rocks like liquid into a sponge. French surrealists would have praised this perception for containing a touch of the "marvelous," although Breton's concept of beauty was more "convulsive" than the tranquillity of Bashō's opening line.

In a 1969 essay, Nishiwaki Junzaburō stated that "the lines by Japan's great poet Bashō, 'inazuma o te ni toru' (to catch lightning in hand) and 'namida o niru oto' (the sound of tears boiling) were forerunners of surrealism." In another essay he quotes Bashō's "aware o kobosu kusa no tane" (plant seeds spilling pathos) and refers to the haiku master as the "Japanese surrealist Bashō."[56] Elsewhere, Nishiwaki called Bashō "Japan's greatest surrealist" and ranked him alongside James Joyce. His perceptive remarks, however, came forty years after he had first introduced surrealism to Japan.

The premodern Japanese worldview contained Buddhas, bodhisattvas, and Shinto *kami*, as well as long-nosed goblins (*tengu*), demons (*oni*), long-necked monsters (*rokuro kubi*), animals with the power to metamorphose—foxes, badgers, and snakes—and other creatures, real and imaginary. Many examples of Japanese art from the Kamakura (1185–1333) and later periods arguably contain "surrealist" imagery. For example, a painting in the *Yamai zōshi* scroll depicts a man lying in bed hallucinating an army of tiny monks. And the *Gaki zōshi* scroll and the *Hyakki yakōzu* screen, with their depictions of hungry ghosts, are vivid instances of the emergence of imaginary, subconscious imagery.[57]

Among the most surrealistic art of premodern Japan are the numerous Edo-period parody (*mitate*) prints, in which two remote realities are juxtaposed, occasionally with the intention of pointing out the non-duality between the sacred and profane realms. One such print is of a gorgeous courtesan using a wooden scoop to clean the wax from Daruma's huge, but dirty, ears.[58] Another shows a man leaning against a radish twice his size.[59] A further example of early surreality is an erotic print by Utagawa Kunisada (1786–1864) of a man and woman embracing, with faces and genitals transposed.[60] There is much overlap of sensibility between Edo artists and French surrealists, despite the wholly different cultures and times that they reflect.

Alien to the Edo artists but vital to the surrealists was the *zeitgeist* of the age of psychoanalysis and the consequent focus on how to dissolve the barrier between dreaming and waking states of consciousness. Nevertheless, Edo graphic work, like surrealist art, is often shocking.

Dozens of cases of surrealistic tendencies in traditional Japanese culture could be cited, but further examples would only emphasize the point that Japanese literati in the late 1920s neglected to acknowledge the predisposition of their culture to accept surrealism, especially its bizarre imagery. Paradoxically, the same past that Japanese treated as a dead entity and wanted vehemently to deny also provided fertile soil for welcoming the new movement from the West. The premodern worldview, technology, and high literacy rate, the same factors that had underpinned the entire modernization project since the Meiji period, cannot be overlooked as key factors in smoothing surrealism's adoption.

Although no Japanese poet before World War II related surrealism and premodern Japanese culture, the painter Fukuzawa Ichirō (1898–1992), who returned to Tokyo in 1930 after seven years in Europe and was eager to expand the movement, did make this point in his introductory book, *Surréalisme* (1937).[61] Fukuzawa's examples of objects he found surrealistic in Japan included packaged traditional candy, a patchwork house designed by a so-called madman (Ferdinand Cheval had also been regarded as insane by his neighbors), the Ryōan-ji temple rock garden in Kyoto, and a picture of a monster's body constructed from the paraphernalia for drinking sake. Some of his choices might strike us as odd, but his attempt to relate the ideas behind surrealism to the Japanese past was a commendable effort to introduce the subject seriously. A full decade had passed between Kitasono's initial efforts at *SMG* and Fukuzawa's in-depth treatment.[62]

In the late 1920s, however, when there were no convenient, introductory books on surrealism,[63] besides the translations of surrealist texts and the original surrealist poetry published in *SMG* and *Ishō no taiyō*, there were no essays on the subject until *Shi to shiron*. In 1929 Nishiwaki Junzaburō's *Chōgenjitsu shugi shiron* (Surrealist poetics) was published by Kōseikaku in the series Haruyama edited on modern art and criticism. Those who were expecting information on the new movement from the articulate Keiō University professor must have felt much confusion upon reading Nishiwaki's scholarly analysis of irony and "surnaturalism" in Charles Baudelaire's poetry. *Surnatural*, a term coined by Baudelaire, was picked up as a universal critical term by Nishiwaki.[64] Since he was dealing with mid-nineteenth-century poetry, an essay by Takiguchi Shūzō, "Dada yori shurearisumu made" (From Dada to surrealism), was appended to bring the subject up to date and justify the title of the book.[65] Nishiwaki, while making a reference to surrealism in his section of the book, added the disclaimer, "This explanation is not that of the French surrealists; it is completely my own."[66] He had planned to title the book *Surnaturalist Poetics*, but "the editor at that time [Haruyama Yukio] chose the newer word *surreal*."[67]

Japanese readers now had to puzzle out the meaning of surnaturalism (*chōshizen shugi*) and its relation to surrealism (*chōgenjitsu shugi*). Their problems were compounded because surnaturalism's counterpart, "naturalism," had not functioned in Japan to criticize the hypocritical values upholding society in general, as it had in Europe. Rather, Japanese authors adopted "realism" as a method and proceeded to write confessional "I-novels" that reflected only their immediate surroundings and quotidian experience.

The 1930 "Shigo jiten" (Dictionary of poetic words), edited by Momota Sōji (1893–1955), was ostensibly intended to help clear up the terminological difficulties.[68] Here are the entries for *surrealism* and *surnaturalism*:

Surrealism is the literary method of surnaturalism. Surnaturalism refers to the object, whereas surrealism refers to the method, as is the case with realism [in relation to naturalism]. Moreover, it can be said that *the literature of surrealism is dadaism, and the surrealism of literature has a formalistic tendency.* [Italics added]

Surnaturalism has been interpreted in two ways: (1) What is called surnaturalist literature is that which treats the non-natural as an object. However, in this case the object is simply surreal, and the descriptive literary method can be naturalistic. As opposed to this, (2) surnaturalism as a descriptive literature is the purposeful combining of the shapes of words, resulting in combinations whose order has no relation to nature. This is the same in the case of naturalist literature and literary naturalism.[69]

These definitions are overly compact and highly erroneous. The statement that "the literature of surrealism is dadaism" must have perplexed readers who believed that the literature of the two movements was different. And, French surrealists who were using automatism as a method would have been dumbfounded to find that their chaotic subconscious outpourings had "a formalistic tendency." (Formalism surely derived from Russian constructivism and not French surrealism.)

In *Shi no kenkyū* (Research on poetry; 1931), Haruyama Yukio accepted Nishiwaki's category surnatural and further expanded on the definitions in Momota's book.[70] According to Haruyama, surnatural works come about in one of two ways: one can write about a non-naturalistic object (a nymph) with a naturalistic method (realistic description, as of a painting of a nymph) or about a naturalistic object (a cat) with a non-naturalistic method (such as formalism).[71] The relationship between surnaturalism and naturalism parallels that of surrealism and realism:

	thought/(object)	*method*	*poem*
1	surreal thing/act	realistic writing	surreal
2	real thing/act	non-realistic writing	surreal

For Haruyama, realism was less valid than surrealism, of which there are two kinds. The first is realistic writing about imaginary subjects, which for him was the same as straightforward realistic description of real objects. The second occurs when the method itself is surrealistic. By this he did not mean automatism, but a wide range of techniques, including his own brand of formalism in which a few ideograms are repeated over and over to distort their lexical content. Here again, Haruyama did not refer to Russian constructivism with its emphasis on form. As examples of surrealistic methods, he gave (1) early formalism (Apollinaire's calligrammes, experiments by futurists); (2) the combining of two remote images (Reverdy); and (3) a stream of words, each more unexpected than the last (Gertrude Stein).[72]

Haruyama took "surreal" in a far more literal sense than the French surrealists had in mind. His theorizing led him (and Kitasono and Ueda Toshio) to experiment with a new type of poetry that would have been unrecognizable as surrealistic to the French, but was thirty years ahead of its time: "concrete" poetry. Haruyama called it "formalism," and he and Kitasono explored the style. Meanwhile, Kitasono and Ueda Toshio also extended the genre to their original "diagrammatic poems."

Haruyama was able to use the Kōseikaku series to bolster his theories. Besides Nishiwaki's *Surrealistic Poetics*, he also published full-length volumes of poetry by Ueda Toshio, Kitagawa Fuyuhiko (1900–1990), Anzai Fuyue (1898–1965), Kitasono Katue, and, in translation, Jean Cocteau, Blaise Cendrars, and Max Jacob.

For Kitasono, it was his first book of poems, and he titled it *Shiro no arubamu* (White album; literally, "Album of whiteness"; see Fig. 11). It

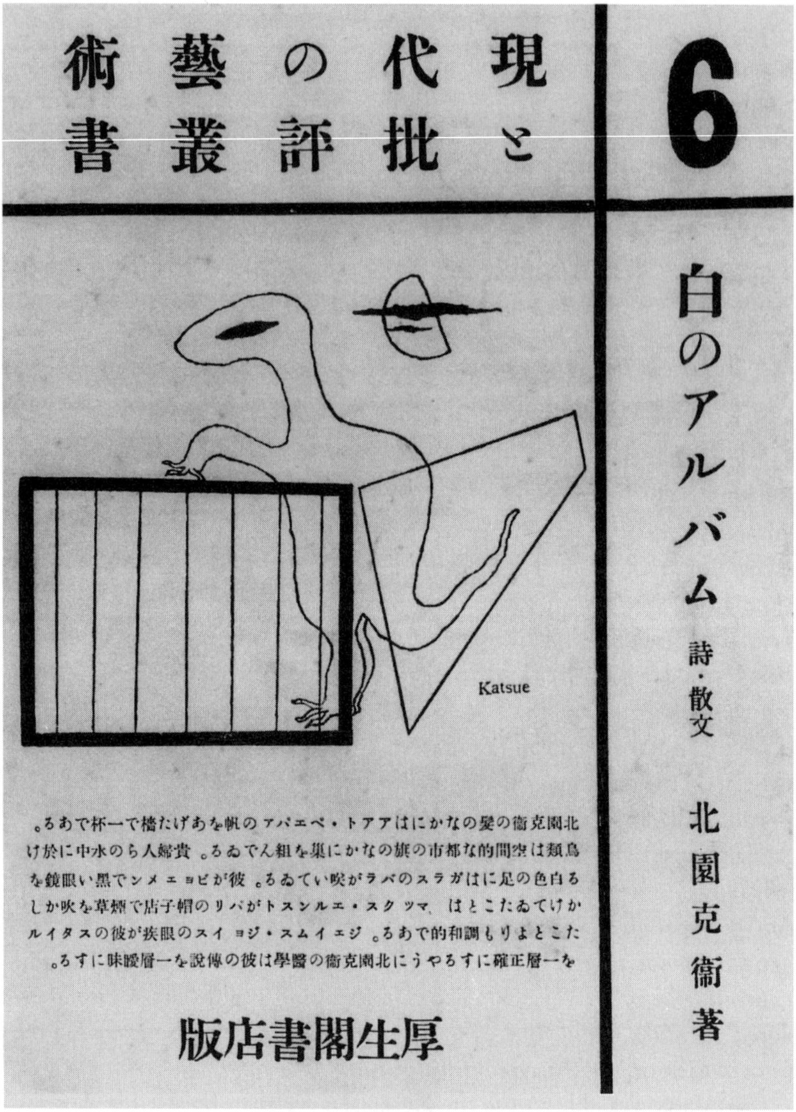

現代の藝術と批評叢書

6

白のアルバム

詩・散文

北園克衞著

Katsue

。るあで杯一で橋たげなな帆の アバエベ・トアアはにかなの髪の衞克園北
け於に中水のら人婦貴 。るゐでん粗な集にかなの旗の市都な的間空は類鳥
な鏡眼い黒でンメエヨビが彼 。るゐてい咲がラバのスラガはに足の色白る
しか吹な草煙で店子帽のリバがトスンルエ・スクッマ　はとこたゐてけか
ルイタスの彼が疾眼のスイ ヨジ・スムイェジ 。るあで的和調もりよとこた
。ろすに昧曖層一な説傷の彼は學醫の衞克園北にうやるすに確正層一を

厚生閣書店版

Fig. 11   Cover of Katue's first book of poems, *Shiro no arubamu* (Kōseikaku, 1929).
Designed by Katue.

contained a preface by Haruyama and was printed in an edition of 1,000 copies, of which 320 were sold.[73] Unlike the roughly five hundred poetry books published annually in contemporary Japan, *Shiro no arubamu* was one of only forty-two poetry books published in 1929.[74] In 1961 Katue reflected on what the book meant to him.

At that time I was not even thinking of publishing a book of my poetry. For me it was no more than the event of a distant world. Maybe that is to say that I had no interest in having a book of my poems. . . .

I remember the freshly printed book and the royalty payment arriving by registered mail. Even by today's standards it is hard to believe the good luck at receiving royalties on one's first book, but especially for that time it was incredible luck. Particularly for someone like me who wrote poems that had nothing to do with Japanese traditional poetry, it is probably more accurate to consider it as having been a wonderful accident. With that in mind, my appreciation to Haruyama Yukio for his courage in printing *Shiro no arubamu* continues undiminished to this day, supporting my affection for all the present avant-garde.

I have published as many as twenty poetry books since then, but all the "patterns" of my poetry are in *Shiro no arubamu*. In that sense, *Shiro no arubamu* is an unfinished volume of many patterns gathered in a jumble, but the book includes all the elements of the poems I will probably write through my entire life.

When I get in a slump, I always take out *Shiro no arubamu*, and like a hunter stalking prey, my eyes wander in the jungle of words where I discover a forgotten pattern, sweep away the dust, and extend it in a new way.[75]

Katue must have decided on the title very late, because the book was advertised as "Hakushoku shishū" (White poem collection) only a month before publication.[76] He was most satisfied with "Kigō setsu" (Semiotic theory) which, as noted above, was a reworking of the poem "Hakushoku shishū." Two stanzas of "Kigō setsu" were quoted in advertisements for the book.

Katue considered his method a major breakthrough in originality:

In 1927 for the first time, without being influenced by anyone, I discovered a space (*ba*). Until then I had been able to write some individual poems using various forms but, for some reason or other, those poems were mixed with other people's "elements." Even now I can recall the thrill of successfully writing what in every sense were my own poems. It was the joy of pure creation, and it was exciting. I remember writing many poems over a six-month period with my newly discovered form.

As for poetry, it is almost impossible to discover a new space without anyone's influence.

My experiment came about as a result of having so severely destroyed the concepts supporting the poetry that had existed up until then. Now [in 1952] it is somewhat accepted as poetry but, to be honest, at that time even I wondered whether my adventurousness wasn't going slightly overboard.

In any case, on a blank sheet of paper, as if painting with a brush on a new canvas, I chose ideograms with simple but vivid imagery and wrote poems with the same conciseness as, for example, we find in Paul Klee's paintings. In short, *I ignored the general content and inevitability in words* and used words as symbols of colors, lines, and dots. This was the principle of my poetic experiment.[77] (Italics added)

Kitasono's description of his profound and joyful experience resembles an account of religious awakening and conversion. However, it is philosophically doubtful whether any creation can come about without a single outside influence. Kitasono's mention of Paul Klee shows that he was presumably not altogether free of influences. He wrote with a keen awareness of poetry as a historical system of evolving forms ("patterns") leading to ever new directions. The crossover application of techniques from the field of art to poetry was indeed an innovation by Kitasono. After years of experimenting, he was now thoroughly convinced of his originality. His peers were the great innovators on the world stage, such as Mallarmé, Apollinaire, Stein, and Joyce.

What Kitasono regarded as the poetry of "Kigō setsu," namely, the arrangement of signs without reference to their meaning, corresponds precisely to the untranslatable portion of the language. His statement that he "ignored the general content and inevitability in words" conversely acknowledged that meaning and the sign holding it are ultimately inseparable. Did he believe he could present word shells unattached to any content? (Those would be sights or sounds, not words.) Was he in effect implying that his ideal reader would not understand the language at all? And when he "used words as symbols of colors, lines, and dots," did he mean that the graphs for colors are to be read for their content (color is perceived from the meaning not the shape) while the other graphs are viewed only as lines and dots? Even granting that he could consciously ignore the meaning of ideograms, could he dismiss the issue on a subconscious level? Kitasono's experiment was clearly impossible in any absolute sense. Nevertheless, given the ultimate futility of the venture as a point of departure, he was bravely testing how far he could deny meaning and highlight the visual aspect of written Japanese with simple and vivid images. Instead of using the page to let his passion gush out, he turned it into a substitute canvas. That represented a new way of treating the language. Traditional Japanese and Chinese calligraphy had also taken language and rarified it into "visual art," an esthetic that may have influenced Kitasono's theorizing. Ironically, he gained more acclaim painting in poetry than he did on real canvases. Recognition as a poet, sweet in itself, was not his goal at this time; he was interested in making his name and living as an artist. Poetry became both a sanctuary where he could display his talent and a playground to avenge his inability to distinguish himself as a painter.

"Kigō setsu" was one response to a larger trend, considered by the avantgarde Japanese poets to be surrealistic, of valuing form over content. For "Kigō setsu," Kitasono relied on intuition in choosing ideograms; yet his method diverged fundamentally from automatism in emphasizing the *conscious* arrangement of material. Critics inevitably cite "Kigō setsu" for its original method of construction and then base their judgment of Kitasono to a large degree on this one poem. Readers, however, rarely approach poems solely as exercises in methodology. In my opinion, nothing has been more harmful to Kitasono's reputation as a poet than the overexposure given the bland imagery of "Kigō setsu" at the expense of his other poems. In this respect, he was as guilty as anyone.

Katue was not as happy with his experiments in formalism, believing that they were contaminated with borrowings from other poets. Perhaps less original than "Kigō setsu," they are, nevertheless, intriguing compositions. One formalistic tendency (shared with Haruyama) is the frequent repetition of one word or phrase. Form is valued over content, and the design of the finished poem is meant to please the eye. His experiments in this vein derived from Mallarmé's "Un Coup de dès n'abolira jamais le hasard" (1895)[78] and Apollinaire's "calligrammes."[79] It must have dawned on Kitasono and Haruyama that the Japanese language, with its one-hundred phonetic characters and several thousand ideographs, was a pictographic gold mine compared to European languages based on the twenty-six letters of the Roman alphabet, although at the time they never explicitly made the comparison.

Among Kitasono's formalistic poems using repetition is "umi no umi no umi no . . . " (ocean's ocean's ocean's . . .), a section of the longer poem "Bara no sanji" (3 P.M. of the Rose). The graphs *no* (の, corresponding to the "apostrophe + s" of English) and *umi* (海, "ocean") appear seventy times each. When viewed as one unit, they combine to give the impression of waves curling on the ocean surface (Fig. 12).

海の海の海の海の海の海の海の海の海の
の　の　の　の　の　の　の　の　の
海　海　海　海　海　海　海　海　海
の　の　の　の　の　の　の　の　の
海　海　海　海　海　海　海　海　海
の　の　の　の　の　の　の　の　の
海　海　海　海　海　海　海　海　海
の　の　の　の　の　の　の　の　の
海　海　海　海　海　海　海　海　海
の　の　の　の　の　の　の　の　の
海　海　海　海　海　海　海　海　海
の　の　の　の　の　の　の　の　の
海　海　海　海　海　海　海　海　海
の　の　の　の　の　の　の　の　の
海　海　海　海　海　海　海　海　海
の　の　の　の　の　の　の　の　の
海　海　海　海　海　海　海　海　海
の　の　の　の　の　の　の　の　の
海　海　海　海　海　海　海　海　海
の　の　の　の　の　の　の　の　の

Fig. 12　Section of Katue's poem with concrete tendency, "umi no umi no umi no . . ."
(ocean's ocean's ocean's . . .), in *Shiro no arubamu* (Kōseikaku, 1929), p. 59.

Kitasono's visually accented poem is open to multiple interpretations. For example, "ocean's ocean" could mean that with each new wave the ocean engulfs itself again. There is little point, however, in dissecting a concrete poem like "umi no umi no umi no" into a myriad of exegetical possibilities beyond its visual content. The potential for multiple explanations holds more significance than any single interpretation.

One of Haruyama's formalistic poems became more famous than any of Kitasono's. The title is simply an asterisk (*), and the poem consists of the phrase "shiroi shōjo" (白い小女, white girl) repeated 112 times.[80] The poem was twice reprinted with the phrase repeated 84 times (Fig. 13).[81]

Haruyama wrote that his poem had been interpreted as (1) an athletic meet ("mass-game") of white girls; (2) a group of white girls; (3) a formation of white girls; 4) "x y" of white girls; (5) "x . . . "; and (6) "y . . . ."[82] His colleagues took sides for and against Haruyama's poem and the formalistic method behind it. Anzai Fuyue commented that all the poetry would have been lost if "white girl" had been replaced by "yellow boy."[83]

One cluster of poems in *Shiro no arubamu* contains what Katue called "diagrammatic explanations." Both he and Ueda Toshio had already published poems with this tendency in 1927.[84] They consist of squiggly and straight lines, mathematical notations, arrows, parentheses, and almost no words. They still remain fresh, continually inviting us to reflect on the nature of poetry and where we define its perimeters. Poems in this mode, such as "Hikōsen no densetsu" (Legend of the Airship; Fig. 14), are well-balanced designs that allow for visual satisfaction while blocking any adequate understanding of them with the intellect. Kitasono's diagrammatic poems are not always so resistant to meaning. Without sacrificing visuality, the content is fairly comprehensible in poems such as "Seikei shujutsu" (Plastic surgery operation; Fig. 15) in which the only word that appears, "zōka" (artificial flower), has links to cosmetic surgery.

Kitasono's transition from "Kigō setsu," with its semi-denial of meaning, through the repetition poems to the diagrammatic jottings follows a trajectory of greater abstraction within similar forms. As frivolous as the poems sometimes appear, because of the experimentation in *Shiro no arubamu*—especially the taxonomic gesticulations—Katue was able to redefine poetry once again beginning in the late 1950s by naming his photographs "plastic poems."[85]

白い少女 白い少女 白い少女 白い少女 白い少女 白い少女　白い少女 白い少女 白い少女 白い少女 白い少女 白い少女 白い少女 白い少女

白い少女 白い少女 白い少女 白い少女 白い少女 白い少女　白い少女 白い少女 白い少女 白い少女 白い少女 白い少女 白い少女 白い少女

白い少女 白い少女 白い少女 白い少女 白い少女 白い少女　白い少女 白い少女 白い少女 白い少女 白い少女 白い少女 白い少女 白い少女

白い少女 白い少女 白い少女 白い少女 白い少女 白い少女　白い少女 白い少女 白い少女 白い少女 白い少女 白い少女 白い少女 白い少女

白い少女 白い少女 白い少女 白い少女 白い少女 白い少女　白い少女 白い少女 白い少女 白い少女 白い少女 白い少女 白い少女 白い少女

白い少女 白い少女 白い少女 白い少女 白い少女 白い少女　白い少女 白い少女 白い少女 白い少女 白い少女 白い少女 白い少女 白い少女

Fig. 13   Haruyama Yukio's formalist poem "*," in *Shi no kenkyū* (Kōseikaku, 1931), pp. 97–98.

Haruyama Yukio's highly unconventional preface to *Shiro no arubamu* erased the barrier between criticism and poetry and came to be regarded as a classic in its own right (it has been reprinted many times). Yukio praises Katue by frequently mentioning his name alongside eminent Europeans such as Baudelaire, Pushkin, Nietzsche, László Moholy-Nagy, and Kurt Schwitters (no Japanese are mentioned): "His [Kitasono's] wearing black glasses in Bohemia is even more harmonious than Max Ernst blowing smoke in a Parisian hat shop. And just as James Joyce's eye disease made his style more precise, Kitasono Katue's iatrology has obscured his own legend."[86]

Yukio's praise is expressed in the cool, half-mocking tone that was coming to be prized by the new poets. Elsewhere, he parodied Katue's vocabulary

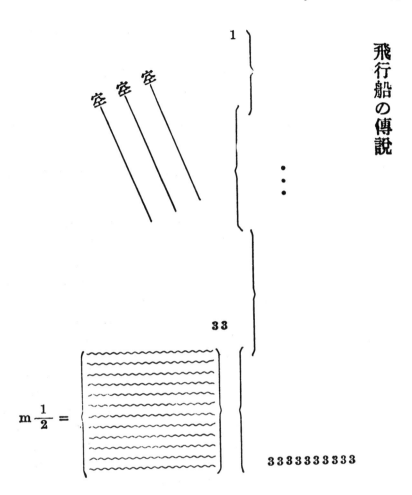

Fig. 14   Kàtue's diagrammatic poem "Legend of the Airship," in *Shiro no arubamu* (Kōsei-kaku, 1929), p. 42; reprinted in *Kitasono Katue zenshishū* (Chūsekisha, 1983), p. 45.

and style. "Kitasono Katue's iatrology" refers to a list of words by Kitasono starting with "p-" (and mostly ending in "-ology") that accompanies a drawing in *Shiro no arubamu:* "phrenology, physiology, physiography, physics, philosophy, phonology, philology, pharmacology, psychology, pistology, and parasology."[87]

Much of the preface has nothing to do with Katue, such as, "Cows, sheep, horses, and deer outside children's stories, when taken as food, are not outside nature. Painted deer don't eat grass."[88] At the core of the preface, however, are pronouncements by Haruyama on the valuelessness of "meaning" in poetry:

A poem overly confused by meaning, instead of losing all its leaves, reminds you of a tree holding a flock of bad-mannered sparrows.

*

A poem without meaning is no more than the application of a minus literary method of not providing meaning.

*

What was written down was no more than literature. Only now for the first time, the unwritten part is called poetry.

*

By writing poetry without meaning, the purity of poetry is demonstrated. To see meaning in poetry is not to see anything beyond literature in poetry.[89]

Yukio had started as a symbolist but was now interested in leaving that weightier treatment of language in favor of surrealistic and formalistic experiments in which meaning was given short shrift.

Shiro no arubamu was advertised in *Shi to shiron* and elsewhere as "surrealistic poetry and prose," although the adjective was not found on the cover of the book itself. Basing himself on Jean Cocteau's broad interpretation of the poet as multifaceted artist and borrowing his categories, Kitasono divided the contents of the book into (1) "poésie"; (2) "poésie en prose"; (3) "poésie de théâtre"; (4) "poésie de roman"; and (5) "poésie graphique."[90] Poetry was the spring from which flowed not only his diagrammatic experiments but also short stories, drawings, and performance pieces. Although Katue lumped all genres of writing and art together under the rubric of "poetry," for him and the other young poets, artistic production itself was only one by-product of the new lifestyle and values sweeping the intellectual world.[91] And in evaluating one another's work, they looked not only at the text but also at the extent of the author's *esprit nouveau*, which was most evident in how far the author stretched the boundaries of literature.

Shiro no arubamu was intended to shock the poetry establishment.[92] Katue gained immediate recognition as one of the main poets from the emerging counterculture. Satisfied with the niche he had carved out for himself in the previous half-decade, he clung to isolation from the mainstream as his badge of authenticity.

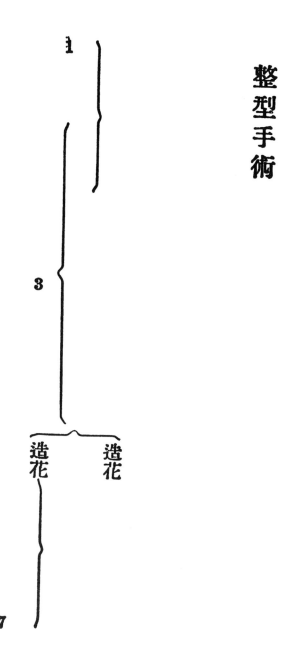

Fig. 15   Katue's diagrammatic poem "Plastic Surgery Operation," in *Shiro no arubamu* (Kōseikaku, 1929), p. 36; reprinted in *Kitasono Katue zenshishū* (Chūsekisha, 1983), p. 39.

This chapter has focused on the introduction of literary surrealism to Japan in the late 1920s and its interpretation there. One aspect of French surrealism that went almost ignored in Japan was the tolerance of sexually explicit material from the subconscious, usually a result of the non-filtering of thought in automatism.[93] Kitasono, Nishiwaki, and most of the other Japanese surrealists, rarely referred to the genitals or sex. One exception is the line "I lick virgin Cleopatra's vagina" in an Ueda Toshio poem.[94] Nevertheless, Toshio was at least liberated enough not to edit out such passages.

The immediate crisis for the few dozen avant-garde poets had been where to go after dadaism. It was fairly easy to discard traditional Japanese literature and write absurd poems bordering on nonsense in the name of a new civilization, but it was more difficult to regain some touchstone of relevance without sliding back to pre-dadaist sentimentalism. The border between dadaism and surrealism at this time was not sharply demarcated in Japan (or in France), but the poems and manifestos coming from France were pointing to a new beginning, a rejection of simple negation. For Breton and his colleagues, the answer was to tap the unconscious. Kitasono and his fellow poets wanted a method that would allow them to write poetry that would reflect their contemporary sensibility. At times the Japanese found the thoughts and actions of French surrealists incomprehensible, for example, the contempt they displayed toward Jean Cocteau.[95] Japanese accepted the surrealists and Cocteau. Likewise, they did not choose between Tzara and Breton but admired both from afar.

Surrealism continued to influence Kitasono's work both before and after World War II. However surrealism was interpreted or misinterpreted, it was certainly more alive in Tokyo than Westerners commonly believe. For instance, Dawn Ades wrote in 1981 that "surrealism did not really become international until 1936, remaining very much a French movement centered in Paris."[96] In fact, Japanese were digesting surrealism from the mid-1920s and actively publishing on the subject from 1927.

Western surrealism grew out of Western soil; Japanese surrealism was a transplant that grew out of Japanese soil. Japanese poets were simultaneously absorbing several movements, and they tended to call the mix *surrealism*. The leap into concrete poetry, a by-product of experimentation in the name of surrealism, was the harvest of a creative misunderstanding.

4 MULTIPLE
MASKS

Japan had a difficult time putting its financial house in order in the aftermath of the 1923 Great Kantō Earthquake. In 1927, while Diet members were discussing Japan's return to the gold standard, word spread that banks in possession of "earthquake bills" were about to default. In the ensuing panic, thirty-seven banks collapsed, causing a nationwide depression. Japan's fragile economy was further jolted when the Great Depression in the United States rippled out to cause chaos in international commerce. Full recovery was not achieved until 1935, by which time the leading industrial countries had broken up into more or less self-sufficient blocs whose economies were preparing for a military confrontation. During the 1930s, Japan's exports and imports were cut in half, and its colonies assumed increasing importance both as a source of raw materials and as a consumer of its manufactures. The agricultural sector (and especially the 36 percent of farm families who engaged almost exclusively in sericulture) was hardest hit by the sudden downswing in prices and collapse of international markets.

As poverty swept through the countryside, stories spread of infanticide and young girls sold into prostitution. There was also high unemployment, giving rise to a popular song with the line *daigaku o deta keredo* . . . (I graduated college, but . . . [can't find work]). In the resulting frustration and despair, intellectuals felt a keen responsibility to help raise the lot of workers, and novelists and poets aimed at emboldening readers with reformist, if not revolutionary, zeal. Accordingly, during the late 1920s and early 1930s proletarian literature gained a wide audience.[1]

Katue acknowledged the dominance of proletarian literature, but he had no use for it. From the perspective of 1950, he wrote:

The proletarian movement vigorously produced a sharp resistance to the societal malaise of the time, and even in the arts it had some resounding successes. Yet with the passage of time, that overly theoretical concept restricted authors' creations beyond what was necessary. When the proletarian arts degenerated into nothing more than the search for propagandistic techniques, they lost their importance and, gradually, their universality as an artistic movement. The seeds of surrealism were sown in the soil of this avant-garde movement.[2]

Kitasono's refusal to associate his own poetry with social and political causes helped strengthen the foundation upon which it was based, while making him appear irrelevant in the eyes of some fellow poets and readers. Even among the modernist contributors to *Shi to shiron*, there was a call for more consciously political literature than editor Haruyama Yukio was willing to publish; consequently, Kambara Tai (1898–1997), Kitagawa Fuyuhiko, and others left in protest and started the magazine *Shi, genjitsu* (Poetry, reality).[3]

One strategy of Japanese poets to emphasize their modernist identity was to adopt pen names. The most extravagant in this regard was Nishiwaki Junzaburō, who went by the Latin name Jacobus Phillipus. Satō Saku sometimes published under the pseudonyms Tosu Kō and Sekimizu Ryū. Most of the lesser known poets also adopted pen names, but no one used as many as Hashimoto Kenkichi (Kitasono Katue).

From 1927 Hashimoto started using the name Asaka Kenkichi (Asaka was the name of a village near his hometown) in the literary journals *Bungei toshi* (Literary city) and *SMG*.[4] In the latter he also signed drawings with the mysterious initials (or name) ASS. Seeming to fancy himself a fusion of Picasso and Miró, in *Bungei tanbi* he signed his drawings "Picalo" (the "r" of Miró changed to "l"). But from July 1928 he published under the name that he would use thereafter almost exclusively—Kitasono Katue (also written Kitazono Katué or Katsue).[5] Treating himself as a third-person phenomenon, he would also sign poems and drawings "Le Katue."

The name Kitasono Katue appears on all his books, but for contributions to magazines he used additional pen names throughout his career. Why he chose the name Kita-sono Katu-e (north-garden-conquer-guard) remains a mystery. Sasaki Kikyō (1922–) is probably correct in speculating that "the 'e' in Katu*e* stands for the 'garde' ['ei' is an alternative reading] of 'avant-garde' (zen-*ei*)."[6] Katué and the surrealist painter Koga Harué at times added an accent on the final "é," when writing their names in Roman script, because they wanted them pronounced as in French. The "sono" of Kitasono, being the second element in a compound, is pronounced "zono," but Katue spelled it with an "s" in imitation of the French in which an "s" between two vowels is pronounced "z."[7] From the name alone one cannot determine the poet's sex.[8] An androgynous name was not inconsistent with the hairdos and other fashions of the Japanese avant-garde of the 1920s. If his choice of name was consistent with his "design" approach to writing poetry, then the characters were settled on as much for their visual and aural qualities as for their meaning. Whatever the reason, Kitasono Katue was certainly a more exotic (hence, literary) name than the commonplace Hashimoto Kenkichi.

Not everyone was aware that Hashimoto and Kitasono were one and the same poet. The *Shidan jinkokki* (1933; Dictionary of poets arranged by native prefecture) contains this brief entry for Mie prefecture:

Although Mie Prefecture gave us haiku-saint Bashō, these days it is not producing many poets. Among the few, there is really only Kitasono Katue, who wrote *Shiro no arubamu*. His poems can be said to extol the esthetics of literature [excerpt from "Kigō setsu"].

Besides them [Kitasono Katue and Ōnuma Jaku], we have Hashimoto Kenkichi and Shibahara Hidetsugu, but one feels a loneliness in the paucity of their compositions. I think that this area, which long ago produced the haiku-saint Bashō, will certainly give birth to an outstanding poet.[9]

The title of the book confirms the great importance attached to the prefectural origin of poets. There is unintended irony in that avant-garde poets were supposedly "cosmopolitan."

In 1930 Iwamoto Shūzō (1908–79), a poet from Uji-Yamada City (where Katue had gone to business school) and a graduate of Tōyō University, who had majored in classical Chinese literature, called on Katue in Tokyo. Over the next decade, they collaborated on three magazines, *Hakushi* (Blank paper), *Madame Blanche*, and *VOU*. After the war, Iwamoto split from Kitasono to start his own group, Cénacle de Pan Poésie, and its organ *Pan Poésie*.[10] But before the war, the two worked closely together. For Iwamoto, as yet unestablished in the capital, the chance to co-edit with Kitasono, already at the forefront of the avant-garde, was an easy introduction to the scene. And for Kitasono, who had been in Tokyo for over a decade, it was his first experience at being a mentor, a role that he would play with dozens of poets for the rest of his life. Katue and Shūzō were first and foremost friends—Katue abhorred the word *deshi* (disciple)—but of the two, Katue was the innovator in artistic direction for the magazines they collaborated on. Shūzō's poetry is some of the most accomplished modernist verse in

Japanese; he was able to create his own style, and yet, according to Ueda Osamu (1915–96), a poet who knew both writers, "Just as without Motoori Norinaga [1730–1801], there would have been no Hirata Atsutane [1776–1843], without Kitasono there would have been no Iwamoto Shūzō."[11]

From 1930 until Japan's invasion of China in 1937, Katue was involved in a bustle of artistic activity. Still set on being a painter, he joined the prestigious Nikakai (Second-tier association) group of avant-garde artists. His first exhibited work, the 1932 surreal oil painting *Umi no haikei* (Ocean background), was destroyed in the war, but a black-and-white photographic print remains (Fig. 16).[12]

Also in 1932, Katue's poetry took a new, lyrical turn, and he published his second book, *Wakai koronii* (Young colony).[13] From the title alone, with the Japanese Guandong Army in the act of colonizing Manchuria and a relatively unknown author, a contemporary reader might have expected a patriotic book studded with images of the Chinese continent and daily life. But Kitasono intended nothing of the sort.[14] Oblivious to any political overtones, he used the word "colony" in the sense of "artists' colony." The setting for the most part is reminiscent of a Japanese seaside resort like Atami, with tennis and summer pleasures.

Busy escaping from the oppressive Japanism surrounding him, Katue involved himself ever deeper in the *haikara* (high-collar) aspiration for, and identification with, the West. In this sense he was the happy inhabitant of a make-believe European colony. As a citizen of imperial Japan, Kitasono was part of the network of annexations of neighboring territories that had begun before his birth—Okinawa in 1879, Taiwan in 1895, Korea in 1910, and, most recently, Manchuria in 1931. When Katue would later claim that he was interested only in "pure poetry" and not in politics, he was not accounting for the fact that not to oppose the status quo was, by default, to support it.

The seventeen poems in *Wakai koronii* are all short, and the book itself is miniature (3.25 × 4.75 inches), the first of a series of poetry books published by Bon shoten that included others by Haruyama Yukio, Kondō Azuma (1904–88), and Takenaka Iku (1904–82).[15] Katue was aware of the book as an integrated object in which format should match contents. Unlike *Shiro no arubamu* with its "jumble of patterns," the poems in *Wakai koronii* are of a single, unified pattern—brief and lyrical, glowing with a romantic but not overly sentimental optimism. For Katue it was a new experiment, seemingly his answer to the question of how to compose modern love poetry in collo-

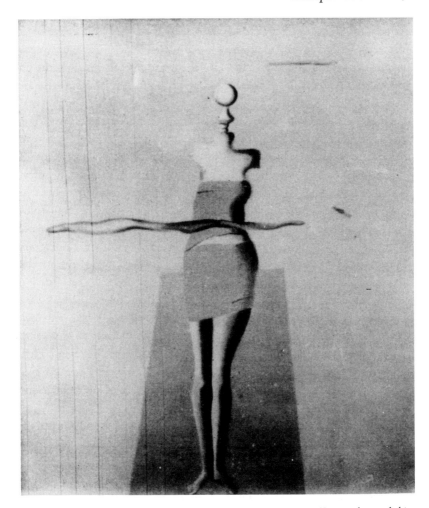

Fig. 16   Katue, *Umi no haikei* (Ocean background), oil painting. 1932. Katue submitted this painting in 1932 to the annual exhibit of the avant-garde group Nikaten. The painting was destroyed during World War II, and only the photograph remains.

quial Japanese. None of the poems stands out as a masterpiece, but in combination they evoke the vigor of a poet in the prime of youth. Kitasono, who until then had been somewhat of a lone wolf struggling to prove his worth, is here more conscious of community—in the title of the collection, in his habit of addressing his audience as "cousins," and in his frequent use of plural pronouns. Both the personal following Kitasono was beginning to attract and his secure place within the budding avant-garde movement may have contributed to his newfound friendliness. The hard, formalistic edge of his first book had given way to a renewed warmth in which people once again inhabit the poems. Because of the surreal edge to his romanticism, the poems manage to avoid the self-pity found in much modern Japanese verse and prose fiction.

Kitasono keeps each poem internally consistent and maintains an even tone of language, although he is, as before, antagonistic to easy, logical connections between lines. His main technique is to create surreal images from a linguistic reservoir drained of all but lyrical vocabulary. Whereas his previous surreal work (as in *Ishō no taiyō*) evoked a fantasy world purely of his imagination, these poems are firmly grounded in modernized Japan—Tokyo and resortlands—and they relate, however indirectly, to Katue's experience. Whereas we may have wondered about the identity of the Kiiiiing and Queeeen in "Vin de Masque," in *Wakai koronii* we have the impression that the characters are he and his circle of friends.

The vocabulary is largely restricted to words that evoke a pleasant vacation: "spring," "birds," "boat," "tennis," "summer," "violets," "glass," "window," "rose," "smile." Mixed in with these are words reminiscent of a Western bourgeois context: "parasol," "bonnet," "angel," "mandolin," "bouquet." There is also much water imagery: "sea," "lake," "mermaid," "waves." The most overused word is "seashell," seemingly a replacement for the ubiquitous "crystal" of previous poetry.

Wakai koronii is most memorable for the sharpness of certain surreal images. Logic and cause-and-effect are cast to the wind, producing lines such as, "The sea vibrates spirit smiles inside pine needles" ("Billet"); and "With your mysterious sensibility won't you pass a derrick my way?" ("Karui tenisu" [Casual tennis]), and the visually more consistent—and therefore more conventional image—"Streetlights simultaneously heat up orangeade" ("Natsu no sanpomichi" [A summer's stroll]). His landscape—"night tennis court / the city's transparent desert"—turns playfully phantasmagoric as "blue flowers bloom / in the cacti . . . rackets" ("Momo no kawa" [Peachskin]). One overused device, here and elsewhere, is striving for a poetic effect by adding a commonplace noun that connotes modernity, such as "derrick," "orangeade," and "tennis court."

Katue's frequent use of personification first surfaces in *Wakai koronii*, and it adds a human warmth consonant with the lyrical surface. Walt Disney cartoons (which the surrealists admired) and French surrealist art often animated non-human objects with human characteristics.

> how many times when opening the car door have we seen
> Spring getting out on eternity's side
> > —"Natsu no kokoro"
>
> opening the window, there was Bluesky[16]
> > —"Jabot"
>
> October rides a boat and comes home
> > —"Une Bienséance"[17]

Erotic surreal imagery is rare in Kitasono's poetry. One anthropomorphic image from *Wakai koronoii*, however, is unabashedly erotic: "stars with sensitive breasts" ("Bonne nuit").

Wakai koronii rings optimistic because the accent is on summer, the height of the year, and on youth, the prime of life. At times the images are superficial and the lines limp, for example, when the French greeting "Bonjour" or "Bon soir" is invoked to carry the weight of a full line in poems of less than a dozen lines ("Umi no nikki" [Diary of the Sea], "Jabot," "Une Bienséance").

The ebullient summer atmosphere is tempered at times, not by contrary dark or wintry imagery, but by a caution that puts a check on the runaway enthusiasm. For example, "in the city not every glass is the queen of diamonds" ("Natsu no ichiya" [One summer night]) can be interpreted as a warning to men from the countryside not to be fooled by the dazzle of city women. And in a retreat from the marvelous to the mundane, he states, "because pointed nails may scar our love / even now I love common, ordinary dreams" ("Natsu no sanpomichi").

This atmosphere, saturated with pleasant images, starts to wear, but Kitasono curtails the naïveté by giving the final sequence of poems the title "Tu es bête" (You are foolish). And when we start to gain the impression that his colony does nothing but sunbathe, we are told that they are "dying in summer." In these ways he keeps an edge of tension in what is otherwise sugary verse.

"Kotoba" (Words) is more compelling than the other poems in *Wakai koronii*, because it does more than simply evoke an atmosphere:

Words

in summer let's buy blue lampshades
to see your and our lovely fingers
in the star city is an angel with seashell fingernails
a selfish, shabby angel
that's you
in the shade of waves of acacia leaves
a true manicure is performed
but

ah, touch the nails and you'll get scarred

this was also a simple, pencil-sketched angel[18]

Kitasono's angel is depicted first ethereally "with seashell nails" and then more humanly as "a selfish, shabby angel." We may wonder, Why an angel? and Where does this angel come from? This three-dimensional angel is suddenly flattened to a two-dimensional figure in the last line, "this was also a simple, pencil-sketched angel." The reading of the poem is undermined by the deflating ending, one of the techniques in Kitasono's poetic arsenal since the nihilism of his neo-dada days. In *Wakai koronii* we find another nihilistic ending, "all is demolished," in the poem "Umi no sukandaru"(The sea's scandal). Mallarmé's poem "Un Coup de dés n'abolira jamais le hasard" and the key dadaist concepts of simultaneity and chance are recalled in "I shake the dice / cars move along / bicycles have blowouts" ("Natsu no sanpomichi").

As in his earlier surreal poetry, Katue continues to use the *kakekotoba* (pivot word) of classical Japanese poetry, but now for lyrical effect.

faraway beach parasol
on hot sand
in the lovely shade we wrote our diary[19]

Here "sand" performs a dual, or pivot, function: "parasol on hot sand" and "on hot sand . . . we wrote our diary."

As part of Katue's experiment with surrealism and the creating of a new lyricism, he regularly takes poetic license and forms ungrammatical expressions. He also switches back and forth between prose and poetry in groping for a new style. Images, sharp in themselves, shine only intermittently and to less effect when buried in prosaic phrases. One such obstruction, to be discarded in his future poetry, is the use of repetitive conjunctions, *shikashi daga* (but, yet; "Kuchi bue" [Whistle]), *mata futatabi* (once again; "Natsu no sanpomichi"), *keredomo shikashi* (yet, however; "Momo no kawa"). Justifiable in terms of rhythm, such tampering with the grammatical apparatus, by calling too much attention to the vehicle, works against the smoothness of the lyrical effect. The experiment, however, eventually bore fruit in postwar poems in which such repetition added a sense of hesitancy, and hence fragility, and was instrumental in building an atmosphere of fragmentation and alienation (see Chapter 7).

Kitasono's most radical technique, however, is the rupture of continuity of meaning from line to line, exemplified at the end of "Karui tenisu":

> after all, thieves are correct
> an egg-shaped cloud circles the chimney
> inhaler makes one tear
>
> well! even when you smoke, you deceive me
>   with meaningless words[20]

The first line above comes out of nowhere. Why are thieves correct? And about what? The next two lines bring together nouns, adjectives, and verbs of roundness—"egg-shaped cloud . . . circles . . . chimney . . . inhaler . . . tear"—as well as subtly embedding a set of images with oppositional flows: "cloud-tear" (implying descent through the inhaler) and chimney-smoke (ascent). There is no singular meaning—the poem opts for an open, not closed, reading—yet the elements fit well enough within the same associational set so as not to give the impression of random nonsense. Although denying a one-dimensional, linear reading, Katue supplies a contextual gap between lines to make the reader's imagination stretch to try to bridge it. The discontinuity from line to line is similar to the *kakekotoba*, "forked" reading in its illogic, except that the latter is more compressed in generating two readings from a single word or phrase.

In spite of Katue's sophistication in constructing parts of *Wakai koronii*, especially the surrealistic imagery, other strands of his thought have a distractive effect on the poems. For example, he shows questionable taste in "on your left hand / make a gold watch shine" ("Umi no paruku" [The ocean park]), or when repeating the word "buy"—"buy blue lampshades" ("Kotoba"), "buy aqua blue hats for the ladies" ("Momo no kawa"), "city people . . . buy bouquets" ("Rokugatsu no mikan sui" [June's Tangerine Juice]). Behind the romantic notion of showing affection to the beloved by giving a present is the implication that men buy women's love with flowers, clothes, and furniture. These lines read like capitalistic advertisements and detract from the momentum of the poems, exposing Katue's ideological and political naïveté about the mechanism of consumerism. The reader of *Wakai koronii* may want to impute irony to his continual use of "buy," but there probably is none, given Kitasono's poetic project.

With excesses of grammar, inconsistent quality, and a mix of strong and weak images, *Wakai koronii* leaves an uneven impression of experimental fits and starts. Yet Katue's ability to discover a new lyricism with surrealistic imagery in the short poem influenced other poets to venture in a similar direction. Curiously, Kitasono never wrote about the book, perhaps because he was embarrassed by the dreamy romanticism beneath the thin, surreal veneer, finding it at odds with his tougher, anti-romantic poetics.[21]

To turn for a moment to Katue's personal life, he was visited in autumn 1932 by an artist-friend who brought along his wife and a friend of hers, the twenty-one-year-old Kobayashi Ei (1910–87; called Eiko by Katue).[22] Eiko was an English major who had recently graduated from the prestigious Nihon Joshi Daigaku (Japan women's college) and was employed in the Ministry of Education as an English typist. At their first meeting, Kitasono presented her with a copy of *Wakai koronii*, and, in her words, "I was swept off my feet by Katue and his poetry."[23] The two met regularly thereafter. She recalled that on one date they were stopped and searched by the police for no apparent reason, apparently as part of the increased suspicion of young people by the authorities.

The following year, 1933, Katue and Eiko married and went to live in Asama. Katue's father, Yasukichi, had passed away the previous autumn, following Katue's older and younger sisters; now only the three boys in the family survived.[24] Katue returned to show his hometown to his bride and to spend time with his brother Heihachi, who occupied the main house with his family while the newlyweds stayed in a small house that had been left to Katue.

For the previous decade in Tokyo, Katue had been surviving on the meager allowance sent first by his parents and later by Heihachi, and by his earnings from freelance writing and design work. The deteriorating economy made it difficult, if not impossible, for a poet to subsist the way he had in the 1920s, and at thirty-one years old with a wife to support and no steady job, he must have felt a certain apprehension along with the excitement over their new life together. After three months in Asama, Eiko left to visit her parents in Niigata, and Katue returned to Tokyo in search of employment.

For the following year and a half, he was unable to find a steady job. Eiko returned to Tokyo after a couple of months, and the two of them struggled to eke out a living, helped along by money that occasionally arrived from Heihachi in Asama and Eiko's parents in Niigata. In 1934, Eiko gave birth to a son, Akio, their only child. The family moved to a tiny house in Magome, a neighborhood on the outskirts of Tokyo. A number of artists and writers lived there, because housing was relatively cheap and it was not too isolated.[25] Katue lived a few blocks away from the avant-garde sculptor Nakada Sadanosuke (1888–1970). Nakada's wife, Yoshie (1902–95), a fine painter in the modern style, did oil portraits of Katue in 1940 and 1958.[26]

For three years beginning in 1930, Katue worked seriously on a new "pattern" or approach to writing poetry, without publishing any work in magazines. He had always considered his poem "Kigō setsu" as a breakthrough into the unexplored, and he now hailed the twenty-two new poems of *Ensui shishū* (Conical poems) as a further extension of the territory.[27] As with "Kigō setsu," Katue made exaggerated claims for *Ensui shishū*, evident in the blurb he wrote for the dust jacket:

With these poems I have succeeded in grasping the dynamics of *poésie*. I think the mathematical construction of tension between each word carries a unique logic that ensures the eternity of abstract poems. The proposition of art's linguistic construction induces "formalism," but, and this should be clearly understood, it is not sustained by it.

The last sentence was presumably inserted to alert readers that he had transcended the strict "formalism" of parts of *Shiro no arubamu*, in which the content of a poem was subordinate to the form. Behind the barrage of scientific jargon in his blurb ("dynamics," "mathematics," "induce," "proposition") is the innovative method of *Ensui shishū*. Elsewhere, Katue gave this description: "If 'Kigō setsu' is experimental poetry in a horizontal way, then *Ensui shishū* is vertical. Put another way, the former is level [two-dimensional] and the latter is cubist [three-dimensional]."[28]

The prose poems of *Ensui shishū* are in direct contrast to "Kigō setsu." The lines in each poem are few and long, giving the appearance of verticality on the page (the book was typeset in traditional Japanese style). The "formalism" of the poems is a harmonious reflection of the content, and the form does not call attention to itself at the cost of the content.

The images in *Ensui shishū* are cubist and multi-layered and demand viewing from several angles. Grammatically, verbs of motion abound. The poems can best be characterized as "sculptures in motion," such as the following:

Miracle
Summer dancer raises leg and sinks. The horizon instantly rips. Above white tower appears violet yacht.[29]

The images in the poem are clear and precise, as is the interplay between horizontality and verticality. The reader pictures the upright dancer, then the leg lifting (with the thigh horizontal), and next the whole body vertically sinking. Then, at any distance from the dancer, the horizon tears. Finally, we imagine a white, vertical tower, above which appears a horizontal yacht with triangular mast. The poem resembles "Kigō setsu" in being a short, impersonal vignette of perceptual shapes, sights, and colors, with the conspicuous absence of any moralizing or reference to the author's daily life.

The following poem, equally short, continues the accent on movement, horizontality, and verticality:

A Boy's Death in a Flask
All of a sudden smashed into something like a wall. Then, hanging suspended, instantly fell.[30]

Other poems encourage the reader to visualize objects from several angles.

Nul
I stare in a crystal globe at a green cat. I stare in another crystal globe at a silvery white plant. I didn't smoke a rolled cigarette.[31]

The Boy's Metal Stripes and the Operating Room's Yellow Circle
Arriving at an outer limit and dangling upside down. Soon the metal spring will come loose. Then, with something resembling a headband with mirror, I search for a yellow cone and, with something like an ink plunger, quietly start inhaling the firefly-colored zone.[32]

Unlike "Kigō setsu," which is theoretically engaging while purposely lacking in dynamism, the poems in *Ensui shishū* are propelled by images in three-dimensional movement. Each image in *Ensui shishū* seems calculated for compatibility with the rest. The restricted vocabulary and minimal framework add density to the poems. Intuition plays a predominant part in Katue's choice of images, many of which are incongruent and surreal. His technique, however, relies more on conscious construction than on probes of the subconscious. In this respect, it is unlike automatic writing.

Katue had already carried out a less-condensed version of the multiangled poetry of *Ensui shishū* in a few prose pieces in *Shiro no arubamu* under the heading "L'Acte." With the horizontality of "Kigō setsu" and the verticality of *Ensui shishū*, he opted to separate and distill poetry into small, conceptually homogenous units in which particular parts of speech are emphasized for a desired effect. His approach is fragmentary, and depends on taking one linguistic direction (for example, accenting nouns or verbs) to the exclusion of others. In so doing, the reader is forced to conjure up the missing elements. Presence implies absence and vice versa.

Modern Japanese poetry before Kitasono had few experiments from the standpoint of poetics as innovative as "Kigō setsu" and *Ensui shishū*. After three years of struggling with the method and the poems, Katue felt proud of his achievement. With *Ensui shishū*, he had cut away excess words and distractive imagery, and the poems pulsate with a condensed vitality.

Kitasono's first important essay, "Spherical cone no kajitsu" (The fruit of spherical cone), dwells on *Ensui shishū*.[33] Despite some incoherent passages, questionable logic, and a rambling, occasionally arrogant tone, the short essay provides valuable insight into his poetics. Katue's starting point is dissatisfaction with the bulk of poetry of the past, especially emotional verse describing a poet's own life experiences. He is characteristically avant-garde in adopting a haughty, antagonistic posture: "The excellent poets of the past worked in a limited framework without method and insight. At any rate, they were lucky children who . . . did not earn but were handed a systematic relationship. When I face the history of such poetry, I let out only a cold, strained laugh."[34]

Once Katue decided to use the medium for more than personal expression, his dilemma was what to write, as he put it, what *sozai* (subject matter, material) to choose:

I decided to have the *sozai* relate to phenomena of physics. And, as for *sozai* to fill in the gaps, I searched among geometry and meteorology, as well as among the most simple substances and organisms. I was fully aware of the danger [of being misinterpreted] and was cautious not to use heavy imagery.[35]

Having decided on the pool of vocabulary and the cubist method, his next step was to compose the images and combine them. Although he labored over the poems, he liked to picture himself as a cool scientist and claimed that "deciding on the *sozai* and unifying it is an extremely simple and dispassionate operation." For him the issue boiled down to "the order constructed by the images and the effect of their activity and elasticity."

The word "elasticity" is important for grasping Kitasono's approach. As a countermeasure to the limited vocabulary, "elasticity," by definition, stretches the *sozai*. This was achieved mostly by the adroit arrangement of images. In *Ensui shishū*, Kitasono calculates the perceptual jump necessary from phrase to phrase and utilizes both continuity and discontinuity of imagery to disorient the reader. The limited vocabulary and calculated "elasticity" act to contain the boundaries of defamiliarization, and the thread of unity that runs through the poems saves them from degenerating into absurdity. Moreover, elasticity encourages re-readings in which the reader's perceptions are stretched in ever different directions.

Katue also made it clear what not to look for in these poems:

If in the subject matter of "Spherical Cone"—for example, *odoriko* [dancer] or *piramiddo-gata no genkai* [pyramid-shaped boundary]—you were to search for a philosophical symbol or an ironic attitude toward humanism, that would be foolish and, moreover, meaningless. We should leave theories of value and problems of taste outside the boundaries of this discussion.[36]

He closed the essay with a challenge to his critics.

In short, my role is like that of an operating-room surgeon who aims at making the patient breathe and walk like a perfectly normal member of society. Or my role is like that of a manufacturer of vaccines. A good critic would discourse about the bacteria of my vaccine or about my abdominal operation. That would be true criticism. But then another critic may discuss the occupation and personal appearance of the person operated on. Or he may discuss the price and label of the vaccine. The critic is always free to choose. But if I don't cast a glance at him, it is certainly not my fault.[37]

Kitasono might be considered a "surgeon" because he extracted sentimentality from his poetry; likewise, his experiments in abstraction vaccinated other poets against penning maudlin verse. He was not modest about describing his breakthrough with *Ensui shishū*, and his claims were exaggerated; yet they should also be seen as a common sign of avant-garde posturing, as described by literary theorist Renato Poggioli. Poggioli has pointed out that the "hyperbolic image" is characteristic of the "agonism" of the avant-garde mentality.[38]

Katue's attitude aside, his approach to writing the poems was highly experimental, and the results are therefore not consistent. But when the *sozai* and the elasticity interact harmoniously, the result is a vacuum space that is compressed and implosive.

> *Those Countless Stairs and Crystal Breasts of the Boy with a Glass Ribbon Tied Around His Neck*
>
> Snail-colored space warps, tears, flies off. Then, from a direction of total liquid, a boy with golden stripes showed the circle of a wise forehead and came sliding here into the proscenium.[39]

The title immediately transports us to a non-realistic setting with "crystal breasts," "countless stairs," and "glass ribbon tied around his neck." The macrocosmic word "space" in the poem serves to set the general atmosphere. It is modified by the microcosmic adjective "snail-colored." Elasticity is evident in the movement as "space warps, tears, flies off." The reader's mind is stretched to imagine: If "space . . . flies off," where does it go? Outside space?

The following snippet, "from a direction of total liquid," makes us suddenly imagine something like a wall of liquid approaching. We are, of course, free to imagine attributes such as the darkness of the unspecified liquid. And the "golden stripes" on the boy can be perceived as vertical, horizontal, or diagonal. The boy nears, and we are able to glimpse "the circle" of his "wise forehead." The lines of the stripes and the curve of the circle are both geometric shapes. The final phrase, "came sliding here into the proscenium" delivers him to a destination while simultaneously placing the reader in the audience visualizing the boy's arrival.

One of the main drawbacks to the poems in *Ensui shishū* is that Kitasono does not hesitate to reuse the same words once he deems them to be poetic. For example, *hotaru iro* (firefly color) and *katatsumuri iro* (snail color) are compelling and highly original poetic words that induce amazement the first time encountered, but when they are recycled a half dozen times in twenty-two poems, the effect becomes diluted. The same can be said of the ubiquitous *suishō* (crystal) and *shōnen* (boy).

Katue claimed that "the originality of *Ensui shishū* lay not in the subject matter but . . . in the originality of the method." Starting with *Ensui shishū*, he would continue to polish his "method" by varying the pool of vocabulary, line lengths, and the arrangement of imagery. Most of his experiments over the next forty years can better be understood in the context of "Kigō setsu" and *Ensui shishū*.

Katue seems to have been his own best reader at this time, and perhaps that accounts for his self-introduction on the blurb. The book's real impact was on the younger generation of poets who became prominent only after the war, including Tamura Ryūichi and Yoshioka Minoru (1919–90). Tamura called Katue's poetry *kaku bunretsu* (nuclear fission) and Yoshioka acknowledged that his second book of poems, *Ekitai* (Liquid; 1941), was an imitation of Kitasono's method.[40] Much of Yoshioka's later poetry, although less directly derivative, takes Katue's oeuvre as a point of departure. In this sense Katue was performing the avant-garde function of blazing a path in unexplored wilderness and leaving it for others to pave.

While working on *Ensui shishū*, Katue was also active in bringing young poets together. He and Iwamoto Shūzō had already published at least fourteen issues of *Hakushi* (Blank paper) when they decided in 1932 to change the magazine's name to *Madame Blanche*.[41] The club's name was also changed, from the Hakushi Kurabu (Blank paper club) to the Arcueil Club (for the club's badge, see Fig. 17), and monthly meetings to discuss current and future directions for poetry were added. Katue provided this explanation (in English) to *Townsman* about the naming of the club in 1938:

At that time we were profoundly influenced by the personality and the attitude for art of Erik Satie [1866–1925]. In the memory of this harmless great artist we used the name of the place [L'Arcueil] where he had lived for our club. The movement of this club rapidly exerted an influence over young poets, and the members increased [the] next year to more than forty, making an epoch in the poetical world.[42]

Because the members paid monthly dues, which helped underwrite publication of *Madame Blanche*, the financial load did not fall on any one person, as it had on Tamamura Zennosuke at GGPG and Fujiwara Sei'ichi at SMG. An outside sponsor was not indispensable but still welcome, and Bon shoten, the publisher/bookstore that had issued *Wakai koronii* and *Ensui shishū*, published and distributed *Madame Blanche* from the third issue on.

Having been directly involved in editing half a dozen avant-garde magazines in as many years, Katue must have been eager to relinquish the monthly chores of planning the issue, collecting manuscripts, delivering them to the printer, proofreading them, and then distributing the finished

Fig. 17   Badge of the Club D'Arcueil. In Japan it is customary for white-collar workers to wear a badge with their company's insignia in their suit lapels. Among poetry clubs, only those started by Katue had badges. For the members, it seems to have represented a stylishness that fit their modernism.

product. He was more likely to find satisfaction in leading a movement in which his own poetry and poetics were the model. Of the initial fifteen members, three were women, a higher than average proportion for a little magazine of the time.[43] Several poets who belonged to the Arcueil Club are now considered among the best prewar modernists, such as Nishiwaki Junzaburō, Sagawa Chika, Ema Shōko (1913–), Kondō Azuma, and Yamanaka Sansei. Conspicuously absent as regular members (with the exception of Nishiwaki) were the surrealist poets Katue had worked with on *SMG* and *Ishō no taiyō*. Their essays and translations were featured in the new magazine, but not their poetry. A typical early issue of *Madame Blanche* opened with a short contribution by a guest, such as Takiguchi Shūzō or Haruyama Yukio, followed by one short poem by each member.

A huge influx of new members just before the fifth issue of *Madame Blanche* swelled the roster to forty-two poets.[44] Most were students in their late teens born in the Taishō era and adaptable enough not to be sunk in old-fashioned language and poetics. Kikushima Tsuneji (1916–89), who was sixteen years old at the time, recalls how he joined the Arcueil Club:

I had been editing little magazines since I was thirteen years old—first there was *Prism* and then *Omega*, and I was acquainted with Iwamoto Shūzō. One day I received an unsolicited illustration from Katue of a high-heeled, slender woman. He offered it as the cover for *Omega*, no. 4. I used it, and a month later Katue sent me a drawing of a tiny giraffe with a note suggesting that I add it to the side of the woman for the following issue! I did. He also contributed poetry, as did Iwamoto Shūzō.

Around that time Katue asked me to join the Arcueil Club. I had heard Erik Satie's music the year before and was knocked out by it. The association with Satie excited me as much as the community of poets. I said I would join but didn't want to abandon my *Omega* friends. Katue got Iwamoto's approval, and the six of us joined the Arcueil Club together.[45]

Ema Shōko was one of a group of women poets who also joined the club at this time. She knew of Katue as a surrealist painter but was not aware that he wrote poetry.[46] At the time, he was writing advertising copy with poet Sagawa Chika in a tiny, narrow office in Ginza, which Ema described as "the size of an eel's bed."[47] The two persuaded Ema to join the Arcueil Club. She recalled their monthly meetings:

Kitasono Katue was very shy, and when he did speak, it was in a hushed voice saying only, "This month's issue is pretty good" or "It isn't very good" or "There are a lot of proofreading errors," and so forth.

The members would give their opinions, sometimes at odds with Katue's, or they would make certain requests of him. Everyone was free in discussing poetry.

It was at the meetings of *Shii no ki* [Chinquapin] magazine[48] and *Madame Blanche* that I came to realize how boring bad poetry is and how much fun good poetry can be. . . .

It was spectacular that among the *Madame Blanche* members were the women poets Itō Masako [dates unknown], Nakamura Chio [1913–82], Hiroe Michi [dates unknown], Kuwakado Tsutako [dates unknown], and others.[49]

Kitasono encouraged the participants to excise verbosity and write short poems. He insisted on duplication of *katakana* symbols for long vowels (proscribing the use of the customary dash; e.g., アア, rather than ア ー), but imposed no other stylistic rules.[50] Kitasono's own poems for the first three issues of *Madame Blanche* are in the tone of *Wakai koronii*. He continues his imagistic mix of geometry and surrealism, such as in the line, "Aren't all memories merely Sunday in an egg?"[51]

Apart from the lyricism of *Wakai koronii* and the conceptual experimentation of *Ensui shishū*, Kitasono also developed a third style of short poem in which he drew vocabulary from the classical world of haikai and waka. He considered it no more than a variation of the *sozai* method, but it marked his first glance backward to traditional verse since his initial encounter with the avant-garde in 1924. He first published this type of poetry in *Madame Blanche*, no. 6 (Apr. 1933), *Bungei hanron* (Outline of literary arts), and the prestigious Keiō University literary journal, *Mita bungaku* (Mita literature), founded by Nagai Kafū (1879–1959), the eminent novelist, and later edited by Nishiwaki Junzaburō. These poems, seventeen in all, were collected and published as *Kon* (1936).[52] *Kon* (Chinese: *k'un*) originally meant tiny "fish roe," but the meaning of the word was purposely inverted by Chuang-tzu (Japanese: Sōshi), legendary Taoist of the fourth century B.C.E., to mean "an unimaginably huge fish":

A fish, "kon," exists in the dark north. It is so large that no one knows for how many thousands of miles it stretches. When it metamorphoses into a phoenix, no one is sure for how many thousands of miles its back extends. Clouds covering our sky are its hanging wings flying off in anger. At times when the ocean becomes turbulent, it absconds to the dark south. The dark south is heaven's pond.[53]

According to Arcueil Club member Ueda Osamu, Kitasono chose the name "kon" as much to demonstrate antipathy to the more powerful Confucian tradition as to show solidarity with Taoism.[54] Chuang-tzu converts little into big by having a fish egg extend for thousands of miles; likewise he returns big to little by referring to "the dark south," home of the gigantic "kon" creature, as merely "heaven's pond." The breaking of boundaries by inverting size—small is large, large is small—must have reverberated with Katue's appreciation of one aspect of surrealism. At any rate, *Kon* depicts a Japan untainted by the West. Here are three of the poems in translation:

> *Kon*
>
> this bronze fish at one time was handed down from a Tendai
>   high priest to my elderly mother
> in summer the valley village was sinking under young foliage
> a gentle breeze blew through the invigorating darkness
>   of the drawing room
> in the gentle breeze the fish gallantly faced north
> between this Brutus-like, majestic fish and a mirror
>   was the pungence of jasmine flowers
>
> *Typhoon*
>
> that one-armed, aged monk put his walking stick aside and
>   pointing to the mountains

expounded on the twisted road of suffering
yet his satin robe was dripping wet
while outside the monastery quarters, rain fell duskily

House of Old

at that time grandfather went out and stood
    in the south of the garden
facing the bamboo forest, he pulled a crumblingly large bow
the bowstring shook the middle of the study's window
sunflowers bloomed in the west of the garden
    my mother loved those white flowers
in autumn, wind crossed the bamboo forest
    and chestnut leaves buried the fountain's spurt[55]

These poems are an excellent foil for his previous poetry. Unlike his dadaist and surreal experiments, all the elements have a clear place of reference in the tradition. In spite of the loose conjuring of horizontal and vertical shapes that Kitasono maintains in these poems, the change in vocabulary and the continuation of meaning from line to line create a wholly new and different effect. The playing with defamiliarization in his future-looking, earlier experiments is abandoned in favor of words steadily anchored in the past.

That a champion of avant-garde poetry could also write in this mode struck even other avant-gardists as contradictory. Friend and fellow poet Murano Shirō (1901–75) considered Kitasono's ability to pen *Kon* and other such traditional verse a "scandal."[56] For Murano and others, the poems detracted from Katue's avant-garde image; they even nullified his experimental poetry in the eyes of some. Despite the lack of political content in *Kon*, its old-fashioned vocabulary and sentiment have made a political issue of the book. Why from 1933 on did Katue turn back to the tradition? (For a photograph of Katue wearing kimono and admiring a sword, see Fig. 18.)

First, can we be sure that his selection of words from haikai and waka does in fact represent a regression? Or is it a step forward or sideways—another experiment in finding different material (which in this case happened to be traditional) for a new pattern? Had writing Westernized poetry perhaps become stale for him, and in a swing of the pendulum, was he discovering something fresh in traditional Japanese poetry? From his viewpoint, was poetry like *Kon* now the most viable "avant-garde" alternative? Put an-

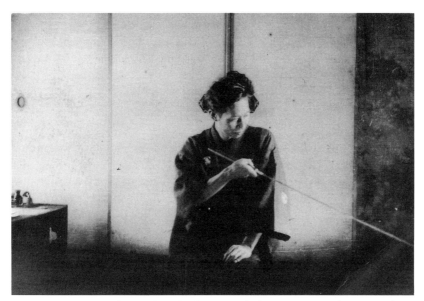

Fig. 18   Katue, ca. mid-1930s, dressed in kimono and admiring a sword. The original photograph is inscribed on the back in French, "à Monsieur Azuma Kondo par Kitasono Katue (Nov. 25)." No year is indicated.

other way, why should a Japanese poet adapting methodologies from the West be precluded from writing in a style that uses vocabulary from his own tradition? Was not casting off the tradition and becoming avant-garde a reflection of the same impulse to break through barriers that he was now attempting again, only in a seemingly reverse direction? Kitasono brushed the matter aside in *Madame Blanche*: "The material of the poems need not have more significance than the several signs of geometry. Accordingly, it is the reader's free territory to make value judgments about the experience contained in the material."[57]

There also may have been personal reasons for his poetic shift. The return home with Eiko following their marriage must have brought back memories of his childhood and parents as well as his early, sentimental poetry written without a preconceived method. That summer he also discovered Matsuo Bashō's poetry in the family storehouse and thereafter began writing haiku.[58] Although mere speculation, it is possible that once he found pleasure in Bashō, his attitude toward Japan's literary heritage may have been affected, and then it was only a matter of time before he used premodern subject matter in his own poems.

Kon also represents a more personal side of Katue as opposed to the impersonality of his Western persona. His family members—mother, brother, and grandfather—appear in *Kon* (whereas only his mother had been mentioned in his avant-garde verse). The book is divided into the sections "Kon" and "Sofu no ie" (Grandfather's house), and the village, mountain, trees, and flowers of his hometown appear in several poems, although Asama is never named directly.

By noting what Katue added to make these poems traditional, we can also see what he eliminated in his other, more experimental writing. First, the surface texture of the language has an ancient patina: ideograms are chosen for their power to evoke the esthetic worlds of *yūgen* (ethereal beauty), *wabi* (cosmic loneliness), and *sabi* (elegant simplicity). Whereas the verbs in Katue's dadaist and surreal poems are intense, dynamic, and even violent—"hang," "rupture," "collide," "tear," and "crush"—those in *Kon* conjure up slower, more graceful movements—"walk," "drift," and "flutter." This relaxed quality is conveyed even more forcefully in his choice of temporal adverbs. Time is suggested in *Kon* in vague units of a season or simply the past—"in spring," "when the leaves fell," "at one time." In his avant-garde verse, on the other hand, time is more focused on a charged moment of immediacy—"suddenly," "abruptly," "instantly."

The traditional poems in *Kon* differ from Katue's avant-garde verse in that they display a unity of scene with all the elements having a definite "place" both in the context of the poem and in the society outside the poem. They are more than merely a change in vocabulary and atmosphere. In the avant-garde verse, words seem to take their place randomly somewhere on the page, and they are unconnected to everyday life.

Besides Katue's personal reasons for writing in a traditional vein, there is also much overlap between Japanese avant-garde poetry and the worlds of waka and haiku (and their comic counterparts *kyōka* and *senryū*). Up-to-date poets who felt liberated from writing verse restricted to thirty-one or seventeen syllables tended to use free verse to write short poems that often adopted the five- and seven-syllable line lengths of the old forms. We have already noted the similarity between haiku's leaps of logic and surrealism's illogic, as well as modern adaptations of the ancient technique of *kakekotoba* (see Chapter 3). *Kon*'s borrowing of vocabulary from the pool of classical poetry makes it hard to distinguish where the old worlds of waka and haiku end and the new world of the avant-garde begins, except in the obvious difference in syllable count, the lack of haiku's obligatory seasonal word (*kigo*), and other conventional rules specific to the old forms.

Katue effectively conjures up two airtight and seemingly contradictory worlds in his Western and Japanese modes. This is not surprising, for twentieth-century life to almost all Japanese has meant the blending of native and foreign elements. What is surprising, however, is that the surrealist side of Katue did not mix them. His insistence on keeping subject matter distinct according to the poem, and not "contaminating" one style with the other, foreclosed the possibility of interweaving his Western and Japanese parts into a wildly new and different mix, which could have been surrealistic to the second power. An unhappy consequence of Katue's refusal to unite the two worlds is that each becomes a stereotype of the atmosphere elicited—classical Japan is tranquil, whereas *l'esprit nouveau* (with the exception of "Kigō setsu" and lyrical verse) is tempestuous. Fear that the fusion would become a parody of both worlds may have prompted his hesitation. In 1961, he expressed interest in merging the diverse strands of his poetry, but found himself lacking a viable, single "pattern" to unite them all.[59]

Katue designed *Kon* and put his family crest, a *mitsugashiwa* (buckbean flower), on the cover. As if somewhat embarrassed by the personal nature of the poems, he wrote in the preface that "*Kon* is not meant to circulate in society; it is put together as an expression of affection for longtime friends."[60] He also paid for printing the book out of his own pocket. He sent a copy to Ezra Pound (about whom more will be said in Chapter 5) with the following explanation: "I send you may [*sic*, my] work 鯤 (Kon) which means an imaginary gigantic fish. I intended, in each poem, to express the classical atmosphere of Tea Ceremony and Zen, the "L'ESPRIT DU JAPON." I made only one hundred copies to give them to my most intimate friends."[61]

Whatever reasons Katue had for evoking the classical atmosphere, his choice paralleled the shift to the right in the political arena following the Manchurian Incident (1931). With Japan's temporary success at colonizing a large portion of the Chinese mainland, there was an upswing of national pride in all things Japanese, including the literature of the past. Interest in Western Europe was still paramount, but slowly the focus was turning to the homeland. Katue's choice to write in two modes—*l'esprit nouveau* (Western) and *l'esprit du Japon*—reflects the short-lived and uneasy plurality of the times. Traditional poetry had been held in contempt by the avant-garde in the 1920s and early 1930s, but by 1940 the traditionalists were able to ban avant-garde poetry. At neither extreme, the mid-1930s saw an acceptance of both styles; meanwhile, the military situation cast a darker shadow with each passing month.

As Katue's poetry took a traditional turn, his essays became more astringent. In *Madame Blanche*, no. 8, he published "Doku no hanataba" (A bouquet of poison) under the pen name Oguri Sen'ichirō, without revealing his dual identity to the other club members (with the possible exception of Iwamoto Shūzō). Kobayashi Yoshio (1912–), who joined the group with *Madame Blanche*, no. 5, recalled visiting Katue at home and spotting an unfinished manuscript with the name Oguri Sen'ichirō on his desk. When Kobayashi exclaimed, "Oh, so you are Oguri!" Katue's reply was only an elusive smile.[62] Proof appeared in 1941 when the Oguri essays in *Madame Blanche* were republished under the name Kitasono Katue in *Haiburau no funsui* (Highbrow fountain).[63]

Why did he want to use a different name? What was he concealing and why? What did the assumption of a different name mean to him? Or to put this another way, what did personal identity mean to him? He never wrote about these matters, but one possible clue is provided by former club member Ueda Osamu, who stated: "Around this time Katue stressed to me that 'to keep pure in this sullied world, I value mystification.'"[64] Oguri Sen'ichirō also became a vehicle for Katue's anonymous attacks on the work of fellow poets. The once-close friendship between Haruyama Yukio and Katue had soured (they would later make up), and Oguri/Kitasono lashed out in *Madame Blanche*, no. 9: "I must say that the conclusions reached by [James] Joyce researcher Haruyama Yukio are extremely unreliable."[65] Oguri also discussed the magazine's name: "People often translate 'Madame Blanche' as 'woman of whiteness' or 'white-colored woman,' but those are bad jokes. Of course, if that had been the meaning, the magazine would be 'La Dame Blanche.' No, it is in 'Madame Blanche' [that is, 'a lady named Blanche'] that the magazine's revolution hides."[66] "Blanche" in his interpretation is a person's name and does not stand for "white woman" or "whiteness," although his defensiveness demonstrates that not everyone read it that way.[67]

Oguri Sen'ichirō continued to contribute essays and translations to *Madame Blanche* and occasionally to other journals, but no poetry was published under the pen name.[68] From issue no. 11 of *Madame Blanche* Kitasono used a third pen name, Kasuga Shinkurō, which only a handful of poets at the time knew was Katue. Unlike the situation with Oguri, Katue never admitted publicly that he was Kasuga Shinkurō.[69] Kasuga's column, in turns humorous and cruel, reinforced Katue's poetics while revealing his defense mechanisms in action. The abrasive style made lively reading and may have helped boost interest in the magazine. The name Kasuga Shinkurō was taken from the hero of a 1924 adventure novel by Yoshikawa Eiji (1892–1962).[70] Yoshikawa's Kasuga Shinkurō is a samurai who finds the gentle arts of poetry and painting more amenable than swordsmanship, and in this he fits the millennium-old mold of Japanese popular lovers from Ariwara no Narihira and Prince Genji to Ihara Saikaku's fictional Yonosuke.[71] Katue used the name Kasuga Shinkurō only for his book reviews. What did he declare behind Kasuga's mask, and how did he defuse the situation when readers pointed accusingly in his direction?

In his column "Shishū no shinpan" (Judge of poetry books), Kasuga doled out praise and blame—especially the latter—as he saw fit. A minor scandal ensued after he wrote: "The review [by Katō Hajime in *Etoile de Mer*, no. 6] of *Radeige iboku* [Radiguet's autograph; trans. by Yamanaka Sansei] ended in miserably exposing the stupidity (*atama no warusa*) of the reviewer."[72]

Besides Kasuga's regular book review column, the following issue of *Madame Blanche* contained a one-page statement by Kasuga Shinkurō, "Watakushi no benkai" (My explanation).

When I heard that some people wonder if Kasuga Shinkurō is the pen name of Kitasono Katue, while others spread the rumor that it is beyond a doubt Iwamoto Shūzō, I was both startled and flattered. I am not sure how to put this, but I hope people will cut out the ridiculous excavating.

On reviewing *Etoile de Mer* in [*Madame*] *Blanche*, no. 12, I said that Katō Hajime was stupid. He was a[n Arcueil, that is, *Madame Blanche*] club member and, unfortunately, quit right away. By so doing, he only proved again how stupid he really is, but I regret that the club has lost a member.

If quitting the club in the future, don't be babyish about it. Rather, fight back logically and learn from the experience. Because I am not famous, I try to remain indifferent to victory and defeat. Therefore, I don't mind apologizing if I lose. But I hope you'll cut out demonstrating your stingy nature by counting your fortune.

I also hope that you'll stop treating me as a *kagemusha* [a behind-the-scenes manipulator].[73]

As if to aid in making these protestations of independence from Katue sound convincing, a calm, traditional poem by him, out of character with Kasuga's raging, was placed on the facing page:

Poverty-stricken

walking among eulalias and it becomes a garden of Bashō plants
in winter the master always offered plain hot water garnished
    with citron buds
and in the shade of the garden a line of daffodils blossomed blue
    and white flowers[74]

How to deal with Katue's poetry should have posed a delicate problem for Kasuga, but he chose to praise the poet unconditionally. *Madame Blanche*, no. 12. for example, has this review by Kasuga of *Ensui shishū*:

[Katue] wrote his own blurb for the book: "With these poems I have succeeded in grasping the dynamics of *poésie*." The book adequately points out the scientific quality that poetry must contain. The general concept related to the mechanism of methodology will be clarified with this book, and errors will be corrected.

In his essays [*Ten no tebukuro* (Heaven's glove; 1933)], which all twentieth-century poets should have, he accurately describes the interfacing of poetry and science as well as the limits of poetic consciousness. He clearly endorses this poetry book [*Ensui shishū*], and I am sure that you will want to take a look at it.[75]

Here, as with mirrors in mirrors, author Hashimoto Kenkichi has created another mask, book-reviewer Kasuga Shinkurō, who is quoting still another mask, poet Kitasono Katue, who in turn is commenting on his own poems. There is as much "poetry" in the multiplication and manipulation of personae as in the verse itself.[76]

Readers of *Madame Blanche*, no. 12, could notice that Kasuga was praising Kitasono. Possibly to chase away suspicions of his identity, Kasuga criticized Katue mildly in *Madame Blanche*, no. 13, for the poetry in classical style that he contributed to the magazine *Bungei hanron* (later collected in *Kon*): "As for Kitasono Katue's 'Sofu no ie,' the first and last poems are successful. However, the overall impression is *sanman* (vague, distracted)."[77] He must have found it difficult to remain critical of himself, for a few sentences later Kasuga claims that "Sleepless Afternoon," a poem by Iwamoto Shūzō on a sword in the same issue of *Madame Blanche*, "does not come close to Kitasono's [poem 'Katana' (Sword)]."[78] Kasuga's comment implies that Iwamoto was unaware of Kasuga's true identity and that Katue considered Iwamoto his rival, however friendly they may have been.

Kikushima Tsuneji claimed that he confronted Katue, his mentor, for being "unethical in hiding behind the pseudonym of Kasuga while attacking fellow club member Katō Hajime."[79] According to Kikushima, Katue admitted being Kasuga in disguise but offered no apologies. In disgust, Kiku-shima and Motoyama Shigenari (dates unknown) quit the club (Katō had already left). Not all members were aware of Kasuga's, or even Oguri's, true identity. Oguri never appeared on the list of Arcueil Club members at the end of each issue. Kasuga, however, appears on the roll call for *Madame Blanche*, nos. 13–17, although he began contributing with no. 11.

While engaging in these machinations, Katue was able to poke fun at himself, or at least allow others to do so. *Madame Blanche*, no. 13, contains an anonymous section, "Anthology Against Anthology," with parody poems spoofing the work of Haruyama Yukio, Kondō Azuma, and others. One poem imitates Katue's style,

> A poem like a white album is more stupid than having your
> 　　feet stepped on
> Oh Venus unable to cover your own flesh
>
> This is witty thinking, isn't it?[80]

Katue was involved in yet another activity at this time—translating from French—a language he had taught himself. In 1933 he published the first book of Paul Eluard's poetry to be translated into Japanese (eleven love poems to Gala), and in 1934 a book of love poems by Stéphane Mallarmé.[81] Carefree and making fun of himself, on the jacket (*obi*) of the latter was written, "The clumsiest complete translation of *Madrigaux*, the love songs of Stéphane Mallarmé."[82]

Surrealism and *l'esprit nouveau* influenced the translations of Kitasono and his contemporaries. Satō Saku, who went on to distinguish himself with many books of translations from the French, recalled the prewar attitude:

Even though they were bad, literal translations, we felt that is what they had to be. Rather than beautiful translations with elegant words like those of Ueda Bin and Mori Ōgai, we believed it was purer to make mistranslations that were strictly literal.

To translate literally was to make it fresh. For example, *rose des vents* I translated as "the wind's rose." If you look it up in the dictionary, the meaning is "compass." Nevertheless, I insisted on translating it literally. How many times I was unsparingly accused of mistranslating! (Laughs). I geared my translation for people who would read it as "the wind's rose" while knowing it meant "compass." Also, *mont-de-piété* I translated literally as "mountain of piety," although I knew very well that the real meaning was "pawnshop."[83]

Satō imagined his audience knew French well enough to re-translate the Japanese words back through their literal meanings to their dictionary meanings. This new, freewheeling attitude was partly justified by the surreal effect sought by the translators.

Katue inscribed a postwar book of his translations with the following comment: "To translate is always a double lie—one directed at the author and one at the reader."[84] He did not specialize in translating, yet his work in this area has been evaluated highly.[85]

Arcueil Club member Yamanaka Sansei corresponded regularly with Paul Eluard and decided to print a hardback book using elegant handmade paper to honor the French surrealist.[86] Included in *Hommage à Paul Eluard* were original poems by Japanese surrealists writing in Japanese, French, and English, as well as translations of poems by Eluard, Breton, and others. Kitasono's contribution was a twenty-two-line poem in English titled "Opera Poetica." Each line ends with a period, and there is little continuity of meaning between any two lines. His choice of images is occasionally compelling, as in the following excerpt:

> The moon breaks as a soup-plate . . .
> The newspaper, solemnly as the Bible, displays the scandals of
>   the last month . . .
> The skeleton of a crushed chair . . .
> A broken fork stretches out his excited hand to the
>   rotten bouquet . . .
> It is miserable that you cannot look out of the three windows at
>   the same time.

No matter how effective any single line is, the overall impression remains diffuse. Considering that Katue had no native speaker of English to help him, he succeeded in writing a poem with crisp imagery. "Opera Poetica" is significant as his first poem written in English. The experience forced him to consider what was communicable in a foreign language, and he responded with surreal imagery.

After one and a half years of publication, the end of *Madame Blanche* was announced on the cover of the seventeenth issue. Several members left for *Nijū seiki* (Twentieth century), a magazine started by younger poets in their twenties that was edited and published by their leader, Gyō Shōtarō (dates unknown). *Nijū seiki* signaled the emergence of a new generation—and a generation gap. The Arcueil Club did not disband, however, for on New

Year's Day, 1935, trimmed to twenty-seven members, it launched a new publication, *JaNGLE*. A second and final issue appeared in April, and then the club broke up. Significantly, Kasuga Shinkurō did not appear on the list of members, and was never heard from again.[87]

Katue gave various reasons for the parting of ways. In his introduction of the VOU Club in *Townsman*, he wrote (in English): "It was by an inevitable result of the tendency of the age that the 'Club d'Arcueil' should dissolve at last without a serious reason and the *Madame Blanche* ceased to be published at #19."[88] In 1963 he claimed that a new poetics had motivated the change: "We discontinued *Madame Blanche* to start up *VOU* because we were shedding lyricism in favor of a high-grade intellectualism."[89] And in 1977 he blamed the large membership (over forty people), saying that "the quality of material was dropping, and therefore the opportunity was taken to dissolve the club in order to regroup with only the most talented people."[90] Whatever the reason was, Katue was still proud of his leadership when he wrote in 1941, "Ninety percent of the excellent young poets around now were in the Arcueil Club."[91]

The club ground to a halt somewhat mysteriously and is usually passed over in the history of modern Japanese literature because of the greater achievements of Katue's VOU Club, which followed it.[92] Nevertheless, *Madame Blanche* provided modern Japanese poetry with a vigorous lyricism that reflected a youthful, upbeat attitude. This was not accomplished solely by the Arcueil Club poets, but their contribution was substantial. The new generation, educated with less emphasis on traditional learning, was more capable of carrying the modern language in fresh, unforeseen directions. The crisis in the wake of the destruction caused by the Pacific War demanded a more politically aware attitude, and the prewar avant-gardists were judged *en bloc* as naïve and frivolous for having penned patriotic verse (Chapter 6), even though many of the younger poets had not been asked to contribute, and we cannot know if they would have. As a consequence, the main achievement of the Arcueil group—writing concise poems with fresh language that attempted to evoke *l'esprit nouveau* of contemporary life—has been almost completely passed over by critics and publishers alike.

Katue led a new generation of poets in *Madame Blanche*. Besides using the magazine as an outlet for his poetry, he also found it convenient as a showcase for his essays and book reviews. Editing, design work, and painting also helped broaden his outlook on poetry. Katue explored several diverse directions during the years 1930–35. One curious question is to what degree his masks (the poetry styles and the pen names) are manifestations of a consistent thread, and to what degree they are self-contained entities isolated from (and in opposition to) each other. Katue's work poses the question while seeming to disavow easy either/or answers. Additional masks created over the following years only served to deepen the emerging contradictions.

5 KIT KAT

and

EZ PO

Ezra Pound and Kitasono Katue—or "Kit Kat," as Pound affectionately called him in the letters—corresponded from 1936 to 1959, until Pound entered his silent period. Approximately 100 letters and cards remain as evidence of their friendship—the longest-lasting one in the modern period between an important Japanese poet and a major Western poet.[1] Yet Pound and Kitasono died without ever having met. That may have saved their friendship—neither man was able to maintain a similarly unruffled relationship with literati of his own country. The two poets were not merely polite and superficial with one another, however; each expressed his thoughts and affections openly. In this chapter I shall draw on their letters and related material in attempting to answer the question: What did Kitasono Katue and Ezra Pound mean to each other—as friends, poets, literary theorists, and intercultural ambassadors?

The correspondence began after two important events in Katue's life. Given the extent of Katue's activities during the early 1930s, there was no indication at the end of 1935 what an important year, in the long run, it would turn out to be. But by the close of his life, it was one of the years most associated with his name, because in 1935 he formed the VOU Club, with its organ *VOU* (1935–40; 1946–47; 1949–78), one of the twentieth century's longest-lasting poetry magazines committed to avant-garde principles. According to Katue, the name "VOU" was empty in and of itself; the activity of the members would generate meaning.[2]

Second, 1935 also saw an improvement in Katue's economic well-being. Until then, he had survived with help from his family and his wife's parents, but the life of the artist-poet in the city was growing more difficult by the month. Especially after the birth of their son, Akio, in 1934, Katue may have felt pressured to find a regular job, since the freelance writing assignments and design work that had been trickling in were not enough to rescue his family from its hand-to-mouth existence.

The offer of a job came from Katue's friend Nakahara Minoru (1893–1990), whose father had founded Nihon Shika Daigaku (Japan dental college) in downtown Tokyo. Minoru was one of the most innovative avant-garde artists in Japan from the mid-1920s until he stopped painting in the early 1960s. His work is invariably exhibited, along with that of Koga Harue, as exemplifying the best art of the early Shōwa years. Nakahara arranged for Katue to research and edit a volume on the history of the dental college on the occasion of its thirtieth anniversary. Katue began work on the project in May 1935 and finished it the following year. Thereafter, he was given permanent employment as Nakahara's assistant in the college library, which at the time housed only a few thousand volumes.[3]

In early 1936, at the time Katue began writing Ezra Pound, the American poet was leading a reclusive life in Rapallo on the Italian coast, and there was relatively little contact between Japan and the West in the mid-1930s.[4] Katue initiated the correspondence when he was thirty-four years old and Pound was fifty-one. His letter arrived in May 1936 by way of Faber and Faber, Pound's London publisher:

Dear Sir,

You will please excuse me that I take the liberty of writing you. For a long time, since Imagism movement, we have always expected you as a leader on new literature. Especially your profound appreciation in the Chinese literature and the Japanese literature has greatly pleased us.

Last year, we established "VOU Club" and have continued our lively strife for the newest art. Now the existence of our group has come to be attentively watched by the younger generations of this country.

We started from Dada and passed Surrealism. And at present we are connected with no "-ism" of Europe. Under the close influence of contemporary architecture and technology, we are making progress in our theory on art and are forming a characteristic form of ourselves.

"VOU Club" consists of poets, artists, composers, architects and technologists. The members are now twenty one, two-third of them being poets.

I send you two copies of our review VOU under separate cover.[5] I shall be very much obliged if you will kindly make some ideas of our group by them.

Hoping you will receive this letter as soon as possible.
> I remain,
> Yours truly,
> *Katue Kitasono*[6]

Katue initially wrote to Pound with the hope of getting a comment on *VOU*. Pound responded to the letter immediately and included a copy of his *Cavalcanti* as a return gift.[7] In subsequent letters, Pound never gave an opinion on the two copies of *VOU* Kitasono had sent him, perhaps because they never arrived, or perhaps because he was embarrassed at being unable to read anything but the romanized title (he was incapable, for example, of matching the *kanji* for the members' names in the table of contents with their romanized signatures on the list they had sent him).

Katue made the most of his association with Pound. Portions of Pound's first letter, received in mid-June, were translated into Japanese for *VOU* and sent to the printer by July.[8] Also in the same issue were three short poems by Pound translated by Katue and published in the "Decoupage" section. The following number, *VOU*, no. 12, featured a translation by Ema Shōko of the first chapter of Pound's *ABC of Reading*, and no. 13 had Katue's translation of the "Medievalism" chapter of *Cavalcanti*. And that was only the beginning. *VOU* was a monthly magazine at this time, and the Pound connection, both personal and literary, had an impact on validating the magazine in Japan. Perhaps to accommodate Pound, club policy was officially altered from issue no. 11 to allow nonmembers to contribute.[9]

Pound suggested to Katue, "Print a few lines of french or english in your magazine giving such news as you want a few european & american poets to get."[10] The advice was quickly heeded. Issue no. 13 contains the following message in English:

To the poets of the world:
We have denied, before, that a poem should be written as a mere reflection of society, religion, politics, etc. It is foolish that poetry should be interfered by them (which contribute nothing to the literary theoretical system of poetry).

We try hard to keep poetry as a new system of thinking [away] from the interference of philosophy, natural science, and sociology.

Poetry has its own function, which is to organize, by a scientific method, the most fresh, pure, and newest world of thinking which is able to be expressed by nothing except poetry.
> VOU Club[11]

Ironically, Pound's ideas of historicism and economics in his *Cantos* and other writings should have made him as guilty from the VOU viewpoint as the proletarian poets whom they were indirectly criticizing. But both Pound and Katue happily overlooked their philosophical differences; perhaps they were willing to be lenient with a foreigner (neither man was tolerant of poets from his own country who held such divergent beliefs about the art), or perhaps it was simply a matter of finding each other irreplaceable.

In addition to the VOU Club message to the poets of the world, the last two pages of the magazine were left empty except for a tantalizing question in English: "Don't you wish to write a poem in this blank?"[12] *VOU* was not only opening its pages to the West with translations into Japanese, but also inviting new work from Western poets in their native languages. No Japanese magazine had made such a direct appeal to foreign readers before. Practically speaking, however, few non-Japanese poets saw that issue of *VOU*. The formal introduction of the club to the West came in the first issue of the London-based avant-garde literary journal *Townsman* in January 1938 (Fig. 19).

Pound's views on literature were taken quite seriously. Below is the full text of his introduction of the VOU Club. He had not seen the Japanese versions of the poems he was describing, and therefore he knew no more about the original work than did the readers of *Townsman*.[13]

It is not a case of asking what would any set of eight European and/or American poets look like if asked to translate *their* poems into Japanese. It is a case of saying that for half a century after Papa Flaubert started writing, any man who wanted to write English prose had to start by reading French prose. And it may be that from now on any man who wants to write English poetry will have to start reading Japanese. I mean modern Japanese, not merely studying Chinese ideogram, as I have been advocating for the past twenty years.

Not as translations but as *actual writing*, these poems are better work than any save those of E.E. Cummings at his happiest. They may even serve to introduce Cummings and Peret to readers who have thought my more obscure younger contemporaries merely eccentric. Yes. You will have to read Mr. Kitasono's introduction twice, and the poems three or four times. The Japanese eye is like those new camera shutters that catch the bullet leaving the gun. You will not understand some sentences as you read them, but only after having got to their ends, see that they reach round and tuck in their beginnings, so that sense is there nicely boxed. I myself feel rather like a grizzly bear faced by a bunch of weasels. It is the Mongoose spring, the chameleon's tongue quickness. All the moss and fuzz that for twenty

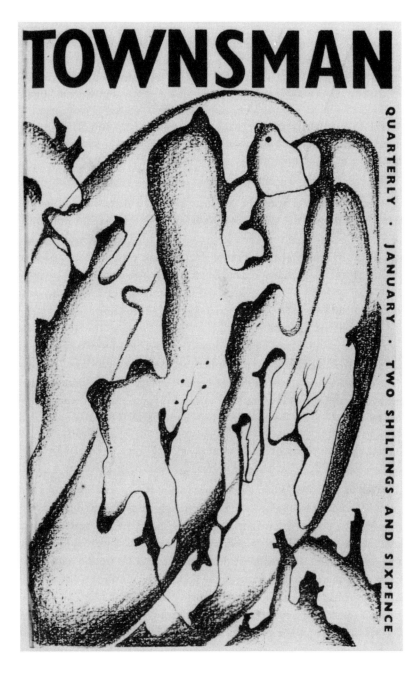

Fig. 19   Cover of the first issue of *Townsman* (London), January 1, 1938, included
poems by Katue and an introduction to the VOU club by Ezra Pound.

years we have been trying to scrape off our language—these young men start without it. They see the crystal set, the chemical laboratory and the pine tree with untrammelled clearness. As to their being *a* or *the* most active new club of poets in Tokio, I doubt if any one city contains two such clubs. I know that nowhere in Europe is there any such vortex of poetic alertness. Tokio takes over, where Paris stopped.

Make no mistake, the thought is not absent from these poems. The Japanese poet has gone from one peak of it to another faster than our slow wits permit us to follow before we have got used to his pace.

Ezra Pound[14]

Pound started by placing the Western poet in a defensive position by making him imagine the difficulty of translating his own poems into Japanese. Next he suggested that the future course of English poetry may be influenced by Japan rather than France. He was not explicit about whether this shift would occur solely because of the *VOU* poems or whether those poems were part of a larger trend (including imports of Nō, tanka, and haiku) that had been affecting Western poetry for some time and was especially influential on the short poem.

Perhaps to avoid mentioning the original poems, which he had not seen, Pound urged the reader not to judge them as translations but "as *actual writing*." Is the reader expected suddenly to erase the fact that these are translations by foreign poets of compositions originally in Japanese? Pound went on to claim that they are "better work than any save E. E. Cummings at his happiest." Considering that Gertrude Stein, T. S. Eliot, Laura Riding, Langston Hughes, H.D., Elsa Gidlow, William Carlos Williams, Yvor Winters, Louis Zukofsky, Kenneth Rexroth, and others were actively writing poetry in English at this time, Pound's generous praise of the *VOU* poets sounds frivolous if taken at face value. If Pound was suggesting that the deformation of the English language wrought by the *VOU* poets (who translated their works into a kind of highbrow pidgin) can be used as a halfway house by readers to penetrate the even more distorted and obscure work of native poets such as Cummings, then what was he implying about the state of the language that he had done so much to reform?

Pound considered himself "a grizzly bear facing a bunch of weasels." The VOUists are the epitome of speed and agility: "the Mongoose spring" and "the chameleon's tongue quickness." The Japanese eye is likened to a camera shutter that can catch "the bullet leaving the gun." To criticize the poems for lack of content would betray an inability to grasp the speed of thought of the Japanese poets, who move "from one peak of it to another faster than our slow [Western] wits permit us to follow." Criticism is foreclosed.

Exaggerated as Pound's claims for the VOU poems are, he was undeniably impressed: "All the moss and fuzz that for twenty years we have been trying to scrape off our language—these young men start without it." Specifically, did he mean that their English is to be commended for starting without "moss and fuzz"? Or did he mean that ideogramic languages (such as Japanese and Chinese) are inherently free of such superfluous words, a phenomenon that can be glimpsed even in the VOU translations? Pound was working under the presupposition that languages based on the alphabet are full of dead words inhibiting clear thought, whereas ideogramic languages, based as they are on pictographs (he thought), maintain a tauter connection between sign and referent, allowing for clarity of thought. Granted that unclear thinking is partially generated by imprecise language (e.g., Orwell's "doublespeak"), still, if Pound assumed that ideogramic languages lack inconsequential words, fillers, and "fuzzy expressions," he was off the mark. Captivated by the festival of signs, Pound ignored undesirable aspects of the characters.

Pound's thoroughly laudatory introduction crests when he pinpoints the VOU Club as the new sensation of the poetry world: "I know that nowhere in Europe is there any such vortex of poetic alertness. Tokio takes over, where Paris stopped."

Why did someone as astute about literary inventiveness as Pound regard these poems so highly? One factor was that he approached the translations while imagining an idealized, though blurred, "original" Japanese text. His almost mystical belief in the ideogram predisposed him to view the poems in a positive light. As with Plato's idealism, the "pure" forms (Japanese poems) could not be seen, only the shadowy reflections (English translations).

But that alone would not have been enough to draw such high praise. The poems were intriguing for their extreme compression of dynamic imagery. The poets, who had absorbed dadaism and surrealism, made their poems flights of fancy unattached to the mundane world. They gathered poetic words from the physical sciences—particularly botany, zoology, geology, and metallurgy—and etched out a modern, "hard" poetry in their mix of images. Katue submitted two poems in his own English:

I

Under the umbrella of concrete, yesterday, we laughed at tomato
     for its carelessness.
Their thoughts have gone rotten by a bucket, and they talk
     of rope-necktie.
A shot is cabbage in the sky over the office.
Dear friend, now is all right the heel.

To-day a duck they dug out in a brush of philosophismus
My laugh is nearer to the condition of Dachshunde-like cylinder than
     the cucumber-shaped idea of Aquinas.
I put on gloves emeraldgreen and start with a book *Membranologie*
     under my arm.
Is there a shop to sell clear bags?

To-morrow beside a bucket a necktie I shall wear for the sake of
     General clothed in vegetable costume.
A weary city is likened to a brush.
Be-gone! a wandering head.
Be-gone! in a fling like an explosive, over the rock through a Geissler's
     brass pipe.

II

In leaden slippers I laugh at the fountain of night, and scorn
     a solitary swan.
A parasol of glass she spreads, and wanders along the lane the
     cosmos flowering.
Over the cypress tree I image, to myself, a hotel marked with
     two golf-clubs crossed;
And move my camera on the sand of night.

In the street, there shining the spindle-shaped amalgam stairs,
     the telephone-bell is ringing on the desk.
In Congo by a barber a parrot is trained and sold at Kabinda.
Then by cheerful young sailors her head is replaced by a leaden one:
Just a glimpse of it a watchmaker catches under cocoanut-trees,
     where is seen a dome tightly closed.

On the table I toss the gloves of antelope, and the gloomy
     fellows I ignore.
A typewriter packed in a raincoat of oil-skin is dead and gone
     on the Le Temps.

She, spreading the parasol of glass, pursues a nightingale, in the
    space between the Le Temps and the cosmos flowers.
Or the new age is born.

Under the hydroplane, "Hamburger Fleugzeugbau Ha 139," a
    duck throws into confusion the battle line.
Among the cosmos flowers vibrate machineguns.
By the drain a young washerman blows up.
O the clearer, the better is the sky over the street.
Flash on the concrete a bright wire and shovel.[15]

Katue confidently tested brittle poetic vocabulary—"Geissler's brass pipe,"
"*Membranologie*," "Dachshunde-like cylinder"—and embedded the words in
what might be called "scientific lyricism," using expressions such as "umbrella
of concrete," "parasol of glass," "leaden slippers," "vegetable costume," "spin-
dle-shaped amalgam stairs."

Following Katue's cue, Fuji Takeshi (dates unknown) used imagery in his
poems that has the reader "sliding down the stair-cases of plants" and then
listening to "the soft duet at the end of tendril," and Yasoshima Minoru
(1906–83) conjured up "aluminium music" and "magnesium light." Pound
never mentioned T. E. Hulme and imagism in his introduction of the VOU
Club, yet the members' poetry combined Hulme's (and Pound's) call for
"angular verse" with their own brand of esthetic surrealism, which had
gained popularity in Japan.

Pound was correct in sensing something fresh in the VOU experiments,
but instead of assigning quasi-mythical powers to the language and exotic,
animal-like prowess to the poets, he could have stated the case more simply
and gotten closer to the facts: the VOU poets had absorbed Western liter-
ary trends, and now their modern, polished, and imaginative perceptions
were able to excite Western readers. For almost twenty years, the Japanese
had been writing verse that would have interested Europeans and Americans
if not for language and cultural barriers.[16] Nevertheless, it is to Pound's
credit that he appreciated their poetry and was willing to place his reputa-
tion on the line for them, especially since no other "major" poet was paying
attention to the Japanese avant-garde. Pound had made a breakthrough by
introducing the Nō twenty years before but had since lost his Japanese con-
tacts, and he was probably eager to prove to his Western friends and audi-
ence that, in spite of his physical isolation in Rapallo, he was still in touch

with East Asia and even discovering the best of modern Japanese poetry. The VOU poets conveniently provided a boost to Pound's prestige by showing he was still an active literary talent scout at a time when people were dismissing him as over-the-hill because of his odd brew of Social Credit economics, anti-Semitism, Confucianism, and fascism.

Needless to say, Katue and the VOU Club were pleased when Pound proclaimed them the latest rage on the world literary stage. Katue the francophile, who had been instrumental in introducing surrealism to Japan, was surely unaware that Pound had been snubbed by the surrealists when he lived in Paris and therefore bore some ill will toward them.[17] Privately, Katue wrote Pound: "Your very sensible introductory sentences for VOU Club saved us from our deficiency. Words fail to express my gratitude for your kindness."[18]

Along with Pound's introduction and the *VOU* poems, *Townsman* published a short essay on poetics by Katue. Pound took the nucleus of that essay, clarified Katue's English slightly, added comments of his own, and reprinted it in *Guide to Kulchur* (1938). The text that follows is the *Kulchur* version (I have italicized Pound's comments). It is Katue's most important statement on poetics to that time and shows the role of Pound as intermediary.

A civilized man is one who will give a serious answer to a serious question. Civilization itself is a certain sane balance of values.

The VOU club supplies me such an answer, not only to my particular question: what is young Japan doing? but to a half dozen others whereon a deal of occidental ink has flowed vainly. The club was started by some admirers of "that great harmless artist Eric [sic] Satie." Katue Kitasono writes me:

Now the most interesting subject to us is the relation between imagery and ideoplasty. Contemporary young poets are all vaguely conscious of, and worry about this. Some of them went over again to its extremity and returned. Others gave up exploration, and found out a queer new country, remaining only as amateur thinkers. But anyone whose standing ground is in literature, can do nothing for it if he ignores the system of literature.

The formation of poetry takes such a course as:

(a) language. (b) imagery. (c) ideoplasty.

That which we vaguely call poetical effect means, generally, ideoplasty which grows out of the result of imagery. Man has thought out to make a heart-shaped space with two right angles. [*Point where the occidental pillars of imaginary geometries fell down.*] This great discovery in plastic, and also that of the conics in mathematics are two mysteries brought by man's intellect.

The relation between imagery and ideoplasty makes us suppose the heart-shaped space which is born by the connection of the same mysterious two curves. We standardized these two curves and got a necessity.

What we must do first for imagery is (in this order) collection, arrangement and combination. Thus we get the first line: "a shell, a typewriter, and grapes," in which we have an aesthetic feeling. But there is not (in it) any further development. We add the next line and then another aesthetic feeling is born. Thus all the lines are combined and a stanza is finished. This means the completion of imagery of that stanza and then ideoplasty begins.

This principle can be applied to poems consisting of several stanzas. In that case ideoplasty is formed when the last stanza is finished.

Though it cannot be allowed as orthodox of poetry that imagery is performed by ideoplasty.

******

This is where the present commentator suggests that his reader pause for reflection.

******

This violence is dared often by religionists, politicians, and satirists. Morality poems, political poems and satirical poems are written, almost without exception, with such an illogical principle.

The phenomena in our life proceed, through our senses to our experiences, perceptions, and intuitions. It is intuition rationally that provides the essentials for imagery, and it is the method of poetry that materializes intuitions perceptively and combines. Consequently, exact imagery and ideoplasty are due to an exact method. Pure and orthodox poetry cannot exist without this theory.

Jan. 6th (or thereabouts), 1937.

Mr Kitasono has arrived at a clearer and gentler statement than I had seen before the arrival of the brief essay here quoted. What he says is not alien to something I once wrote re Dr Williams' poems, nor is it contrary to Gaudier's sculptural principles. I do not for a moment suppose Mr Kitasono wd. insist on the "theory" being consciously held. Intuition may even provide the essentials in this domain.

Against this is set the sickly and pasty-faced appearance of the lower deck men as seen some years ago, here, Rapallo, when the British fleet used to put into the harbour. "Can't have 'em always around on deck," said the chaplain.

[abridged][19]

Webster's Dictionary defines "ideoplasty" as "the power of imagination." Katue defined it as "that which we vaguely call poetical effect . . . which grows out of the result of imagery." It is akin to the term coined by Samuel Taylor Coleridge, "esemplastic," meaning "to shape into one."[20] "Esemplastic," according to James Engell, approximates the German *Einbildungskraft*, which includes the concept that an image impresses itself "in the soul or mind where it will naturally mix with and become part of other images that will aggregate, fuse, and be shaped by the active power of the mind into a larger whole or 'one.'"[21] Pound and Katue shared a belief in the poem as an autonomous object in which the operation of image-integration takes place, and which the reader merely discovers there. Critical theory of the past two decades would interpret Katue's comment that ideoplasty happens only after the last line to mean that it occurs in the mind of the reader, not that of the writer.

In philosophical and scientific vocabulary, Katue is advocating "poetry for poetry's sake" and is opposed to the usurpation of art by special interest groups seeking to propagandize their cause. His call for ideoplasty to come from imagery and not vice versa was especially aimed at the proletarian poets, who started with a set idea and used imagery to persuade. In a sentence excised from the English translation, Katue claims that "as long as we don't explain by what reason our imagery occurs, this principle [ideoplasty] can't help falling into mysticism."[22]

Outside his endorsement of "pure poetry," however, his use of "ideoplasty" is not altogether clear, for how can there be "exact ideoplasty" when the effect of a poem on each reader (and at each reading) is bound to be different? Moreover, his statement implies that the ideal reader holds the esthetic feeling from each line in a state of suspended animation until the poem ends and then all the images suddenly coagulate into a total effect. Although little is known about how the brain "reads" poetry, the process is surely less neat than Katue would have it. Some images no doubt register vividly, and others do not. Images may interact and fuse in the mind at irregular, unpredictable intervals—in the middle of a stanza or even midway through a line—and not necessarily only after the last line of a poem.

In Katue's Japanese version of the same essay, for "ideoplasty" he coined the word *ōka kannen* (応化観念; "idea adjustment"; literally, "response-transform-notion"), implying that the *ō* (response) is either tucked into the autonomy of the text or in the reader's domain.[23] His emphasis on closure makes explicit something taken for granted in Western poetics, namely, the way a poem closes itself as an atemporal, esthetic "object."

Katue's ideas are presented more lucidly in an earlier essay that he considered the first half of the ideoplasty essay. In it he claimed that pre-dadaist poetry was based on rhetoric with lines linked grammatically, whereas poets since that time have related lines by a logic based on balance and symmetry.[24] Katue's purposeful denial of a single thread of meaning running through a poem as well as his visual, constructivist approach are in evidence here. For him, ideoplasty probably was connected with the "elasticity" he valued in poetry (see Chapter 4). When he abandoned a narrative approach in favor of abstraction, the relation between the lines and the closing of the poem became increasingly problematic, but he did not discuss these issues in his writings. One way out of the stalemate of line after unrelated line would have been to end with a punch line (*ochi*), but Katue did not take that approach. Instead of zeroing in on specifics, he theorized about ideoplasty as one way of perceiving the effect of the poem holistically.

Despite the importance of ideoplasty in Katue's poetics at this period, critics almost invariably make only passing mention of it. For example, Fujitomi Yasuo (1928–), while believing that it should be highly evaluated, offers no analysis of his own.[25] The rare exception is Iwanari Tatsuya (1933–), who cites the dictionary meaning as "idea formation" and goes on to state that "behind the surface of the descriptive content [of words] is generated the receptor of another content."[26] He does not, however, elaborate on the nature of what lurks behind the surface of words.

Instead of starting from the end and working backwards to explain the effect of a poem, it is perhaps more illuminating to quote the basic VOU attitude toward writing, most succinctly stated by Fuji Takeshi, "Poets cannot transmit their thoughts without language, but we certainly aren't going to use language merely to transmit thoughts."[27]

Pound's comments on Katue's ideoplasty essay are circuitous: he suggested that there is no need for "the 'theory' being *consciously* held" and that "intuition may even provide the essentials in this domain." In a sense, he was urging readers to be impressed with Katue's intelligence but stopped short of insisting that they had to take the trouble to understand the content of his assertions. Pound invoked William Carlos Williams and Henri Gaudier-Brzeska (as he had invoked E. E. Cummings before) but gave no concrete hints of how Katue's idea resembles theirs. Taking an apophatic stance,

Pound claimed that Katue's statement was "not alien to something I once wrote re Dr Williams' poems, nor is it contrary to Gaudier's sculptural principles." The same could be said about many people's poetics; Pound was again resorting to the tactic of name-dropping to add to Katue's prestige.

Privately, Pound was exasperated by Katue's stance in favor of "pure poetry." In one letter, Pound mixed his blend of politics and economics and finally exclaimed, "If these subjects bore YOU, put me in touch with your grandfather, and stick to plastic values and verbal nuances."[28] Pound was well aware that he and Katue differed in approach, as is evident in the following comments—the first appeared in an article he wrote for *The Japan Times* and the second in a letter to Katue:

If I start going into it [several historical questions he poses] I might fall into the snares of power psychology or even of monetary psychology, and this, your admirable poet Kitasono Katue would find, I fear, unpoetic on my part. (Mar. 4, 1940)[29]

******

And as soon as we have a sane peace with FUNK's european plan in action and proper monetary system, I will stop boring you to death with econ/politico/geo/etc. and behave like an æsthete/ occupying myself with dramady/poesy/music etc. as a true inhabitant of Miaco. (Aug. 25, 1940)[30]

Pound understood Katue's position but could not resist trying to change him. In a part of a letter to Kitasono that he offered for publication in *VOU*, Pound had an anti-Semitic paragraph followed by criticism of the VOU stand on pure poetry: "It is proper that up to the age of crucifixion (32) the poet be lyric. After that he withers, I think, if he does not feel some curiosity as to the LOCUS of his own perceptions and passions. By LOCUS I mean their movement in relation to the humanity about him" (Dec. 31, 1940).[31]

The tensest moment in the three-decade-long friendship occurred over the same issue, namely, the content of poetry. Pound, who had lived through the futility of World War I, believed that poets could not afford to stand idly by and be pulled into future wars.

We are having a LOAN-Capital war. Some say a jew war against the aryan population of Europe. . . . Some call it Kuhn Loeb and Co's war on Japan.

At any rate there is no understanding of the present wars without understanding of war loans / loans by the SAME MEN to the Same men. De Wendel the banker pays the French people's money to De Wendel the gun maker. And SO FORTH.

and all this is subject matter for literature.

(Oct. 28, 1939)[32]

Katue usually ignored such comments, but after an earful about politics and economics to be told directly that "all this is subject matter for literature" was more than he could stomach. Katue, sticking to his position that the poet does not stoop to involve himself in the mire of the world, an attitude sanctioned by Japanese tradition (notably Zen artists), retorted:

I'm sorry, but I must confess I think economics is, too, one of such uncertain sciences as medical science, psychology, etc. You can imagine how firmly I stand to this belief, as I . . . studied political economics and philosophy in university. Please excuse me, if I'm mistaken, but I guess yours is political economics. In fact it's another field to which economics should extend, but I fear which may change economics into a nasty sandwich.

For my part, I prefer to look at the vague cosmos of Marquis de Laplace,[33] standing on my poetical philosophy of life, hanging down a ribbon from my collar, printed "I don't need such a hypothesis."

(Dec. 5, 1939)[34]

Katue's reference to Laplace is, in retrospect, indicative of his own desire to stay outside (or above) politics. It was also an insightful but unheeded warning to Pound, who after World War II barely escaped execution for treason and, to evade a jail sentence, was confined for thirteen years in St. Elizabeth's Hospital, a federal asylum in Washington, D.C.

Pound was occasionally irked by Katue's estheticism and expressed mild disagreement, but he was interested more in using his Japanese pen pal as ammunition in his tirade against the evils of Western civilization than in breaking their friendship over a quarrel on poetics. In the *Kulchur* essay quoted above, Pound contrasted Katue the Japanese intellectual with the boorish British sailors who docked in Rapallo, his point being that Japan is more civilized than England. Pound was attempting to counter anti-Japanese sentiment in the West with his own propaganda.

In *Kulchur*, Pound always mentioned the VOU Club and Kitasono in a positive light. The following comment could not have failed to impress Pound aficionados:

I did not speak of Shakespeare in that opusculus [*ABC of Reading*], and still believe the bard is both read and ably discussed by others almost sufficiently. The VOU club thought that my meaning was clear and that they at least were sufficiently conversant with Elizabethan drama not to be led astray by my indication of other peaks in our poetry.[35]

Pound seems to have enjoyed using Katue to embarrass the West. As leader of the VOU Club and editor of *VOU*, Katue could publish whatever he liked; Pound nevertheless presents his friend's literary activity as heroic: "I spend 8 years demanding a proper English edtn. of Frobenius. K Kitasono has an article on Paideuma in *VOU* within the minimum time after receiving the volume (Feb. issue 1937)."[36] And in one of the letters Pound suggested that Katue try to get W. E. Woodward's *New American History* into the Japanese curriculum, even though his friend had no affiliation with the Ministry of Education: "It would be a great joke if you started using it in your schools and giving a better teaching of U.S. history than is given in American schools."[37]

Pound not only wrote in advocacy of the VOU group, but also helped get Katue and VOU published in three countries. In January 1938, Katue was featured in the Italian magazine *Broletto*, with a photo, a facsimile of his signature, and an Italian translation of his essay on ideoplasty.[38] *Townsman* (1939) printed seven Katue works in translation.[39] In New York, James Laughlin, poet and publisher of New Directions Books and a Pound disciple, introduced the VOU Club in his annual of experimental poetry. The twelve-page spread presented new translations, Katue's essay on ideoplasty, and a short introduction by Laughlin in which he candidly explained his motives: "I am particularly glad to be able to publish them because of two dissociations which they can effect. They will show first of all that militaristic imperialism has not wiped out artistic activity and secondly that there *is* live poetry in Japan."[40]

For many Western readers of *New Directions*, *Townsman*, and *Broletto*, Katue and the VOU Club were the sole link with contemporary Japanese literature. The VOU poems, with their sharp imagery, helped in a small measure to counter Western jingoists intent on presenting Japan as a nation of "savage warriors." Significantly, the strategy of cultural hegemony always requires the presence of a few "civilized" people among the "savages," and there was nothing particularly assertive or threatening to the Western reader in Katue's poetry; rather, he was quite useful and serviceable.

Laughlin reiterated the extra-literary value of poets as cultural ambassadors in his 1940 introduction of the "international chainpoems," in which a number of VOU members participated: "At a time when England and Japan are on the verge of war, it is rather good to think that poets of the two countries have been working together on this project."[41]

On ideograms and ideoplasty Laughlin rehashed Pound's ideas:

The first thing to think about in studying these poems is the fact of the ideogram. The Japanese language, derived from the Chinese, is still very much a picture language. In spite of the intrusion of the phonetic characters the Japanese can still see in many of the words which he writes the picture of the thing itself. What is the result in terms of poetry? Naturally there is more verbal reality, a closer relationship between the thing and its name, some of the essence of the thing in the name.

But of course that quality is not carried over into a translation. So we can only surmise that the oriental poet and poetry reader are, in this respect, "better off" than we are, and let it go at that.[42]

We are, as with Pound, predisposed to accept the translations favorably, if only on the basis of the superiority of the original language. The myth of the ideogram influenced Laughlin's perceptions of the translations. Summarizing Pound's viewpoint on the Japanese language (while, unlike Pound, making no pretensions to understand the language), Laughlin stated:

If I understand Japanese syntax aright it has, to an even greater degree than an inflected language like Latin, a minimum of dead words—that is, words which have no charge of meaning apart from their grammatical function—articles, prepositions, etc.—all the useless little words which clutter up a positional language like English and thin out the vigour of the poetic line.

I think anyone must concede that one of the most important factors in poetry is verbal inter-activity—word working upon word, the sense-aura of one word fusing and contrasting with those of the words near it. The dead little words of English lessen this activity by separating the meaning-bearing words. Thus in English we only get in small segments of the line—in adjectival and adverbial phrases for the most part—the kind of tension that we often get in a whole line of Latin, where there will be perhaps only one word out of seven that does not carry a meaning. The same sort of thing, I think, is possible in Japanese; certainly these poems confirm that thesis.

And the poets of the VOU Club are very well aware of the rich possibilities of their medium. They would not perhaps use the word "tension" but they have coined the word "ideoplasty" to express the esthetic effects which the close juxtaposition of verbal images makes possible.[43]

Laughlin was correct in perceiving the visual possibilities in the Japanese language, both in the concreteness of individual graphs and in the compact alignment of striking imagery. Ironically, what Laughlin noticed about the language was even truer of Katue's formalism of the late 1920s than it was of these experiments in abstraction. Laughlin was attributing characteristics to the Japanese language primarily based on his understanding of the *VOU* po- ems. Modern Japanese is, however, full of dead words—particles, cluttering fillers, doublespeak, uncharged words—that the VOU poets were careful to avoid using. Instead of idealizing the inherent nature of the Japanese lan- guage, Laughlin might have thought that Katue and colleagues had a similar attitude to their language as Pound and others had toward English: clean up sloppiness of expression and use vivid, charged words. Perhaps because it did not help perpetuate his myth of the ideogram, Laughlin chose to excise the following section of Katue's essay:

The subject which most engages the attention of contemporary poets is still about functions of words. The words we use have become too flat, petrified into marks and loaded with so many conventions. (It is fine, to-day.) In this sentence, there is no sky so blue as sulphate of copper, no verdure, and no green leaves trembling like jellies. We are but to know that it is not necessary to take an umbrella.

On the contrary, in days of yore, our ancestors must have said, (The sky is like the sea.) (The sun is on the cocoa-nut palm.).[44]

By no means as lucid as similar statements on the subject by Pound or Laughlin himself, Katue nevertheless did put himself in the same camp by asserting that the Japanese language also has conventional expressions that the VOUists were intent on discarding.

Almost fifty years after his *New Directions* introduction of 1938, Laughlin gave a glimpse of the "Ezuversity" at Rapallo and showed that he had swept away his previous misconceptions about the ideogram:

A Chinese dictionary compiled about 800 A.D. shows only 8% of the characters as ideoglyphic, the rest being phonetic or syntactic. But Pound believed that he could find picture-meanings in every character. I saw him trying to do it in 1934. After lunch in Rapallo he would stretch out on his bed, with his big black hat shading his eyes from the sea light, a Chinese dictionary propped up on a pillow on his stomach. He would stare and stare at the characters, trying to see the pictures in them which he might reconcile with the dictionary meanings. If he didn't find the picture, he might invent it. So some of his English phrases are more Pound than Kung [Confu- cius].[45]

Laughlin, in spite of his occasional inaccuracies and omissions, was in- strumental in promoting the VOU Club both before and after World War II in his annual New Directions anthologies. *Townsman* ceased publication in 1946, but New Directions, with many avant-garde writers on its roster, grew in influence with the passage of time. Through Pound and Laughlin, Katue was in touch with the central network of experimental poetry in the English-speaking world. Charles Henri Ford, an American surrealist poet, enlisted the VOU group in the writing of "international chainpoems," which were the first examples of a new, cooperative genre that has since spread in popularity.[46]

Other Western poets took notice of the VOU translations. High praise came from Hugh Gordon Porteus, who wrote in *Criterion* in 1939, "The most fruitful experiments with language are likely to continue to emerge from those who concern themselves with *images* and their relations, rather than with idle wordspinning. Nothing more novel and exciting has been done lately, along these lines, than by the poets of the Japanese *Vou* group."[47] He went on to elaborate about the VOU Club. His comments raise several points already discussed, namely, the Japanese language, translation, and VOU's role in the international avant-garde prior to World War II.

Vou is a meaningless name, like *dada*. But the poetry of the *Vou* club, which is animated by the theories of "ideogram and ideoplasty" of its founder, Mr. Katue Kitasono, is to be distinguished from the superficially similar poetry of the *dada* and *surrealist* movements. It is written in *kanamajiri*, that is, in a mixture of Chinese ideograms and Japanese phonetic script, and it is devoid of all rules, though bearing some resemblance to the traditional *kyoka*, or comic epigrammatic verse. The *Vou* club prints its work in a magazine which deserves notice for several reasons. In the first place, this publication proves that there is a vital and original spirit still at work in the Far East. In the second place, it proves that despite the most formidable political, national and linguistic barriers, cultural exchange is still possible between literary innovators of the East and the West. The July issue of *Vou* prints (in Japanese) the first half of the suggestive essay on "Language and the Experimental Writer" by James Laughlin IV which appeared in 1937 (in English) in *New Directions*. And three of the poems in this issue have also appeared, translated by their respective authors, in the second number of *The Townsman*. I don't know what the Japanese are likely to make of J. Laughlin IV. But it should be pointed out that the poems, as translated, are inadvertently more *quaint* than their Japanese originals. There is more than a touch, here and there, of "English as she is Japped." A suspicion that *The Townsman* enjoys exploiting this element, (i.e. the *leg-pull* element present in much experimental art, of the *dada* order) is confirmed by the transliteration of Mr. Nagayasu's name as 'Syuiti Nag.' Here it may be noted that as good art has been done with the tongue in the cheek as with the most solemn intention; and, art aside, we should invariably prefer the clown to the magician.[48]

Porteus understood Japanese better than Pound did. He even compared the original poems with the translations and found the latter "quaint," because the target language (English) was not the native tongue of the translators. He also claimed that the poems resemble traditional *kyōka* (mad verse). Certainly the VOUists relished displaying their *esprit* in humorous lines of verse as much as in fashionable dress, but they also took their work seriously and considered their poetry a type of "natural science." Katue, at least, would have objected to his poems being labeled purely comic, since he proscribed satirical poems along with political and religious verse for their preconceived, one-dimensional standpoint. Porteus must have understood the mix of brittle images from the sciences, which the VOUists considered poetic vocabulary, as mere leg-pulling.

Porteus accused *Townsman* of purposely leaving in grammatical mistakes as a dadaist gag to catch the reader off guard. A letter to Katue reveals that Pound tampered with the translations only to the extent of clarifying ambiguous words and correcting misspellings.[49] Neither Pound nor Duncan, editor of *Townsman*, altered the syntax or improved the writing. Since at the time at least six weeks transpired between sending a letter and receiving an answer, it may have struck the poets as too much trouble to haggle back and forth. Nevertheless, they could have corrected grammatical mistakes that unnecessarily distract the reader.[50]

But more important than the poems themselves seems to have been the communication between East and West that the VOU Club engendered. Porteus was in agreement with Laughlin and the others on this point. Western poets and editors, powerless to affect their governments' tailspin into war, used the solidarity with VOU poets as a gesture of protestation. Frank Jones and Arthur Blair, the editors of *Diogenes*, also solicited a contribution from Katue, which turned out to be the last poem published abroad by a VOU poet before the suspension of mail service in spring 1941.[51]

After the war, Katue and VOU became even more a part of the international avant-garde movement. Katue was praised by William Carlos Williams and Charles Olson, and a brief volume of his poems in English translation was published by Robert Creeley.[52] Later, Kenneth Rexroth acclaimed Katue as one of the best of the international concrete poets active during the 1950s and 1960s (see Chapter 8).[53] Kitasono and the VOU Club rose to prominence and achieved international recognition on the strength of the imagery in their poems and because of their persuasive promotion by Ezra Pound.

Although the relationship between Kitasono and Pound was inextricably bound up in the literary activity generated by their correspondence, there was also another, less tangible, factor—the mutual affection the two men felt for each other. The ice was first broken in an exchange regarding the number 21. Kitasono in his initial letter had written of the VOU Club, "The members are now twenty one, two-third of them being poets."[54] Pound replied, "May the club, whatever the number of its members, stay 21 years young."[55] Katue then sent a letter signed by the VOU members with the following comment, "We, the Japanese younger generation, heartily wish to success [sic] in our work, staying always at the twenty-one years old, as you hoped in your letter."[56] Katue was actually thirty-four years old (and Pound fifty-one), but as they bantered the casual remark back and forth, the way was cleared for discussion of more serious topics.

Polite as they were with each other from the beginning, their friendship blossomed after the subject of Pound's then twelve-year-old daughter, Mary (now Mary de Rachewiltz), entered into their letters. Kitasono, wishing to send Mary a greeting for Christmas 1937, asked Pound for her address in America. Ezra replied that she was not in America; he would, however, send an essay she had written in Italian about the life and customs of the Tyrol, where she was living, as soon as he had finished translating it into English. Katue was impressed with his friend's affection for his offspring and wrote back: "No Japanese papa would make such a pleasing booklet for his daughter."[57] He decided to translate it into Japanese (no doubt finding the style less terse than Pound's own prose) and was able to place it, with photos, in *Reijokai* (Young ladies' world), a leading monthly magazine for teenage girls.[58] Pound proudly wrote to his friend in America, Mary Moore, "My own daughter has just made her literary debut in Japan."[59]

The language gap between Kitasono and Pound was occasionally exacerbated by typing mistakes, as in this amusing letter:

Dear Ezra Pound,
I fear I might have astonished the bon papa of Mary by writing in my former letter, "I received a very lonely letter from Mary."
    It was, of course, a very lovely letter that she gave me.
    Please disregard the mistype of my forefinger.
        ever yours
        Katue[60]

Pound was restless with the long name Kitasono Katue, and so he abbreviated it "Dear K.," or "K/K," or "K²" until he hit on the nickname "Kit Kat," which he first used in 1940 and thereafter favored almost continuously.[61] Pound also wittily abbreviated his own name. Having translated Li Po's "The River Merchant's Wife," he signed one letter "Ez Po" and, in case Katue missed the point, added, "debased form of Rihaku" (romanization of the Japanese reading of Li Po).[62]

Katue started out as Pound's distant pen pal but soon became his translator, editor, and publisher. By 1939, on the eve of Pound's first trip back to the United States in eighteen years, Katue also became Pound's job procurer and banker. Especially helpful to Pound was Katue's arranging for the older poet to contribute articles to *The Japan Times*. After mail delivery was cut off between the Allied and Axis blocs, Pound's sources of income began drying up. Because Italy and Japan were on the same side, communication continued for some time. Despite a request that Pound restrict his comments in *The Japan Times* to the cultural sphere, his penchant for discussing economics and politics inevitably crept into his opinion-laden columns. His articles were not as inflammatory, however, as the propaganda broadcasts over the Italian airwaves that resulted in his arrest at the close of the war.

Pound's most constructive idea was his call for trilingual editions of "the hundred best books of Japanese literature." He chose English and Italian from Western languages, and "ideogram, with the Japanese sound (syllabic) comment" as the third language, an idea that suggests that he believed all *kana* are *furigana* (optional marks to indicate the sound of *kanji*).[63] Later he revised this plan and advocated roman letters instead of *kana* for phoneticizing. He was interested in using the new technology of microphotography to reproduce the finest texts inexpensively, so as to make them easily affordable to Western students.

Katue's friendship inadvertently proved useful for Pound at his sanity hearing on Feb. 13, 1946. Pound was found unfit to stand trial because of his delusions. Dr. Wendell S. Muncie, the psychiatrist hired by the defense, gave the following testimony:

He has a number of rather fixed ideas which are either clearly delusional or verging on the delusional. One I might speak of, for instance, he believes he has been designated to save the Constitution of the United States for the people of the United States.

I will come back to this item in a minute.

Secondly, he has a feeling that he has the key to the peace of the world through the writings of Confucius, which he translated into Italian and into English, and that if this book had been given proper circulation the Axis would not have been formed, we would be at peace now, and a great deal of trouble could have been avoided in the past, and this becomes his blueprint for world order in the future.

Third, he believes that with himself as leader, a group of intellectuals could have gotten together in different countries, like Japan, for instance, where he is well thought of, to work for world order. (Italics added)[64]

Although no single delusion mentioned above constitutes insanity, Pound's lawyer, Julian Cornell, on cross-examination had Muncie agree that together they added up to a delusional framework. Katue thus had a crucial, though indirect, role in saving Pound's neck.

After the war, the Occupation censors would not permit Katue to receive Pound's *Pisan Cantos*. And since Pound's outgoing mail was checked by psychiatrists at St. Elizabeth's Hospital, the older poet found it more convenient to convey his messages to Katue through his wife. After being released from St. Elizabeth's, Pound wrote Katue two spirited last letters before entering into his long silence.

In their thirty-year friendship, Pound and Katue always played the role of representatives of their respective cultures. Katue was known in Japan for introducing Western literary trends, and Pound had a similar reputation in the West for introducing Japanese and Chinese culture. Yet, ironically, the two poets in their letters always act like an ambassador of their own country. They might have carried on their discussion in terms of a larger internationalism to which they both belonged, but their strong ethnic identities foreclosed such a possibility.

In retrospect, did Katue and Pound influence one another's poetry? Since Pound could not read Japanese and was familiar only with a dozen or so of Katue's poems in translation, we can assume that they exerted no influence on his *Cantos*, no matter how enthusiastically Pound introduced them. Katue, for his part, mentioned Pound directly only in one poem in *Saboten tō* (Cactus island; 1938). The reference is playful and ambiguous:

> Ezra Pound's world grows rectangular, spiral-shaped, and distant.
> Wyndham Lewis's world, while spinning and inclining, approaches with the
> sound of drums.[65]

Katue might have been more influenced by Pound had he just begun writing poetry, but he had already established himself over the preceding decade as an original poet who wrote in a half-dozen different modes. The fundamental styles of Pound and Katue are almost polar opposites—Katue strove for a transparent simplicity built on abstract imagery, and Pound for an opaque style constructed of concrete and idiomatic fragments. The two poets converged in creating verbal assemblages and in their insistence on "making it new." Katue was continually experimenting; as soon as he found a niche he would abandon it and think up a different approach. His attitude toward art paralleled Pound's poetics, and it made for a compatibility between them.

Katue's poetry was also affected by Pound in another minor but not insignificant way. In the kind of osmosis that goes on among friends, Katue vicariously took on some of Pound's literary attributes—for example, his Mediterranean imagery, his anti-academic stance, his role as reviver of classical culture, and his self-proclaimed authority to pronounce confidently on the past, present, and future of poetry. None of these can be traced directly to Pound, but they were reinforced by the association. Above all else, Pound's friendship gave Katue the luxury of ignoring his rival poets in Japan outside the VOU group. That confidence in turn allowed him to pursue his poetry experiments quietly over the following four decades with an inner assurance that he had been validated by someone whom he believed truly mattered—Ezra Pound—his friend and one of the most influential poets and literary powerbrokers of the twentieth century.

Katue and Pound developed a close working relationship. Each sent his works to the other; each promoted the other in his own sphere of poetic and critical production. But this does not mean that either poet understood the other poet's work or theory. As a matter of fact, one of the most fascinating things about this relationship is their failure to understand each other, and indeed their indifference to this failure. Their need for each other was quite real, but served different purposes. For Katue, Pound's support and praise were important for self-promotion: he was unabashedly self-Orientalized, and any recognition from a famous Western poet was—as it still is to many Japanese writers—an invaluable endorsement. But this does not mean he understood Pound, either his imagism, ideogramic method, or fascist ideology. Katue was serious about his avant-garde poetry and VOU principles; so he should not have accepted Pound's historicism, for instance. For Pound, on the other hand, Katue was useful, simply because no one knew who he was or what Japanese modern poetry was. Pound could thus claim that

Japanese poetry was radically new, and no one in Europe or in the United States could refute him. Pound needed to prove that he was familiar with the latest and newest in the world. He could show off his Japanese poet-friend together with his Fenollosa and Chinese characters to his fellow poets. Also, Katue provided him with a Japanese publisher whose royalties were precious for a poet with limited resources. This does not, however, mean he truly understood Katue's poetry. Pound read no Japanese and little Chinese, and Katue's translations of his own manifestos were incomprehensible. (Of course, Pound's claim that he understood these incomprehensible tracts was used by Pound to impress rival poets and critics.) The mutual pact of pretended familiarity and real indifference—a rather cynical agreement for the sake of mutual promotion—is nothing unique: it still goes on today, maybe on a larger scale. Perhaps Pound and Kitasono were themselves among those taken in by it.

6 THE QUICKSAND

of

FASCISM

Many avant-garde or proletarian Japanese poets of the 1920s and 1930s were coerced during World War II (1941–45; also called the Pacific War) to demonstrate their loyalty to their country by writing jingoist verse. Should the patriotic compositions of those years be overlooked when assessing the lifework of the poets? Almost all Japanese literary historians think so, as do the majority of poets themselves, and they disregard or downplay the "fascist" propaganda poetry as irrelevant.[1] Some justify their position on the grounds that the verses were written under pressure and were the only form of camouflage available to the downtrodden poets. They reason that Japan consists of a few islands, geographically isolated, and Japanese poets had nowhere to run. Had the avant-garde poets gone to California, for example, they would have been placed in internment camps, in contrast to Caucasian writers and artists from Europe such as André Breton who went into a safe self-imposed exile in the United States.

A few critics and poets take a much stricter view and fault the avant-garde poets for succumbing to government pressure.[2] They argue that the avant-garde involvement of the poets consisted of no more than a thin outer coating of dilettantish cosmopolitanism grafted onto an unshakable nationalist core nurtured by an educational system based on emperor worship and the myth of Japanese invincibility. These critics cite the heroics of certain Western poets such as Paul Eluard—who risked his life resisting German fascism—with the situation of Japanese poets who bent under duress and revealed their ideological spinelessness. As a corollary to this viewpoint, prewar avant-garde poetry produced by adherents of futurism, dadaism, surrealism, and proletarianism is evaluated as second-rate, "false" literature, and less experimental poetry (related to *tanka* and *haiku* but in free verse) penned by traditional Japanist groups such as Shiki (Four seasons), Nihon romanha (Japanese romantics), and Kogito (Cogito) is held to be inherently more authentic.

This polarization between apologist and accuser ignores the complexity of the situation. To dismiss the wartime poems as insignificant without exploring the circumstances surrounding their creation is evasive. Kitasono's biographer, Fujitomi Yasuo, in an otherwise pioneering study, elides Katue's wartime activity. Instead of revealing the patriotic poems written by Katue, in a play of mirrors he quotes Nakano Ka'ichi quoting Watanabe Masaya (1929–), who apparently stated (although he cites no sources), "He [Kitasono Katue] did not write so-called patriotic poems."[3] And with that the subject is dropped. Those on the opposite extreme believe that one war poem is sufficient to discredit the entire lifework of a poet.[4] The gap between the two arguments is unbridgeable. Those who forgive usually prefer to do so by silence or by denial, for open support of the patriotic poets invites ridicule as a fascist sympathizer. Therefore, the handful of accusers seem to win by default. Now that over a half-century has elapsed since the end of the war, it is appropriate to take a fresh glance from various perspectives.

One fundamental problem surrounding the issue of patriotic poetry is whether the Japanese have *shutaisei* (subjecthood, individuality), in other words, a sense of identity approximating that which we take for granted in the West. If not, it is perhaps a fruitless task to attempt to understand these poets as individuals when their society did not allow them to function as such. The *shutaisei* problem, and the forced *tenkō* (conversion) that many poets were subjected to, is succinctly summarized by Masao Miyoshi:

With the coming of the Asian and Pacific War . . . the resistance was easily neutralized and absorbed into the mainstream bourgeoisie, as individual writers underwent ritual conversions (tenko) whereby they abandoned their critical opposition and adapted themselves to the imperial programs. Some writers continued their passive noncooperation by remaining silent, while others collaborated actively. None were guiltless, since nearly all writers were at least acquiescent. None of them were, however, wholly guilty either, since they were all under coercion. In this grey mix of guilt and innocence, the contours of the individual were blurred into the background of the state totality.

This dialectic of the self and the Other changed very little after the catastrophic defeat in 1945. Swiftly moving away from the rightist position of the war years, writ-

ers renamed themselves "humanists" and "modernists," "democrats" and "interna-
tionalists." There was an ironic repeat performance of "conversion": in proclaiming
their *shutaisei* ("individuality") in unison, the writers were unwittingly reaffirming
state collectivism. The oaths of readaptation were chorally orchestrated. In fact, as
the cold war commenced in the mid-1940s, there was still another need for a turning
back, totaling three zigzag reversions for some writers: from the left to the right in
the 1930s, from the right to the left after the war, and from the left back to the right
in the 1950s. The Japanese state seems to have remained unaltered throughout these
gyrations; with or without the emperor as its symbol, it has animated the people and
loomed ever larger in the common mind every waking moment.[5]

A related issue is whether Katue would have conceived of actions or poli-
cies of the state as "political." Imperial authority in Japan had a quality that
put it above "politics" in the minds of most Japanese, who tended to associate
"politics" only with out-of-power agitation for change.[6]

I approach the war poetry by taking Katue's activity from 1939 to 1945 as a
window through which to view the problems confronting all Western-
influenced poets in Japan at that time. Virtually every avant-garde poet co-
operated with the war effort, although to varying degrees and in different ca-
pacities. Almost any poet could serve equally well as an example, and a simi-
lar scenario of capitulation would be observed. My main concern is to follow
the shifts in Katue's work after the first police crackdown on avant-garde po-
ets, the Kobe Incident of March 1940 (discussed below).[7] My purpose is to
illuminate the circumstances in which Katue found himself and the choices
he made. After the war, he never wrote about his wartime activity, and the
younger generation of his postwar VOU group considered it bad manners to
broach the subject.[8] The patriotic verse of this time deserves close scrutiny
because of its relative neglect, and because in the subsequent revival of poetry
along Western lines after the war it served as an omnipresent reminder of
the past, a negative point of departure.

During my interviews for this book, questions about wartime activities
usually elicited an embarrassed silence. Many poets denied having published
pro-war poems, and yet time and again I would discover such compositions
in anthologies. Once I was even told point-blank by the poet Hattori Shin-
roku (1913–98), who, ironically, did not himself pen patriotic verse, "The
subject is taboo."[9] Finding the surviving poets tightlipped, I draw less on in-
terviews here than in the other parts of this book. Locating material on this
period was a piecemeal and laborious process. The staff of the Library of
Modern Japanese Literature in Tokyo (Nihon Kindai Bungakukan) in-

formed me that poets are extremely sensitive about this subject, and some have even physically removed their patriotic contributions to wartime anthologies before donating materials to the library's collection.

I introduce seven of Katue's patriotic poems, published between 1939 and 1945—probably his entire production—and note his other wartime activities. Of the seven poems, four have previously been republished by critics Sakuramoto Tomio (1933–) and Yoshimoto Takaaki (1924–), although their studies do not focus on Katue. In the second half of the chapter, I introduce Katue's wartime diary in order to consider him in terms of his everyday struggles and not only as a propaganda poet in the abstract. The public and private portraits of him at times reinforce and at times contradict one another. Finally, I examine his postwar attitude toward his wartime involvement.

The controversial issue of how to evaluate patriotic poetry is too complex to settle here, especially since it is tinged with identity politics. For example, even though some of Katue's colleagues in the poetry world denounced him after the war for writing patriotic poems, Japanologist colleagues of mine have suggested that for me, an "American," to take the same position would amount to "winner's justice." Despite the pitfalls, I trace the trajectory of his ideological shifts from liberal to conservative and, after the war, back to liberal again, not to make a categorical judgment about his complicity or culpability, but to demonstrate his responses to the shifting political situations.

Katue's wartime activity took place within a political context that had undergone a tremendous transformation since the mid-1920s. In 1925, the enactment of universal manhood suffrage more than quadrupled the number of eligible voters, from three to thirteen million. That same year the Ministry of Justice created a special section to monitor "crimes of thought" (*shisō hanzai*); meanwhile, the promulgation of the Peace Preservation Law (Chian Iji Hō) signaled an intensification of the anti-radical campaign. These draconian measures, ostensibly intended to curtail communists and anarchists, were devised partially to counterbalance the unknown power of the newly expanded electorate. From the earliest systematic roundup of socialists on March 15, 1928, until the total war mobilization of 1941, there were over 60,000 arrests. The target was first the political left, then the literary left, and eventually any author "tainted" by the West, no matter how apolitical. The crackdown was directed more toward novelists than poets, because their books had wider circulation, but by 1940 even poets were scrambling for safety and devising camouflage tactics.

Until autumn 1940, Katue was free to write in whatever style he liked. Along with members of the VOU Club, he had spent the years 1935 to 1940 writing abstract poetry that reflected the methodological gains of dadaism, surrealism, and other Western-inspired movements of the twentieth century. The VOUists considered themselves poetic scientists searching for formulas to display the boundless possibilities of human conceptualization in a laboratory of words. Other poets could concentrate on putting their maudlin sentiments into old forms such as tanka and haiku or into the newer "free verse," yet the VOUists, for their part, aimed at replenishing the intellectual content of poetry through explorations of hitherto uncharted realms of the mind. From their viewpoint of pure poetry, they scoffed at the net entangling the imagination of most poets, whether committed proletarians or more mainstream poets, who took as their subject matter the experiences of everyday life. Further pulling the VOU groups toward abstraction was the opportunity they had been given to translate their own poems for publication in Western magazines, which made them aware of the universality of powerful imagery as opposed to words and phrases that convey only a specific mood in a particular language.

Katue, while involved in the abstract poetry movement with his VOU friends, was also writing in a variety of other styles during the five years preceding the Pacific War.[10] These included lyrical poems,[11] aphoristic poems on literary criticism and philosophical subjects,[12] poetry in a neo-traditional vein,[13] conventional haiku,[14] as well as one patriotic poem ("Sensen no aki"; to be discussed below). These last three categories—neo-traditional, haiku, and patriotic verse—seem to run counter to his previous experimentation in Western forms. Although the language of any single poem or book is relatively consistent, Katue was not the type of purist who rejects all but one style. His literary production during the war years further widened his scope.

Katue found himself in a paradox: he desired to continue writing abstract poetry that, by definition, transcended the mundane world, yet the mundane world of militarist Japan found his transcendence subversive to the law and order it wished to impose. Starting with the Manchurian Incident of 1931, which led to the Sino-Japanese War (1937–45), the military establishment increasingly dominated civilian life and by the late 1930s was exercising a stranglehold over the population, including the way people were allowed to think. The Tokubetsu Kōtō Keisatsu (Special higher police; abr. Tokkō) had been created in 1911 to suppress left-wing movements. The Tokkō, specializing in crimes of thought, were commonly referred to as the "Shisō Keisatsu" (Thought police).[15] Poets considered apolitical were not targeted until 1940.

Ironically, a police crackdown on ideologically motivated authors would have made more sense during the first half of the 1920s—the earliest wave of avant-gardism in Japan—when dadaism was inextricably associated with anarchism. By the late 1920s, however, there had developed a clear split between politically committed proletarian poets and the politically apathetic *esprit nouveau* poets. Katue always considered himself apolitical, as did most members of the clubs he headed. But in 1940 the Thought Police, on orders from the Diet, widened the definition of "thought criminal" to include anyone influenced by the West, and Katue's stance became untenable. Avant-gardists were suspected of harboring villainous thoughts merely for using loanwords of European origin.

In the government's view, too much Westernization had made intellectuals decadent, and this played into the hands of the imperialistic West, with its goal of world domination. Government spokesmen argued vehemently that Japan must carve out its own autarkic bloc, but this could be achieved only with civilian solidarity. In the process, not only Japan but all of Asia would be rescued from the clutches of corrupt Western civilization. The policymakers concluded that intellectuals had to take a leadership role in nurturing fellow Asians in the Japanese version of their "shared Oriental heritage." If Japanese poets continued their immersion in Westernism, they argued, it would send a counterproductive signal to both Japanese and the inhabitants of Japan's colonies. Poets would have to desist from emulating Western models and instead create a poetry relevant to the new Asian order. Poets who joined the vital endeavor would be rewarded; those who resisted would be punished severely. The middle ground of previous years was no longer tenable.

In 1938 Osada Tsuneo (1902–77), avant-garde poet and VOU member, founded the Tōkyō Shijin Kurabu (Tokyo poets club) in an attempt to overcome the factionalism dividing rival cliques and allow poets to speak in a single voice in support of the Japanese war effort on the Chinese continent.[16]

According to a note in *VOU*, no. 24, Osada arranged a poetry reading called "Shōhei ni okuru sensō shi no yū" (An evening of war poetry dedicated to the wounded soldiers) on October 26, 1938, at which Katue read his first patriotic poem, "Sensen no aki" (Autumn at the front), along with Apollinaire's "Four Nights."[17] Some 700 people attended, by far the largest audience up to that time for a reading by avant-garde poets. Osada organized a second public reading of patriotic poems in January 1939, and the thirty members of the Tokyo Poets Club shared the stage with ten older poets (*senpai*). Injured soldiers and one theater group served as volunteer staff. Kitahara Hakushū, a leading poet who was in the hospital dying of causes unrelated to the war, contributed the opening message; he stressed that soldiers were sacrificing their lives for the homeland, and poets should do their part willingly to fight with words.[18] It was a case of the pen should try to equal the sword rather than the pen is mightier than the sword. By all accounts, the evening was a success.

Osada asked the poets to contribute to the anthology *Sensō shishū* (War poems; Fig. 20), and it was published in August 1939 by Moriya Hitoshi (1897–1969) of Shōshinsha (which had issued Katue's *Hi no sumire* in 1939).[19] Katue's contribution to the anthology was substantial: he designed *Sensō shishū*, including the cover (a photo of the Japanese cavalry in China), and contributed the poem he had read in public, "Sensen no aki." *Sensō shishū* is the first anthology of Japanese war poetry from the 1930s, and curiously, it was produced not by known nationalist poets but by so-called avant-gardists.[20]

Was Osada, who criticized much war poetry for its oversentimentality and was not known as a nationalist, acting simply out of patriotic zeal? After all, several of the Tokyo poets were being maimed and killed across the sea on the Chinese mainland. VOU poet Nagashima Miyoshi (1917–), for example, was sent to the front in January 1939 and by April he was hospitalized after being struck by a mortar round in the left leg and blinded in one eye.[21] Or were Osada's activities, including the blessing and contributions from elder statesmen poets, motivated by a desire to protect freewheeling poets (and publishers such as Moriya) from right-wing attacks? In other words, were the poets exhibiting two faces (avant-garde and patriotic) or were they attempting to cover their avant-garde face with a patriotic mask?

Contrary to what one might expect, poets in groups who were not internationalist in temperament and wrote in a style inoffensive to the Thought

戦争詩集

東京詩人クラブ編

Fig. 20　Katue's cover for *Sensō shishū* (Shōshinsha, 1939); he also contributed a poem.

Police—such as those in the Kogito, Nihon romanha, and Shiki groups—
did not issue war poetry anthologies as the avant-gardists did, leading one to
suspect that *Sensō shishū* was, at least in part, a defensive action aimed at as-
suaging the increasingly vocal ultra-nationalists inside and outside the poetry
establishment.[22] There was no formal conspiracy among the poets, and no
impositions or restrictions were put on the compositions for *Sensō shishū* ex-
cept that they were to be about war.[23] A number of the poems are not stri-
dently patriotic, and a few can even be interpreted as anti-militaristic in their
evocation of sympathy for the waste of human life. Nevertheless, the title,
design, and contents of the book would have provided a convenient shelter
when the Thought Police, backed by public opinion, searched for scape-
goats. Osada and the avant-garde poets must have realized that their past
writing, based on Western models, was perilously out of step with the times.
A proverb often-quoted in Japan—"The protruding nail is hammered in"—
expresses the predicament of the conspicuous poets,[24] and it echoes the *shu-
taisei* problem looming in the background. Government censorship of the
press over the preceding 150 years, when enforced, had been so harsh that
writers, artists, and publishers customarily preferred to engage in self-
censorship, believing that more could be salvaged by reining in oneself than
in openly confronting the system and being silenced completely, or possibly
killed.[25]

Katue never discussed in print his contribution to *Sensō shishū*, "Sensen no
aki":

> *Autumn at the Front*
>
> autumn wind blows again at the front this morning
> above the enemy's base
> arrangement of cannons and intense cabbages
> enemy bullets
> scrape invisible steel wire above head
>
> the whole day confronting the enemy in view
> the chance for all-out battle is not yet ripe
> three light injuries
> moonlit night arrives
> covering the boundless midnight sky
> mammoth movement of airforce
>
> then the dawn's gentle breeze like fresh water
> crosses a vast field of pampas grass

below a single weed with slightly blooming flowers
in the instant of attack
a first-time calmness of the race spreads out interminably[26]

The text presents a mixture of Katue's styles and techniques. One is VOUist abstraction, exemplified by the cannonballs seen as "intense cabbages" and by the bullets speeding past that "scrape invisible steel wire above head." Despite the seriousness of the subject, these images inject a light, playful touch into the poem, while revealing that Katue was out of touch with a real battlefield. The terror of war is absent, and his tone approximates that of a sports announcer dramatically setting the stage for an athletic contest. A second feature of the poem, contrasting with the first, is the evocation of a traditional Japanese atmosphere, reminiscent of his writing in *Kon*, but with an added emphasis on the uniqueness of the race. In addition to the last line, examples of such traditional images of serenity include "moonlight night arrives / covering the boundless midnight sky" and "the dawn's gentle breeze like fresh water / crosses a vast field of pampas grass." A third element, unseen in Katue's poetry until this time, is the subject matter of war. His use of the words "enemy," "base," "chance for all-out battle," and "attack" violates the essence of his previous poetics—art for art's sake—which he had elucidated so adamantly only one year earlier as VOU spokesman in *Townsman*: "Though it cannot be allowed as orthodox of poetry that imagery is performed by ideoplasty, this violence is dared often by religionists, politicians, and satirists. Morality poems, political poems and satirical poems are written, almost without exception, with such an illogical principle."[27]

The fact that "this violence" was now, for the first time in his writing career bluntly "dared" by Katue himself is proved by the poem's very existence. He could no longer claim, as he had with his shift toward Japanism in *Kon* (1936), that he was simply utilizing a pool of vocabulary (*sozai*) or content: "Sensen no aki" is both a morality poem and a political poem. From its publication until the end of the war on August 15, 1945, Katue rightfully can be accused of contradicting his own avowed poetic principles. His prewar poetry evinces no overt resistance against the system, which suggests a lack of an inner mechanism that would have stopped him from writing political poetry. Critics oversimplify Katue's case, however, when they lump his prewar, experimental poetry with his patriotic poetry and claim that the two are essentially of the same mold because they come from the same mind.[28]

"Sensen no aki" does demonstrate Katue's technical skill at composing a poem. He built an effective tension by juxtaposing sets of opposites: first, tranquillity—expressed in "autumn wind . . . this morning," "moonlit night," "gentle breeze like fresh water," and "calmness of the race"—versus the agitated atmosphere of "intense cabbages" and "airforce movement in sky." Also, in the panoramic scenario, distance ("enemy's base") and proximity ("weed") are invoked, as are macrocosm ("war zone," "boundless midnight sky," "mammoth movement of airforce," "a vast field of pampas grass") and microcosm ("single weed"). Katue deftly understated the uneasy time preceding an intense skirmish with "the chance for all-out battle is not yet ripe / three light injuries." His remoteness from the actual killing gives these lines an unreality similar to the action-drama poems in *Shiro no arubamu*.[29] His imagistic manipulation of verticality and horizontality is also much in evidence: verticality in the airplanes and in the single weed; and horizontality in the arrangement of cannonballs, in the speeding past of bullets overhead, in the breeze blowing across the pampas grass, and in the envisioned spreading out of calmness. On the whole, the poem gives the impression of a mixture of lofty VOU somersaults of the imagination and sober thinking on the mundane world of the war. The contradictory poetics in "Sensen no aki" suggests struggle and confusion within Katue.

Around the same time that he was contributing to *Sensō shishū*, he was publicly expressing his ambivalence toward the war in China: "Although Japan is thoroughly winning the war, the consequences certainly are not good."[30] And in *Bungei hanron* (Sept. 1939), he lashed out against the creeping loss of freedoms:

The *hinomaru bentō* [lunchboxes with white rice and a pickled red plum in the middle to resemble the Japanese flag and inspire patriotism], the mixing of hulled and unhulled rice, [the encouragement of traditional] *geta* [wooden clogs, due to lack of shoes], the crew cuts of today's students, the forbidding of permanents,[31] the disuse of air cooling, and other trivial policies have been enacted as if to incite a populace that is already suffering from the war and the high cost of living. Even though . . . the administrative bureaucrats whose duty it is to protect culture . . . can't come up with the slightest show of favorable treatment toward cultural idealism or spiritual expansion, they ceaselessly spout off on the Japanese spirit and its cultural mission in the Orient. Their Japanese spirit truly consists of nothing more than old-fashioned Japanese conventionalism.

However, that is not what I want to discuss here. I want to warn the ultranationalist poets who, brandishing their antiquated spirits and exploiting rash-like trivialism, plot scandals of foul play against the world-class level of the poetry and theories we have been speculating on and refining for over a decade: we will certainly never be driven to silence.[32]

Katue's refusal to stand silent at this time was a forthright expression of rebellious individualism. A year later the same refusal to stand silent signaled the reverse—timid conformity within the narrow ideological spectrum prescribed by the Thought Police, as evidenced by his willingness to write patriotic poetry. The strong stand in *Bungei hanron* was Katue's last insistent call for free speech, although occasionally he still commented along the same lines, such as in the penultimate issue of *VOU* (no. 29, June 1940): "Old vocabulary is preserved by old thinking. One old word takes away the effect of dozens of new words."[33]

When interviewed about the VOU Club's activities by Indian author Amar Lahiri for his *Japan Talks*, Katue again stood firm: "While the works of 'old directions' can be construed to contain rightist ideals, our poems can be classified as leftist literature. Both have their value. In this metallic universe, leftist poems expose the ideals, thoughts and expressions of unconventional monisticism; whereas the rightist ideals are still clinging to conventional morality and tradition" (July 30, 1940).[34]

In September 1940, the Thought Police came to Katue's residence to question him about his literary activity. At the time, he was at his regular place of employment, the library of the Japan Dental College, and his wife, Eiko, answered the door. She recalled the incident:

Two Tokkō [policemen] stepped into the house and demanded to see the magazine Katue published. I handed one of them *VOU*, no. 29, the most recent issue, and he leafed through it with a puzzled look on his face, as if it didn't make any sense at all. He asked, "What kind of magazine is this?" and I replied, "It contains poetry, essays, drawings, and photographs." He confiscated *VOU* and told me to tell Katue to report to the police station the following morning. They then left the premises.[35]

From the time Katue returned home until he went to his interrogation the next morning, he must surely have contemplated how he could defend himself. What were the laws he was confronting? What position was tenable for him to take when questioned about his artistic activity?

Having stood at the cutting edge of the avant-garde poetry movement for the previous fifteen years, Katue surely must have sensed that he was a prime target for the Thought Police. If they needed a directory of avant-garde poets to find him, they could have consulted, for example, *Nihon shidan* (The

Japanese poetry world), which listed about 250 functioning magazines and 1,350 poets.[36] In the entries for the Tokyo district, *VOU* is listed third among 76 publications and is one of only two with roman letters in the title (*KOQ* is the other). Katue's name and address appear in the registry.

Katue was well aware that experimental poets in Kobe had been rounded up and arrested as subversives in March 1940, an act that sent shock waves through the nationwide community of poets. And in Nagoya the self-proclaimed surrealist poet and photographer Yamamoto Kansuke (1914–87), a friend of Katue who joined the VOU Club around that time, was hauled in for questioning for publishing *Yoru no funsui* (Night's fountain), an elegant surrealist magazine of poetry and drawings using Japanese handmade paper, to which Katue also contributed.[37] Yamamoto was subjected to questions such as, "In this surreal poem of yours, what do you mean by the third line of the second stanza? and, how does your surreal photography aid in Japan's war effort?" According to him, "It was a frightening experience. I needed to evade their questions while not saying anything that the police might interpret as incriminating me."[38] Yamamoto was released on the condition that he no longer publish *Yoru no funsui*.

Nakagiri Masao (1919–83), who edited the magazine *Luna* (1937–May 1938; renamed *Le Bal*, June 1938), was interrogated sometime after Katue. Nakagiri found it safest to feign ignorance of the political issues underlying the avant-garde movement based on Western models and insisted that he was writing love poetry merely to impress his girlfriend.[39] His strategy was effective partially because he was in his early twenties. Katue, on the other hand, was thirty-seven and had been at the forefront of the movement for fifteen years, a fact that precluded him from adopting Nakagiri's simplistic ploy.

Regardless of whether Katue thought he had done anything wrong by writing poetry using foreign loanwords and communicating with foreign poets, the laws were stacked against him. The Thought Criminal Probation Law (Shisōhan Hogo Kansatsu Hō), passed by the Diet in May 1936, provided for a probationary period, usually two years, for "thought criminals" arrested under the Peace Preservation Law of 1925. An alleged thought criminal need not even be indicted.

Also being enforced was the National Mobilization Law of 1938 (Kokka Sōdōin Hō), which marshaled civilians into sacrifices for the war effort against China. Western-influenced poetry could be construed as unpatriotic and in violation of the mass mobilization effort and its slogan *ichioku isshin* (100 million [people], one heart). The National Service Draft Ordinance of July 1939 (Kokumin Chōyō Rei), promulgated under the National Mobilization Law, was the legal machinery by which a number of writers suspected of left-wing tendencies suddenly found themselves called into service at the front. The draft notice, commonly referred to as *aka gami* (red paper), at times was no more than a directive ordering the draftee to prepare summer clothes, a canteen, and other basic supplies and await further instructions as to where he would be sent.[40]

Katue must have been aware of the possible consequences when he arrived for questioning. If things went badly, he could be held for months or be recommended for the draft. *VOU* magazine and the club's existence were also in jeopardy. What line of thinking did Katue stress in his encounter with the police? The haughty and rebellious stance taken in *Bungei hanron* would have been extremely dangerous, and an appeal to liberal ideas was also no longer a viable option. September 1940, when Katue was held for questioning, was one turning point in the long war. Diplomatically, Japan concluded the Tripartite Pact with Germany and Italy, an agreement that in effect enabled Japan to exploit Southeast Asia under the banner of the Dai Tōa Kyōeiken (Greater East Asia Co-prosperity Sphere). The country was in an optimistic mood, because Japan seemed destined to extend its territory to the tropics and beyond.

We have no record of what occurred at Katue's interrogation, but we can speculate on the few choices he had as he confronted the Thought Police. Making much of his friendship with foreign poets, especially English and American, would only have exacerbated his tenuous situation. Unable to deny his past, the most logical course for him was to stand as an "avant-garde patriot," however oxymoronic that may have sounded. His VOU Club was, after all, responsible for the widest penetration of modern Japanese poetry in the West up to that time. His achievements, he could rightfully claim, brought glory to Japan at an opportune moment, when the homeland was being culturally belittled in the West.

Katue's prewar activity on the international poetry stage had in fact always been as a kind of poet-ambassador for Japan. The Katue-Pound correspondence reveals a Katue always conscious of representing his country or Asia in general. One example is a letter with an illustration titled "Cactus Island," with which he sent a snapshot of himself and drew a Japanese flag blowing in the wind.[41] Katue never seemed to transcend his awareness of nationality in favor of a one-world utopianism, despite his constant desire for more communication among poets of different countries. In one letter to Pound he wrote, "I only hope the coming of the day when we shall be compensated for the sacrifice we are now making for superior culture in the West and in the East."[42]

It would have been safest for Katue to tell the Thought Police that his avant-garde involvement reflected a deep-seated patriotism and that he was unaware of having done anything wrong. As further defense, he could have mentioned his non-avant-garde poetry. *Kon*, with its traditional poetry and design, and his haiku would presumably have pleased the authorities as acceptable behavior. But, more than anything else, his active participation in the war anthology, *Sensō shishū*, would have stood him in good stead. In any case, for Katue to downplay his Westernization in favor of his traditional and patriotic work would have been a commonsensical course to take.

Also, he could have stressed the consistent anti-communist stand he had taken in *VOU* and elsewhere. Unlike most of the apolitical poets, who simply ignored the rising popularity of proletarian poetry, Katue had openly condemned it as stifling to the imagination and contrary to his poetics of art for art's sake. The Thought Police would have been sympathetic to Katue on this point and maybe even persuaded of his good intentions in raising the image of Japanese poetry in the West, but the focus of the encounter inevitably would have narrowed to their differences of opinion.

Katue never wrote about his interrogation, but we can extrapolate from the results of the encounter and assume what probably took place. The interrogator probably offered a coercive "deal": Katue would cease participating in the abstract movement he had led but could continue publishing if he changed the direction of the magazine to suit the patriotic mood of the times. The roman letters V-O-U of the title would have to be replaced by something more appropriately Japanese, and Katue's project of publishing a book-size anthology in English—with VOU poems and new work by Pound, Duncan, Laughlin, and others—would have to be shelved indefinitely.[43] For the new magazine to receive paper in a time of scarcity, it would have to comply with recently issued guidelines prohibiting loanwords from foreign languages. The mood of the country was such that from 1937 the Spiritual Mobilization campaign had tried to eradicate English because it was the language of the enemy. Although the government never officially banned English and other foreign languages, the police never interfered when right-wing zealots pulled down public signs with roman letters and replaced them with Japanese equivalents.[44]

Katue was backed into a corner. There was the stick of punishment if he offered resistance and the carrot of a new magazine if he acquiesced. The authorities preferred an exploitable writer who underwent an ideological conversion (*tenkō*), whether official or not, to a rebel, because the former could be used as an example in suppressing other writers.

It is clear that Katue was made to stop the VOU movement with its internationalist thrust, but for some time after his interrogation he continued publishing Japanese translations of letters from Ezra Pound and other Western writers, as well as news of poetry and art from abroad, and even abstract and surreal drawings and photographs. The Tokkō were apparently most concerned with controlling the use of romanized language. The cover of issue no. 29 of *VOU* (June 1940), the copy seized from Katue's wife, is guilty of an abundance of "language violations": no Japanese words appear, the title *VOU* is repeated three times, the names of all members are written in roman letters, and the rest of the information is in French.

From reports of others interrogated at that time, it seems that the Tokkō wanted primarily to gauge one's loyalty to Japan, with one's attitude toward the emperor as a litmus test. Perhaps the interrogation focused on those issues; that would partially explain why Katue's literary output after the interrogation became ambiguous and contradictory.

Was Katue's desire to carry on the VOU Club more important to him than adhering to the poetic principles of abstraction that he had passionately advocated within the pages of *VOU*? Or was he afraid for his safety and that of his family, as well as for the members of the VOU Club and their families? Did he imagine that one false move would place him in the center of a much worse nightmare? Or were the proceedings altogether more cordial?

What is not known, and may never be known, is whether Katue was coerced to show positive signs of reform, or whether he was given the option of disbanding the VOU Club and remaining silent. Ueda Osamu, who had been a member of Katue's Arcueil Club in the early 1930s and who also underwent interrogation by the Tokkō on separate, non-literary charges, related the following: "Although Katue never told me about his experience with the Tokkō, this is what I imagine: The Tokkō in all probability said to him, 'Why are you dealing with those *kichiku-beiei* [American and English devil-beasts]? You must do something for your country!' Katue—or any avant-garde poet in that precarious situation—would have bowed his or her head and replied, 'Yes, I understand.'"[45]

Katue had edited almost a hundred issues of avant-garde magazines up to that time, and much of his identity was intricately bound up with his leadership role. To cling to silence and await an uncertain future as an outsider may have been too painful for him to bear.[46] Katue, unlike avowed communists, never underwent an "official" *tenkō* in the sense of being sent to a rehabilitation center and then reintegrated into society.[47] Nevertheless, critics Nakano Ka'ichi and Tsuruoka Yoshihisa (1936–) apply the word *tenkō* to Katue's experience: official or unofficial, his subsequent change in artistic direction amounted to a conversion of principles.[48]

Katue's interrogation occurred as issue no. 30 of *VOU*, with much abstract poetry and news from the West, was about to go to press. He left that material intact and, preceding the table of contents, inserted a manifesto justifying the VOU movement. The final paragraph announced the new direction of "ethnic art" (*minshū geijutsu*). The manifesto is signed "The VOU Club" but, according to Torii Ryōzen (1913–), a member at the time, "It was written by Katue himself without consulting the rest of us. As leader of VOU, he was taking responsibility for all of us, so we thought it appropriate that he would make the decision on what to do with the club."[49]

After the war, Katue claimed, "In 1940 we were forced to abandon publication of the magazine. I succeeded somehow or other in keeping VOU poets from arrest."[50] Perhaps more remarkable than his capitulation to the authorities is that, in spite of the independence shown by the VOU members as poets and artists, none of them reacted against the 180-degree turn from internationalism to nationalism by quitting the club. Of course, anyone who protested conspicuously might have found him- or herself in danger. The change in direction was apparently never discussed by the club as a whole, which returns us to the thorny question, What was the identity as individuals (*shutaisei*) of the members?

Katue's manifesto declaring the dramatic shift from abstract to indigenous poetry deserves quotation in full.

Manifesto

It has been six years from the appearance in July 1935 of the VOU Club's first issue, *VOU*, no. 1, until the present issue of October 1940 [*VOU*, no. 30].

During this time we have expended energy in establishing and developing new art theories on poetry, music, painting, photography, and architecture. We have presented our experimental poems and essays in the magazine *VOU*, which has been distributed within this country and in Manchuria, China, Germany, Italy, England, the USA, France, Spain, Argentina, etc. We have revealed the originality and progress of Japan's new production in the arts.

To begin with, the proposition of the formative grasp of thought at the base of the artistic theories we have been advocating compares with [artistic movements of] other times such as surrealism. It also has technical aspects in common with the German artistic theory of *neue Sachlichkeit* [new objectivity] as well as methodological aspects that overlap with artistic currents of the Tang [618–907] and Song [960–1279] periods in China. Among the Japanese classics, what has been elucidated in *VOU*—in taking the world of speculation on visual imagery as its object—is closer in literary function to the *Man'yōshū* [ca. 759] than to the one-hundred-year later *Kokinshū* [905] or to the *Shin kokinshū* [1205]. Since VOU's inception, we have unceasingly dealt with the relationship between pure thought and matter.

Amar Lahiri has described this systematic line of thinking in relation to the birth and conclusions of the New Hellenism, and how there existed a clear Japanese blossoming of the ancient spirit that flowed along the Silk Road through the natural defenses and deserts of dark Turkestan.

The fresh unveiling of this ancient spirit that we have shown in the pages of *VOU* has been introduced abroad in the following periodicals: *Literatur* (Germany); *Broletto, La Riforma Literaria, Meridiano di Roma* (Italy); *Townsman, Criterion* (England); *View, New Directions* (USA), and others. Having stimulated artists in the above countries, we have gained recognition as modern Japanese artists for the intensity of our theoretical investigation as well as for our creativity. Thus we can claim a certain satisfaction in the cultural contribution made on behalf of our country.

However, at the present time Japan is involved in the resolute action of constructing a new order in East Asia and establishing that new system. For us, as individuals of the nation, it is a natural obligation to take a direct stance and call up all our intellectual strength in cooperating with this endeavor. Therefore, with the current [thirtieth] issue we are bringing to a close the artistic movement that we have carried on for the past six years. To contribute directly to the promotion of an ethnic spirit, we hereby proclaim the beginning of the establishment and appropriate practice of an indigenous art theory that will be both unique and brand-new.

October 1940   The VOU Club[51]

A few words are in order about Amar Lahiri, the Indian author who had interviewed Katue a few months earlier. Lahiri published three books in

English between 1939 and 1940, and his writing abounds with wholehearted support of the emperor system and Japan's military designs in Asia.[52] His Japan always glows in the rosiest light, as in this example from the end of his volume, *Japanese Modernism*: "The Land of Kami is guided by Kamikaze and the ancestral spirit of the Imperial Family, and, therefore, her indestructibility is most likely to be preserved."[53]

To what degree Lahiri and Katue shared opinions on these and other matters is unknown. One supposes that Katue would have felt uncomfortable with the following assessment:

The Western style of music, dancing, painting and writing which she [Japan] has incorporated into her cultural fold, are merely for the purpose of proving to the world her claim to become the "Treasure-House of the World Culture." . . . The noteworthy feature is that these foreign things, when treated and retouched by the Japanese, do not show foreignism, but give a glimpse of "Western Japan." The products of Japanese Westernism are, however, not essential parts of Japanese modernism, but are side-shows carefully preserved to please other foreign nationals with her Japanized exposition of things foreign. Strictly speaking, the Japanese foreign culture does not bear any out-and-out similarity with the West. Japanese Westernism which has come to stay in the country is not a vital part of the national modern culture, but a decorative show to entertain foreigners. Her modern culture is the product of her re-Orientation and all the ingredients therein are Oriental and things Japanese.[54]

With the outbreak of the Pacific War a year later, Katue would adopt the same line as Lahiri on the frivolousness of his own previous involvement with modern Japanese poetry, but at the time he was still corresponding with Ezra Pound and a handful of other American and European poets and, perhaps equally important for his self-identity, he was still being published in the United States. Proud of the VOU Club's achievements abroad, as evidenced by his comments in the manifesto, Katue surely would have been unwilling to view his own Westernization in the shallow terms suggested by Lahiri. Perhaps Lahiri's ultra-nationalist view of Japan—in light of the fact that he was a foreigner—provided a shelter for Katue. On the other hand, quoting Lahiri could simply have been an expression of gratitude to an ally willing to interview him and plug the VOU Club. In *Japan Talks*, another book by Lahiri, Pound is referred to as "the sage of Rapallo."[55] Katue sent the book to Pound, who responded,

Dear Kit Kat
HAPPY New YEAR [1941]. And thanks for Lahiri's book. How much does he know? How seriously am I to take the book? Several dozen questions . . . .[56]

The announcement in the last paragraph of the manifesto of the future change in direction for the VOU Club is of far greater consequence than the reference to Lahiri. VOU and the Western-inspired movement were to be abandoned in favor of a new Japanese poetry, presumably to serve as a model for all Asia. Once Katue had made the decision to continue publishing, he must have wanted to evade the contradictions in his compromised position and put the best light on the task ahead. Even though he had not spent a great deal of energy writing neo-traditional verse, it was familiar to him. Years before, when sending Pound *Kon*, he had called his style "l'esprit du Japon."[57] And, according to Lahiri, Katue claimed, "We are not ignoring the established conventional ideas. We are trying to re-establish those ideas on a new foundation of universal symphony dusting off the age-old rusts."[58]

The problem that confronted Katue and the VOU members was to devise a new course for traditional poetry. To "make it new" was the challenge, but with the imposed ban on Western words and imagery, the situation posed a peculiar dilemma: How could a poet properly evoke modern Japan while remaining within the ideological mold dictated by the Thought Police with its accent on returning to the "pure" Japan of the mythological past? Were not the Thought Police essentially demanding "age-old rusts"?

Shin gijutsu (New techniques), the VOU Club's new magazine, appeared on December 25, 1940. Its format was smaller than that of *VOU*, and the cover symbolized the change: Japanese writing replaced the previously conspicuous roman letters, and a nondescript photo of a cat peering out from a large ceramic pot stood in place of abstract photos. If Katue put up any resistance at all, it was in numbering the first issue no. 31 (*VOU* had ceased at no. 30) and in listing the VOU Club as publisher.

Katue's article "Shimei kaishō" (Renaming the magazine) contains nationalistic buzzwords that he had never used before—*Dai Nihon Teikoku* (Great Imperial Japan) and *hakkō ichiu* (the eight corners of the world under one roof). The issue also contains his "List of Writing Prohibitions":

Hiragana will be the standard script for poems and essays. The following practices are to be avoided:

—using a dash after a character [to indicate a repeated vowel sound; instead, the kana symbol must be duplicated];
—uneven line lengths, especially in poems;
—parentheses and brackets, especially in poems;
—dotted lines, especially in poems;
—solid lines, especially in poems;
—*kanji* of more than 22 strokes (except for proper nouns and other special cases);
—*kango* [Chinese words] (exceptions allowed);
—foreign words (except proper nouns and other special cases);
—dots on the sides of characters [for emphasis, like italics];
—lines on the side of characters [for emphasis, like underlining];
—*furigana* [small kana symbols written on the side of characters to indicate the phonetic reading];
—roman letters written from top to bottom [these would align with writing in Japanese but the reader needed to shift his or her eyes ninety degrees];
—*odoriji* [a sign to indicate a repetition, akin to a ditto mark];
—dialects;
—conventional poetry words (exceptions permitted);
—special type fonts such as gothic, etc.[59]

Katue's list reflects the change in direction proclaimed in the manifesto. As an editor who also did the layout, he aimed at standardizing certain elements to unify the design. He had previously printed lists of prohibited marks and words in *VOU* (and continued doing so after the war), but this was the longest and strictest list of all.[60] Several items reflect his personal quirks, such as the elimination of distractive punctuation marks to keep the page clean, but the ban on foreign words was undoubtedly intended to appease the government. Katue's proscription of bookish Chinese and native dialects suggests that he wanted to make the new direction accessible to a wide readership rather than limited to the elite who understood the written language of the past or that of a particular locality. Perhaps he intended to reach the young in his own country and any Asian who could read basic Japanese. His lack of tolerance for linguistic diversity, however, can also be seen as an elitist and coercive position.

At first, VOU members had difficulty changing gears and heeding the new rules. For example, next to the statement banning words of foreign origin appears an article by Torii Ryōzen whose opening sentence contains words that were supposedly prohibited (italicized in the quotation): "A young girl wearing white *jacket* white *beret* white *skirt* and white *sandals*—and blowing out *cigarette* smoke—shows up with a sanitary pig."[61]

Katue's first poem in *Shin gijutsu* is equally confused, with abstract tendencies and prohibited foreign words in *katakana*, namely "glass," "spiral," "tinplate," "lens," "asphalt," "flask," "encyclopedia," "pipe," "terrace," "tulip," "chloroform," and "beer":

> *Hard, Curved Line*
>
> wearing a hood of grapes
> the act of squatting inside a curved line
> is a light act
>
> thinking of violets
> with an ant of the glass's circle's shadow
> stepping on egg-shaped seashells
>
> above alabaster cone
> are wire glasses
> and a shining spiral of water
>
> for a soft pivot
> leaning smoke and
> that wobbling cogwheel
>
> the morning of
> cutting a tinplate cylinder
> and washing a dissolving lens
>
> in the blue sky
> an asphalt driveway twists
> ah
>
> a red stripe stutters
> toward a column's bitter
> whiteness
>
> octopi in a flask
> bleached
> become a swarm of transparent curves
>
> finally I shut the encyclopedia
> light a pipe
> and go out on the terrace of budding tulips

I sit on a chair
circular in the shape of the sabbath
and suddenly sneeze

removing a long and narrow pillar
smelling of chloroform
I bend my finger and close my eyes

then, drinking a little beer
for a severely spherical plaza
I discover a brittle locust[62]

Shin gijutsu started as a hodgepodge; the contributors mouthed new poet-ics about technique while more or less continuing to write in the old vein. The contradictions inherent in the sudden reversal of artistic direction occa-sionally take on farcical proportions. Nagayasu Shūichi's surreal drawing of a bird-headed woman holding a cocktail glass becomes even more surreal with the absurd—but officially acceptable—caption "Kyōshū" (Longing for hometown).[63] Other examples of a lack of reform are abundant in both photos and text, such as the following essay by Osada Tsuneo, the editor of *Sensō shishū*:

One theory has it that war poetry is wonderful because it is full of life, but this is tricky thinking. Value is attained not merely by inducing primitive excitement.

We are told by the majority of people that our [abstract] poetry is difficult to understand or just plain gibberish. Elementary school children seem to have a far easier time with our poetry.[64]

Despite Katue's commitment to abandon the abstract movement at home, he was still intent on being published abroad. *Shin gijutsu*, no. 32, con-tains an announcement stating that seventeen VOU poets had contributed forty-three poems in their own translations for New York poet Charles Henri Ford's planned "View Poets International Anthology."[65] Included in the same issue was a note "To the Readers Overseas": "As you see in the 31st issue, the VOU will be called, hereafter, by new name, 'SINGIJYUTU.' The name VOU had no special meaning, but 'SINGIJYUTU' means new technique."[66] Foreign readers were, of course, oblivious to the specific cir-cumstances surrounding the name change. Arthur Blair, editor of *Diogenes* (in which Katue had been published), responded approvingly, "I like VOU's new name very much. It has a wonderful sound."[67]

All in all, the first two issues of the new magazine were neither completely submissive nor significantly rebellious, and they indicate more a lack of viewpoint than any newfound direction. The switch to poetic content that matched the nationalism expressed in the manifesto came slowly but surely.

Although Katue was earnestly mulling over his new poetics and starting to write in the "indigenous" style reminiscent of *Kon*, he was still not altogether denying his Western-style achievements. The fruits of his avant-garde years before the 1940 manifesto came out in two books in 1941—his abstract poems in *Katai tamago* and his essays on poetry in *Haiburau no funsui*.[68] When asked to contribute a poem for the 1941 *Gendai Nihon nenkan shishū* (Annual of modern Japanese poets), Katue submitted a surreal selection from *Saboten tō* of 1938 and not a poem in his recent indigenous mode, suggesting a measure of discontent with having had that experimental collection overlooked.[69]

In the meantime, the Tokyo Poets Club, headed by Osada Tsuneo, decided to go nationwide and regroup as the Nihon Shijin Kyōkai (Japan poets association). Katue joined the organization and, given this forum to make a wide appeal to Japanese poets, wrote the lead article on poetics for the premier issue of the new organization's magazine, *Gendai shi* (Modern poetry).[70] His article is worth studying mostly because it illuminates his methodological confusion. Having decided to abandon abstract poetry and any reference to foreign objects in his poems (for political reasons), he now made the absurd claim that the new poetry should not be subservient to political ends. Although he seemed to be groping for a pacifist alternative within the restricted linguistic and imaginative framework allowed by the Thought Police, judged retrospectively, his advocacy of poetry free from politics and propaganda while complying with the political directives imposed on him shows his thinking was imbued with self-deception and opportunism.

In his article, which one would expect to be a blueprint to propel Japanese poetry in a new direction away from Western, especially Anglo-Saxon, influence, paradoxically he quoted four poems in English (including his own abstract verse in translation, "The Life of a Pencil," published in *Diogenes*) and not a single poem in Japanese. His briefly stated conclusion is that Japanese poets need to have more contact with the New Objectivity movement in Germany, a goal consonant with the wishes of the political authorities.[71]

Apart from the inherent contradictions in his approach, Katue did provide insightful hints about his conception of *kyōdoshi* (hometown poetry). Perhaps as a natural consequence of the taboo on mentioning Western artifacts, he stated that "the purest objects for poetry are those closest at hand," meaning nature and the Japanese objects surrounding him. Rather than advising poets on what subjects to write about, he urged them to discover a new form in unexpected moments when the mind is temporarily distracted. As examples of this state of mind he cites, "the instant when, walking on a rainy day, suddenly you turn a corner" and, "the moment a smoker lifts a match to a cigarette," indicating that his first thoughts on hometown poetics were less concerned with nationalism than psychology. According to him, "The brain clouds over during chance moments and, like a flash of lightning, consciousness is interrupted. Some effort is required to get back to what you were thinking about. Everyone experiences this several times in the course of a day. . . . This form of consciousness is pure in that it is free of any particular concept."[72]

Katue then quoted a study of temporary amnesia (now commonly referred to as "short-term memory loss") and chastised Western authors for not acknowledging the creative potential of the unconscious during momentary lapses of linear thinking. Katue's points are interesting in themselves and show him desperately trying to find an idea on which to base a new poetics at some remove from blatantly propagandist verse. He was not explicit, however, as to how an appreciation of amnesia translates into a new poetics. It is tempting to interpret his essay as rebellious self-parody—the poet studying up on amnesia to learn how to forget the past he was forced to deny—but Katue probably had no such intention, judging from his serious tone and the *realpolitik* of the age. The cloudy, trance-like state of mind that he promoted will be reintroduced later with examples of his hometown poetry, for it is there that we find him using blank moments of consciousness to induce a sense of timelessness. Here, suffice it to say that his much anticipated new poetics was still attached to Western concepts and models; his quotations make that abundantly clear. Because of this article and the appearance of Katue's two avant-garde books in 1941, fellow poets who had heard that he was embarking on a fresh course but had not read the new poems must have been at a loss to determine the relationship between what he was advocating and "hometownism."

Katue's avant-garde *Katai tamago* and *Haiburau no funsui* were reviewed in August 1941 by the modernist poet Kinoshita Tsunetarō (1907–86), who had translated Ezra Pound into Japanese.[73] His review is a barometer for gauging how Katue was perceived in the literary world. Kinoshita praised the poet's previous originality and then applied peer pressure in urging him to excel as a nationalist. Kinoshita allowed Katue only two choices: he can be a brilliant has-been, or he can take the opportunity at hand, show his mettle, and rise to the pinnacle of the Japanese poetry establishment. The Katue of old would have scoffed at the crumbs of such mainstream glory, but his internationalist stance was now fully eroded with the umbilical cord to Pound and the West severed since the spring 1941 suspension of mail service. The new opportunity dangled temptingly before Katue.[74] Below is a translation of Kinoshita's article.

Current Appraisal of the Poetry World

Recently Kitasono Katue published the essay collection *Haiburau no funsui* and the book of poems *Katai tamago*.

Each of these fine works represents the magnificence of the Japanese poetry world. While reading them, I was surprised at the high level of civilization to which Japanese poetry has risen. Of course, this does not signify that the standard in the Japanese poetry world has improved overall; rather, it only points out the excellence and originality of Kitasono Katue.

But, seen from the perspective of the times, these good works already belong to the past, and the writer himself has conceded that. I have high expectations for the forthcoming activity of this poet, who possesses good sense and overflows with originality.

The cultural role of poets, all poets, is to use their mother tongue to console, encourage, and invigorate the common people in society. In other words, beauty and skill are employed to induce knowledge. By such reinforcement, their lives are glorified both as human beings and as citizens of the state. One assumes that a poet recognizes these facts. It is also important that he possess a keen ability.

Katue's fearsome poetic ability has already been acknowledged by everybody. He competently waged battle with foreigners on the international stage for his mother country. And *Haiburau no funsui* and *Katai tamago* are the crest of those achievements.

With his awesome abilities, Katue is now singing about his native country and its lifestyle, competing with other poets of his homeland.

He is battling it out with poets Takamura Kōtarō [1883–1956], Miyoshi Tatsuji [1900–1964], and Okazaki Sei'ichirō [1900–1986], among others. Without losing his originality, Katue should put his effort into piercing through to a new world. And then he should let his capabilities blossom in a Japanese way. I believe it would be quite easy for him in light of his intelligence and poetic ability.

I'll state it once again: poets are a consoling hand and providers of vitality and hope for the Japanese people. In these times of hardship for the mother country I wait with earnest hope for the coming day when Kitasono Katue will lend a con-soling hand and be a revitalizing force in the painful life of the people.[75]

Kinoshita's metaphor of battling poets, both internationally and domesti-cally, shows his competitive view of the poetry world. As mentioned above in connection with Kitahara Hakushū, poets commonly considered it their duty to parallel the role of soldiers in the field. Kinoshita was unable to de-fine poetry outside the realm of such propaganda. Poets, especially the avant-garde fringe who had not been taken seriously by the general public in the 1930s, suddenly found their patriotic poems given wide exposure in newspapers and on radio. Clearly, many of them found the limelight too tempting to refuse. Another point—overlooked by almost all poets at the time (and in this sense they were deficient in their role as Seer)—was that writing propaganda poetry entails assuming responsibility for inciting people to risk their lives and kill others. Kinoshita did not seem to realize that giv-ing people the bravado and fervor to perform further sacrifices proved to be more burden than consolation.[76]

Under pressure from police and friends, by the third issue of *Shin gijutsu*, Katue was little by little enclosing himself in a cocoon of Japaneseness. To generate a dynamism sufficient for producing new poetry, he found it in-creasingly necessary not only to plunge deeper into a traditional lifestyle but also to deny his previous Westernization. Whatever pressure he was under while writing the manifesto ending *VOU* was absent by the time he wrote the following statements in *Shin gijutsu*. He was willingly fulfilling his prom-ise to turn his energy to native, hometown poetics.

The manifesto in *VOU*, no. 30, perhaps came three years too early for us. But it was bound to happen sometime or other. An international standard for poetry in any age is achieved only by an advanced group of poets with a high standard in their own country. We should not rest satisfied simply because the poetry of one country [Japan] has attained an international standard. . . .

I think that the various elements making up the cultural conditions of our poetic thoughts are certainly a blend. This can be understood by calling to mind the phe-nomena appearing in our so-called daily life that we experience in any given 24-hour period. In reality, daily life in a large city is like a mosaic of cultural fragments drawn from all peoples of the world. It takes firm resolve and much effort to face the diffi-culty of producing pure [Japanese] ethnic activity in this cultural climate. But we cannot afford to ignore this difficulty if we are to create fine poetry aloof from the times. This problem goes beyond mere taste in vocabulary or technique of imagery and relates to the overall attitude at the core of our thoughts on poetry.

As one part of this attitude a return (*kaiki*) to hometownism (*kyōdo shugi*) seems inevitable.[77]

Katue further explained the new attitude in the following issue of *Shin gi-jutsu* in which he adopted the metaphor of battle while further distancing himself from his Westernized past:

It has already been ten months since abandoning the battle on the international po-etry stage. The effect on me has been to gain an abundance of time and a surplus of energy. It has been an unexpectedly wonderful condition. Perhaps salvation is this kind of fertile idleness. Now I do nothing but sink into the earth, plant myself down in this Japanese lifestyle, let my thoughts run toward the styles, customs, and inter-ests of the past and present, and I grow older with the emotions of the seasons.

Two approaches to writing [patriotic] poetry reach the root of the nation's ori-gin. One is "fighting poetry," and the other is more composed. The former sets in-ternational culture as its target, while the latter sets native culture as its target. I am presently going so far as to suck the marrow of the bone of traditional native culture as a means of bringing about an escape route from [previous] indigenous poetry which has not been blessed with originality.[78]

After pondering the direction that the new poetics should take, Katue concluded that not only a change of vocabulary but an overhaul of his life-style was in order. Within the confined linguistic and imaginative space left him by the Thought Police, Katue was set on distinguishing his calm ap-proach from the supercharged emotionalism of stridently patriotic poets (such as Takamura Kōtarō [1883–1956]). However, when he stated, "I am presently going so far as to suck the marrow of the bone of traditional native culture," he sounded like a puppet of the Thought Police.

When writing Western-influenced poetry, even in the March 1941 line "I go out on the terrace of budding tulips," Katue had used settings from his imagination and not from his own life. Henceforth, for the cause of so-called purity and an authenticity based on "reality" (which he could not claim with his Westernized verse), Katue surrounded himself with things Japanese while discarding Western artifacts. Lacking direction and originality and yet needing to lead the VOUists somewhere, all he could come up with to sur-pass his Western experiments was that his Japanese words derived from a Japanese lifestyle. By his previous standard of ideoplasty (poetic effect), which he was now eagerly rejecting, for Katue to write racially pure poetry based on a racially pure lifestyle was paradoxically to write impure poetry, for he was appeasing political and moral agitators inside and outside the government.

The problem Katue had to confront was that his strength did not lie in writing lyrical poetry in a traditional vein wearing kimono and deftly handling brush and ink. He had been in the habit of looking down on old-fashioned poets, and now he was imitating them. Katue had always been conspicuous for his daring experimentation and outlandishness, but his native poetry was at best mediocre when compared to the work of Japanese poets who had from the beginning written along traditional lines. Nevertheless, the softened imagery and calm atmosphere of some of the poems have a seductive beauty.

In 1941, while Katue was making his conformist adjustments, the Thought Police widened their dragnet and jailed two avowed surrealists—poet and art critic Takiguchi Shūzō and painter Fukuzawa Ichirō.[79] According to one account, both men were apprehended on the same day (March 5, 1941) and released on the same day (November 11, 1941).[80] The Tokkō considered them surrealist agents working clandestinely for the international communist movement. They spent over half a year in separate detention centers, in line with the common judicial practice of not indicting suspects but wearing them down with interrogations and confinement for months or years under miserable conditions. Among Japanese surrealists, Takiguchi and Fukuzawa received the harshest treatment, yet they were fortunate in being released before Pearl Harbor. Prisoners held after the outbreak of the Pacific War often did not fare as well because of the shortage of supplies, and a great many of them died of malnutrition and disease.

Katue's call for hometownism was consistent with the shift in national attitude following the February 26, 1936, coup d'état attempt by junior army officers. The rebel officers praised the virtues of the countryside (where most of them came from), especially its role in feeding the nation, and they blamed urban corruption for Japan's wayward economic and political policies. Their coup failed, but the ideas they stood for increasingly gained prominence. The tension between city and country persisted throughout the war. One farmer expressed the common animosity toward city dwellers: "When we farmers occasionally went to Tokyo, people would be gathered in a huge crowd in front of the kabuki theater trying to buy tickets. We could not bear the idea of sweating so hard to produce rice to be sent to city people who amused themselves like this."[81]

In January 1943, Katue published his tenth book of poems, *Fūdo* (Climate), a collection of twenty-five new poems based on his hometown poetics and written between February 1940 and August 1942. The writing is along the same line as *Kon* (1936). Several were previewed in *Gendai shi*, *Mita bungaku*, and his own *Shin gijutsu*.

In contrast to the impersonality (or transparency of personality) in Katue's abstract verse, he expressed himself more directly in *Fūdo*. Not only has the vocabulary been trimmed to "suitable" Japanese and Chinese words, but we also find a number of other substitutions: natural images replace man-made objects; fragrance replaces vivid imagery; and a blend of tranquillity, reflection, and simplicity replaces restlessness, action, and complexity. In Katue's Western experiments words have no "place" outside their randomness on the page, but with *Fūdo*, as with *Kon*, the words have a place in the literary tradition and in the society outside the poem.

> *Night*
>
> at night
> crickets circle the house
> chirping
>
> camellia
> flowers and leaves
> in the alcove
> cast a slight shadow
>
> the fragrance of *sumi* ink
> faintly
> drifts past
>
> dreary days
> visited me
> like one drop of pure water
>
> already
> there is nothing
> yet soft fulfillment
>
> late at night
> on the desk
> I stretch out paper blankly

ah
nothing to say
my thoughts race out
to my hometown's night of falling leaves[82]

The poem is nostalgic, sentimental, and compliant enough to make a
Thought Policeman smile. Katue's endorsement of "a return (*kaiki*) to
hometownism (*kyōdo shugi*)" was a jumble of contradictions. If he were intent
on a back-to-the-roots lifestyle, why did he not make an effort to return to
his own hometown, Asama, if only for a visit? Last seen five years before and
never again visited during the remaining thirty-five years of his life, Asama
was an object of contemplation that had become rarefied in his imagination.
Tokyo had been his pivot for the previous two decades, with his poetic pen-
dulum tipping to Paris and then swinging back to Asama. The theme of
"longing for hometown," used as a device for lyrical manipulation in his po-
etry, must have held more significance for him than the reality of the place
itself. In *Fūdo*, Katue uses the highly charged word "hometown" seven times
but never mentions Asama by name, perhaps because it is not his aim to de-
scribe his own roots but to objectify the generic concept of hometown for
the reader to identify with, as in the lines, "my hometown is far away / and
already only a name."[83]

"Yoru" (Night) is typical of the poems in *Fūdo* with its accent on a black-
and-white world, reminiscent of ink paintings, to evoke a "Japanese" effect.
Auditory and olfactory senses take over in the dim light; the "I" of the poem
hears crickets and smells *sumi* ink. The piece of paper being stretched out
blankly (lit.: "whitely") on the desk is all that he sees directly, and it stands in
bold relief against the dark objects visualized either indirectly ("camellia . . .
shadow") or in memory ("dreary days," "night of falling leaves"). Such careful
modulation of shading, sense perception, and vocabulary was not only part
of Katue's stock of *shin gijutsu* (new techniques), but a variation on his basic
design approach to writing poetry. In this sense everything, even the persona
in the poems—a solitary hermit with meandering thoughts, who is definitely
not Katue the commuting librarian or the concerned familyman—is an ob-
jective construct, a calculated building block of the design.

The poems in *Fūdo* are pervaded with a keen sense of the esthetic princi-
ple of *ma* ("interval," i.e., use of blank space) giving them a relatively unclut-
tered appearance. This effect is partially achieved by referring to people and
objects as absent. What had been a bombardment of visual perceptions in

his avant-garde poetry is now reduced to a few chosen images, giving an overall impression of sparcity and compression.

> *Almost Midwinter*
>
> winter sun
> shines on
> slight moss
> like on damask
>
> I put on deer
> armor
> and sit in a
> narrow hallway
>
> with the passing days
> thoughts are light
> bright
> and futile
>
> one bitter drop
> contained
> as in a Chinese bowl
> cold and futile
>
> there is nothing
> I should know by now
> also, no books
> and no visitors[84]

During the second coldest part of winter (*shōkan*), the persona of the poem wears deer armor and sits down to contemplate. The action stops, and hereafter we follow his thoughts. When he states that "thoughts are light / bright," we are apt to interpret it as his stoic resignation amid hardship in wartime, but he undermines that reading by adding "and futile" (*munashikatta*: "in vain," "empty"). The passing days are liquefied as one drop, leading to the association with a Chinese bowl. The days, the one drop, and the bowl are all in vain. In the last stanza the persona concludes that knowledge cannot save: "there is nothing / I should know by now." The poem ends with an affirmation of absence: "no books / and no visitors." The continual reference to nothingness and absence in the *Fūdo* poems can be interpreted as a rechanneling of the nihilistic strain in his neo-dada poetry of the mid-1920s (see Chapter 2).

Time in *Fūdo* is conceptualized as eternal: perception of sensations occurs within immobile contemplation, and even the slightest fluctuation of a leaf can appear magnified. Time is never specified beyond day and night. "The passing days" are treated as a single unit, and the past and the future are referred to in millennia.[85] Katue explained in an essay how he induced the trance-like state of suspended time: "I place a bowl on the desk. Then I stare at it as if it has been there for thousands of years. I also stare at it as an eternal shape, immobile for thousands of years to come. That is one basic thought pattern for 'hometown poetry.'"[86]

Katue's appreciation of the state of temporary amnesia adds a haziness to the atmosphere, removing the poems from the present to an unspecified, nebulous time. One example is the ending to another poem, also titled "Yoru" (Night).

> slightly
> I open the *Saden*
> I close the *Saden*
>
> sadly
> I faced the
> wind and smoke[87]

Saden is the abbreviation for *Sashiden*, the thirty-volume work written during the Warring States or Sengoku period (1467–1568). Katue presumably introduced it because the solitary "I" of the poem is also living through war. He opens and closes the book and then, lost in daydream, turns to face the wind and smoke. Similarly, we do not know what Katue's persona in the following excerpt specifically thinks about Bo Juyi's death (which was apparently of old age in the year 846)—the emphasis is rather on the atmosphere of foggy contemplation:.

> alone
> I slide the paper door closed
> I read poems by Bo Juyi
> and ponder his death
>
> all day long
> small birds chirped brightly
> a faint cloud drifted by
> suddenly darkening the desk[88]

The serendipity of discovering the desk darkened by the shadow of the passing cloud arrests the persona's consciousness and interrupts his train of thought. Katue finds the subtlety in such overlooked moments consistent with the indigenous atmosphere he wished to conjure up, although he never clarifies the connection.

His most lucid exposition of the poetics of hometown poetry appears in an essay serialized in *Shin shiron* and reprinted in *Gendai shi*. Previously having advocated no more than a return to traditional Japanese culture, he now unveiled the fruits of his own immersion. His approach is a recycling of his Western-inspired poetics (which he had supposedly abandoned), shorn of the label "ideoplasty" and its Japanese equivalent, *ōka kannen* (see Chapter 5). On the key point of imagery Katue stated: "The new value of imagery in poetry is not as a means of expression but as a method of perception. In other words, imagery is not employed as a technique to express one's thinking but as a tool of thought. In this way poetry's 'automaticity' inevitably prevails."[89]

After long deliberation on hometown poetics, Katue, unsurprisingly, had arrived full circle at what he had once promoted under the banner of abstract verse. At that time he did not explain the philosophical base supporting his concept of ideoplasty. Now he lifted the veil and declared that the intuitive world of Zen is the foundation of his hometown poetics, leading us to suspect that an appreciation of Zen, although unnamed, had not been absent from his Western-influenced poetics, either. In this sense, Pound's response to ideoplasty was right on the mark: "Intuition may even provide the essentials in this domain."[90]

Katue regarded his turn from abstract to hometown poetry as "a shift from estheticism (*bigaku*) to ethics (*rinrigaku*)."[91] He then negated the easily identifiable equivalencies found in the use of metaphor by most poets in favor of a Zen "ethics" based on illogic, disclosing that his *Fūdo* poems are underpinned by the same Zen permeating the worlds of haiku and the tea ceremony.[92]

We don't have a tea room and utensils, nor the [proper] haiku style. Yet, this new method [hometown poetics] gains elasticity when combined with Zen. It also forecasts possibilities for the birth of an abundantly fluid literature. I have been trying to explore these possibilities in my hometown poems since last year. Needless to say, as modern poetry they are fundamentally different in poetic method from pastoral poetry and folk songs. In other words, the content does not express, introduce, or praise the scenery of the countryside and tell stories about it in poems. On the contrary, in the primitive scenery of hometown poetry, by seeking to confer ethical meaning and value, there is a self-refinement that molds an idealized and perfected human being as a "figure."

I emphasized before that the new value of imagery in poetry is not as a means of expression but as a method of perception. This is directly consistent with the Zen approach to thinking. The contents of the *Hekiganroku*, written by the great Zen monk-scholars Setsu Chō [980–1052] and Engo [Kokugon; 1063–1135] of the Sung dynasty (and presumably the first book of the sect), straightforwardly indicates the character of Zen thinking. The most typical example would be in response to the question "What is the law [of Zen]?" one monk silently displayed 3 *kin* [a measurement] of hemp and another monk, instead of a [verbal] reply, raised one finger. But it is completely mistaken to assume, therefore, that Zen thinking is metaphorical. Engo clearly explained the subtle context of the age in the *Hekiganroku*, but if the 3 *kin* of hemp were meant, for example, to explain the law in some way, then it [the illogical correspondence] would not make sense as a metaphor. The 3 *kin* of hemp was most probably used as a wedge to divert thought. For that instant, however, it also held an absolute meaning, which couldn't be replaced [by something else]. Today we cannot understand what that was because we have only the written words. All we can know is that 3 *kin* of hemp in that case performed an important role in ordering thought.

The above is almost equally applicable to the condition of the "figure" in [my hometown] poetry.[93]

Katue, hoping not to be misunderstood, added in another essay that the Zen method is to be used for poetry and "there is absolutely no need for poets to preach Buddhism."[94]

The reader may be tempted to draw parallels between the persona in the *Fūdo* poems and a Zen monk sitting in contemplation, because both perceive an ultimate emptiness in the phenomenal world. But Katue's persona, cultivating poetry and not enlightenment, often invokes objects and thoughts for their ability to conjure up powerful emotions rather than to overcome attachment to emotions. Katue wanted to adopt the Zen method free of Buddhism. Nevertheless, seen from the perspective of Zen proper (in which the novice abandons connection to family and, significantly, to hometown), Katue's brand is *yako zen* ("delusional, self-styled Zen").

At times the poetry in *Fūdo* echoes a racial pride lurking at the bottom of Katue's ethics, as in his ending to the poem "Fue" (Flute).

Flute

twilight
shuts away the village
in a bottle of blue glass
no wind
road continues to the forest

for a while
smell of dirt drifts by
water flows past
then the water flowing in the darkness
turns into the sound of a flute

I lean against
a rock railing
and think of far, southern mountains and rivers
and a huge *muku* tree on a prairie

ah
I recall the *taiko* drum people
and the flute's pale echo
barely
crossing over grasses of unseen fields
and flowing over my hot eyelids[95]

Written in August 1941, this was one of the first poems in the hometown mode. One can notice lingering VOU imagery in "the village / in a bottle of blue glass" and "my hot eyelids." More significant is the innocuous folkloric pride evoked in the poem that was meant in the context of the era to function as a cultural pillar, paralleling the government policy of militarist expansion in Asia and its categorical denial of Western values.

The successful attack on Pearl Harbor sent Japan into a nationalistic frenzy. Almost every poet celebrated the auspicious opening of hostilities with the United States and England. Katue admitted in February 1942 that he had the desire but not the ability to write a good patriotic poem: "I feel ashamed that I have not been able to write a patriotic poem with satisfactory form and content, and I will not publish any until I am satisfied. Lately, this is one of the matters that has been irritating me."[96] He cites a *Man'yōshū* poem (no. 4373) as the ideal expression of patriotic sentiment:

> from today on
> there is no looking back
> for me who sets out
> as the emperor's unbending shield.[97]

Two months later Katue achieved a breakthrough: "The first poem I have written about the Greater East Asia War is 'Hawai kaisen senbotsu yūshi ni okuru shi' (Poem sent to the brave soldiers killed in the Hawaiian naval battle). Since then I have not been able to write a poem that satisfies me, but *in that one poem I aimed at condensing all my gratitude for the Greater East Asia War*" (Italics added).[98] In another essay Katue mentioned having published this poem in the *Yomiuri shinbun* (Yomiuri newspaper), but unfortunately it does not exist in the newspaper's microfilm records.[99] A patriotic poem by Katue titled "Seiki no hi" (The day of the century) and published in the anthology *Kuni o kozorite* (The country gathered) is probably the Hawaiian poem retitled.[100] The publication of *Kuni o kozorite* was postponed for almost one year because of the death of editor Satō Sōnosuke (1890–1942). His assistant, Katsu Yoshio (1902–81), who completed the task, explained in the afterword that the editorial principle was "to gather patriotic poems about Pearl Harbor that had already been published in newspapers or had been broadcast on radio, rather than allowing poets to select their own favorite compositions."[101] All the manuscripts arrived within the month of December 1941. Since he submitted his poem in 1941, it is unclear why Katue declared in early 1942 that he was unable to write a patriotic poem. His poem describes the buoyant mood following Pearl Harbor, suggesting that "The Day of the Century" is a renamed version of "Poem Sent to the Brave Soldiers Killed in the Hawaiian Naval Battle."

The Day of the Century

winter morning
the sun shone brightly
on a silver fir tree

a Japanese day
like yesterday
quietly began again today
but this time
the radio
calmly proclaimed the start of a decisive battle

ah around the palm of my hand
rushed the great sword's sheath
it was a gallant sentiment
how the multitudes of people
eyes brimming with passionate tears
absorbed the excitement of the moment!

in the city
citizens
were walking silently

their faces one by one
were cheerfully
full of determination

it was the face of mighty Japan
the face of the one who
builds the century

walking along the pavement
or sitting at a teahouse
everywhere I saw the face of Japan

on this destiny-determining day of battle
I saw the face of a master
quiet as a forest

from today
no parents no brothers no wife no children
we are all comrade-in-arms

oh from this day on
we have no death no life
a single heart congeals, committed to smash America and Britain[102]

This was Katue's second patriotic poem, and the first since "Autumn at the Front" in the anthology *Sensō shishū* of two and a half years earlier. "The Day of the Century" is a blatant propaganda piece infused with patriotic enthusiasm. Katue seems genuinely caught up with his fellow countrymen in the emotion of national pride. The lack of VOU-style abstraction gives his sentiment added sincerity. Katue's hometownism can be seen in "I saw the face of a master / quiet as a forest." However, in writing "we are all comrade-in-arms / . . . / we have no death no life / . . . committed to smash America and Britain," Katue was not only violating his theory of ideoplasty but also betraying the supposedly cool rationality of his hometown poetics, which aimed at an ethnic pride based on the tranquillity and profundity to be found in the tradition since antiquity and not in emotional flagwaving.

Katue's third nationalistic poem, "Fuyu" (Winter), was written three weeks after Pearl Harbor and presumably not long after "The Day of the Century." It has a similar mix of hometown and patriotic rhetoric, although it is less strident in tone. Katue's emotionalism, embedded in stanzas of calm imagery, irrepressibly bubbles to the surface.

> *Winter*
>
> the winter day
> began windy
> and ended windy
>
> the frosty garden
> was muddy
> all day long
>
> atop a hazelnut tree
> a star
> was shining in the wind
>
> but
> on tropical islands
> the imperial army is fighting gallantly
>
> ah
> carrying East Asia's fate for the next 1,000 years
> soldiers with unswerving loyalty!
>
> that brave
> and incomparable
> distant attack!
>
> I faced my desk
> all day long
> beside a small bowl
>
> in a dark room
> thoughts flow
> a faint light drifts by[103]

After the war, Katue was embarrassed by "Fuyu." When all his poetry books were reprinted as part of a single volume in 1955, he refused permission to include "Fuyu."[104] Other poems in *Fūdo* could be justified as resulting from his experimental method, but "Fuyu" was too blatantly militaristic, and he wanted it suppressed.

Katue was able to prove to himself with *Fūdo* that he could develop a style of poetry independent of VOUist abstraction. With the emphasis on Zen and the reference to traditional Japanese artifacts, the poems exude a stoic calmness. Yet Katue's linguistic and imaginative wings had been clipped, and the poems reflect that curtailment, as well as the general humorlessness of the age. The question remains why he felt compelled to write anything at all.

Fūdo was issued in an edition of 1,500 copies.[105] A Chinese poem (*kanshi*) of four lines with five characters per line appears on the back cover. The uncredited lines are the opening of a series of five poems by Chinese poet Tao Qian (367–427) titled "Returning to the Farm to Dwell," which he penned upon retirement from official life in the year 405. It is one of the most famous poems in the Chinese canon:

> When young I lacked a disposition that suited ordinary men
> My true nature is to love hills and mountains
> Mistaken, I fell into a dusty net
> After I left [home], thirty years passed

The verse is a confession of life wasted in frivolous urban pursuits and has the dramatic compression found in the finest Chinese poetry. Unlike Tao Qian, a man of great integrity who found himself at odds with the strictures of the ruling establishment, Katue's use of the same poem, seen within the politics of his age, is at once an obedient and deep bow to his repressive government and a mockery of the Chinese poet's spirit of resistance.

In 1942, Katue published three more issues of *Shin gijutsu*, but with several of the poets conscripted and paper in short supply, he found it increasingly difficult to continue.[106] There was nothing within the pages of issue no. 37 of *Shin gijutsu* (September 1942) to indicate that it would be the final number and the last activity by the VOU Club until it regrouped again after the war.[107]

By early 1942, Katue was already putting most of his energy into co-editing (with Murano Shirō) a sixteen-page, monthly magazine called *Shin shiron* (New poetics).[108] The magazine had already been appearing since 1937, but Katue and Murano took over as co-editors beginning with issue no. 57 (Feb. 1942).[109] A few VOU members took an active role, but contributions from anyone were welcome.

Katue and Murano churned out *Shin shiron* for twenty-one consecutive months, until exigencies of the war forced them to abandon even this thin vessel. Katue's essays in *Gendai shi* (cited above in the discussion of his ideas on hometown poetics) were first serialized in *Shin shiron*. After engrossing himself in what he considered the best aspects of Asian culture—poetry, music, pottery, philosophy, and religion—he poured his discoveries and opinions onto the pages of *Shin shiron*, which was Katue's main outlet during the years 1942 and 1943. Japanese scholars have largely neglected mentioning the magazine because it has been relatively difficult to locate. By reading all the issues, one can monitor Katue's changing mental and physical condition during these months, especially by consulting the editorial column.

For example, the August 1942 issue (no. 63) contains this politically noteworthy announcement from Katue: "The Poetry Section of the Nihon Bungaku Hōkokukai [The patriotic association for Japanese literature; hereafter referred to as Hōkokukai] has been formed, and, unexpectedly, we [Katue and Murano] have obtained the position of *kanji* [managers]. Therefore, we pledge to continue to do for poetry all we can in any way possible."[110]

The Hōkokukai was the literary wing of the Taisei Yokusankai (Imperial rule assistance association; hereafter Yokusankai), an umbrella organization formed to unite all Japanese by profession to aid in the war effort. The Hōkokukai was divided into eight sections—Novel, Drama, Poetry, Criticism, Japanese Literature (Kokubungaku), Tanka, Haiku, and Foreign Literature. Section heads were chosen by the Yokusankai's cultural division, but the positions within each section were probably filled by volunteers.[111]

The Poetry Section had the following organization:

Position (Japanese title)	Poet(s)
1 Section head (*bukaichō*)	Takamura Kōtarō
1 Director (*riji*)	Satō Haruo
1 Head manager (*kanjichō*)	Saijō Yaso[112]
6 Permanent managers (*jōnin kanji*)	Murano Shirō, Osada Tsuneo et al.
14 Managers (*kanji*)	Katue Katue et al.
5 Honorary members (*meiyo kaiin*)	Noguchi Yonejirō et al.
5 Councilors (*hyōgiin*)	
8 Secretaries (*sanji*)[113]	

The Hōkokukai was from its inception the nation's central literary organization for whipping up patriotism. In January 1943 the poetry section had 322 members.[114] Katue was in a powerful position near the top of the pyramid. We cannot be sure what he said and did as manager, but as one of the main committee members, he was involved in, among other activities, planning and producing anthologies of patriotic poetry. Those anthologies served as propaganda for citizens at home and the troops abroad. Unlike the situation two years earlier, Katue was not now in the slightest danger of being suspected as a thought criminal. On the contrary, with his entrance into the ranks of the higher echelon of the Hōkokukai, he was now on the same side of the fence as the ultra-nationalists, some of whom were bent on punishing errant authors and agitating indifferent ones into writing more inflammatory verse.[115] Katue probably took the position of manager as much for personal gain as for the opportunity to express his loyalty to the state. He had previously been outside the poetry establishment (and his poetry consequently had suffered from relative neglect), but now he was cozily situated among the leading mainstream literati. He had unabashedly become a propagandist for government policy, both in his function as administrator and in his own writing.[116]

In his essays, he continued emphasizing the virtues of Asian culture and Japan's vital role in the global equation, noting that "the war is important to [the goal of] changing Japan from an imitative culture to a creative one."[117] Elsewhere, he bewailed the loss of native Japanese civilization by the spread of Chinese, and later, Western culture. In the April 1942 issue of *Bungei hanron* (the same publication that had carried his liberal essay in 1939), we find Katue's fourth nationalistic poem, "Hata," celebrating the Japanese occupation of Singapore, Manila, and other outposts in Southeast Asia.

> *Flag*
>
> finally
> the day has come for our flag
> to flutter in the tropics
> like a star
> like a flower
> finally
> far away
> brightly

in rainstorms
in sunshine

finally
the day has come for our weapons
to slaughter enemies of East Asia
like lightning
like wind
finally
sharply
fiercely
in jungles
in waves

finally
the day has come for us to cross the equator
and achieve our ideal
like a god
like the moon
finally
widely
beautifully
on the sleeping countryside
on various islands

the day has come for our culture
to advance for Greater East Asia
like fire
like voices
finally
young
intense
in the lively people
in the new history

in sunshine
in rainstorms
brightly
far away
finally
like a flower
like a star

the day has come for our flag
finally
to flutter in the tropics[118]

In the mid-1920s, Katue (still using his birthname, Hashimoto Kenkichi) compiled a scrapbook of his published poems and articles. For the cover he made a collage that included a sentence printed in Japanese: "The flags of all countries are lonely."[119] In sharp contrast to that sentiment, which encapsulates the idealism and defiance of his youth, the poem "Hata" epitomizes the staunch conformity of his middle age.

With Katue working for the government as one of the managers of the Hōkokukai's Poetry Section, his editorial statements in *Shin shiron*, one of the few surviving poetry magazines, take on a polite and sympathetic tone toward his fellow poets. No longer slinging mud at the poetry establishment from the sidelines as in his *GGPG*, *Madame Blanche*, and *VOU* days, Katue now profusely thanks contributors and wishes his readers good health. He had matured over the decade but, in the process and under the circumstances, had lost his edge.

Katue's return to a traditional lifestyle is highlighted in the editorial column of *Shin shiron*. His continual references to nature and pursuits such as reading Chinese poetry and painting with sumi ink are reminiscent of a life of leisure in the middle ages. In *Shin shiron*, as with the *Fūdo* poems, the reader is given the impression that Katue was living alone in the countryside, because he never referred to urban life. In contrast, co-editor Murano Shirō mentioned personal matters ranging from the crowded conditions of his morning commute to the tragic news that his younger brother had been killed in battle. He even quoted from his brother's final letter, forwarded from the cemetery: "From now we will be advancing for a forced landing against the XX enemy. As the time approaches, my mind becomes clearer and clearer, like water."[120]

Katue, despite his reclusive pose, did not hesitate to give detailed reports on the state of his health. Besides time spent at his regular employment and at the Hōkokukai meetings, he was writing poems, essays, book reviews, and the editorial column for the monthly *Shin shiron*, all the while sharing the various chores associated with putting out the magazine. Overexertion and malnutrition gradually began to take their toll on him.

Officially the war had already dragged on for over five years (unofficially eleven years), and the heavy loss of life compounded with the shortage of supplies was being felt acutely at home. The early days of morale-lifting victories had passed, and the Japanese were sobering up to the reality that the war was no longer going in their favor.

Murano was the first of the two editors to succumb to fatigue. His doctor prescribed Vitamin C and told him to rest.[121] The editorial burden now fell solely on Katue, causing his stamina to wane rapidly. From September 1942 on, he gave monthly accounts of his health, but only in the December issue did he reveal that he was suffering from pleurisy. Despite his debilitation, he remained optimistic: "Maybe it's due to my age [having just turned forty], but I seem to be recovering quite rapidly. Once a week I receive 500–700 cc of air injected between my ribs. I have heard that this treatment can have very beneficial results."[122] Katue was referring to the then-popular treatment in which pleurae sacks are filled with air to alleviate strain on the infected area and to facilitate breathing. The treatment is no longer considered effective and has been discontinued.[123] Katue persisted in editing *Shin shiron* despite his physical troubles. In the February 1943 issue, he addressed an angry message to insensitive contributors: "Since Murano and Kitasono have recently been ill, there has been a rapid influx of poems about respiratory diseases. This reminds us of what we are trying to forget, shows no consideration, and is wretched."[124]

In the June issue Murano expressed concern about Katue's tendency to succumb to summer heat. Then, in the August issue, Murano reported that his prediction had unfortunately come true and his colleague, after gathering half the manuscripts, had been stricken with a fever. Katue was back the following month, after having gone to Numazu to visit his younger brother, Shōji (1907–64), and recuperate by the seaside. Murano noted in passing that poets Sasazawa Yoshiaki (1898–1984) and Haruyama Yukio were also ill, the latter having lost one-third of his former weight.[125]

The health reports stopped in September 1943 with *Shin shiron*, no. 77, the final issue. The decision to cease publication was made not by the editors but by the government, which decided to merge the then-existing 195 nationwide poetry publications into two new journals—*Nihon shi* (Japanese poetry) and *Shi kenkyū* (Poetry research). The bland names symbolize their unimaginative approach; the two publications took no chances, tried to please everybody, and, at best, achieved mediocrity. Similar unifications were occurring in every sphere of society, as small units were forcibly merged into large, blanket organizations that facilitated the government's regimentation of life. Poetic creativity, meanwhile, turned into a pale and somber caricature of what it had once been.

The daily travails of a war with no end in sight were wearing down Katue's body and spirit, and the success of his attempt to spread hometownism as the new direction for modern poetry was, at best, lukewarm. He won minor acclaim when *Bungei hanron* did a special issue on hometown poetry, the term Katue had coined, and he was asked to write the lead article.[126] Also, his book-length collection of essays on the subject, *Kyōdo shiron* (Hometown poetics), was published in the largest edition (3,000 copies) of any book in his lifetime.[127] To place his contribution in perspective, he was not the leader of a budding movement but was simply the self-proclaimed coiner of a term. His hometown poems were merely one variety of the nationalism imposed on all writers by the government. Certainly, no one hailed Katue's advocacy of temporary amnesia as a great innovation.

In fact, the pages of *Shin shiron* abound with indirect criticism of Katue's position by various poets, starting with co-editor Murano who prefaced his remarks with, "I respectfully beg to differ with Katue's approach to hometown poetry." Murano condemned both the exploitation of poetry by political leaders and the way "poetry's inevitable beauty is being sacrificed for empty rhetoric."[128] In a later issue of the magazine, Ueda Tamotsu expressed discontent with the contemporary trend: "I can't help feeling that the new creativity in Japanese culture will not come from simply abandoning the West and reviving the native culture of the past." Ueda qualifies his bold remarks, critical of government policy, by making the concession that the renewed contact should be "to assimilate the West in order to conquer it."[129]

The cultural importance of Tokyo, the center of modernization for eighty years, receded as the war, fought on foreign soil, took center stage. Tokyo poets expected the best poetry of the new age to emerge from those who had firsthand experience of the war, and especially pinned their hopes on soldier-poets stationed in China. Miyakoda Ryū (dates unknown), sent *Shin shiron* an article from China in which he credited *VOU* and *Shin shiron* poets for "seriously worrying about the thrust of poetry in the coming age."[130] But he noted only the concerns of the Tokyo poets and not their results, a subtle blow to Katue's hopes for hometown poetry to be seen as applicable throughout Asia.

A further criticism of hometown poetry, also indirect, appeared in an essay by former VOU poet Kuroda Saburō (1919–80), who had been sent to fight on the Chinese continent: "I wonder whether poetry is necessary at all in this age. For people like us who are engaged in combat, we also wonder in what ways the reality in poetry has been changing. . . . It is not [important] how closely poetry approximates reality, but rather what kind of reality the poem presents before our eyes."[131] The implication is that hometownism, abstract verse, and other ethereal poetry had become irrelevant now that the battlefield was imposing its harsher reality. Kihara Kōichi (1922–79), another former VOU poet and frequent contributor to *Shin shiron*, made the point more bluntly right after the war: "In the midst of war's cruelty, I became aware how vapid the 'pure poetry' sought by VOU really was."[132]

Despite Katue's lofty aims, hometown poetry in the end amounted to nothing more than the basis for his own personal style and never became a movement. What at first had been a challenging new direction for him became with the passing months a stale routine.[133] A friend warned him in early 1943 that his hometown poetry had reached a dead end, but he continued to write in that style until the war ended some thirty months later.[134]

Katue's physical ailments, his daily struggle with survival, and his lack of success with hometownism stretched his nerves to the breaking point. The attempt to discipline his mind with Zen stoicism in wartime added enormous stress, as he admitted in an article on haiku for *Shin shiron*.

I started writing haiku only a few years ago, and by now I have written approximately sixty to seventy. I consider writing haiku a balsam or an antipyretic.

Recently I think that my poems are too reasoned and have become pained. Writing poems has become a kind of hand-to-hand combat. Of course, there is also the pleasure accrued from high-level creativity. But this pleasure is transparent. The pleasure of finally slaying some of the numerous enemy. Rather than calling it pleasure, it is probably closer to the relief of being resurrected. When I solve a problem I have been working on in poetry, I feel relieved. First, I try not to think of painful poetry. Swordsmen of old in desperate situations thought of the "non-sword," and I can understand why. In this sense I regard haiku also as a "Way." It is a Wayless Way. When you observe the Wayless Way, then the mountains, rivers, and everything else become the Way. This is the same as the law/non-law of the Zen sect. In other words, if you are enlightened about law/non-law, then there is nothing in the entire universe that is not law.[135]

Katue's "entire universe" does not, however, encompass the enemy. The following stanza from Stephen Spender's poem "Two Armies" (1942), which would have been unpublishable in Japan, rings truer to the all-embracing spirit of Zen than Katue's partisan verse.

> Clean silence drops at night, when a little walk
> Divides the sleeping armies, each
> Huddled in linen woven by remote hands.
> When the machines are stilled, a common suffering
> Whitens the air with breath and makes both one
> As though these enemies slept in each other's arms.[136]

Katue ends his article with an attack on professional haiku poets:

Haiku by professionals is mostly for [social] haiku gatherings. Instead of fresh, imaginative wings, their haiku makes you think of childish wings. It is as if their devotion makes them exert all their energy to take something vulgar and express it in a non-vulgar way. But that is its own world, amounting to the overprofessionalism of professionals.[137]

In spite of Katue's initial acknowledgment that his "antipyretic" haiku were of a different order than those by learned professionals, his tone thereafter turned sour, signaling a return to combative impoliteness, reminiscent of his polemical onslaughts in the 1930s on avant-garde poets whom he had deemed incompetent. Katue, who had made his mark in the Japanese poetry world with his Western-style experimentation, now found himself backed into a corner, unable to distinguish himself in the competitive world of old-fashioned letters. Paradoxically, now that he was hovering near the power center of the poetry world, his own work was having far less impact than it had in the 1920s and early 1930s when, willfully, he had situated himself at the margin.

From January 1944 through August 1945, when food and paper were in extremely short supply, Katue kept a small desk diary (*takujō nikki*; Fig. 21) in which he entered brief notations of whom he had met, what he had bought, and at what hours bombs had fallen.[138] For the most part, Katue did not record his opinions of people or describe events; he merely jotted down names, places, and numbers. With an abundance of free time and sensing the immediate danger to himself and all Japanese, he felt compelled to record the historic moment in some form, however abbreviated.[139] Unlike more substantive wartime diaries that were later altered to conform to the new political climate of the Occupation, there is no indication that Katue later tampered with the facts to show himself in a more positive light.

Despite the brevity of the entries, the diary records his everyday comings and goings and provides a picture of his life that is not accessible through his poems and essays. Of course, we also learn much trivia, superfluous to a reading of Katue's poetry but fascinating in itself; for example, he took a bath about once every two weeks. The fragmentary entries allow us to see how one poet lived under the daily threat of death from the frequent and intense aerial bombardments. From our side of history, we use a magnifying glass or microscope to look down at objects and scrutinize them closely, whereas Katue's gaze was forced upward, toward the airplanes of annihilation.

Katue's diary remains unpublished and has never been seen outside his immediate family. Katue wrote the diary in formal *bungotai*, a style influenced by classical Chinese prose and conveniently compact for the limited space; it also fit with the image of a literatus absorbed in traditional pastimes that Katue was projecting during the Pacific War. He continued publishing in 1944 and 1945, although his output was necessarily slowed by the effects of the prolonged war.

Mention of his nuclear family—his wife, Eiko, and their only child, Akio—is almost completely absent from his poetry and essays. In the diary, however, the name Eiko appears 42 times and that of Akio 46 times. A portrait emerges of Katue the concerned parent. For example, before ten-year-old Akio was relocated on October 4, 1944, as part of the government's program of evacuating primary school students, Katue frequently took him out for the day, usually to Ginza for a visit to the planetarium, to shop, or to see newsreel films.[140] Akio owned toys enjoyed only by fairly well-to-do children, such as a projector (for 16mm film) and binoculars. The binoculars cost Katue a whopping ¥203, more than his monthly salary. His affection for Akio is noticeable in the respectful and independent way he treated his son: even after Akio relocated again—this time with his mother in November 1944 to Sanjō City in Niigata prefecture, home of her relatives—Katue continued to write them separate letters. Instead of placing both letters in a single envelope addressed to his wife, Katue must have wanted his son to have the pleasure, rare for a child, of opening his own mail.

Symbolic of both the pathos and the absurdity of war, the most memorable reference to Akio is the entry for May 25, 1945, the day after the Tokyo suburb of Magome, where Katue lived, was heavily bombed.

Fig. 21 Katue's desk
diary of 1944
(*top*: year 2604)
and 1945 (*bottom*:
year 2605).

Stayed home all day.

Kihara [Kōichi] came to visit. News that the house of Ogihara [Toshitsugu, composer, 1910–92] was burned to the ground and his younger brother is missing.

Sent Akio his rationed underpants.

The diary entries, besides touching on family matters, also provide a reliable picture of Katue's economic situation. (For a full list of his income and expenditures during the final twenty months of World War II, see the Appendix.) By no means wealthy, he was nevertheless free of financial worries. His friend and boss at Japan Dental College, Nakahara Minoru, paid him a hefty salary of ¥185 per month plus twice a year bonuses of ¥80–130. For his part, Katue displayed loyalty by risking his life and remaining in Tokyo, commuting to work at the college library even during the heaviest bombing, when surely he could have evacuated earlier. Beyond representing a danger to his life, however, his job as librarian at this time meant little more than showing up for work and putting in a few hours three or four days a week. Considering that his time and energy were hardly tapped, his salary was a windfall, placing him on equal monetary footing with top-level managers (*buchō*) in industry, at a time when carpenters earned only ¥60 a month, and a college graduate starting in a bank earned ¥80.[141]

Katue also had a number of side jobs, mostly book design and prose writing. For the latter, his pay ranged from ¥10 to ¥50 per manuscript. He wrote for *Gendai shi* and *Shi kenkyū*, the two remaining poetry journals sanctioned by the government, and even penned an article for the Bureau of Weights and Measurements. Katue once engaged in unspecified, part-time labor over a two-week stretch for which he received ¥2.3 per day. By far the best-paying side job he took was writing the school song for Tōkyō Kōgyō Senmon Gakkō (Tokyo industrial college). He met the school president, visited the campus, composed the lyrics, and then received a hefty payment of ¥500 (April 11, 1945), equivalent to six-month's wages for the average laborer. Being a poet had its occasional advantages, even in the thick of war. Ironically, Katue had never before enjoyed such financial security as in these unstable months of physical danger.

One striking aspect of the diary is that Katue meticulously registered gifts of food received from friends.[142] While the entire population faced malnutrition and a large segment of it survived on nothing but potatoes for months, he managed to have considerable nutritional variety. Naturally, the Kitasonos encountered the same shortages felt by everyone, but the generosity of their friends seems to have made the situation bearable. Akio's experience provides a reliable register of the difference between the average person's diet and that of the Kitasono household: after being evacuated with his schoolmates, Akio escaped and attempted to walk the sixty miles to Tokyo "because I was hungry and the food at the relocation center was so bad."[143] He was thereafter transferred to Sanjō, where Eiko's relatives furnished him with more nourishing meals.

Katue's friends helped him when they could, and he in turn was generous with them. While never extravagant, he was thoughtful, sending a compact (cost: ¥8.50) as a wedding present for Torii Ryōzen, VOU poet and photographer, and ¥20 to a poet relocating in Kyoto. Besides sharing food and bestowing presents—including ¥90 worth of summer gifts (*chūgen*) in 1944, Katue and Eiko also took in a friend whose home had been devastated by firebombs.

By 1953, when there was already a noticeable distance between the war and his memory of it, Katue reminisced: "I did not fight. I only picked up a pen and wrote, picked up a brush and painted. And also from now on I don't want to do anything else."[144] The diary confirms that Katue spent his free time mostly absorbed in the arts. In his role as national poet, he corresponded with wounded soldiers who had returned to Japan and some who were still fighting at the front.

Jan. 17, 1944: Received a letter with many signatures (*yosegaki*) from wounded soldiers at the Muramatsu Sanitorium for the War Disabled in Tochigi prefecture. Sent reply.

Feb. 19: Sent postcards to friends at the front.

Mar. 15: Gave a consolation lecture (*imon kōen*) at Chiba Sanitorium. Title: "The Sword and the Poem" ("Katana to shi").

Jan. 31, 1945: Signed flags of soldiers being sent to front.[145]

Katue remained active in the Hōkokukai. According to the diary, he attended five Hōkokukai meetings in 1944.[146] He would have attended a sixth meeting, on July 6, 1945, had the building in which it was scheduled to be held not been reduced to rubble by an American bomb.

The role Katue played in the organization is difficult to ascertain. Two entries in the diary are enigmatically laconic.

March 10, 1944: I resigned as manager of the Poetry Section of the Hōkokukai.

May 8, 1944: Went to Hōkokukai meeting, where I was [again] chosen as manager.

Did Katue quit temporarily because of discontent? Did he have moral objections to the group's activities, or was his resignation due to physical exhaustion? After resigning, why did he again take up the post two months later? Did an internal political squabble prompt his action? The diary notation is intriguing, but lack of supplementary evidence leaves these questions unanswerable. Katue retained his membership in the Black Iron Association, attending meetings on January 26 and October 28, 1944.[147]

Besides exerting himself in these official capacities, Katue paid frequent visits to his publishers. A special edition of *Fūdo* was issued in sixty copies by Shōshinsha in 1944, each with an original Katue watercolor painting of a ceramic bowl. From the diary we learn that the authorities granted Shōshinsha permission to issue *Kyōdo shiron*, a compilation of Katue's essays since the manifesto in *VOU* on hometown poetics, rejecting Westernization in favor of a return to East Asian traditionalism. Permission was granted on April 27, 1944, but the book did not appear until five months later (September 20). Katue also made occasional visits to Hōbunkan, the publisher responsible for *Shi kenkyū*, the official poetry journal. For *Shi kenkyū*'s first issue, he sent a hometown poem, "Natsu" (Summer), which, in contrast to the contributions by other poets, is notable for its lack of reference to the war.

> *Summer*
>
> the wind
> blew
> through the young tree leaves
>
> summer
> in this way
> began in the valley homes
>
> from a faraway poet
> whom I've never met
> a letter arrived
>
> alone
> again today
> I boil water
>
> and with my hand
> hold up
> one bowl's worth of tea
>
> suddenly

I was facing
irises

the end of June
bright moon
people and thoughts again new[148]

Typical of his hometown poetry in general, the imagery of "Summer" is sparse, and the action slow-moving. The only break in the sober rusticity comes in the last line when the mood suddenly becomes optimistic—"people and thoughts again new." Katue's slightly uplifting tone came on the heels of Kinoshita Tsunetarō's call for poetry "to console the people." Katue appeared to be keeping a "stiff upper lip" in spite of the adverse situation, but his optimism also served to reinforce the blind hope of Japan's dream to set up a new order in East Asia.

Even after the government's regulation of poetry and paper shortages forced *Shin shiron* and other unofficial magazines to shut down by December 1943, Katue circumvented the law by publishing privately.[149] On February 10, 1944, he notified a handful of poet-friends still in Tokyo that he was organizing a club, Mugi no Kai (Wheat association), and that he intended to circulate a newsletter of poetry and short articles, *Mugi tsūshin* (Wheat dispatch), exclusively to club members. Any publication, official and unofficial alike, was supposed to relate to the war effort; even though Katue was far from advocating antiwar sentiments in *Mugi tsūshin*, its very existence presented a challenge, however meager, to the military's control.

Printed in minuscule numbers, no complete set of *Mugi tsūshin* presently exists. A number of references in Katue's diary provide the only publication data available.[150] The two issues I have seen are undated and unnumbered, but they are paginated "25–28" and "29–32," respectively.[151] Internal evidence reveals that the war ended between the writing of these two issues (nos. 7 and 8). Katue noted on page 25: "It is the fault of the enemy (*teki*) [the United States] that the first issue [of 1945, no. 5] was four months delayed," yet on page 32 the object of criticism, although unnamed, is now Japan's defeated military leaders: "The war is over. As for exposing the deception (*giman*) of the people, we are now linked only by this single sheet newsletter, reflecting on the happiness of being alive."[152] These words close the penultimate issue.[153] With a swift imputation of blame, Katue eluded taking any personal responsibility.

Several of Katue's friends were sent to war, many of his acquaintances were killed at home, and his family was relocated after having lived for months under threat of death. During this period of hardship, *Mugi tsūshin* seems to have been an integral part of his identity. Apart from the literary value of the poems, which is minimal, the newsletter's very existence acted to bond the poets. With the American aircraft flying over Tokyo and dropping tons of bombs on civilians, Katue secured safety and food for his family and, whenever possible, sought the companionship of a small circle of like-minded poets. Exactly what rebelliousness, if any, *Mugi tsūshin* represented is hard to assess, but Katue demonstrated quixotic passion and formidable perseverance in publishing a poetry magazine after almost everyone else had given up. His diary entry for June 16, 1944, poignantly juxtaposes the horror of the headlines with his private reality:

Went to school [the Dental College].
    Kita Kyūshū, Southern Korea, Chichijima of the Ogasawara Islands, Iojima, Saipan, etc., bombed.
    I mailed out *Mugi tsūshin*, no. 1.

The somber and uninspired contents of *Mugi tsūshin* (pp. 25–32) are similar to those of *Shin shiron* except for the necessary brevity imposed by the four-page, instead of sixteen-page, format. Contrary to his practice in *Shin shiron*, Katue in *Mugi tsūshin* took the liberty of introducing each poem with a short appraisal, something he had never done in two decades of editing almost a hundred issues of literary journals. Ironically, his attitude resembles that of a professional haiku master passing judgment at a gathering, a posture he had previously condemned.

Sprinkled between the poetry and essays in *Mugi tsūshin* is news of club members. Katue's bland topical poem "Ie" (House) is strategically placed to reverberate with the heartrending news item following it.[154]

> *House*
>
> again, once again
> came a day of silence
> desolation surrounded my forest
> filled my creek
> oh wind
> oh small birds
> my fingers are wild
> my watery eyes stare north

Letter

As of the end of June, club members Osada Tsuneo, Murano Shirō, and Takeda Takehiko [1919–] have suffered calamities [incendiary bombs had leveled their houses]. We wish them heartfelt sympathy.

Katue's tenacity in continuing to publish despite the adverse circumstances has earned *Mugi tsūshin* a place in Japanese literary history as one of the few poetry "magazines" bridging the war and postwar periods. Two months after *Mugi tsūshin* ceased publication, Katue began editing the new journal *Kindai shien* (Modern poem garden). Japanese chronologists are occasionally unaware of *Mugi tsūshin* and credit *Kindai shien* with being one of the first postwar poetry magazines.[155]

The desk diary contains one original, unpublished haiku by Katue, scribbled in the margin for December 4, 1944, the day after the second air raid of the year:

tekki aru	enemy planes
sora no aosa ya	the sky's blueness
ichō chiru	gingko leaves scatter

Katue's straightforward sketch, technically unremarkable by haiku standards, is probably the best poem he penned during the war in that he makes direct use of the historical reality unfolding before his eyes. The unnamed persona appears composed in the midst of uncertainty. The full-blown drama of the war is elicited skillfully in the opening five syllables—*tekki aru* (enemy planes). The next seven syllables—*sora no aosa ya* (the sky's blueness)—add a sharp visual contrast, pitting the dangerous, man-made machines against a backdrop of nature's blue sky, vividly immobile. Although the enemy planes conjure up a moving image, on the linguistic level their existence is flatly stated (*aru*). The sky's blueness, on the other hand, immobile as image, is marked as dynamically poetic by the interjection of *ya*. This linguistic inversion of the moving/static dichotomy within the visual sphere emphasizes the persona's attitude of stoic resignation. In spite of the obvious danger, an impression is given that fear cannot obscure the protagonist's appreciation of the blue sky. The ending five syllables—*ichō chiru* (gingko leaves scatter)—appropriately fulfills the "seasonal word"(*kigo*) requirement for haiku, pinpointing the time frame—early December—when the gingko trees shed their leaves. Katue's choice of the verb *chiru* (scatter) rather than *ochiru* (fall) brings the verse full circle by hinting at the destructive potential of the enemy planes to scatter life and property indiscriminately. Yet the re-lationship between the enemy planes and the leaves scattering on the ground is left open-ended; perhaps there is a causal linkage, or perhaps the leaves scatter simply because of the season, unaffected by the world of man and his machinery. In either case, the juxtaposition of the brutal metal aircraft with fragile gingko leaves highlights the acute sensibility of a protagonist caught in the web of circumstance.

The haiku is noteworthy for its evocation of macrocosm (sky, with imagined dropping of bombs vertically on the city below) and microcosm (the wind horizontally or diagonally scattering petals). The imagery is pow-erful because no judgment is made on the situation; the poet merely de-scribes objectively, as if the haiku were a telegraphic news and weather re-port. The reader is drawn by the understatement to sympathize with the horror of a human being who is sensitive to nature and made to endure re-peated bombing attacks.

Although Katue published no haiku during the Pacific War (or for the remainder of his life), it is noted in the diary that he attended haiku parties on September 24, 1944, and May 20, 1945. The meetings focused on poetry, while providing an opportunity to exchange information and share camara-derie for a few precious hours. After returning from the second gathering, Katue noted contentedly in his diary: "In the afternoon I went to a haiku party (*kukai*) at the house of Jō [Samon; 1904–76]. I got thirteen points, the highest score. Received prize. Took my own dinner (*bentō*). Towada [Misao; 1900–1978], Ise [?], Iwasa [Tō'ichirō; 1905–74], Sasazawa [Yoshiaki], Kihara [Kōichi], and Yasoshima [Minoru] attended. Returned home at 9 P.M."[156] By taking their own food, perhaps Katue and the others were showing one another their purity of purpose in gathering to write haiku. In the midst of the war, it was easier to share poetry than food.

Katue also attended five "book exchange parties" (*shomotsu kōkan kai*), mostly with the same group, at the house of Iwasa Tō'ichirō during the first half of 1945.[157] One gets the impression from the diary entries that the haiku and book exchange parties were the peaks of Katue's social life.

The diary segments that make by far the most compelling reading are those dealing with the numerous air raids and warnings. It is difficult to as-sess at what point in the war Katue realized that Japan's defeat was unavoid-able. Information was tightly controlled, and negative news about the course of the war, such as casualty figures, was concealed. The government faced the contradictory task of having to instill morale for its "inevitable victory" while preparing its citizens for the bombing raids they were about to encounter. Bad news was revealed only when it could no longer be suppressed, often months after the outcome of a battle. Katue's entry for June 16, 1944, mentions the fall of Iojima, which occurred in mid-March. Likewise, his September 30, 1944, notation that "the massacre on Tinian and Guam is made public" came seven weeks after the fact.[158]

More consequential for Katue than the time delay (of which he may not have been aware) was the reality behind the bad news: American fighter bombers, with newly acquired bases in Japan's fallen territories, soon would be in striking range of Tokyo. When Katue recorded the fall of Guam, we can assume he knew it was only a matter of time before he would need the bomb shelter he had been building in his garden since February 27, 1944 (there were no government-supplied bomb shelters for the people; each family had to fend for itself).

In May came the first air raid warnings. In mid-June, he recorded participating in three days of reserve military training, part of the general mobilization to defend against the upcoming invasion.[159] The war was casting its shadow over the life of all Japanese, yet the forty-two–year-old Katue appears to have coped relatively well and gone about his business as normally as possible until November 29, 1944, the day the systematic bombardment of Tokyo began. (The American Air Force had conducted one surprise raid two years earlier, on April 18, 1942.)[160] During the six months between November 1944 and May 1945, when he finally relocated to Sanjō to wait out the last weeks of the conflict, Katue was in constant danger of losing his life.

In 1954, with a decade of hindsight, he recalled the air raids:

After evacuating my wife and son, I lived alone and cooked for myself. I used to wear a war hat and national costume with gaiters, just like everyone else at that time. . . . Finally, every part of Tokyo was being firebombed. When the Ōmori area [which included Magome, Katue's residence] was firebombed, poet Jō Samon and novelists Towada Misao and Yamamoto Shūgorō came to inquire how I had fared. Seeing I was all right, their tense faces relaxed.

Then one of them said, "Hurry up and burn already!"

"Thanks," I replied, "but it seems Roosevelt has decided the bombing will proceed from your house outward!"

In this way we would joke back and forth. I was prepared to die at any moment.[161]

According to the diary, Katue endured 46 air raids and 22 warnings.[162] He merely recorded them, often adding the time of day and noting the number of aircraft, but without additional comment. What becomes readily apparent is the psychological warfare employed by the Americans in the choice of timing. For example, on New Year's Day, 1945, Katue notes that enemy planes bombed at midnight—the moment being celebrated—and again from 5 A.M. The most destructive raid on Tokyo was carried out on Armed Forces Day, March 10, 1945; 80,000–100,000 people died, and 63 percent of Tokyo's commercial district was burned to ashes.[163] Most of the devastation occurred at quite a distance from Katue's residence. His diary for March 10, 1945, records, "150 enemy planes bombed from around 2 A.M. The city is devastated. Casualties are extremely high."

Poet Sō Takahiko (1915–96) witnessed the carnage from close range and managed to survive. He recalled his panic at the time:

In the chaos that followed the March 10 saturation bombing of Tokyo, rumors spread that 2,000,000 city residents had been killed. After time passed, the general estimate of casualties came down to 100,000. It isn't as if 100,000 deaths is not a sufficiently mind-boggling number, but the fear running through us at the time was that it had been even much more catastrophic.[164]

The high morale and strict discipline of Japan's armed forces enabled them to make conquests early in the war. America's strategy was to wear Japan down to the breaking point. Joseph C. Grew, American ambassador to Japan in the decade before Pearl Harbor, emphasized the psychological factor as crucial in his influential appraisal of the situation.

When they [the Japanese troops] struck, they made no provision for failure; they left no road open for retreat. They struck with all the force and power at their command. And they will continue to fight in the same manner until they are utterly crushed.

We are up against a powerful fighting machine, a people whose morale cannot and will not be broken by economic hardships, a people who individually and collectively will gladly sacrifice their lives for their Emperor and their nation, and who can be brought to earth only by physical defeat, by being ejected physically from the areas which they have temporarily conquered . . . by complete defeat in battle.[165]

British subject John Morris, who was one of the last foreigners to leave Japan during the war, agreed with Grew:

I believe it to be of the utmost importance for the war to be brought home to the people of Japan themselves. They know so little of what is happening in the world today, that only when the war is actually brought to their homeland itself will they realize they are beaten. Nothing less than an occupation of the country will be necessary; not necessarily a very long one, but one long enough to make the fact of *our* victory and *their* defeat incontestable.[166]

The viewpoint of Morris and Grew, namely, that Japan would have to be brought to its knees, became the basic Allied strategy. Katue, along with the rest of the nation, endured enemy firepower until the August 15 surrender. Katue estimated in his diary that 150 planes took part in the March 10, 1945, raid; in later attacks he mentioned even more aircraft. Usually tens of airplanes, but occasionally hundreds of them streaked the skies. On May 29, 1945, Katue used an old literary expression, *tenjitsu tame ni kurashi* ("the sky is obscured by clouds"—the "clouds" were 600 American bombers). Then on February 15, 1945, he recorded that 1,000 planes struck. At other times a single plane buzzing over Tokyo was enough to awaken Katue—and presumably the rest of the city's inhabitants.

From the diary alone, we cannot grasp the effect of these attacks on Katue. Of his friends at that time who visited him at home and at the Dental College, only poet Kobayashi Yoshio is alive. Kobayashi had worked with Katue on the literary journal *Madame Blanche* in the early 1930s, and they had kept in touch since. There are a number of references to Kobayashi in the diary, including the following: "June 20, 1945: I asked Kobayashi to mail a package for me by fourth-class mail."

Kobayashi related the following anecdotes that portray Katue in a different light than the self-portraits of stoic resignation projected in Katue's essays and poems:

Katue's bomb shelter was fastidiously neat and well supplied; he had taken extreme care in building it, which wasn't the case with most people.

Katue was well liked and had many connections. In those days it was difficult to get domestic baggage sent. When the post office refused the parcel he wanted to mail to his family in Sanjō, I offered to send it through the publishing company where I was employed. Katue brought the package, and I asked what was inside. He listed so many items that I could not believe he had squeezed them all into such a compact space. It must have taken him much thought. But he had a talent for that, which was also noticeable in his bomb shelter.

Katue was thin and a bit on the nervous side. I visited him at the Dental College one day when an air raid suddenly began. I almost burst out laughing when he put on his *bōkū zukin* [a hood worn over the head as a kind of shock absorber], because his was three times larger than the average. I had never seen such a huge hood! The alarm sirens sounded, Katue's face turned ghostly pale, and his body began trembling. He was a psychological wreck. Of course, everyone was frightened, but Katue seemed to take it even worse than most people. Watching him, I thought to myself, "That man truly understands fear."[167]

Kobayashi's picture is at variance with the cooler image Katue projected of himself as a modern-day hermit with samurai powers of endurance. If Kobayashi's account is reliable, then the stoic persona appreciative of traditional culture that appears in Katue's wartime poetry and prose is at least partially a construct of self-mythology, having little to do with his fear-filled reality.

When Katue's residential area of Magome was the direct target of attack, for the first and only time in the diary he expressed emotion—a deep despair.

April 4, 1945: From about 1 A.M. until about 3 A.M. enemy attacked with the utmost ferocity. Gas and electricity cut off. Gas has been out for the whole day. Letter from Eiko with news that she received my letters of 21st and 23rd.

Depressed, I have nothing to say.[168]

The war situation is getting worse and worse.

After almost one week without bombing, the attacks resumed full force. The entries are sketchy, but read in sequence they conjure up the drama of the time:

April 12, 1945: Approximately 100 enemy planes attacked (around 10 A.M.).
April 13: Roosevelt died.[169]

Went to school. Kobayashi [Yoshio] came by. In the afternoon I dropped by Tokyo Industrial College on my way home.

Kunitomo [Chie; dates unknown] came by and brought my ticket [for Sanjō, the city in Niigata to which Katue's wife and son had evacuated].

From around midnight 100-plus enemy planes attacked. All-clear siren rang at around 3 A.M.
April 14: Stayed at home.

All train lines are shut down as a result of last night's enemy attack, which lasted until dawn.

Rested at home all day.

April 15: Stayed at home all day.

Kunitomo, Jō, Towada, and Iwasa came by. We talked and had dinner together.

From 9:30 P.M. the Keihin-Ōmori belt [which includes Magome] was bombed heavily by 200 airplanes.

April 16: Alert called off at 3 A.M. Kuroda [Yoshiaki; dates unknown] stayed overnight.

In the afternoon the Kunitomos came over, and we discussed my travel [to Sanjō].

Iwasa dropped by with news that Imaki's house had burned down.

The ticket to Sanjō that Katue had requested on April 3 arrived ten days later, but because the train lines had been bombed, he was held up for another three days. Early in the war Katue had written with optimism in a patriotic poem, "our flag is flying in the tropics"; now he was having trouble escaping from the rubble of burned-out Tokyo.

Katue stayed in Sanjō for sixteen days and then returned to Tokyo, where he endured five more weeks of air raids before evacuating for the last time. While in the capital, he recorded paying ¥30.50 on May 23 for fire insurance, with a premium of ¥5,000, and ¥16.87 for life insurance on May 28. Katue must have supposed that if he died, the premium would take care of Eiko and Akio. In purchasing insurance, Katue showed that he had not abandoned the sense of fiscal responsibility he had learned as an economics major in college.

No matter how much Katue was suppressed during the war—first by the Japanese police who interrogated him in September 1940 and later by the American air attacks—the whimsical and stylish side of his personality, much in evidence during his years at the helm of the VOU group, did bubble to the surface at times. Among all the precise notations of reserve training, air raid alerts, and shelter repairs, we find the following entry: "June 30, 1944: Went to school. No change. In the afternoon I dropped by Mitsukoshi and Takashimaya [department stores] and bought tropical fish." Katue, for the most part a realist in war, also needed to forget: tropical fish and poetry provided two escape routes.

Up to this point I have discussed four patriotic poems published by Katue through 1942.[170] During the last three years of the war, he published at least one more propaganda poem per year.[171] Altogether, the seven poems make up the bulk of what he produced in the genre, and they constitute a critical mass of nationalistic fervor. He wrote the first four poems while Japan was piling up stunning victories, but the last three were penned after the military situation had deteriorated.

The most noteworthy project of the Hōkokukai during 1943 was the production of *Tsuji shishū* and *Tsuji shōsetsu shū*, for which all leading writers were enlisted.[172] The books were widely distributed; each had an initial print run of 10,000 copies. Their bite-size doses of patriotism (poets were given two pages and novelists one page) were meant to be read by citizens on busy street corners in order to raise donations for battleships. Feeling the pinch after the military setbacks in the Pacific, Japan's leaders realized that access to its lifeline of vital natural resources, the colonies, was assured only if battleships could keep the sea-lanes open. The government implored its citizens to donate metal, and the massive drive brought in everything from ancient temple bells to record-player needles.[173] For *Tsuji shishū*, Katue contributed the poem "Fune o omou":

> *Thinking of [Battle]ships*
>
> since ancient times the Japanese people
> have made ships in the shape of swords
>
> to slaughter the bitter enemy
> we maneuvered them like swords tempered 100 times
>
> this is the autumn of the crucial showdown
> I think of battleships carrying the people's life
>
> raising a spray of water
> I contemplate battleships boldly cutting their way
>   forward like daredevils
>
> with their gale-force speed and their thunderish fierceness
> I contemplate the battleships of inevitable victory[174]

Katue blended the poetic image of sword-shaped ships cutting through waves and spraying water high into the air—displaying a futurist's awe at the grandiosity of modern machinery—with the standard political rhetoric forecasting "inevitable victory" over the "bitter enemy" after the "crucial showdown."[175] The battleship, for which people were being asked to donate, is symbol of the nation at war and, ultimately, preserver of "the people's life" (*minzoku no seimei*). Had Japan won the war, "Fune o omou" and Katue's other patriotic verse would have been hailed as instrumental elements in the spiritual backbone behind the victory. But such was not to be the outcome.

In 1944 Katue published the poem "Sōshun no sakyū ni" in the large pa-
triotic anthology *Dai Tōa* (Greater East Asia), which was compiled to sup-
port a sanatorium for wounded and sick soldiers. Appropriate to the occa-
sion, Katue's poem expresses gratitude to a recuperating soldier.

> *On a Sand Dune in Early Spring*
>
> on April sand with budding dandelions
> sat a man wearing white
> he sat facing the ocean
> the wind was slight
> the sun high in the sky
> a single patrol aircraft
> like a sharp needle
> circled under the altostratus clouds
> the man wearing white
> watched it intensely
> with stern eyebrows
> and precisely shining forehead
> ah
> young wounded soldier
> you will blossom in the skies of early spring
> like a magnolia
> you returned from the bloody and muddy battlefield
> to a rigorous purity
> the slight smell of disinfectant
> drifts like the dusk
> and on April sand with budding dandelions
> I can feel that smell
> caught in a glass-like loneliness
> but wounded soldier
> before long, like a young lion
> you will bravely rise to your feet again
> and as the child of the mountain yearns for mountains
> you will surely pick up your loving sword
> and return to the blood and mud of the battlefield
> until the day the arch-enemy is annihilated
> even if knocked down you will rise to your feet
> again and again you will fight on ceaselessly
> I think about this

> while walking across dunes of early spring
> and I pray to the gods for the day of your recovery
> with fervent desire
> and full of boundless love and appreciation[176]

The sand dune, the spring, the slight breeze, the sun high in the sky, and the poet's sincere prayer all give the surface of the poem a seductive, love-of-life quality. But underlying these images Katue reinforces the harsh government policy encouraging soldiers to sacrifice themselves as a means of spiritual purification. He himself was unwilling to engage in combat, and his exhortation of others is hypocritical in light of his postwar statement, "I did not fight. I only picked up a pen and wrote, picked up a brush and painted." The poet, of course, was not responsible for creating the military policy requiring soldiers to return to the battlefield once their wounds had healed sufficiently, but Katue's unquestioning acceptance of the status quo contributed to its perpetuation.

In "Thinking of [Battle]ships" the battleship is the focal point for poet, soldier, and reader in their solidarity as citizens of the Japanese state. Similarly, the sand dunes in "On a Sand Dune in Early Spring" represent a common ground—Japanese soil—where the poet walks, the soldier sits, and the reader imagines the scene.

When the protagonist of the poem assures the wounded soldier that "you will blossom in the skies of early spring / like a magnolia," is he implying that he will recover his health, or that he will attain a state of spiritual purity by dying for the country? Unlike the idealism found in Katue's previous patriotic poems, this one assures no bright future. The wounded soldier, who wears the white hospital outfit of a recuperating patient, "like a young lion," will pick up his sword again "as the child of the mountain yearns for mountains." Even if knocked down, the soldier will "rise . . . / again and again" and "until the arch-enemy is annihilated / . . . fight on ceaselessly." Rather than praying for the soldier's recovery (which would mean his return to battle), Katue would have made his emotional rhetoric more persuasive if he proposed magnanimously to take the veteran's place in the battlefield, enabling him to recuperate without concern for future injury. But Katue was unwilling to risk his own life, even in the imaginative world of the poem. Besides Katue's unambiguous ideological position, the poem is also remarkable for one line—*garasu no yō na sekiryō ni torawareta* (caught in a glass-like loneliness)—a brief re-emergence of his imagistic VOU days.

Katue's last patriotic poem, "Kigen setsu" (Empire day)—targeted toward children—was printed in February 1945. The poem was perhaps a result of the agitation regarding the surveillance aircraft and air raids of Tokyo, which began on November 29, 1944. Katue, perhaps irritated by radio and newspaper reports concerning the upcoming invasion, wrote in his diary for November 12, 1944: "Stayed home all day. I sent an angry poem (*fungeki shi*) to the Hōkokukai." The circumstances surrounding Katue's comment are unclear, and his "angry poem" may never have been published, or he may have been referring to "Empire Day." His anger was apparently aimed at the enemy, not the Japanese military establishment, to whose literary arm, the Hōkokukai, he was willingly sending his poem.

Patriotic poetry had already gained wide exposure among adults through newspapers and over the radio, and gradually the propaganda machine was directed at children. Murano Shirō, already in January 1943, had written an essay on the emerging popularity of patriotic poetry for children in which he hailed the phenomenon as a new opportunity for poetry, declaring that "poets could to a large degree fulfill the cultural obligation they ought to be shouldering."[177] He also conceded that certain pitfalls should be avoided, such as merely describing one's childhood recollections.

Katue's poem for children, "Empire Day," refers to the February 11 holiday, arbitrarily chosen in 1872, which celebrates the accession of legendary Emperor Jimmu to the throne in 660 B.C.E.[178]

> *Empire Day*
>
> long, long ago there were the children of Kume and other warriors
> under Emperor Jimmu's flag
> elated, they struck unceasingly
> subjugating rebel throngs
> the beautiful day the land of the rising sun was founded
>
> for the long stretch of 2605 years
> not once losing to an enemy
> the Japanese nation so strong and correct
> singular throughout wide East Asia
> the day the magnificent country was founded
>
> oh countrymen—young and strong and yet so few
> today is the day to take the firm oath
> to become warriors like the children of Kume

and defend Japan
smashing all those hateful American and British soldiers[179]

In this flagrant propaganda piece, Katue tried to instill courage in mid-twentieth-century Japanese boys by reminding them of the glorious feats accomplished by Emperor Jimmu in the ancient past: "take the firm oath / . . . like the children of Kume" and "smash all those hateful American and British soldiers." He also alludes to Japan's invincibility—"for the long stretch of 2605 years / not once losing to an enemy"—as he had in "On a Sand Dune in Early Spring." Japan's unbroken line of emperors through its long history, symbolic of the undefeated nation, underscores the moral rectitude of the Yamato race. Katue completely accepted the government's propaganda line. No longer putting up even a modicum of resistance, he was now actively instructing children to believe in the same nation-building myths that adults were forced to accept. The fact that World War II resulted in the deaths of more than fifty million people and that modern weapons represented a threat in themselves were inconsequential arguments to the propaganda machine of which Katue was but one cog. To him, the courage of a few dozen soldiers on the Yamato plain millennia ago could serve as a means to boost the morale of young soldiers. Far from harmless, such propaganda takes a macabre turn when placed in the context of a popular American saying of the time: "The Japs take all kinds of chances, they love to die."[180] Immediately after the war, Katue would denounce such facile myth-spinning as an example of the weakness for sentimentality in Japanese culture, but this poem supplies ample evidence that he himself served as a conduit for spreading such beliefs. Katue, however, never admitted his complicity.

"Empire Day" is in a continuum with his other patriotic poems. While exhorting the nation's youth to be courageous, he managed to send his own son, Akio, to school far away from Tokyo in the relatively safe city of Sanjō. There is a revealing gap between Katue's encouragement of his countrymen to be brave in the poems "On a Sand Dune in Early Spring" and "Empire Day" and his fear as described by fellow poet Kobayashi Yoshio. In the paradox of the "frightened stoic poet," we can find Katue's frail humanity. Although Katue could not have publicly expressed his fear or doubt about Japan's assured victory, it is equally true that he need not have participated as actively as he did in the war machine.

Katue waited out the war's conclusion in Sanjō with his family. His brief diary entry for August 15, 1945, records Emperor Hirohito's surrender:

Japan finally [*tsui ni*] agrees to unconditional surrender.
　The emperor broadcast a speech.
　I listened to it at Ichijōin [temple] in Sanjō.
　Bought train tickets for Tokyo.

Katue's anger and grief at the shattering of the dream are compressed in *tsui ni* (finally, in the end). The following day he and his family returned to their Magome home to restart their lives.

　Now, more than fifty years after the cessation of hostilities, Katue's wartime activities are still little understood, and misconceptions regarding his role abound, in no small part because he shrewdly distanced himself from the past as soon as the war ended. Many readers who have seen only his postwar writings mistakenly believe that he was uninvolved in writing patriotic poetry, partially because his war writings have been excised from recent reissues of his poems and essays while his antiwar statements are preserved. Here I will chronicle briefly how Katue deceived the literary world after the war and emerged more or less unscathed even after being exposed.

　In the post-surrender *Mugi tsūshin*, Katue indirectly accused the military of "deceiving the people." In two other writings directly after the war, he implied that he had committed no wrong and deserved to be accepted again as an avant-garde leader. The first was an essay published in the *Yomiuri shinbun* four months after the war under Katue's byline and the headline "The Duty of Poets: Be Pioneers of the Revolution—Let's Bring Back the Passion for Human Welfare."[181] Knowing that Takamura Kōtarō and other poets had been far more stridently patriotic than himself, Katue drew a line between their activity, which he censured, and his own, which he ignored. Notice how he deftly switches from "we" to "they" in his deflection of responsibility.

The morality of poets who have fallen to earth. Over the past ten years *we* have physically experienced a pathetic and shameful history that will have to be spelled out by historians at the end of the century with pens of great indignation. And now, as citizens of a defeated country, *we* are looking at reality head on, without turning our eyes away.... While it is necessary to make clear who is responsible for having brought about this shameful situation, at the same time *we* must reflect on what factors in the tradition of our people allowed *them* to exist as a kind of singular herd. ... It can be said that some poets gave their services to promote the desire for war, and now with the defeat, *they* have not faced the people and written a single line of penitent poetry, thereby displaying *their* impudence, which is akin to the attitude of the irresponsible leaders. ...

Now, taking up a pen in one hand and a bell (rather than a wine cup) in the other, it is time that *we* must write living poetry standing on the burned-out grounds that resemble the Grecian wilderness. Poets—facing the present and future of cultural Japan—should prepare with a resolute will to write [even] one line of responsible poetry.[182] (Italics added)

In September 1946, Katue penned "Futtōteki shiron" (A seething essay on poetry) in which he blamed others and, seemingly struck with "premeditated amnesia" (which he had once advocated as an ideal of his hometown poetics), conveniently refrained from reminding readers of his own wartime activity. On the other hand, had Japan emerged victorious, Katue naturally would have written something entirely different, because he had also positioned himself cozily for that eventuality by his hard work in the Hōkokukai and his production of patriotic poetry.

A Seething Essay on Poetry

The period from 1940 to 1945 was a golden opportunity for the military leaders of this country to exploit poetry. And *they* certainly profited to a degree. However, strictly speaking, the poets (and poems) they exploited were not those standing at the avant-garde edge of modern poetry; *they* had already retreated in the 1920s and lost their raison d'être. This will become apparent when taking a glance at the poems broadcast from 1940 to 1945, in which nothing but pity can be found among the vulgar posing and sentimental agitation. But good poets of the future should perhaps have some appreciation for the existence of *those poets*, because within a packaged existence *they* were able to avoid being victims of the tragi-comedy of this idiotic century. At any rate, *those poets*, together with the perishing ruling class, will surely sink again like straw sandals beyond the horizon into the past. Let's allow the sinking ones to sink! Unexpectedly for them, blood and tears for that single dance were squeezed out of the entire populace in an irrecoverable sacrifice.

Nevertheless, now an age of fresh poetry has dawned with new poetry magazines sprouting up nationwide. I earnestly hope that these poetry groups will enjoy a fine future and develop favorably.[183] (Italics added)

On reading Katue's comments, it is striking that he chastised others without mentioning his own participation in the war anthologies, in the Hōkokukai, and in the Kuroganekai on behalf of the militarist government. He would have been more credible had he spoken in the first person about his own experience: "Within a packaged existence [I was] able to avoid being [a victim] of the tragi-comedy of this idiotic century." Attempting to cast his future in the best light, he probably justified his war poetry to himself by recalling that other poets had been even more nationalistic than he, and therefore his own activity was negligible (i.e., not worth mentioning) in relation to theirs.[184] His avant-garde roots went back farther than almost any other Japanese poet, and he had the opportunity to resume where he had left off, if only he could put his wartime poetry behind him. Katue gave up not only patriotic poetry (which obviously was unwelcome during the Occupation) but also hometownism and the traditional poetics supporting it. He now called for poets to pick themselves up from the rubble and write a new type of poetry, taking into account the reality of their present situation. This sudden switch, as understandable as it was coming right after Japan's defeat, was strikingly similar in pattern to Katue's abandonment of avant-garde poetry in October 1940, following interrogation by the Thought Police. He detected the winds of change and followed them, seeming to fear cultural death if he stagnated.

How are we to evaluate Katue's abandonment of Western poetics in favor of patriotic poetry and hometownism, and then, after the hostilities were over, his re-embrace of Western poetics and abandonment of Japanism?

The metaphor of a reversible jacket aptly describes Katue's drastic zigzags in mentality and lifestyle in 1940 and 1945. Unprincipled and contradictory as his two swings of the pendulum may appear in retrospect, they reflect the general course of the country both in its pro-Japanism phase during the war and in its integration along American "democratic" lines following the war. The sudden discarding of fifteen years of work in 1940 and then the disclaiming of his wartime work in 1945 are readily explainable by historical facts—the former by his interrogation by the police and the latter by Japan's surrender. More difficult to assess is the impact of these traumatic transformations on Katue and his subsequent poetry.

I asked Katue's wife, Eiko, why her husband had written patriotic poetry during the war, and she made the following points:

Katue was full of fear, and he was certainly not willing to confront the authorities on their terms of brutal power. Also, we were misinformed about the real course of the war and were unaware, for example, of Japan's mistreatment of people in the colonies (including atrocities such as human experimentation by Unit 731 in Manchuria). Katue, it should be remembered, was a product of the Japanese educational system that had indoctrinated all of us to believe in the country's invincibility, especially after the defeat of Russia in 1905. Moreover, it wasn't easy to "love your enemy" when we were taught that if America won, they would kill every last one of us.[185]

As we have seen, Katue's literary activity from 1925 to 1945 included avant-garde poetry, hometown and patriotic poetry, haiku, and other styles. For convenience, I categorize hometown and patriotic poetry in the same group. Even though the hometown poems were usually more subtle than the jingoistic patriotic poems, they nevertheless were written in deliberate conformity with the ideological framework prescribed by the Thought Police, and Katue himself considered them ethical outpourings of patriotism.

In the West certain poets considered themselves both avant-garde and fascist (Ezra Pound in Italy, the New Objectivity poets in Germany, among others), in wartime Japan the term "avant-garde fascist" would have been an oxymoron. Katue's hometown poems can be seen as an attempt to be both avant-garde (without admitting the Western origin of the notion) by opening a new frontier for poetry and fascist by lending cultural support for the propagation of master-race theories and nation-building legends.

Katue's activity from 1940 to 1945, taken as a whole, can be subsumed under the four hypotheses:

1. He was essentially avant-garde, and his patriotism was a camouflage.
2. He was essentially a patriot, and his avant-garde activity was dilettantism.
3. He underwent a genuine transformation from avant-garde to patriot and back to avant-garde again.
4. Both avant-gardism and patriotism were masks, and he was absent.

Each of these is plausible. Katue would no doubt have claimed the first choice, and indeed, all his postwar work reads as if he had hibernated during the war and been saving himself for the day he could resume his avant-garde feats. In time and quantity his avant-garde production from 1925 to 1940 — eight books of poems, and approximately one hundred magazines edited — is quadruple the output of his five-year nationalistic phase. If he was camouflaging his true self because of police coercion, then his hometown poetry and patriotic poems must be seen as *playing at being Japanese*.

The camouflage hypothesis, however appealing it is to readers who appreciate Katue's avant-garde poetry, is untenable. There is too much contrary evidence. For example, the following statement by Katue on his reconversion to Japanism, written in 1943, seems too persuasive to interpret as merely an elaborate ploy.

In actuality, since writing the first poem in *Fūdo*, I have not looked at one page in a foreign language. And I have not looked at any magazines, books, or newspapers concerned with [Western] painting, sculpture, architecture, science, film, and fashion. Not only that, but I have completely put that kind of cultural lineage outside my mind, replacing it with things that are purely Japanese. And, at the same time, I have completely changed my lifestyle. Everything my eyes come into contact with has changed along those lines. Concretely, instead of a [Edward] Weston photograph, I hang a scroll with a Chinese poem; and on my desk, instead of *Life* or *Vogue*, lie magazines devoted to handicrafts or research on local customs. Instead of painting with oil, I now use ink. And my interest in lighters and mechanical pencils has been transferred to fragrant brushes and [India] ink. In this way, everything I see with my eyes and everything I think about has changed. Only by having changed this much was I able to write the first line of *Fūdo*. Some people know what [a difficult transformation] I am talking about: poetry does not simply change by making minor adjustments [i.e., your lifestyle also needs to be drastically altered].[186]

Because of statements such as these, Katue's critics reject the camouflage idea outright and instead favor the second—and opposite—hypothesis. Yoshimoto Takaaki and Sakuramoto Tomio, in a blanket condemnation of the two generations of writers who complied with the authorities, asserted that the prewar avant-gardism of Katue and others was simply a dilettantish flirtation with the West and that at heart they were model patriots.[187] The term used to refer to the shallow avant-gardism of prewar Japanese poets and artists is *gaikoku kabure* (lit. "to wear foreignness"), implying that the adoption of foreign tastes, literary and otherwise, is as phony an exercise for Japanese as putting on a disposable hat.[188] Sakuramoto, for example, blasts Katue as a dilettante indulging in *hakuraihin sūkei* (a reverence for things foreign). To belittle the previous fifteen years of a poet's achievements because of his capitulation to coercion in 1940 seems an unfair basis for making a historical judgment. For his part, however, Katue unwittingly fueled his critics' argument by rejecting his Westernized past and embracing Japanism.

Following this line of reasoning, Sakuramoto and postwar VOU poet Andō Kazuo (1929–) deny that Katue would have needed to camouflage himself at all, claiming that he could have removed himself from the poetry establishment altogether and could have satisfied the Thought Police with "safe" haiku.[189] Rather than camouflage, they argue, opportunism was the driving force that impelled Katue to compromise himself. They conclude that Katue's patriotic services in writing poetry and essays, attending committee meetings, and revamping his lifestyle—whether initially prompted by a desire for self-preservation or not—virtually nullify his prewar avant-gardism.

A less categorical assessment, but one that also finds his patriotism genuine, is the third hypothesis, namely, that Katue was genuinely avant-garde from 1925 to 1940, but thereafter underwent a sincere change of heart, initially prompted by the Thought Police, and he gradually became more and more deeply involved in propaganda activity. This evaluation is more satisfactory than the preceding ones because, rather than seeking an absolute either/or answer, it allows for complexity and change, two undeniable aspects of the human predicament.

The argument that he embodied two contradictory sides, each sincere in its time, still raises problems. For example, if his patriotic poetry genuinely reflected his beliefs, Katue somehow becomes more culpable than if he had been disguising his true, avant-garde self. After all, if he had not penned patriotic verse, his avant-garde reputation in Japan would be more solidly intact. Conversely, if he had not carried the stigma of being a modernist, the Thought Police and nationalist poets would not have found him suspect in 1940–41.

The fourth argument is to some extent a natural outgrowth of the third, namely, that Katue was both an avant-gardist and a patriot, and to the extent that the two positions are mutually exclusive, they neutralize each other, leaving the fundamental identity of the author unrevealed. Accordingly, neither Katue's avant-garde posturing nor his patriotism is seen as authentic. Rather, Katue (or, more precisely, Hashimoto Kenkichi) is seen as a kind of dream weaver who writes in numerous styles—including avant-garde, hometown, and patriotic—that are no more than fashionable masks purposely kept at a remove from himself. This argument is more applicable to Katue than to other poets because of the variety of his writing styles and his interest in impersonal poetics. From the mid-1920s on, he had continually shown a preference for objective poetry, especially notable in his graphic compositions (*Shiro no arubamu*) but also abundantly evident in his lyrical experiments (*Wakai koronii, Natsu no tegami*). Katue's surrealism from 1927 and his abstract experiments between 1935 and 1940 were further plunges into his imagination and had only the flimsiest connection with his everyday life. Although many mainstream poets wrote verse approximating *shi shōsetsu* (I-novels), Katue accented wholly other concerns such as design and the gap in meaning from line to line. At first glance, his hometownism would appear to be an exception to his impersonal stance, especially in light of his claim that the poetry in *Fūdo* blossomed from his immersion in Japanese culture. Yet, the pattern he sought in his hometown poetry was mostly an objective construct, as was the persona of the poems. In short, his hometown poems were as much journeys into the recesses of his imagination as his avant-garde poetry had been, and perhaps the sharp contrast in styles did not signal a switch from objective to subjective poetry.

The second and fourth arguments differ from the first and third in judging Katue's avant-gardism to be an insubstantial mask rather than a central ingredient of his personality. His belief in mystification and use of several pen names (Chapter 4), when considered with his "theory of ideoplasty" (Chapter 5) bolster the contention that the poet purposely absented himself from his writings. The fourth hypothesis, although tinged with cynicism, helps to explain Katue's return to avant-garde poetry after the war, without acknowledging his prewar avant-garde commitment as authentic.

In this analysis, I have interpreted the currents in Katue's poetry from various angles. With the reputations of avant-garde and proletarian poets eroded by their documented participation in the propaganda mill for the Japanese war effort, several critics have taken a wholly different perspective in viewing the question of wartime literary culpability. Their argument, which has gained currency, is that all poets were guilty of participating in the nationalist cause; therefore, instead of blaming them, we should shift our focus to *after* the war, when poets were again able to express themselves freely, and notice the sincerity of their self-examination (or lack of it) concerning their wartime activity. Takei Teruo (1927–), an accuser who was born too late to be coerced himself, makes this point about Tsuboi Shigeji (1897–1975), the proletarian poet who underwent *tenkō* (conversion) but reverted to left-wing thinking as soon as the war was over: "I am not pursuing Tsuboi's wartime responsibility. I am questioning the postwar responsibility that began with the evasion of wartime responsibility."[190]

Yoshimoto Takaaki, with similar reasoning, acquits Takamura Kōtarō, the *kaichō* (head) of the Hōkokukai's Poetry Section and perhaps the most influential patriotic poet.[191] Unlike Katue and Tsuboi, Kōtarō was truly penitent after the war, shutting himself away from the world in a small cottage in Iwate prefecture for seven years. Kōtarō went through an intense introspection and loathed himself for indirectly having caused many deaths with his poems based on fanatic worship of the emperor.[192] Kōtarō, broken but repentant, wrote some of his most moving verse, similar in sentiment to Ezra Pound's confessions of failure in *The Pisan Cantos*, while reflecting on his past errors.

In terms of postwar admittance of wartime guilt, Katue fared quite badly, as we have seen. His evading of discussion of his patriotic poetry and voluntary work for the Hōkokukai has lost him respect among critics who evaluate poets on the basis of their penitence and are aware of his activity. Although we can sympathize with this humanistic standard—especially in light of the inhumanity of the war years—allowing for only a confessional response unwittingly reinforces the old-fashioned attitude, discarded decades before by abstract poets, that demands that poets must express their thoughts and feelings only within a personal and direct framework.

Rather than condemning Katue's war poetry or excusing it as a perfectly acceptable expression under oppressive circumstances, the fairest way to evaluate Katue's situation is to take a chronological look at what he did, as has been attempted over the course of this chapter. Thereby, we can see that he did put up a modicum of resistance ("I want to warn the ultranationalist poets . . . we will certainly never be driven to silence"; September 1939), but after having capitulated he became a fervent "convert" to the cause ("I am presently going so far as to suck the marrow of the bone of traditional native culture"; November 1941). We should also distinguish between the differences in circumstances surrounding the war when it was hot only in distant China ("Autumn at the Front"; 1939) and the end of the Pacific War, when Katue was enduring almost daily saturation bombing and penning nationalistic poems such as "On a Sand Dune in Early Spring" (1944) and "Empire Day" (1945). While not denying that the two poems are unabashed propaganda, it is also fair to ask: If one's life is in continual danger, as Katue's was, and the nation feels threatened with genocide, as Japan was, what do a few nationalistic poems amount to, anyway? The questions raised by the issue of wartime responsibility remain thorny. It is fitting that critics have been baffled by Katue's swings from avant-garde to patriot and back again, because he seems to have been equally confused by his own behavior. He admitted the following in a 1943 essay:

When I run into friends whom I don't see regularly, they always tell me, "Your poetry has really changed lately." I agree it is unforeseen that I should write the [hometown] poetry of *Fūdo* within 500 days of writing the [abstract] poetry of *Katai tamago*. Their concern that I have gone crazy is not unreasonable. But to explain at great lengths is a bother, so I just say that it is a continuation of *Kon*.[193] The friend inevitably replies with a look of complete comprehension, "Yes, if you put it that way, the poems do resemble those in *Kon*." Then I am the one left unable to make sense of it.[194]

Katue was easily frightened by the summons from the Thought Control Authorities and eschewed his long-avowed avant-gardism and enthusiastically self-generated Orientalism, adopting instead nationalistic, traditionalist, home-culturalism. His surrender seems painless. Here one ought to remember that there were few writers who resisted the military suppression— except for a handful of brave members of the Communist party who dared the authorities at the price of imprisonment, for over a decade in the case of Miyamoto Kenji (1908–), and his wife, Yuriko, who was in and out of jail and ill throughout the Fifteen-Year War. Besides, most writers were ignorant of the realities of the war. Thus, Katue's collaborationism was not quite as criminal an act as that of writers in Nazi Germany such as, say, Martin Heidegger or Hermann Hesse. Still, his re-reversal to Westernism after the war was, it must be recognized, painless and unembarrassed. Katue even tried to conceal his wartime activities and writings.

His compromised attitude, never admitted publicly, and the experience of the war had an effect on his postwar poetry as a negative stimulus, always forcing him forward to more adventurous experimentation.[195] By late 1945 he could see what he had been blind to in 1939: one step into the quicksand of fascism and there was no escape until the war had run its course. Katue swallowed the bitter pill of his responsibility in silence.

Perhaps the main value for him of having written patriotic poetry was that it propelled him thereafter in the opposite direction. His postwar poetry, the subject of the next two chapters, is the record of a poet who, although never tested again in a similar way, pursued his artistic explorations as if he were eager to demonstrate that he would never again compromise himself.

7 SHREDDING
the TAPESTRY
of MEANING

After Japan's surrender on August 15, 1945, Katue was like a man just released from a long stay in prison or hospital. He may have believed that he was resuming his avant-gardism, but in retrospect we can see that he was merely regaining his bearings. His poetry of this interim period is filled with anger at the militarist system for having demanded such futile sacrifices of the people. Directly after the termination of hostilities, Katue, while still not conceding any personal responsibility, did begin expressing a personal viewpoint about the reality before his eyes. He had almost never done this in his prewar poetry, and his wartime poetry had fit the propaganda "reality" demanded by the Thought Police. The sheer historical significance of the moment perhaps impelled him to record Japan's defeat and the uncertainty of the Occupation. A poem by Katue from 1946 is reminiscent of Du Fu (712–70), who bewailed the decline of Tang civilization (618–907) while walking among the rat-infested ruins of a palace.

> *In a Lost City*
>
> piercing through the brain
> violet-colored light flashes
> thrown on exhausted insides of white bones
> from where a truly wretched peace was born.
> I won't forget this instant for eternity.
> the entire capital is razed
> together with the blazing flames
> those dandy, cocksure,
> lovable city people have perished.
> yesterday suffering the despotism of militarists
> today wandering in the tyranny of appetite

nothing but a mob covered with rags.
I slightly climb up a heap of bricks
people!
before this unsightly page of history
without tears, what
what can we scream?
taking hands, crossing knees
tearfully gnawing on hopeless bones, what else to do?
blown in the bleak autumn wind
I appeal to heaven
to make this stupid century pass even a moment sooner![1]

Whereas the United States rebounded quickly from the war, Japanese continued to suffer shortages of food and staples for three long years after the surrender. "In a Lost City" was written at the height of the despair following the defeat, and it is not included in Katue's *Zenshishū* (Complete poems).

This unabashed realism proved to be short-lived. By 1949 Katue had started to publish in his revived *VOU* magazine the abstract poems that would be gathered into perhaps his most renowned book of poems, the 1951 *Kuroi hi* (Black fire; Fig. 22). Following the wartime coercion and an attempt at expressive realism, he shifted to the subversion of meaning itself. *Kuroi hi* is difficult to understand unless one reads it as a deliberate attempt to block the process of deciphering meaning. With the freedom to write whatever he liked, Katue chose incoherence.

Katue never directly related his poems to politics, but he has been called an anarchist, and he told one of his closest VOU colleagues, Kuroda Iri (1929–), that he considered himself one.[2] How this anarchism meshes with his wartime poetry is, needless to say, highly problematic. Nevertheless, the excavation of some peculiar possibilities in Japanese—what Kuroda Iri refers to as "Kitasono language"—if indulged in by everyone in society, surely would result in a chaotic state of noncommunication, an anarchy of incoherence. For example, what soldier would obey an order if language consisted of only free-floating signifiers without signifieds, as found in *Kuroi hi*? In fact, the world would break down if language were to lapse into such imprecision. Katue was, of course, not presenting his poetry as a means of communication in the ordinary sense; rather, he self-consciously created poetry by selecting and combining words to evoke imaginative possibilities. If his poetry can be considered anarchic, it is primarily in a functional or esthetic sense, with implications for ideology and politics buried in the subtext.

Fig. 22   Katue's celebrated book of poems, *Kuroi hi* (Shōshinsha, 1951).
He designed the cover with the title in French.

What techniques does Katue use to distort the Japanese language? The following analysis illustrates how, using avant-garde methods, he created poetry unlike any seen before in Japan. I begin with a translation of one of the poems in *Kuroi hi* and comments on the original by three of his contemporaries, followed by a brief introduction to the postwar Katue and the volume. Lastly, I introduce comments by Western critics on Western avant-garde poetry because they are applicable to Katue's experiment in *Kuroi hi* and because they suggest alternative avenues of interpreting his supposedly indecipherable text.

Night Elements

bone
that hopelessness's
sand's
doorknob

hole
in
stone's
chest
or hole
in
stone's
arm

loneliness's
mouth's
bone
held up by
night
of
the idol

toward
one
eye
one
turtle's
wisdom

or
inside
fertile hole
the diagram
toward love
rejecting
eternity
of
love

dream

of
gloomy
mud
torn
by
circle
of
night
of love's
pubic hair

that darkness's
phantom's
cocoon
of
fire

that
phantom's
death's
black sand
of rapture
or
that
black rapture's
bone doorknob[3]

I do not think that there is any more difficult poem among the works of modern [Japanese] poets. And I do not think that anyone could explain it in a detailed and appropriate way. Even the author probably could not provide an explanation that would satisfy the reader.[4] (Murano Shirō, 1950)

In Kitasono's recent work can be found the special positioning of words that form vivid images. Moreover, the skillful changing of the imagery and the obstinate co-agulation of a unique visual sense in the author exert a gravitational pull that ap-proaches the phenomenon of magnetics.[5] (Yamanaka Sansei, 1951)

As for Katue's literature, how on earth could one interpret the poems? Can they really be broken down, analyzed, and annotated? I think that would be impossible. Therefore, it is no surprise that the explanations of Yamanaka Sansei and Murano Shirō are insufficient; yet, at the same time, they are appropriate regarding the way poetic methods should be. In other words, by examining these explanations of Katue's poetry, we can discover the limits of the possibilities of modern poetry. Be-cause his poetic method shows one extremity, the commentaries by the two of them—as something spoken at the extreme—are on a high level. We cannot hope for any better explanation in the future.[6] (Itō Shinkichi, 1955)

Over forty years have elapsed since Katue wrote the poems in *Kuroi hi*. The abstract, self-referential language and the clipped form of one or two graphs per line have continued to dumbfound critics; yet some interesting points have been made about them over the years.

Itō Shinkichi is correct that "Night Elements" and the other poems in *Kuroi hi*, as with any work of art, are irreducible and can never be fully interpreted. Certainly more can be attempted, however, than has been done until now. Articles have appeared in Japanese on the special qualities of Katue's language—especially his repeated use of the particle *no* の (to be discussed later) and his style of combining one or two graph lines with の.[7] But no one has explained, with examples, the specific stylistic techniques that Katue used to create his effects. Consequently, a mystique and a distractive piety surround his work; it can be demystified while still appreciated if we examine his usage of conventional and unconventional poetic devices. "Night Elements" is not as impenetrable as the critics would have. The wealth of images related to death and eroticism read as a meditation on postwar despair and the loss of the cultural and the individual self.

The considerable polarization in evaluations of Katue's wartime poetry (see Chapter 6) can also be found in discussions of his postwar avant-garde verse, but for different reasons. Critics blasted his wartime verse for their strong patriotic fragrance, but dismiss his avant-garde verse as not political (i.e., left-wing) enough. The proletarian poet Tsuboi Shigeji, for example, lambasted Katue for the lack of reality in his poetry: "In the end Katue approaches mysticism."[8] Katue, who never professed an interest in writing realistic verse, did not respond in print to Tsuboi's condemnation.

On the other extreme, his advocates have tended to credit his abstract poetry with an intuitive perfectionism. Okunari Tatsu (1942–) notes that "in many articles on Katue's poetry we find it praised for 'abolishing all decoration,' 'containing not a superfluous word,' and for its 'precision' and 'degree of completeness.'"[9] Okunari, who experiments with similar clipped forms in his own poetry, argues in his essays that the fluid process of Katue's style is more significant than the crystallized end products.[10]

Katue translated seven of the twelve poems of *Kuroi hi* into English and published them in avant-garde magazines in the United States.[11] Although the original versions perplexed Japanese critics, his English translations were not reviewed by American critics, who must have found them too marginal to the literary scene, if they noticed them at all. Nevertheless, over the years a number of first-rate Western poets have lavished high praise on Katue's work, including Ezra Pound, Ronald Duncan, and James Laughlin before the war, and Charles Olson, Robert Creeley, Kenneth Rexroth, William Carlos Williams, and Haroldo and Augusto de Campos after the war. Charles Olson, for example, commented that "Katue Kitasono is already marked as one of the few important contemporary poets."[12]

Katue became known in the West for *VOU* and for *Black Rain* (1954), his first book of poems and drawings in English, published in Mallorca, Spain, by the American poet Robert Creeley.[13] William Carlos Williams read *Black Rain* and wrote Creeley a letter, which Creeley forwarded to Katue: "It is remarkable that Kitasono has been able to get rid of the formality of the strictly Japanese modes of his ancestors and approach the West. That is som[e]thing that only an artist, among all the craftsmen in all the trades, could effect and a man with [not only] a free mind but a steady heart."[14]

Because of the language barrier, Western poets who knew only Katue's English translations were unaware of the complex ways in which he was distorting the Japanese language, but they were nonetheless impressed with his work in translation and the creative spirit they sensed in the original. How much of the self-referential nature of his poetry came across in English is hard to assess, yet it did not seem to pose a problem to Western poets who had themselves conducted similar experiments in a variety of literary and artistic movements ranging from surrealism and objectivism to abstract expressionism and minimalism. Even though most of the Western poets who praised Katue's work had read it in English translation only—the shadow, as it were, of the original—they intuitively sensed something contemporary and unique in his sensibility. This was in part because their own avant-garde experimentation with language used a variety of defamiliarization techniques. Pound, Williams, Rexroth, Olson, and Creeley all were successful at carving out individual styles and making breakthroughs in form and content.

The various ways that Katue's poetry has been categorized, and his idiosyncratic approach to writing, give some sense of the manner in which Katue rejected the common notion of style in creating his own. Katue classified his poetry into three styles: classic lyricism, modern lyricism, and experimental verse.[15] His biographer Fujitomi Yasuo adopts the same categories but adds a fourth to cover miscellaneous works such as the aphoristic *Saboten tō* and the English *Black Rain* (1954).[16] Kuroda Iri modifies Katue's divisions.[17] He retains the category "experimental verse" but, taking his cue from the labels "classic lyricism" and "modern lyricism," he lumps the two together under "lyricism." He also adds a third category, "synthetic poetry," which he sees as starting with *Mahiru no remon* (Lemon at high noon; 1954) and its "fusion" of the experimental and lyrical modes.[18]

Despite different emphases, each classification agrees on the division between Katue's avant-garde experimentation and his lyrical poetry (in Kuroda's case until 1954). That assessment, although fairly accurate, is misleading because the two categories are not mutually exclusive, even in Katue's prewar poetry. Lyricism, however slight, is not altogether absent from his avant-garde verse, and many of the technical devices found in his experimental poems appear in his lyrical works. Katue's lyrical works are never straightforward love poetry but contain surrealist imagery, occasional dadaist negation, and other devices intended to appeal as much to the intellect as to the heart of the reader.[19] His attempt to carve out a new lyricism that reflects modern city life contains glimmers of innovation perhaps because running through the poems is the paradoxical tension generated by a romantic who abhors sentimentality. It is a matter of taste whether one prefers Katue's avant-garde verse with its search for new concepts and forms or his lyricism with its accent on musicality, imagistic sharpness, and the theme of love treated euphemistically. There is, in any case, considerable overlap from one style to the other. The lyrical stream—which predates his avant-garde verse of the 1920s (see Chapter 1)—often is more appealing when sublimated in his experimental poems than in his overtly lyrical poems.

Unlike most poets who settle on one or more styles, he systematically limited the form, grammar, and vocabulary of his poems to attain various effects. His first book, the 1929 *Shiro no arubamu* (see Chapter 3), contained a number of composite "patterns" or styles (such as surreal poems, graphic poems, and diagrammatic poems), but each book thereafter represents a single pattern with an identifiable combination of key "elements." As he altered these component parts, his poetry continually took on new appearances. In the twenty-three poetry books published in Katue's lifetime,[20] he did not repeat the patterns mechanically; rather, within each book a different pattern resolves itself at a logical extreme.

Katue used at least thirteen elements in diverse combinations as modular blocks to form his individualistic style:

1. *Line length*[21] (whether he opted for short, medium, or long, there is little variation within any given book);

2. *Classical vocabulary* vs. *modern vocabulary*;

3. The inclusion or exclusion of *movement* (kinetic imagery vs. stagnant imagery);

4. *Rural* vs. *urban imagery*;

5. Grammatically *complete sentences* (implies a narrative flow, statements) vs. phrases, hesitations, and other *incomplete utterances*;

6. The presence or absence of the *first person*, *second person*, and *third person*; or any combination of the three;

7. Use or non-use of *metaphor* and *simile* vs. *metonymy*;

8. The presence or absence of *dialogue*;

9. *Colors*: light vs. dark imagery; or black-and-white vs. color imagery;

10. Words used for *design* vs. words used for *sound* vs. words used for *meaning*;

11. *Horizontal* imagery vs. *vertical* imagery vs. their combination (*cubist imagery*);

12. *Open-ended* poems vs. those with a sense of *closure*; and

13. *Word poetry* vs. *photographic ("plastic") poetry*.

There were also a few constants in Katue's choices, although his dependence on them varied from book to book:

1. The habitual use of *primary colors, black & white,* and *geometric shapes*;

2. The habitual use of *surrealist imagery* (see below for further divisions) and other types of *illogic*;

3. The concept that each graph, each poem (or photograph), and each book is a self-contained *objet* ("art object");

4. A liberal use of *blank space—ma* (間)—physically and conceptually; in other words, absence is a palpable presence in his work; and

5. *Foreign words* included for their exotic sound, often unavailable in Japanese, as much as for their meaning.

Each category could be subdivided, and the list extended, but these lists allow us to see the types of choices Katue made in constructing a poem. When he mentions, for example, that "the abstraction in *Katai tamago* is carried on in *Kuroi hi*,"[22] a glance at the two books—both in the "experimental" style—makes their structural similarities and differences evident. Katue was correct in asserting that both books combine elements in similarly abstract ways, but the elements themselves are quite distinct. For example, in *Katai tamago* we find long lines forming complete sentences that describe colorful imagery with the presence of human subjects, whereas *Kuroi hi* features short lines, lopsided and fragmented grammar, primarily black and white imagery, and an absence of human beings.

Similarly, a comparison of two books in the "lyrical style," *Natsu no tegami* (1937) and *Vinasu no kaigara* (Venus's seashell; 1955), yields a closer-grained analysis than the categorizations of Katue, Fujitomi, and Kuroda:

Similarities: colorful imagery, full sentences, surrealist illogic.

Differences: *Natsu no tegami*—long lines; rural imagery; rare use of first or second person; frequent use of simile; no dialogue; underlying theme of infatuation with youth, love, and friendship, but no presence of a tangible lover.

Vinasu no kaigara—medium-length lines; urban imagery; frequent use of first and second person; few similes; occasional dialogue; theme of love relationship with frequent presence of the beloved.

It is apparent from these contrasts of books within the "experimental" and "lyrical" modes that both labels conceal as much as they reveal. Katue's poetry is better viewed as a variety of combinations of technical elements or key building blocks, such as those outlined above. His unusual approach channeled and limited the form and content of his poems. Certain choices—especially that of the line length—had great influence on the tendency of other elements to cluster. For example, a medium or long line implied that there could be full sentences with verbs, thus enhancing the possibility of lyrical and dramatic content, words used for meaning, and closure. Conversely, a one- or two-graph line with almost no verbs is usually associated with an abstract content, incomplete sentences, less use of the first and second person, no dialogue, words for design and sound (rather than for meaning), and a consequent lack of closure.

We can imagine the previously listed elements as threads of different color and material that Katue selected and combined to weave the "pattern" of any given book. He obtained a considerable part of his poetic effect by leaping from pattern to pattern with each subsequent book, thereby challenging readers to decipher the current work while inviting expectations of continuing change in the future. The leap in pattern from book to book parallels the leap in meaning between lines (or stanzas) in individual poems; both force the reader's imagination to bridge the elusive gaps. Those readers (often themselves poets) who astutely gauged the twists and turns of Katue's poetry could take pleasure in comparing previous and current patterns and wondering what he could accomplish next. In this sense, he was more avant-garde than writers who clung to one style and made it their trademark, because he opened paths in uncharted directions while demonstrating possibilities at stops along the way.

Katue published thirteen poetry books during the thirty-three years from the end of the war until his death in 1978. He has been dubbed "the banner-bearer of the avant-garde,"[23] and it seems appropriate to focus on *Kuroi hi*, one of his most acclaimed avant-garde experiments, rather than on books in the somewhat less exploratory lyrical style.

A good way to understand the experiment in *Kuroi hi* is to contrast it with *Shiro no arubamu*, Katue's first and most varied book of poems. Both volumes are among his most experimental verse, yet they also contain some opposite qualities. First, there is an immediate polarization in the two titles: "white" versus "black," and "album" (implying preservation) versus "fire" (destruction). Also, white is symbolic of the optimism of his youth (he was twenty-six years old when *Shiro no arubamu* was published) and the general buoyancy of the early Shōwa period before the exigencies of the war crushed aspiring literary movements, whereas the black of *Kuroi hi* suggests the pessimism of the lost war, the uncertain present with Occupation troops stationed throughout the country, and his own middle age (he was almost fifty years old). In *Kuroi hi*, instead of the common realistic images "black smoke" and "red fire" (with their customary associations of campfire warmth), Katue used the unnatural "black fire," which is suggestive of large-scale devastation such as the incendiary air raids on Tokyo and the atomic bombs dropped on Hiroshima and Nagasaki.

The experiments in *Kuroi hi* and much of *Shiro no arubamu* share a concern with form, and both have been labeled "formalistic." In the poem "Kigō setsu" from *Shiro no arubamu* (see Chapter 3), for example, Katue listed words side by side as if he were composing a word collage on the blank screen of the reader's mind. The incremental layering of graphs with their designed look and ineradicable meanings clashed with the non-meaning inherent in the relation between individual words and between line and line. The poem emphasizes the signaling potential of graphs and reinforces the title, "Semiotic Theory."

In *Kuroi hi*, Katue again resorted to listing words that evoke perceptions and to leaving relations undefined, but there is a difference. Unlike "Kigō setsu" (and "Hakushoku shishū"), in which Katue had divided words by listing them on separate lines, in *Kuroi hi* he interposes the particle "no" and thereby related words directly (although often in semantically unintelligible ways that simultaneously—and paradoxically—act to divide them). By relating words in this odd manner, he generated a complex mechanism in which ambiguity flares up to block a unified reading. The consequence of this suppression of clarity of meaning is that the web of relations itself becomes the signification of the poem.

Katue designed *Kuroi hi* by himself. In contrast to the common rectangular shape of most books, it is almost square. Each page contains only one or two lines, positioned near the top of the page. These fill approximately 5 percent of the page, thus creating a tension between the type and the blank space. If Katue had not shortened the page, the disproportion between print and emptiness would have been even more pronounced. Another striking feature of the design is that the poem titles are printed in red ink and the poems in black, thus reinforcing the theme of a "black fire."[24]

More radical than the short line lengths and the two-color lettering is the innovative way the poems of *Kuroi hi* are to be read: top to bottom and *right to left*. For other modern Japanese poetry, the eyes move vertically down one line and then shift a line to the left and proceed down it, and a page is read right to left; or, when the type is laid out sideways as in the case of European languages (common these days), it is read from left to right. Katue essentially throws his readers off-balance by forcing their eyes to move horizontally in the "unnatural" direction of right to left. (On the rare occasion when Japanese was written horizontally in the past, the common direction was from right to left, and in a sense Katue was reverting to an old practice; it is, however, new to modern poetry.) He was the first poet in Japanese, as far as I know, to use a "double axis" of vertically down and horizontally right to left, thus rattling the reading process. Following is a transcription into directional signs for reading (down and right to left) "Kuroi shōzō" (Black portrait), one of the most extreme poems in the double-axis mode. Each letter or number stands for one graph; letters are read vertically (top to bottom) and numbers are read horizontally (right to left), starting at the top right-hand corner:

```
a 10 9 8 7 6 5   4 3 2 1 a 3 2 1 a 4 3 2 1 a 1 a
b                b       b       b b
                 c       c
                 d
```

```
a 1 a 1 a a 3 2 1 a   a 2 1 a 1 a 4 3 2 1 a
b b  b b       b b   b b       b
               c       c
               d
               e
               f
```

This schematic, devoid of meaning, does make visible the musicality in the repeating and non-repeating patterns, as well as the strong visual concern with form that would engage Katue further in his concrete poetry (Chapter 8).

The underriding constant in these poems is "discontinuity in continuity" and "continuity in discontinuity."[25] Because as readers we expect continuity, the text abruptly changes. Then, just as we adjust to expecting discontinuity, the text suddenly provides parallel constructions of syntax, or vocabulary repeated in close proximity, to give a semblance of continuity and overall unity. Continuity and discontinuity (akin to expansion and contraction) are alternated to prevent the dissipation of energy in any single direction. We can imagine that the process of constructing a poem of this sort is quite intuitive.

The following is a brief handbook of literary devices used by Katue (consciously or unconsciously), with specific examples drawn mostly, but not exclusively, from *Kuroi hi.*

Automatic Writing

Katue and other Japanese surrealists (with the exception of Takiguchi Shūzō) were not particularly interested in automatic writing. For them, surrealism was less an exploration of the subconscious than a conscious search for images that were strongly charged as poetry. Katue's surreal imagery can be divided into various types (outlined below). He had little regard for automatism, preferring to use his conscious, albeit spontaneous and instinctive, mind to compose esthetically pleasing (or disturbing) images. Katue's poetry has little to do with automatism—and, by implication, with European surrealism—because his method is conscious generation of poetry (Chapter 3).[26] Despite the author's stated intention, however, we can discover in his poetry what Michael Riffaterre defines as the "automatism effect" on the reader:

The syntax of an automatic text is in no way different from that of an ordinary text.

What is different is the automatic text's total departure from logic, temporality, and referentiality. In short, it is different because it violates the rules of verisimilitude and the representation of the real. Although normal syntax is respected, the words make sense only within the limits of relatively short groups, and there are semantic incompatibilities between these groups; or else the semantic consecution of the sentences is normal, but their overall meaning is obscured by smaller nonsensical groups. Because logical discourse, teleological narrative, normal temporality, and descriptive conformity to an accepted idea of reality are rationalized by the reader as proof of the author's conscious control over his text, departures from these are therefore interpreted as the elimination of this control by unconscious impulses. This is precisely what creates the appearance of automatism. This appearance may well be artificial, the product of very conscious work on form.

Whether this appearance is obtained spontaneously or through imitation, I shall call it the *automatism effect*. Any text in which this effect can be observed belongs to the genre labeled "automatic writing."[27]

Varieties of Katue's Surreal Imagery

The "standard" (incongruous) surreal image. One fundamental method for creating a surreal effect is the simple juxtaposition of seemingly unrelated images. The model surreal image is Lautréamont's "chance encounter between an umbrella and a sewing machine on an operating table." The substantive words (nouns and modifying adjectives)—"umbrella," "sewing machine," and "operating table"—are hardly strange in themselves, but in combination the incongruity evokes a sense of absurdity and even eeriness. And yet, according to Breton (and mystics), there is a part of the mind in which all apparent contradictions lose their problematic nature and are perceived in harmonious accord.

Katue relied on a number of techniques in constructing his brand of surreal imagery. To many Japanese poets, surrealism in words meant describing what they saw in a surrealist painting (e.g., Salvador Dali's frequently used image of a "melting-clock face"). Katue also indulged in such painterly images on occasion, but more often he favored images that would be impossible to paint (e.g., "glass wind"). His poems are strewn with a variety of illogical, abstract images, which it is convenient to group under the general rubric "surreal," for lack of a better term. In the following section, I break down more precisely than has been done to date the types of imagery Katue used, from the simple to the complex. These categories are by no means mutually exclusive; on the contrary, it is the use of them in combination within a given poem that adds accretively to the overall effect (or what Katue called "ideoplasty"; see Chapter 5).

Replacing one element in a metaphorical phrase.   One of the simplest ways of generating a surreal image is to replace one part of a metaphorical phrase and twist the relationship askew. For example, the title of Katue's *Lemon at High Noon* is a takeoff on the common expression "the sun at high noon."[28] The lemon's round shape and yellow color make it a suitable substitute for the sun, and there is surreal humor in imagining a lemon hanging in the sky. The image "lemon at high noon" can also be taken as having no metaphorical associations. The ambiguity in such an expression allows the reader to conjure up various interpretations and examine them in relation to other semantic flows or disjunctures in the text. If the expression were to occur within a poem, for example, comparison could be made with surrounding expressions or lines.

A similar example of substituting terms in a fixed metaphor is *kumo no nadare* (avalanche of clouds), in which the expected word *yuki* (snow) is replaced by *kumo* (clouds).[29] A formation of puffy clouds rolling across the sky can seem like an avalanche of snow. (Curiously, Katue never used the word "snow" in his over 500 poems—which is certainly unique among Japanese poets of any era.) The surreal image obtained by replacing part of a cliché, as in "avalanche of clouds," is perhaps the easiest and least satisfying technique, although it can occasionally yield felicitous results.

Personification.   The attributing of human qualities to non-humans is an ancient and well-worn poetic device. Personification in combination with other surrealist and abstract phrases deflects the reader from relating words mimetically to tangible objects in external reality. Katue used personification of objects and abstract notions in his prewar poetry in lines such as "when opening the car door / how many times have we seen / spring getting out on eternity's side?"[30] In *Kuroi hi*, we find further examples of personification:

winter / wettened by hope / walks the muddy city[31]

April / grows dark / in viridian / rain[32]

a star / sits down crying[33]

In other contexts that are more ambiguous than these examples, the reader may opt for personification as the easiest way to make sense of the relation between incongruent words.[34] Personification is one of several keys to Katue's poetry; as a conceptual tool, it functions to convert the impossible in nature to the possible in language. Katue also used similar transpositions within a number of categories for surreal effect, although these were usually not concerned with the human.

Inversion. A simple device with a complicated effect is inversion of the normal grammatical relationship of possessiveness between two nouns. Two examples from Katue's poetry are "shadow's egg"[35] and "death's turtle."[36] Whereas we can understand a "turtle's death" or an "egg's shadow," the reverse word order violates common logic and forces the reader to perceive strange new relationships.[37]

Inversion also occurs when a physically large object is conceptualized as being contained within a smaller one.

bed / inside / wet bull[38]

pantomime in a sugar cube[39]

Conversion of categories 1: substances made of unlikely materials. Before the war, Katue was already composing images of ordinary objects made of unlikely materials, such as the articles of clothing "tinplate cap" and "silver-paper necktie."[40] After the war, he also skillfully mismatched objects and materials for surreal effect. Three of his most frequently used substances were lead, glass, and bone:

lead flag; lead lily; lead sun[41]

glass flag; glass macaroni[42]

bone wings; bone/rose[43]

Conversion of categories 2: solids, liquids, and gases cross boundaries into one another. a. "glass wind."[44] The most potent surreal image with the word "glass" is "glass wind." Katue did more than substitute one solid for another (a glass flag instead of a cloth flag, or glass wings instead of feather wings); rather, he forced us to conceptualize a gas (wind/air) as a solid (glass). The transparency of the glass and the wind makes them seem compatible, and the reader converts a transparent, empty gas (wind) to a transparent, solid space (glass), much like imagining water at the instant it freezes into ice. Similarly, an image like "dripping lead car"—in which we imagine a liquid car—gains greater resonance than images relying only on shifts in material within the same physical state of liquid, solid, or gas.

b. "liqueur star."[45] We usually conceptualize stars in the sky as tiny, solid dots. To imagine a liquid star made, however, of liqueur is humorously surreal.

c. "while stuttering like rubber."[46] Katue describes invisible substances (voice, sound) in terms of the visible. The bounce and resiliency of rubber is cleverly linked to the repetitiveness of stuttering.

d. "a wad of sound."[47] The word *taba* (wad) is used only for objects tied in a bunch or bundle, such as straw, paper, keys, spinach, and flowers. To imagine sound as limited to a definite shape instead of in waves is an example of a surreal play with language that cannot be painted.

Katue's "surreal meta-image."[48]   Perhaps Katue's most intriguing contribution to literary surrealism is the "surreal meta-image," a combination of images generated by the juxtaposition of two or more incongruent nouns. From the two or more nouns, the reader imagines separate surreal images (A and B and C); these multiple images then stand juxtaposed to one another to produce a "surreal meta-image" (D). I use "meta" in the sense that the final, juxtaposed image is not generated directly by the initial two words but arrives only after the first two or more sets of images have presented themselves as possibilities based on the ambiguity in the initial words. The reader first perceives either image A, B, or C, and then the others come into focus as possibilities; only after two or more have been perceived individually can they stand in relation to each other, and thus give rise to the juxtaposed "surreal meta-image."

A typical example is *kūki no hako* (airbox), the title of Katue's 1966 book of poems, in which again we find at least three ways of interpreting the initial two nouns; the three images (A, B, C) in relation to one another then generate the meta-image (D):

kūki no hako[49]   *kūki* (noun) = air
no (particle) = 's/of
hako (noun) = box

Material	Literal Meaning	Image
A: air + box	airbox; box of air	a box with air inside (i.e., an empty box)[50]
B: " "	" " " "	a box [suspended] in air[51]
C: " "	" " " "	a box made of air (i.e., air in the shape of a box)[52]
D: images A + B + C		a box with air inside vs./+ a box [suspended] in air vs./+ a box made of air

A second example of a surreal meta-image generated by ambiguity is *hone no kago*.[53]

hone (noun) = bone(s)
no (particle) = 's/of
kago (noun) = cage (or basket)

Material	Literal Meaning	Image
A: cage + bone	cage of bone	a cage made of bone[54]
B: " "	a bone's cage	a cage within a bone[55]
C: " "	cage for bones	a cage for keeping bones[56]
D: images A + B + C		a cage made of bone vs./+ a cage inside a bone vs./+ a cage for keeping bones

There are additional multiple images that function in similarly ambiguous ways in Katue's postwar poetry, and they compactly catalyze the reader's attention in imaginative directions. These encounters with two nouns serve the contradictory purposes of blocking a singular interpretation of meaning by accenting ambivalence while simultaneously conjuring up individually clear images, three at a time in the examples given. The surreal meta-images provide an esthetically satisfying (or disturbing) balance of ambiguity and clarity.[57] In cases to be described below, ambiguity is also used to great effect, but the resultant imagery often becomes overcharged to the point of sensory overload, leading to a logic-jammed state of confusion, which is an altogether different "poetic" effect. The lucidity of the surreal meta-imagery gives way to an opacity that perhaps lacks the same esthetic poignancy but has the undeniable ability to sway readers into feeling semantically confounded.

A / that B / 's C. Half of the poems in *Kuroi hi* rattle the reading process from their opening stanzas. Whereas Lautréamont's image can be reduced to the formula A+B+C with A, B, and C as the unrelated words "umbrella," "sewing machine," and "operating table," Katue takes three equally unrelated objects but, instead of lining them up A+ B + C, he thrusts them into the semantically more unstable, "warped" relationship of "A/that B/'s C" (A/sono B/no C). The effect is more bizarre than would result from simply lining up unrelated words and connecting them with the conjunction "and."[58] Katue's objects B and C in the equation stand in a grammatically tense relationship, with the first dominating or containing the second, because the particle *no* acts as a possessive. Furthermore, with the use of *sono* (that), "A" is functionally linked to "B's C." These correspondences can be formulated as "A = B > C."

Katue used this odd grammatical construction at the beginning of several poems. The first word (a noun) is understood as meaningful; then, because of the word *sono*, we expect the noun following it to refer back to the first noun in a meaningful way; when it does not, we return, confused, to the word "that" and wonder "what?" Logic is blocked.

At times Katue presents two (or more) possessives consecutively, making the resulting mix even more opaque. Even in the opening stanzas of a handful of poems in *Kuroi hi*, we find abundant and quite varied examples of the formula:

> chair / that needle's top's / rainbow[59]
>
> star / that black melancholy / 's bone / 's rose[60]
>
> tragedy after tragedy / 's flow / that bone / 's shadow[61]
>
> dream / that / lead / 's lily[62]
>
> bone / that hopelessness / 's / sand / 's / doorknob[63]

The reader, at a loss to relate the three objects meaningfully, is further muddled by having to relate them in the ungrammatical way they are presented with *sono* and *no*. Michael Riffaterre, in suggesting new ways to interpret Western surrealist texts, takes up "ungrammaticalities," a problem equally pertinent to Katue's poetry: "[The reader's] linguistic competence enables him to perceive ungrammaticalities; but he is not free to bypass them, for it is precisely this perception over which the text's control is absolute. The ungrammaticalities stem from the physical fact that . . . the poetic verbal sequence is characterized by contradictions between a word's presuppositions and its entailments."[64] With Katue's use of "A/*sono* B/*no* C," the reader cannot ignore the presuppositions in the words *sono* and *no* that bind them in a relationship with the nouns they modify; yet no coherent meaning emerges from the relationship.

The word *sono* plays a key role in these poems. Katue's way of relating nouns tends to abstraction, but the specificity in "that"—pointing at the noun following it—builds tension by focusing attention on a single point (that + noun). This honing or tapering effect counteracts the opposite tendency toward mental expansion and dispersal of energy experienced when encountering illogical abstractions. Much of the underlying dynamism in the poems would be dissipated if *sono* did not perform its linguistic function of riveting the mind in specificity, in spite of the absurdity generated.

The plurisignation of the particle no *and "forced" relations between concrete and abstract words.* The analysis that follows focuses on the meaning of words to probe subtle shifts in how one can read a text. Naturally, the actual process of reading allows a more impressionistic, associational relation between words and images that develops in the manner of visual collage or cinematic montage.

Katue had made frequent use of the particle *no* between two nouns in his first book, *Shiro no arubamu* (1929). One poem was simply "ocean's ocean's ocean's . . . " with the graph for "ocean" appearing seventy times (Chapter 3).[65] In *Kuroi hi*, he varied the nouns interspersed between *no*. Occasionally Katue linked a series in this way, resulting in a high density of ambiguity. Technically, the word "ambiguity" implies an "either-or" relation, whereas in his case "plurisignation" is a more suitable term, because it implies a "both-and" relationship.[66]

No is primarily a possessive, and this appears to be its main function in *Kuroi hi*. The particle, however, has a much broader range of meaning than the English translations "'s" or "of" would indicate. Katue adroitly exploited the multiple possibilities of interpretation generated by *no* to thwart the reader's ability to decode the text. Paradoxically, the text's resistance to decoding is its main message.

According to Ōno Susumu's analysis of *no* in *Kogo jiten* (Dictionary of archaic words), the particle originally signified a "place of existence."[67] Thereafter its meaning widened to include "the events and products of a locality" and "the manufacturers or makers." As an extension of "place of existence," the usage also broadened to include "the one who possesses" (i.e., the possessive case). Ōno then makes a point relevant to the plurisignative manner in which Katue uses *no*: "To *possess* something and to be *an attribute of* something are opposite in terms of their power relationship [the former dominating the latter]; however, there are many examples from antiquity of 'confusion between the possessive and the attributive,' and *no* is found as the relational particle between nouns in both of these cases."[68] In other words, the possessive and the attributive often overlap.

In English a distinction is generally made between the possessive ("A's B"—e.g., "*fire's* cocoon" in which the fire is larger than the cocoon and contains it, and the attributive ("B of A"—e.g., "*cocoon of* fire" in which the cocoon is on fire but the fire is not larger than the cocoon itself).[69] The meanings, as we can see, overlap to some degree. In Japanese both the possessive and the attributive are written "A *no* B," and, the correct interpretation in a given situation can only be judged by context. Katue compounded this uncertainty by pairing two unrelated nouns, leaving the reader unable to distinguish whether the meaning is "A possesses B" or "B is an attribute of A" or both. For example, in the fragment *inmō / no yoru* ("pubic hair" + "night"), either the pubic hair is personified and "possesses" the night ("pubic hair / 's night")—which would be consonant with Katue's use of personification elsewhere—or the night is an attribute of pubic hair ("night of pubic hair").[70]

The degree of precision or imprecision generated by *no* is always determined by the context in which it appears. Below is a list of ways in which the formula "A *no* B" can be interpreted, with examples from *Kuroi hi*. Although by no means exhaustive, these are possible choices made by a reader who, confused by the plurisignative nature of the text, tries to decipher meaning from the seemingly unrelated words surrounding the particle *no*.

1. possessive—"A's B"
   ko no ha[71] (the tree's leaf)
2. attributive—"B of A"
   genei / no / kagami[72] (mirror of illusion)

3. genitive (adjectival)—"A [+ adj. suffix] B"
   yūshū no me[73] (melancholy eyes)
4. case particle—"A is B" (*no* replaces the particle *ga*)
   shi / no tsukisasaru / objet[74] (death piercing through the object)
5. simile—"B is like A" (A *no yō na* B)
   sumire no [yō ni] tareta namari / no kuruma[75] (lead car drooping like a violet)
6. for—"B for A" (A *no tame no* B)
   ningen no totte[76] (doorknob for humans)
7. made from—"B is made from A" (A *kara dekite iru* B)
   hone no tsubasa[77] (wings made of bone)
8. with—"B with A" (A *no aru* B)
   shima no aru kami[78] (god with stripes)

A translator, needing to choose from the above possibilities, cannot adequately convey the wealth of suggestiveness in the original. Based on the eight categories outlined above, the following list contains meanings generated by the relation between the two nouns "hopelessness" and "vodka." The phrase *zetsubō no uottoka* is taken from the opening of a poem in *Kuroi hi*.[79]

1. hopelessness's vodka
2. vodka of hopelessness
3. hopeless vodka
4. hopelessness is vodka
5. vodka like hopelessness
6. vodka for hopelessness
7. vodka made of hopelessness
8. vodka with hopelessness

I am, of course, not suggesting that every reader is likely to imagine each of these possibilities, but Katue's stubborn wringing of the language for opacity demands that the reader confront plurisignation. Internal logic builds meaning by selecting what makes more sense over less sense, but in the upside-down logic of Katue's *no* experiment in *Kuroi hi*, we are thrown into the paradoxical situation in which the brain's logical apparatus is continually tempted, against its inclinations, to side with those possibilities that present themselves as making *less* sense, because somehow they seem closer to the general drift of the poems.

Katue used two types of plurisignation. In the first type, explained above, the relation between any two nouns (e.g., *zetsubō no uottoka*) can be read in multiple ways; I call this "stationary plurisignation" to distinguish it from a second, even more complex type, "dynamic plurisignation," in which the point of linkage between nouns strung together with *no* (e.g., A *no* B *no* C *no* D . . .) is unclear, resulting in a multiplicity of possible readings.[80] For example, the most common way of reading this series of words would be as a string of possessives, "A's B's C's D," yet it is also equally conceivable to interpret the units of meaning in terms of other grammatical arrangements; for example, as dangling modifiers to be attached to nouns at some further point (as long as the progression is on the line from A toward D and not vice versa). In terms of mathematical probability, there are nine dynamically plurisignative ways of reading the relation between the following four nouns, even within the single stationary plurisignative category of the possessive (* indicates a complete phrase; [ ] indicates ellipted words in which meaning is suspended):

shi (A) *no kame* (B) *no yoru* (C) *no kyori* (D)[81]
death (A), turtle (B), night (C), distance (D)

A's B	death's turtle [ ]
B's C	[ ] turtle's night [ ]
C's D	[ ] night's distance
A's B's C	death's turtle's night [ ]
*A's B's C's D	death's turtle's night's distance
B's C's D	[ ] turtle's night's distance
A's C's D	death's [ ] night's distance
A's D	death's [ ] distance
B's D	[ ] turtle's [ ] distance

In coaxing sense from language, we absorb some words as meaningful immediately but defer understanding of others until later. In *Kuroi hi* there is continual suspension without final resolution. "Dynamic plurisignation," as opposed to "stationary plurisignation," is a time process in which the reader, barraged by potentialities from the text, tries to relate any pair or group of nouns meaningfully. The two means of plurisignifying are different, yet both result in the same transmission of *indeterminacy*.

The range of possible meanings on the vertical axis of "static plurisignation" and the possible meanings on the horizontal axis of "dynamic plurisignation" compound to evoke a rich web of potentialities. The translator is at a loss to determine which threads of meaning to follow. For example, the translation "death's turtle's night's distance" assumes that each *no* is used as a possessive, but if some relationships are interpreted as attributive rather than possessive, each of these three very different versions would be equally valid:

death's distance of the night of the turtle

death's turtle of the distance of night

distance of night of the turtle of death

More important than the accuracy of any given translation is the fact that the text does not present further clues to help us determine which of the riddles of meaning should be read as more valid than others. In the process of reading, we expect the phrase fragments to be clarified in further contexts, but no clues arrive to unravel the text. On the contrary, the contexts that follow present themselves as other problems to interpret in relation to the last and next, and so on. Poetry is then appreciated not for what can be drawn out in terms of specific meanings, but simply for the way in which the words create a crescendo of sharp, and yet half-formed, perceptions in the reader, while holding a condensed storehouse of alternative possibilities at each and every muddled turn.

In this and other ways, Katue molded the Japanese language into a new type of poetry. Before pondering the significance of "meaninglessness" in these poems, I briefly summarize a handful of other devices that are instrumental in creating the overall effect found in his postwar poetry.

Word order for effect. One of Katue's standard techniques is the use of word order to induce maximum surprise. Much of this is lost when a translator, for syntactical necessity, reverses the word order. In the following stanza, for example, Katue introduces fragile images only to bewilder the reader by having them explode violently:

yume no	dream's
chō	butterfly's
no haretsu	*burst*
kudakareta sara no ue	on top
ni	of smashed plates
nao yūen ni	still voluptuously
kaoru	fragrant
kuroi jukki[82]	black *firearm*

The reader imagines the abstraction "dream," followed by the fragile "butterfly" which suddenly "explodes." Had this fragment been translated not as a possessive but as an attributive, the reverse order would yield "*burst* / of butterfly / of dream," and the surprise effect would be diminished. Likewise, "black *firearm* / still voluptuously / fragrant" would lose the impact of the original in which the reader is kept unsure what is being modified by "voluptuous" and "fragrant" until encountering the word *jukki* (firearm). Reversing the word order would amount to telling the punch line midway through a joke. The examples could be multiplied but, suffice it to say, Katue's poetic effect is enhanced by his playing with word order to set up, decoy, and thwart the expectations of the reader. Katue partially explained his process of writing in terms that resemble the spinning of an imaginary, roulette wordwheel: "If 'red' comes out and I make it 'yellow,' that is a gamble. Anything will do, like 'sky' becoming 'ashtray' or 'tower,' yet that is also gambling."[83]

Writing the same word in two different scripts. By forcing the reader to see the same word presented in two different ways in adjacent lines, the vehicle of the language and the design of the text call attention to themselves. The closest parallel in English perhaps would be capital and lowercase letters, or different fonts.

> kimi no junsui / no ki wa *shitatari* [kanji and okurigana "*ri*"] / sono junsui no ko no ha wa *shitatari* [hiragana]
>
> kagami no naka / no kame / no tamago / no *haretsu* [kanji] / natsu no *haretsu* [hiragana]
>
> *garasu* [kanji] / no naka / no *garasu* [katakana][84]

Function versus meaning: connectives. Katue at times seemed to disregard the "inevitability"—or inherent kernel of meaning—in words like *sono* (that) and *no* (of) and pushed their relational function to the forefront. He frequently used the connectives *aruiwa* (or) and *soshite* (then). Here is an example with *aruiwa*:

> hopelessness's
> vodka's
> purple
> beard
>
> *or*

shadow's
egg
inside
cage
of
bones[85]

The context undercuts any coherent understanding of the terms on each side of *aruiwa*. "Or" could be replaced by "and," "then," or "but," yet the essential meaning of the images would be unaffected. The word "or" is necessary here only for its structural *balancing* of the stanzas before and after it. The function of "or" intrudes itself on the surface of the poem and invites itself to be questioned; this differs from its common usage in which it looms in the background of a sentence as the reader engages in following a logical narrative. By pointing to the word's function instead of allowing it to remain transparent, Katue prompted the reader to reflect on the mechanism by which thought, through language, assembles itself into patterns of meaning. By doing so, Katue stimulated the process called for by Breton and the French surrealists of using art and literature to reveal the "blueprint of thought."

The poems in *Kuroi hi* resist metaphorical interpretation, as do the "overcharged" images of *Mahiru no remon*, in which the individual lines are conceptually too far apart to relate meaningfully:

kinpatsu	blond hair
no bara no	's rose's
suna	sand
no sara	's plate
no	's
mata aruiwa[86]	or

In this fragment Katue used *no* as much to isolate words as to bring them into relation with one another. He could have achieved a similar effect with the particle *to* (and). Unable to visualize "blond hair's rose," "rose's sand," "sand's plate," and "plate's or," the nouns become read as if they were items on a list: "blond hair + rose + sand + plate." Even when the nouns on either side of *no* are read as possessives or as standing in some other relationship, they are conceptually so distant that associations are difficult to conjure up, and the words spring apart as self-contained entities. Katue's persistent inclination to give the particle *no* a full line was a radical departure from the practices of Japanese poetics up to that time.

Because Katue rejected the common usage of words in which connotations are limited by the denotative framework suggested by the context, his words become signifiers floating without signifieds. Since they do not denote anything outside themselves, they retain their full potential to connote. Words used in this abstract way revert to their intrinsic dictionary meanings. The blocking of a single line of meaning through the poem acts to release the individual words to mean indefinitely.

In spite of Katue's tampering with the relations between words and parts of speech, he still could not erase the kernel of meaning stubbornly residing at the core of each word. In introducing *no* and *sono* in ways that seem to counteract their functions, he was not obliterating meaning altogether; rather, he was stirring the reader to perceive new combinations of meaning amid the incoherent collisions of the old.

Sound. A crucial element in *Kuroi hi* is the rhythmic sound of the words, which act in conjunction with visual aspects such as the design of the book and the imagery in the poems. Even though Katue had pioneered the modern poetry reading in Japan, debuting on stage in 1935 and reappearing in 1936, he never joined the trend of public poetry readings after the war. He adamantly disapproved of other people's versions of his poems, whether put to music or sung.

My poems are often put to music, but I can't stand them. The pitch and stress of the words in the lines of my poems are measured. People who put the poems to music or sing them approach the material with a different concept; so they accent the words differently and clash with what I was trying to do when I wrote them. That is why I don't like my poems to be read to music or sung. Once you put them to music, you have to rethink the line divisions.[87]

The words in *Kuroi hi* are musical, because of the repetition of *no, sono,* and other sounds. For instance, in the following seven-line fragment from "Shiroi retorikku" (White rhetoric), a poem in *Mahiru no remon* (1954), several sounds are repeated:

garasu teki	glass-like
no hige	beard
to	and
higeki	tragedy
no	's

hata	flag
to[88]	and

The first two lines have the sequence "ki-no-hi-ge" and the fourth and fifth lines "hi-ge-ki-no"; the vowels sequence is a-a-u-e-i-o-i-e in the first stanza and o-i-e-i-o-a-a-o in the second; the first sequence moves from back vowels to front vowels and end with the tongue forward and high in the mouth; the second sequence ends with back vowels, with the tongue low and relaxed.

No closure. A reader who is blocked from the start of the poem from pulling the myriad of perceptions into a consistent whole may anticipate that the ending will offer resolution by casting a new light on what has come before. The ending, however, as we would expect from Katue's approach, is just as unrelated to the rest of the poem as the beginning or middle. To state the matter boldly, any stanza in *Kuroi hi* could be switched around within the same poem with little difference in effect (except, of course, in the crucial order of the imagery). The abstraction ends where it started—carving out a chaotic space filled with fragments of objects from everyday life.

Major subtractions: people, verbs, and bright colors. One of Katue's techniques in *Kuroi hi* is to reduce or eliminate those elements a reader might expect to find in a poem, for example, verbs, bright colors, and human beings. Only in the fourth poem, already one-third through the book, do we first encounter *boku* (I). Humans are usually alluded to as body parts—*kubi* (head or neck), *inmō* (pubic hair), *ago* (jaw), and *mabuta* (eyelids). When the body is whole, it is a *gūzō* (statue/idol) or a *tokeru toruso* (melting torso). Humans in *Kuroi hi* and elsewhere are objectified as visual perceptions (colors and shapes) and appear as equally inconsequential as non-human entities. This denial of the special position of human beings serves as an indirect criticism of societal values.

Further shredding the tapestry of meaning. After *Kuroi hi* and *Mahiru no remon*, Katue's next refinement of surrealism, abstraction, and minimalism was exhibited in *Garasu no kuchihige* (Glass mustache; 1956).[89] In the postwar period, Katue first published his poems in *VOU* and other little magazines; when he had collected enough high-quality poems growing out of a particular experiment, he would issue them in a book. The poems in *Garasu no kuchihige* were first published between April 1954 and August 1956, and they are similar in form to those in *Kuroi hi*—short lines, few verbs, geometric imagery, as well as use of the particle *no* for sound, plurisignation, and design. Yet there are also subtle differences in content, such as an emphasis on depicting imprecise, momentary appearances and disappearances. Also, "dilution" becomes a key word and concept for expressing phenomena at the flickering edge of consciousness. The title of one poem in *Garasu no kuchihige* best sums up this view, "An Extremely Clear, but Unknown, Object." Whereas Katue had made frequent use of *aruiwa* in *Kuroi hi* to juxtapose static images, here he favored the conjunctions *soshite* (then), *sore kara* (and then) and *mata* (again), all of which propel the action forward in time without the addition of verbs.

Having pursued the surreal possibility of placing everyday objects in disconcerting contexts (which Katue continued to do in *Garasu no kuchihige*), he now seemed bent on describing the impossibility of description. In other words, he conjured up perceptions only to doubt and then erase them. One technique for doing this was to make the grammatical subject indefinite, for example, *nanika* (something) and *sore* (that). In *Kuroi hi* Katue had written "shadow's egg," reversing the ordinary perception of the relationship; in *Garasu no kuchihige*, as part of the general dilution, the object has been stripped away and the "shadow" alone now takes center stage, ironically becoming the object.

> some shadowlike thing continually crossed space
> that shadow
> and
> within shadows
> something exceedingly green
> and or there was purple[90]

In the first line a mysterious, "shadowlike thing" is noted as having crossed space. Where is the protagonist? He seems to be in space or in an omnipresent, indefinite place (the void). The word "shadow" (*kage*) is mentioned three times: "shadowlike," "that shadow," and "within shadows."[91] At first the shadow is expressed vaguely, but by the third appearance the shadow has been penetrated. The range from incertitude to atomization in a few lines reflects the shimmering state of the protagonist's mind as it traverses the same space that he has seen being crossed by the "shadowlike thing." The hesitance of "and or . . . purple" adds a choppiness, undermining the unnamed protagonist's ability to decipher clearly. When compounded with the three shadows, it creates an intriguing yet confusing atmosphere. With a dozen or so words the reader is drawn into a science-fiction setting.

Although the structure of the poems in *Garasu no kuchihige* is built line by line, in certain stanzas the content works simultaneously to undermine and destroy, giving the poem a brittle tension. After the erasure, all that remains are references to absence, a pointing at nothingness. This technique is already familiar from the opening stanza of "Kihaku na tenkai" (A diluted development) quoted above. Below are the opening stanzas to four poems from *Garasu no kuchihige*; within each we can notice the process of erasure, as Katue named only to take away.

> once
> there
> like in the cylinder
> of the torn
> wind
> it wasn't[92]
>
> those
> convulsively had disappeared
> then
> within
> a distant perspective
> something slightly scattered
> there was an extremely
> dark landscape[93]
>
> that
> had a shape like wind
> in a dot[94]
>
> then
> and then
> stone had suddenly vanished[95]

In *Garasu no kuchihige* a dialectic is carried on between the surreal and the invisible. Whereas poems such as "Kuroi shōzō" in *Kuroi hi* are bursting with plurisignation, the thrust in *Garasu no kuchihige* is in the opposite direction—the inability to mean at all. This is particularly effective, albeit annoying, in the communication breakdown in the poem "Méssiaen Tobacco," quoted in full below.

Méssiaen Tobacco

I

it rapidly
was
torn

in
that infinity
brittle
wall
's

is called
wind
's
green

water
's
orthodoxy
's

is
called crystal
's
circle

like
an extreme
-ly
black shell

is
called
a solid
's
hard vision
's
and
right angle
's

is
called sand

's
stripe

   2

's

it
rapidly
yellow

like
surface
's
inside
's
glass
's
shadow

and
elbow
's
fragment

about
it
intense
-ly

something
's
paper
's

and

   3

blue trigonometry
's
head

and

right angle
's
noon
's[96]

Katue retained the format he had used in *Kuroi hi*; the poems occupy the top of the page with a blank area below, but now the blankness extends into the meaning. By beginning and ending stanzas with *no* ('s), Katue challenges the reader to fill in the gaps. Whereas in *Kuroi hi* meaning had been overcharged and the context provided few clues to assay the plausibility of an interpretation (whether, for example, *no* was possessive or attributive), here we grope for even fragments of meaning while being led on a series of minuscule detours, with *no* at times forced to mean what it cannot, turning itself into a caricature of itself, a particle warped into a noun.[97]

Ironically, Katue's experiment with incoherence in *Garasu no kuchihige* is rich in philosophical overtones. His "vanishing poetry" is a world set in motion only to remind us of its imminent disappearance. Appearance and disappearance—both mysterious moments—in this poetry become questions posited at existence. By publishing *Garasu no kuchihige* as one volume, Katue was also signaling that he had reached a dead end with this line of experimentation and was ready to switch gears in a new direction.

Donald Keene has written of Katue, "His poems, whether of the 1930s or the 1950s, are abstract, often consisting of a series of images, one to each short line, carefully disposed but providing no single thread of meaning."[98] By presenting words that yield possibilities but no definite "thread of meaning," as well as imagery whose visualization strains the imagination, the poems in *Kuroi hi* and elsewhere prod the reader to consider how words combine to form meaning. Consequently, unlike the case with realistic poetry, the processes of writing and reading become fundamentally more important than the finished product. The experiment here is at an extreme of poetry, and the reader is forced also to ponder the nature of poetry and the limits of abstract poetic expression.

Katue's highly individualistic work was a step ahead of the literary mainstream in Japan but converged with the general trend of twentieth-century experimental poetry in Europe and the Americas. Roland Barthes's concept of "writing degree zero" is relevant to Katue's use of words in his postwar abstract poetry.[99]

Fixed connections being abolished, the word [in modern poetry] is left only with a vertical project, it is like a monolith, or a pillar which plunges into a totality of meanings, reflexes and recollections: it is a sign which stands. The poetic word is here an act without immediate past, without environment, and which holds forth only the dense shadow of reflexes from all sources which are associated with it. Thus under each Word in modern poetry there lies a sort of existential geology, in which is gathered the total content of the Name, instead of a chosen content as in classical poetry and prose. The Word is no longer guided *in advance* by the general intention of a socialized discourse; the consumer of poetry, deprived of the guide of selective connections, encounters the Word frontally, and receives it as an absolute quantity, accompanied by all its possible associations. The Word, here, is encyclopaedic, it contains simultaneously all the acceptions from which a relational discourse might have required it to choose. It therefore achieves a state which is possible only in the dictionary or in poetry—places where the noun can live without its article—and is reduced to a sort of zero degree, pregnant with all past and future specifications. The word here has a generic form; it is a category. Each poetic word is thus an unexpected object, a Pandora's box from which fly out all the potentialities of language; it is therefore produced and consumed with a peculiar curiosity, a kind of sacred relish.[100]

Katue had already made breakthroughs in Japanese avant-garde poetry in the mid-1920s with a fresh vocabulary, a formalistic arrangement of words, and, most important, an impassioned disregard for conventional ways of meaning. Twenty-five years later, with his abstract experiments, he extended and refined his sense of meta-meaning into a strategy with the various technical devices mentioned above. One reason that Barthes could be describing a poem from *Kuroi hi* is that Katue consistently avoided using words metaphorically, taking the same attitude that John Cage described in *Silence*, "I'd never been interested in symbolism. . . . I preferred just taking things in themselves, not as standing for other things."[101]

Although Katue avoided metaphor, his imagery is not completely random. He chose words not only for their sound and visual appeal but from a limited pool of words whose meanings evoke black and white, or dark colors, and geometric shapes. By aligning words that seemingly have no connection but share a recognizable visual line of contiguity (e.g., the limited field of colorless, geometric shapes), Katue was able to build a strong surface tension; that would have been forfeited had there been no organizing principle whatsoever.[102]

For example, rather than reading the concrete imagery in the poem "Kuroi shōzō" as mere discontinuity—which is a strong tendency, especially when it is read against the bulk of modern Japanese poetry—the poem's eerie effect is perhaps better understood as the result of a "metonymic network" in which words essentially stand for themselves within a prescribed range of black and white, geometric imagery.

purple	dark
beard	triangular; or the alternative reading, "mustache"—rectangular
bone	white; rectangular
basket	round
shade	dark
egg	oval; white or brown
turtle	dark; round shell
night	dark; shapeless
black rain	round dark drops
ladder shape	rectangular frame with parallel and perpendicular lines
wall	flat, rectangular
cone	conical
part	unspecified

By limiting his imagery in this way, Katue was intuitively able to give a sense of underlying unity, however tenuous and unconventionally formed, which would have been dispersed if he had added verb-propelled movement or bright colors. Curiously, his word choices are not as random as they may at first appear to be. For example, the titles of poems in *Kuroi hi* are also composed primarily, but not exclusively, of words that evoke dark, geometric shapes:

dark room
poem of death and umbrella
autumn's solid
monotonous solid
black rain
dark april
black mirror
black portrait
a une dame
black distance
night elements
ou une solitude

The titles are practically interchangeable in one respect: they are unre-
lated to the content of the poems. Yet they share the same field of contiguity
as "Kuroi shōzō," namely, *black* (rain, mirror, portrait, distance), *dark* (room,
april, umbrella, night) and *geometric* (room—cubic, umbrella—cylindrical,
rain—circular, portrait—rectangular, mirror—rectangular).

Marjorie Perloff in *The Poetics of Indeterminacy* contrasts T. S. Eliot's "high
modernism," which she finds has "a perfectly coherent symbolic structure,"
with the "enigma texts" of John Ashbery's "post-modernism."[103] She quotes
Ashbery's "Lacustrine Cities," and then analyzes it in a manner applicable to
much of Katue's postwar poetry.

1) [There is] no external referent.

2) The poem blocks all attempts to rationalize its imagery, to make it conform to
a coherent pattern. Fragmented images appear one by one . . . without coalescing
into a symbolic network.

3) There seems to be no whole to which these parts may be said to belong. To-
tality is absent.

4) Connectives . . . create expectations of causality, of relatedness that the narra-
tive never fulfills.

5) Disclosure of some special meaning seems perpetually imminent. . . . As read-
ers, we are thus left in a state of expectancy: just at the point where revelation might
occur, the curtain suddenly comes down.

6) Arresting but unanchored image[s], whose evocations are indeterminate.[104]

Perloff traces the "poetics of indeterminacy" from Arthur Rimbaud to
John Cage and includes Gertrude Stein, Ezra Pound, and William Carlos
Williams among its practitioners. She concludes that indeterminacy is the
hallmark of the anti-symbolist, "other tradition": In the poetry of this 'other
tradition,' ambiguity and complexity give way to inherent contradiction and
'undecidability,' metaphor and symbol to metonymy and synecdoche, the
well-wrought urn to 'an open field of possibilities,' and the coherent struc-
ture of images to 'mysteries of construction' and free play."[105] Perloff avoids
the argument of where to draw the line between the moderns and postmod-
erns, but if John Ashbery's extreme indeterminacy is a sign of his postmod-
ernism, as she seems to suggest, then perhaps the plurisignative abstraction
in *Kuroi hi* and elsewhere is similarly indicative of Katue's postmodernism.[106]

Michael Riffaterre, in *Semiotics of Poetry*, provides insights relevant to
much of Katue's postwar poetry. Riffaterre notes in his observations of
French surrealist poetry that there are two levels or stages in reading a work,

the *mimetic* (i.e., literary representation of reality), in which "meaning" is grasped in units of words, phrases, or sentences; and the *semiotic*, in which the text is read as a single semantic unit, which he calls "signification." This distinction between meaning and signification provides one way to interpret *Kuroi hi*; for the term *ungrammaticalities*, we need only recall Katue's use of *no* for plurisignation, the unconventional usage of *sono*, and the unrelatedness of images. The semiotic mechanism, according to Riffaterre, functions in the following manner:

The ungrammaticalities spotted at the mimetic level are eventually integrated into another system. As the reader perceives what they have in common, as he becomes aware that this common trait forms them into a paradigm, and that this paradigm alters the meaning of the poem, the new function of the ungrammaticalities changes their nature, and now they signify as components of a different network of relationships. This transfer of a sign from one level of discourse to another, this metamorphosis of what was a signifying complex at a lower level of the text into a signifying unit, now a member of a more developed system, at a higher level of the text, this functional shift is the proper domain of semiotics. . . .

The reader's acceptance of the mimesis sets up the grammar as the background from which the ungrammaticalities will thrust themselves forward as stumbling blocks, to be understood eventually on a second level. I cannot emphasize strongly enough that the obstacle that threatens meaning when seen in isolation at first reading is also the guideline to semiosis, the key to significance in the higher system, where the reader perceives it as part of a complex network.[107]

Seen in this light, Katue's plurisignation is not a by-product of the way he combined words, but the text's chief semiotic message of indeterminacy. The text is ultimately a discourse about itself, about language. In the words of David Lodge, such indeterminacy leads to "the creation of labyrinths that have no exit."[108]

Riffaterre further explains the mechanism:

The poem is a form totally empty of "message" in the usual sense, that is, without content—emotional, moral, or philosophical. At this point the poem is a construct that does nothing more than experiment, as it were, with the grammar of the text, or, perhaps a better image, a construct that is nothing more than a calisthenics of words, a verbal setting-up exercise. The mimesis is now quite spurious and illusory, realized only for the sake of the semiosis; and conversely, the semiosis is a reference to the word nothing.

This is an extreme case but exemplary, for it may tell us much about poetry's being more of a game than anything else.

The cancellation of mimetic features leads to a pointless semiosis . . . but of course the significance really lies in the gratuitousness of the transformation: it exemplifies that process itself, the artifact per se.[109]

These analyses of Western avant-garde poetry by Barthes, Perloff, and Riffaterre provide useful viewpoints for assessing texts such as *Kuroi hi*, which until now have been treated as impervious to interpretation of any sort. Their approaches are certainly not the last words on the subject, but they are reliable first steps to counter Itō Shinkichi's assertion that "we cannot hope for any better explanation in the future."

Are Katue's experiments with fragmenting language a political statement, a subversion of societal values, an anarchic kick at language? Or, is the seemingly impersonal poetry really a disguised confession of the torn insides of the poet who had survived the brutal war? Critic Suzuki Masafumi (1947–) takes this approach: "After Katue's self-betrayal during the war, he was spiritually shattered. The fragmentation in his poetry, first evident in *Kuroi hi*, is the linguistic mirror of his minced innards. It was the most honest and direct way for him to express his loathing of mankind in general and of himself in particular."[110]

Katue's experiments are a complex product of the times and his psyche, and the poems of this period are ultimately unfathomable. What we can say is that the same abstraction in his poems that invites a wide range of interpretations also refutes any one interpretation as definitive. His poems show a determination to break down phrases into words and recombine them in new ways, sometimes only in syllables. By shredding the tapestry of meaning, Katue was able to satisfy readers who can discover poetry within linguistic chaos.

8 MUTATION

of the

IDEOGRAM

Kitasono Katue died of lung cancer—he had been a chain smoker much of his adult life—on June 6, 1978, at the age of 75, after having been hospitalized for two months. In homage to Katue, the members of the VOU Club (which disbanded shortly after Katue's death) compiled *Kitasono Katue and VOU* (1988).[1] The book contains a section of letters and short articles by several of Katue's literary friends from Europe and the Americas that provides a vivid picture of his reputation among the international avant-garde. James Laughlin, poet and publisher of New Directions books, wrote:

For forty years or more, Kitasono Katue was a most valuable link between the literary cultures of Japan and the United States. The magazine "Vou" was, to my knowledge, the only one which made a systematic effort over the years to present Western avant garde culture to Japan. And his contribution to the dissemination of visual poetry was especially great. He was a man of high taste and sensibility.[2]

Eugen Gomringer, one of the founders and chief theorists of the international "concrete poetry" (J: *gutaishi*) movement, contributed a heartfelt message to *Kitasono Katue and VOU*:

as i have in this moment no better word or poetical expression in honour to our dead friend, and in honour to all those who continue in his spirit, i wanted to say how much all concret poets (digne de ce nom!) are owing to kitasono katue. we were always very proud to have a brother like him in japan and i remember quite well the surprise when i first saw one of his poems printed in brasil (by the help of the noigandres friends), because this was just the same spirit we felt in writing our own concret poetry. i think that the memory for kitasono katue will help all of us to never forget what concret poetry really wanted to be, how pure, simple and rich all in one it can be. he was- he is a great concret poet = a great poet.[3]

Concrete poetry is a type of verse in which words (or parts of words) are manipulated visually through the use of typography, color, or line arrangement to augment the intellectual and emotional content for esthetic effect. The concept was to take poetry from the confines of the book and display it as art. Variously referred to as "imaged," "shaped," "cubist," or "pattern poetry," concretism emphasizes spatial design over conventionally printed poetry. In the 1950s concrete poetry became an international movement with considerable impact on semiotics, design, painting, and photography.[4]

Kenneth Rexroth, in his contribution to the festschrift, succinctly concludes, "Katue was, for many years, the only Japanese poet known to the international literary community."[5] Rexroth does not pinpoint which years Katue was Japan's sole literary ambassador, but we can imagine that he meant the four decades from 1938 until his death. Echoing Laughlin, Rexroth alludes to Katue's dual role as importer and exporter of avant-garde poetry.

He was certainly the poet who did most to introduce modern poetry—"the international idiom"—to Japan, in superlative translations. . . . Not only that, but he was open to [Japanese] writing of what was then the youngest, post Pacific War, generation which was often very unlike his own. . . . Furthermore, he was himself an excellent poet—a true leader and exemplar. Not least, his "concrete" poem, ringing the changes on "white" in several languages, is the best thing of its kind anywhere.[6]

Katue simultaneously occupied two positions in the West: first, as representative of avant-garde Japanese poetry in general and, second, as a fellow participant ("brother") in the international avant-garde, a loose network with less definable boundaries than those of the VOU Club, but analogous in that poets found camaraderie in confronting the same theoretical issues, influencing one another's work, and being published together in journals worldwide.[7] Since the remarks of Laughlin, Gomringer, and Rexroth were made to commemorate Katue, their friend, after his death, we can expect them to be laudatory. Nevertheless, they give a good idea of how his peers perceived him.

Besides Ezra Pound and the three Western poets quoted above, Katue corresponded with Henry Miller, Kenneth Patchen, Charles Olson, and Robert Creeley, all of whom were part of the New Directions network. Katue also exchanged books with Tristan Tzara and André Breton in Paris and sent *VOU* to a number of literati around the globe. As a consequence of his ever-expanding literary connections, Katue's drawings and poetry (in English translation) gradually gained wide exposure.

Because of Pound's generous introduction in 1938 (see Chapter 5), Katue was already known in the West and considered a part of the *Western* avant-garde literati, although in retrospect his role was more marginal than central. Between 1939 and 1958, no other avant-garde Japanese poet was part of the Western scene. Among North American poets, including Allen Ginsberg and the Beats, familiarity with Kitasono Katue and *VOU* magazine was regarded as a sign that one was cosmopolitan. After 1958, the year Katue's concrete poem "Tanchō na kūkan" (Monotonous space)—mentioned by Gomringer and Rexroth—was first published outside Japan, he rose from being someone who was merely recognized to become a central figure in the emerging movement.

The concretists were usually designers as well as poets, and many gained instant international fame as the new genre became fashionable. Katue was an exception among the concretists in already having a solid reputation as a poet in his own country before becoming a leader in the international movement.[8] His work gained prominence because of his artistic ability and his literary connections, as well as fortuitous timing. Katue's reputation was established largely on the strength of "Monotonous Space." In the words of Haroldo de Campos, one of the founders of the movement, "This was the first concrete Japoem and the bridge for the movement in that country."[9] It was also Katue's only "official" concrete poem, although he later wrote similar poems that he labeled "optical poetry."

There is no need here to supply proof of Katue's well-attested stature, or document step by step his publishing record in attaining it. Suffice it to say that he came to occupy as prominent a position in the international avant-garde movement (in which no one was aware of the patriotic poetry he had written during the war) as he held at home, where a new generation of poets inside and outside VOU was also taking the initiative in defining postwar poetry.[10] Katue's newfound international fame provided him a cozy buffer against any real or perceived isolation at home.

Following the publication of "Monotonous Space," whenever Katue was requested to submit a concrete poem for a Western publication, he refused to send word poems.[11] Instead, he sent photographs, which he called "plastic poems" and which are now more commonly referred to as "visual poetry." His plastic poems, published in a dozen countries from his 1966 manifesto on the subject until his death in 1978, consist of photographs of newspaper cutouts and other assembled objects.

In this chapter I introduce Katue's passport to international success—"Monotonous Space" (see Fig. 23)—analyze its content, and explain its function in the Western movement. Then I discuss the form and content of his plastic poetry, and the poetics supporting it.

Monotonous Space

1

white square
within it
white square
within it
black square
within it
black square
within it
yellow square
within it
yellow square
within it
white square
within it
white square

2

white
within it
white
within it
black
within it
black
within it
yellow
within it
yellow
within it
white
within it
white

3

blue
triangular
mustache
's glass

white
triangular
horse
's umbrella

black
triangular
tobacco
's building

yellow
triangular
star
's handkerchief

4

white square
within it
white square
within it
white square
within it
white square
within it
white square[12]

The dynamics of "Monotonous Space" suggest some of the conceptual riches lurking beneath its concrete surface. The poem is fundamentally a perception game in which the reader visualizes a series of images, some of which are not present in the text but generated from the interaction of given images. Structurally, the poem's division into four parts reinforces the dominant image of the square (four-sided). Each section consists of a few key images: eight in Parts 1 and 2, five in Part 4, and four categories of images in Part 3. There are no verbs, yet there is the semblance of movement in space. From the beginning to the end of the poem, with each successive color,

北 園 克 衛

1

白い四角
のなか
の白い四角
のなか
の黒い四角
のなか
の黒い四角
のなか
の黄いろい四角
のなか
の黄いろい四角
のなか
の白い四角
のなか
の白い四角．

2

白
の中の白
の中の黒
の中の黒
の中の黄
の中の黄
の中の白
の中の白

青
の三角
の艶
の
ガラス

白
の三角
の馬
の
パラソル

黒
の三角
の煙草
の
ビルディング

黄
の三角
の星
の
ハンカチィフ

4

白い四角
のなか
の白い四角
のなか
の白い四角
のなか
の白い四角
のなか
の白い四角

Fig. 23　Katue's concrete poem "Monotonous Space,"
first printed in VOU, no. 53 (Dec. 1958).

shape, or object, perception simultaneously increases and tapers: increases in that a new element is being introduced, and tapers in that the new element is always located *within* the already given, composite picture. Much of the esthetic effect is generated by the one-directional tapering of perception.

In Part 1 the reader is presented with a series of repeated images: enclosed within one square is another square and, within that, yet another square, and so on for a total of eight squares.[13] The color of each square is repeated once, starting the following chain of perceptions: first, a single white square is envisioned; next, a separate, smaller white square is imagined inside the first white square; then, because the color of both squares is the same, the smaller square dissolves within the larger one. The dissolving action evokes a meta-image (an image not directly in the text but created in the reader's mind by the interaction of the two given, static images), paralleling Katue's surreal meta-image (see Chapter 7). Next, a black square is enclosed inside the white square, breaking the movement of the previous dissolution, and causing a composite image to be perceived again as static. Then, a smaller black square within the first black square repeats the dissolution scenario, until once again stasis is reintroduced with an enclosed yellow square, and so forth. Part 1 ostensibly presents eight squares, but four squares are "erased" along the way. Despite the surface simplicity and repetition, a subtle and complex undercurrent alternates stasis and movement, continuity and discontinuity. The poet resembles a magician with eight boxes of decreasing sizes who performs a trick in which half of the boxes mysteriously vanish into thin air.

In Part 1, the repeating pattern and the symmetrical arrangement of the words on the page create another illusion: the reader invariably imagines each new square placed symmetrically within the preceding squares, although the words do not preclude other configurations, such as one square placed diagonally or otherwise askew within the preceding larger square. The act of cognition is uncannily ordered by the layout of the words on the page, and the poem draws attention to this psychological shaping process.

The opening image, "white square," can also be interpreted as a blank screen before a reader awaiting visual stimulation or, alternatively, as pure space or nothingness. The "white square" thus serves to focus the reader's attention on a neutral or zero starting point. The blank image thus evoked acts as a transparent bridge between the reader's state of mind before arriving at the poem and the succeeding parts of the poem. Analogous to the in-

2

Fig. 24   Part 2 of Katue's "Monotonous Space," in Katue's book of poems *Kemuri no chokusen*
(Kokubunsha, 1959). The layout alters the concrete space.

troductory process in an initiation rite, the invocation of the white square
draws the reader into liminal space.

Part 2 is physically the most concrete section of the poem. The graph
shiro (white) stands apart, and then three of the four columns contain a sin-
gle graph iterated seven times. The bottom row breaks the symmetry by pre-
senting graphs for three different colors (see Fig. 24). Part 2 repeats the
imagined enclosing action of Part 1 with the same duplication of colors in the
same order, but the omission of the word "square" releases the colors from a
geometrical framework. The reader is challenged to imagine a color within
another color that has no designated shape. Here the symmetrical arrange-
ment of the words on the page conflicts with the asymmetrical invitation
posed by the lack of stated shape. If the reader, conditioned by Part 1, pic-
tures the colors as square-shaped, the perception is extra-textual, having
been framed by memory. The reduction of stimuli enacted by the square's
absence in Part 2 accentuates in a new way the general, inward tapering of
perception throughout the poem. Parts 1 and 2 together function as a kind of
warm-up exercise to distract readers from whatever they were thinking
about before approaching the poem and to slow down their rate of percep-
tion by focusing attention on a few, simple stimuli. The umbilical cord to
everyday life is severed, leaving the reader open to conceptual leaps. Resem-
bling the technique of slow-motion dancing used to elongate an audience's
sense of time so that later, only slightly quicker, movements appear ex-
tremely rapid, the poem also experiments with relativity and distortion.

Part 3 of "Monotonous Space" contrasts sharply with Parts 1, 2, and 4 in
both form and content. The layout, although of an esthetically pleasing de-
sign, is not conspicuously concrete or shaped to the extent of the other parts;
also, the content consists of four separate images (not one composite image),

each of which consists of two recognizable "objects." The abrupt shift from shapes and colors to concrete objects makes the previous minimalism seem an introductory foil. There is continuity in the presentation of colors and a repeated geometric shape, but discontinuity in the appearance of a new color (blue), a new shape (triangle), and pairs of objects joined in inverted, illogical relationships.

In Part 3 Katue uses the particle *no* in the dynamically plurisignative way analyzed in Chapter 7. The iteration of *no* after each word leaves the reader unsure where to cut the series of modifiers. For example, in the second stanza, "white / *no* triangle / *no* horse / *no* parasol," the reader is left to wonder if the adjective "white" modifies "triangle," "horse," "parasol," or all three or, indeed, any combination of two of these three. Likewise, "triangle" could modify "horse" and/or "parasol." Compounding the ambiguity, the word for triangle followed by *no* (*sankaku no*) can be read separately as "triangle + 's" ("triangle's" or "of triangle"), or in combination as the adjective "triangular." Naturally, there are a variety of ways to translate the stanza, depending on how it is interpreted.[14] The four images in Part 3 are more complex than the scarcity of graphs and simple layout would suggest.

The order of the four parts of the poem maximizes the esthetic impact. If the order of Parts 1 and 3 had been reversed, for example, a great deal of the intensity of Part 3 would have been dissipated. Each pair of objects in Part 3 seems magnified precisely because of the disorienting buildup of Parts 1 and 2. Katue set up the reader to expect further subtraction in Part 3, but then suddenly broke the pattern with a flurry of imagistic addition of pairs of whole objects.

Part 4 repeats the square within square motif of Part 1, except here we have only one color ("white") and five squares (not eight). The five white squares are perceived individually, and then they merge, one by one, into the first white square, duplicating the stasis–movement alternation of Part 1. The poem opens with a white square in Part 1 and closes with a white square in Part 4, suggesting that the two squares are one and the same. The reader has taken a perceptual journey and experienced a number of subtle shifts along the way, before returning in a circular (or square?) route to the same blank screen or "white square." To revert to the metaphor of an initiation rite, we can see that Parts 1 and 2 introduce the reader to liminal space, Part 3 enacts the drama of a new kind of knowledge (in which objects are seen as if for the first time), and Part 4 reintegrates the reader to the outside world by delivering him back to the starting point.

"Monotonous Space" blends two of Katue's previous styles: Parts 1, 2, and 4 coming from his late 1920s experimentation with formalistic repetition of graphs (Chapter 3), and Part 3 deriving from his postwar experimentation with the plurisignative possibilities of *no* (Chapter 7). The blend seemed to fit what people were searching for in the concrete movement.

"Monotonous Space" was originally written in response to a request by Haroldo de Campos of the Noigandres group in São Paulo, who recalls:

In 1956—one year after Décio Pignatari's historical meeting with Eugen Gomringer at Ulm, Germany—the year when "concrete poetry" was launched as an international movement by both Gomringer and Brazilian "Noigandres" group, I started to study Japanese, in order to have a better understanding of the Kanji way of writing. I was also interested in establishing some contacts with Japanese *avant-garde* poets, having read a selection of poems by Kitasono Katue in New Directions magazine n. 4, 1953. Later on, in 1957, having in mind Ezra Pound's words in *Guide to Kulchur* concerning Kitasono's "ideoplasty" and having obtained *Vou* Club's address, I wrote to Kitasono with the purpose of introducing to him our new concrete poetry. . . .

Living in Japan for several years, since 1958, the Brazilian composer and poet L. C. Vinholes became a natural and very effective connexion between Brazilian and Japanese poetic activities in that field. Vinholes started the interchange by organizing an exhibition of "Brazilian Concrete poetry" at the National Museum of Modern Art, Kyobashi, Tokyo, 1960. We had the honour, at this occasion, of being introduced to the Japanese readers by Kitasono Katue, whose prefatory text was displayed during the exhibition along with our own "pilot plan for concrete poetry."[15]

L. C. Vinholes claimed that "the reason we contacted Katue was not because we considered his previous poetry 'concrete,' but simply because we regarded him as the best poet in Japan, the one most likely to understand what we were trying to do."[16]

In 1975 Katue recalled how he had come to be involved in the movement: "The people who pulled me into concrete poetry were the South American Campos brothers [Haroldo and Augusto]. I didn't plan it, but at some point I just slipped in smoothly. . . . They always sent me their publications and seemed quite active. Ezra Pound introduced us. He suggested that Campos and I correspond."[17]

To elucidate the significance of Katue and his concrete poem for the movement, I will briefly introduce the Noigandres and their "Pilot Plan for Concrete Poetry" (1958).[18] The Brazilian group took its name from Ezra Pound's Canto XX, no doubt as a nod of respect to the aged poet.[19] Its members were the de Campos brothers and Décio Pignatari, poets and theorists in their late twenties.[20] They traced the origin of concretism to Stéphane Mallarmé's poem "Un Coup de dès n'abolira jamais le hasard" (A throw of the dice will never abolish chance; 1897) in which the title, the layout of the words in various font sizes, and the poem's content all blend to appeal to the eye, ear, and intellect.[21] Also noted as integral stages in "the critical evolution of forms" were Guillaume Apollinaire's formalistic experiment in *Calligrammes* (1918), the "ideogramic method" expounded by Ernest Fenollosa and Pound, James Joyce's "word-ideograms," visual innovations associated with futurism and dadaism, and E. E. Cummings's "atomization of words." Although by no means original in pointing out the visual trends in twentieth-century avant-garde literature, Noigandres was one of the first postwar groups to accent the visual aspect of poetry.[22] Augusto de Campos wanted his poems to be "luminous letters that could automatically switch on and off as in street advertisements," suggesting an intent to co-opt for poetry the mass appeal of advertising, especially its persuasive utilization of design elements. Accordingly, the usual linear arrangement on the page was discarded for a "structure of space and time"; Gomringer, for example, labeled his early poems "constellations." For Noigandres, the concrete poem was defined partially in terms of the "ideogram":

ideogram: appeal to nonverbal communication, concrete poem communicates its own structure: structure-content, concrete poem is an object in and by itself, not an interpreter of exterior objects and/or more or less subjective feelings. its material: word (sound, visual form, semantical charge). its problem: a problem of functions-relations of this material. factors of proximity and similitude, gestalt psychology. rhythm: relational force. concrete poem, by using the phonetical system (digits) and analogical syntax, creates a specific linguistical area—"verbivocovisual"—which shares the advantages of nonverbal communication, without giving up word's virtualities. with the concrete poem occurs the phenomenon of meta-communication: coincidence and simultaneity of verbal and nonverbal communication; only—it must be noted—it deals with a communication of forms, of a structure-content, not with the usual message [of] communication.[23]

Noigandres's aim was to corral and extend the pictographic qualities that had been introduced into Western poetry since the beginning of the century. The poets regarded ideograms as having an inherent therapeutic value if applied conceptually to poetry in languages based on the alphabet.[24] For them, the challenge in part was how to reshape the alphabet—perceived as visually backward since it had only twenty-six letters compared to the thousands of ideograms in Chinese and Japanese—to act as an ideogramic language. Twenty years after the "Pilot Plan," Haroldo de Campos credited concrete poetry with having enacted a cross-fertilization of East and West.

Concrete Brazilian poetry reverted to phonetic, digital languages (alphabetic) the techniques of analogical, ideogramic writing. On the other hand, Japanese *avantgarde* poets reimparted to Japanese written language (a partially ideogramic medium) the "diagrammatization" techniques of Occidental concrete poetry. This illuminating dialectical process points toward a very important correspondent phenomenon: *avantgarde* poets, either in the West or in the East, are trying to disclose the *universals of poetics.*[25]

The concrete poetry movement, which officially started with the linking up of Noigandres and Gomringer, was interpreted in a multitude of ways by its various practitioners, and the concept itself changed over time. Emphasis on the concrete poem as a self-contained, visual "ideogram" lent credibility to the growing realization that poetry was leaving the security of its traditional locus—the pages of books—to be displayed on walls or as word sculpture, bringing it into a close, and problematic, relationship with the visual arts. Poetry in the 1960s was also leaving the written page in "sound poetry" and in popular poetry readings, often accompanied by jazz or avant-garde music.

Concrete poetry grew into a worldwide movement during the 1960s in part because it broke down linguistic barriers among cultures. The Noigandres "Pilot Plan" declares: "concrete poetry aims at the least common multiple of language. hence its tendency to nounising and verbification."[26] In the age of television and the so-called global village, all literature was proving impregnable to transcultural communication, and it had to take its place, by default, as the least international of the arts. Unlike music, painting, architecture, dance, and photography, which need no intermediary to be appreciated across linguistic borders (although cultural barriers may remain), words need to be translated. Technology in the 1960s began to transport information with previously unimagined speed—beamed out to space satellites and then retrieved back on earth—causing writers to feel acute frustration at the ineffectuality of their medium to allow direct and meaningful participation in the newly opening frontiers. Concrete poetry responded to this crisis by stressing transcultural communication through linguistic condensation and minimalism. Because concrete works ordinarily require translation of only a half-dozen words, whatever their visual or symbolic complexity, linguistic incompetence ceased to be a hindrance. Readers of concrete works were able to decode previously inaccessible languages on a poetically sophisticated level, no matter how few or simple the words might be. Rather than regretting what was being lost by concrete poetry's "appeal to nonverbal communication," poets and readers considered themselves compensated by its cosmopolitan or transnational character.

The erosion of linguistic barriers in concrete poetry challenged the hegemonic position enjoyed internationally by the French and English languages since Charles Baudelaire's pioneering poetry of the mid-nineteenth century. Significantly, neither English nor French was the native language of the founders of concrete poetry: the Noigandres group wrote in Portuguese, and Eugen Gomringer, who was born in Cachuela Esperanza, Bolivia, and educated in Switzerland, wrote primarily in Spanish and German. The fact that the founders and spokesmen for the movement worked in languages regarded as peripheral to the international mainstream reinforced the linguistic decentralization already advocated by the poets in using only a handful of well-chosen words per poem. The theorists never discussed concrete poetry in terms of subverting the dominant position of French and English, because they preferred to draw a line between types of script (the alphabet versus ideograms) rather than within a group of languages sharing a common script. In their search for an inclusive, universal poetics, they welcomed concrete poetry in any language. Their insistence on pluralism was one aspect of their postmodernism. It is difficult to assess how conscious Noigandres and Gomringer were of the relation between their so-called Third World roots and concrete poetry's assault on the privileged position of English and French among the hierarchy of languages.[27]

The marginal status of both Portuguese and Japanese may have been one felt, but unstated, reason for solidarity between Brazilian and Japanese poets. We can deduce from the Noigandres "Pilot Plan," with its idealization of the ideogram (and, correspondingly, the implied devaluation of the alphabet), that the nascent concrete poetry movement had everything to gain and nothing to lose by enlisting an avant-garde poet whose native language was ideogramic. Katue was not only the most famous Japanese poet among the Western avant-garde, but he was also the sole poet writing in an ideogramic script who was widely known to the international literary community. Given Noigandres's fascination with the ideogram and Katue's affiliation with Pound, whom they admired, it was natural that the group would eventually contact the Japanese poet. One of the many ironies of twentieth-century literature is that the de Campos–Kitasono correspondence—resulting in the historic meeting of East and West in concrete poetry—was orchestrated behind the scenes by a mental-hospital patient, Ezra Pound.

By the time Haroldo de Campos wrote Katue requesting a concrete poem in Japanese, the movement had already gained headway among poets in the West, but all works had been written in alphabetic languages—Portuguese, Spanish, German, French, and English. Concrete poets had been forcing one script (the alphabet) to function as its idealized other (the ideogram), but now the founders were seeking an authentic composition in the idealized script as one means of validating their esthetic principles.

Haroldo de Campos was delighted with "Monotonous Space." He wrote an article in 1958 titled "Poesia concreta no Japão: Kitasono Katue" for the literary supplement of the newspaper *O Estado de São Paulo*, in which he gave a Portuguese translation of Parts 1–4, Part 2 in both romanized and the original Japanese, and a glossary for the five graphs in Part 2. He also analyzed the poem and described the separate parts, but not their interrelationship. As might be expected, de Campos emphasized the concrete aspects of the poem. The article gives a good sense of his view of ideograms in general and of Katue's poem in particular.

Except for Part 3, the poem can be considered concrete . . . especially Part 2. The *kanji* used in Part 2 have a certain visual similarity: *shiro* [white], *kuro* [black] and *ki* [yellow] incorporate a small square cut by lines through the middle; in the next *kanji* the rigor and simplicity of the elements is raised to a maximum with the introduction of *naka* [inside], a word that is written in *hiragana* in Parts 1 and 4, but in *kanji* also has a small square. The final graph, (*no*), is in *hiragana* and possesses a quasi-geometrical shape.

The most surprising effect of these graphs is precisely that they give the idea of a general ideogramic structure of the poem by a real unity of composition, which is not digital but ideographic (for example, *kuro*, according to *Vaccari's Pictorial Chinese/Japanese Characters*, is an abbreviated picture of a cauldron above firewood ashes, from which derives the idea of "soot," hence "blackness." However, with the passing of time, it has become lexiconized as a metaphor (on this point, see R.A.D. Forrest, *The Chinese Language: The Written Character*), and no doubt exhibits a truly visual etymology (Fenollosa: "In Chinese the etymology is constantly visible," and "[graphs] retain the impulse and the creative process, visible in action"). On the other hand, the general ideographic structure is conducive to a new principle of selecting elements according to factors of proximity and resemblance, providing unforeseen opportunities of the very rich graphic possibilities in *kanji*. The ideographic character, then, is treated as a new unity, and its original etymology cedes in favor of a new, formal, Gestalt association.

The achieved result in the poem of Kitasono redounds visually with the idea of a series, of a progressive continuity: uniformly varied in Parts 1 and 2, and invariable in Part 4 where the same elements are reiterated. Of the whole poem, Part 2 represents the apex of order and compositional economy. Part 3 inserts itself in a descriptive-impressionistic manner, closely bound to prior experiences of the poet. However, we can observe with curiosity how the author unifies his diverse experiences of the exterior world through two colored triangles that identify, at last, the chosen objects of his perception. As if we had said: "the blue dress with white polka dots" or "small flags with red stripes and one star."[28]

In Haroldo de Campos's analysis, we can detect his fascination with the pictorial element in Chinese characters. He hints that kanji can be reinvigorated by concrete poetry: "Its . . . etymology cedes in favor of a new, formal, Gestalt association." Unsure how to relate Part 3 to the rest of the poem (elsewhere Campos wrote, "Part 3 hints of a very peculiar Japanese kind of visual surrealism"),[29] he seems to attribute the imagery to "how the author unifies his diverse experiences of the exterior world." Then, for an inexplicable reason, he compares the images in Part 3 with ones from his own poetic imagination that parallel the originals only in their accent on color and shape, but not in their playful ambiguity and inversion of relative sizes.

Eugen Gomringer, in a special section on concrete poetry in *Spirale*, no. 8, included Parts 1 and 4 of "Monotonous Space" in his German translation, Part 2 romanized, and a photo of Katue (Fig. 25).[30] Gomringer, however, did not discuss the poem.

Katue, in an article entitled "Geijutsu to shite no shi" (Poetry as art; 1967), quoted Parts 1 and 2 of "Monotonous Space" and commented: "People say that for poets the problem 'What is poetry?' is forever an inexplicable riddle. That is probably true, yet it can be said that poetry is an apparatus

kitasono katué   japan

shiro

nonaka no shiro

nonaka no kuro

nonaka no kuro

nonaka no kiiro (ou ki)

nonaka no kiiro (ou ki)

nonaka no shiro

nonaka no shiro

weiss

innerhalb des weissen

innerhalb des gelben

innerhalb des gelben

innerhalb des schwarzen

innerhalb des schwarzen

innerhaib des weissen

innerhalb des weissen

weisses quadrat

innerhalb

weisses quadrat

innerhalb

gelbes quadrat

innerhalb

gelbes quadrat

innerhalb

schwarzes quadrat

innerhalb

schwarzes quadrat

innerhalb

weisses quadrat

innerhalb

weisses quadrat

Fig. 25   Photograph of Katue and text of "Monotonous Space" (Part 2 romanized, Parts 1 and 4 in German translation), *Spirale*, no. 8 (1960).

(*sōchi*) that makes possible the pure continuity of liberation in newly invented forms."[31]

Without providing an interpretation of the poem or saying a word about concrete poetry, Katue went on to quote from his 1966 book of word poems, *Kūki no hako*, which he considered at the time to be a breakthrough to the "antipoème" (upon later reflection, he wrote, "I dubbed them 'antipoems' but, when I think about it, every new poem is an antipoem in relation to poetry of the past").[32] From all indications, concrete poetry did not mean much to Katue. He previewed "Monotonous Space" and introduced concretism in *VOU*, but with no more zest than he introduced Italian dolorism and other foreign-inspired avant-garde trends of the postwar period. He had been in touch with Western Europeans and North Americans for decades, but Noigandres was his first interaction with the avant-garde of South America. Even though Katue never went on record as advocating concrete poetry, his sole contribution to the movement enabled his work to be widely diffused around the world.

Judging from "Monotonous Space," Katue was not interested in the concrete layout of the poem on the page and its sound to the exclusion of other considerations. His poem also contains, as we have seen, dynamics of movement and stasis, continuity and discontinuity, as well as the plurisignative imagism of Part 3, all of which are superfluous to concretism per se. Perhaps his lack of enthusiasm for concrete poetry derived from its similarity to diagrammatic poetry, one of the genres he had invented thirty years earlier and published in *Shiro no arubamu* (1929). Ironically, Haroldo de Campos and other Western concretists were unaware of Katue's earlier experiments in diagrammatic poetry. Instead of writing "Monotonous Space," he could just as easily have fulfilled the Noigandres request for a concrete poem by sending "ocean's ocean's ocean's . . . " or a number of other poems from *Shiro no arubamu* (see Chapter 3).

Katue may have refused to write other concrete poems in Japanese because he considered them a sell-out to foreigners who appreciated only the pictorial quality of graphs in the awed manner of beginning language students. "Monotonous Space" is poetic in Japanese because of its complex ways of inducing perceptions, not simply because of its concrete shell. Although other Japanese poets, notably Niikuni Sei'ichi (1925–77) and his ASA (Association for Study of Arts) group, composed excellent concrete poems using graphs, the venture was always fraught with the danger of impressing foreigners at the expense of appearing silly to Japanese readers. Niikuni was a master at exploring possibilities unique to ideograms in much the same way as the Noigandres group and other Western concretists were exploiting words. For example, Niikuni would replace or eliminate ideogramic components and play on their meanings by superimposing *kuchi* (mouth) and *kyo* (empty) on one another to imply their combination, *uso* (lie, falsehood).[33] A functional relationship is revealed in the process of separating and merging the parts. De Campos was correct in asserting that Japanese concretists were influenced by the "'diagrammatization' techniques of Western concrete poetry." Katue, however, was never interested in dissecting and recombining graphs.

On the whole, "Monotonous Space" seemed to mean more to foreign poets than it did to Katue himself, and, for whatever reason, he published no more concrete poems. The movement, however, did have a great effect on his work in supplying him and the VOU Club with a vast new international network of publishers and galleries requesting their visual compositions. In addition, the theoretical issues in concrete poetry provided Katue with a point of departure for his leap into plastic poetry. While negating concrete poetry, he, along with other concretists inside and outside Japan who had previously worked predominantly with words, skillfully advanced the movement in the more open direction of visual poetry.

In 1966, first in *VOU*, no. 104, and then prefacing his book of plastic poems, *Moonlight Night in a Bag*, Katue published his manifesto (in English) on the subject, in which he belittled concrete poetry[34]

A Note on Plastic Poetry

Poetry started with the quill and should come to an end with the ball-point pen. Presently it seems that poetry has reached a fork leading either towards ruin or greater potential; the direction will entirely depend on what kind of tool modern poets will use instead of ball-point pens to express themselves.

The camera is fit to be used expressively by poets. The camera can create a lovely poem even from trifling objects.

Words are the most uncertain symbols devised by human beings for communication. Further, Zen, philosophy and literature, etc., have driven them away to worthless rubbish.

It is a pack of nonsense that poems, the products of poets, are for antiquated mental constitutions of Zen and philosophy.

A plastic poem which needs neither lines nor stanzas is the figure of a poem itself; in other words, it is a "device for a poem" for which rhythm and meaning are not essential factors.

A flow of experimental poetry [that] originated from the sources of futurism, dadaism, and cubism has left small ponds of concrete poems here and there, but they will dry up sooner or later.

Poets: You should not expect to win general applause for your being the most skilled craftsmen of words. Such an applause will never be brought to you, however long you may wait for it.

I will create poetry through the viewfinder of my camera, out of pieces of paper scraps, boards, glasses, etc. This is the birth of new poetry.[35]

On the following pages are "plastic poems" (Figs. 26–31) interspersed with Katue's comments on the genre from the only interview he gave in his life, conducted in 1975 for *Yū* (Play) by Matsuoka Seigō (M) and Sugiura Kōhei (S). I quote the sections pertinent to the discussion at hand.

On Concrete, Visual and Plastic Poetry

KK: Concrete poetry offered compelling designs in its own way. Even with that alone, I think it accomplished something useful. And from the viewpoint of quantity, recent works are increasingly using photographs. Whatever has been done until now, with or without a camera, has been referred to as concrete poetry, but lately people are differentiating between concrete and visual poetry.

S: Like futurism, do you think concrete poetry has already had its day?

KK: Yes, at least it is finished in terms of a school. Recently I am thinking in terms of plastic poetry.

M: In the manifesto-like "Note" you wrote about plastic poetry, you state, "Poetry started with the quill and should come to an end with the ball-point pen." Your statement can be taken as a kind of discourse on *ecriture*. What is the true meaning behind it?

KK: What I have been thinking about most is that within words there are many words and in each country they are different. What a bother it all is. My meaning is: "Let's stop using words!"

S: Before you were active with other concrete poets, but now you are working on plastic poetry. Therefore, the gap between the two becomes an issue.

KK: I can think of infinite ways to alter the configuration of shapes and sounds, but you get trapped and unable to get outside that horizon. It is useless to keep repeating, and so there is nothing left to do but dissolve the gap.

On Photography as Poetry

M: Isn't the switch to plastic poetry a coexistence with poetry rather than a shift in poetry itself?

KK: Things have not developed to the point where "it must be like this." Rather, "it is probably something like this."

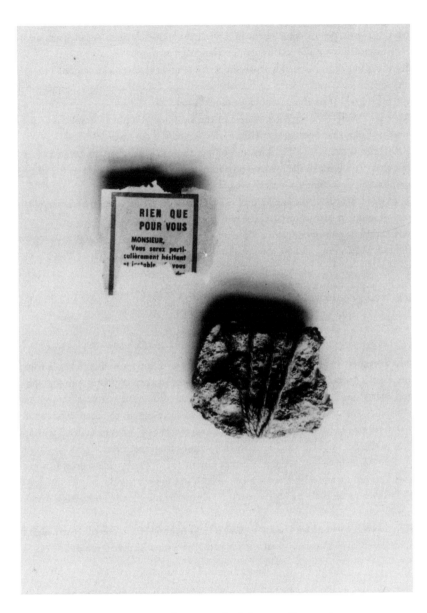

Fig. 26   Katue, "Plastic Poem," *VOU*, no. 160 (June 1978): 17.

M: Do plastic poems come about in a method completely alien to language, or are they intended to be a breakthrough for a language method?

KK: It is not that thoroughly worked out; I just use it as one means among others. I am advocating plastic poetry, and if others do it too, I think a common language will establish itself. If so, things would get much easier.

M: I see. Well, then isn't it a matter of the medium? To put it simply, isn't your starting point that photographs have more possibilities than words?

KK: That is correct. [J. F.] Bory and others also call what they do "visual poetry," but there is a limit to the forms typography can take. It is preferable to use photographs, etc., and compose with the visual in mind.

S: In other words, there is a kind of difference in media because you transcend the serviceability of typography and use photographs.

KK: You see, photographs have more possibility to expand. Sound and meaning are limited. When you examine the possibilities [with typography], you soon arrive at a dead end.

M: Photographs have more depth of reality, is that it?

KK: Yes. It is a liberating method because you cut out a piece of external reality consonant with your own poetic imagination.

On Design

KK: Design is the foundation of what is important to my sensibility. That is why I am always cautious with it. . . . I think design is necessary in poetry, photography, and everything. . . . Most of all, the fundamental consciousness that cultivated my sensibility about objects was the introduction of the Bauhaus to Japan. And my interest continues to remain there. The constructivism and "objects as dots" that appear in the poems is the residue of my impressions from that time.

I do not believe that various materials just enter the lens by themselves. It is necessary to set the material in some form, to lay it out in your mind.

S: Do you mean that the objects must be arranged to return in some basic formation?

KK: Yes. Of course I am not saying that it is all right for any material whatsoever. If some material is necessary, then one can compose with whatever is around.

On the Layout of "VOU"

KK: People usually put the title and name in large type in the middle of the page, but that dirties the space. As much as possible, I want to leave a clean look. I want to see a blank area.

On Ideology

KK: I have always felt a distance from ideology. Ideology is a blank sheet of paper. What is important is method.

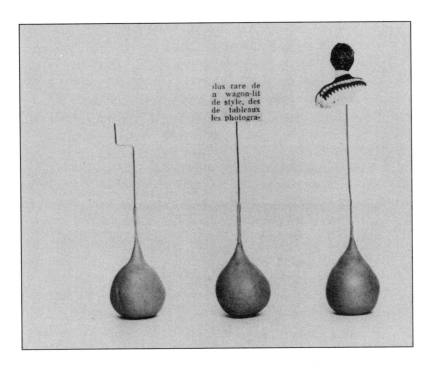

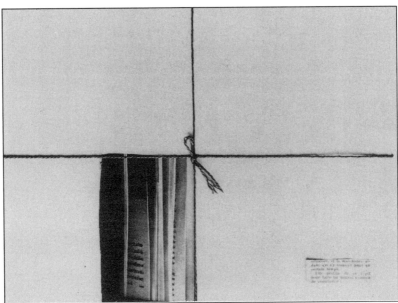

Figs. 27 (*top*) and 28 (*bottom*)　　Katue, two plastic poems, ca. late 1960s

Fig. 29　Katue, untitled cover of *VOU*, no. 85 (Apr.–June 1962).

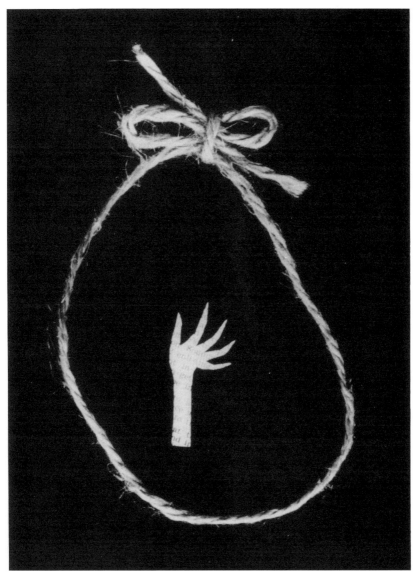

Fig. 30   Katue, untitled plastic poem, ca. late 1960s

Fig. 31   Katue, "Both side[s], 1969," *VOU*, no. 121 (Dec. 1969): 23.

Katue's plastic poems are photographs of everyday objects arranged to evoke a poetic effect. Along with the images—whether considered photographs, poems, both, or neither—the enigmatic label "plastic poetry" is worthy of consideration. In the following section I review statements Katue made over the years on the interrelation of poetry and the arts that reveal how he came to name his photographs "plastic poems."

Katue's switch to plastic poetry was neither a sudden move nor a categorical abandonment of the pen in favor of the camera, as his "note on plastic poetry" might seem to imply. He continued to publish word poems in a number of styles until his death, calling his most concretish works "optical poems." When asked to contribute to concrete and visual poetry anthologies around the world, he sent plastic poems. His packaging of photos as plastic poems was new, although the poetic possibilities of photography were certainly not new to him, to the VOU Club, or to the international avant-garde.[36]

In 1956, after the Korean War had rekindled Japan's economy and made photography affordable to the middle class, almost every issue of *VOU* had a section devoted to the latest experimental photographs by club members, along with reports on VOU exhibits called "keishōten" (形象展; literally: "exhibit of shaped figures").[37] The exhibits featured photographs but also included paintings, collages, mobiles, sculptures, silkscreens, 8mm films, and tapes of poetry read to experimental music. Katue's photos were exhibited regularly; he was by no means the most technically accomplished photographer in the club.[38]

VOU's leading experimental photographer was Yamamoto Kansuke, himself the son of a photographer. Kansuke, a key figure in spreading surrealism in the Nagoya area during the late 1930s, was rounded up by the Thought Police for his artistic activities in 1940, soon after joining the VOU Club. Yamamoto was the driving force behind the club's postwar commitment to exploratory photography. He also wrote poetry and painted, but his talent with the camera and in the darkroom outshone his other achievements.[39] He published his photos infrequently in *VOU* and elsewhere, while remaining a member until the club broke up with Katue's death in 1978. Katue admired Kansuke's work, as his rave review in *VOU*, no. 53 (1956), makes evident. In calling the series of photos in Kansuke's exhibit "poetic" lay the seeds of what would evolve into Katue's own merging of poetry and photography in plastic poetry.

Fig. 32   Yamamoto Kansuke, "photo story: Kūki no usui boku no heya" (My thin-aired room), *VOU*, no. 58 (Nov. 1957): 24–25. (*continues on facing page*).

Yamamoto Kansuke's one-man photo exhibit at Matsushima Gallery in Ginza for one week from November 24 [1956] was a touch on the refined side. His career as an avant-garde photographer can be traced back to the mid-1930s, at which time he joined the VOU Club.[40] His long-time avant-gardism is displayed in the polished photos, and the VOU poet in him shows through in the titles. The color photos "Utsukushii tsūkōnin" [Beautiful passerby] and "Hana hiraku rekishi no sujō" [The lineage of blossoming history] are excellent examples of how subdued color tones can be used. The same can be said for the romantic work "Kaze ga watakushi no mae o yogiru" [The wind crosses before me] and "Kaaten no hako" [The curtain's box], which resembles an abstract oil painting; in both we can recognize the glittering of his unique spirit. Furthermore, his originality is indicated brilliantly in the four-panel "photo story: Kūki no usui boku no heya" [My thin-aired room; see Fig. 32].[41] For avant-garde photographers, this series of poesy-filled photos provides revelations of a new world. The camera—that quaint old machine—has been able to carry a poet's voice by means of this genre breakthrough.[42]

Katue praised Kansuke's titles and regarded the photos themselves as "filled with poesy" and "carrying a poet's voice." For him, all the arts converged, and poetry was equal to photography. He also made it clear in 1975 that already in the mid-1920s "I used to give the same weight to photographs and paintings."[43] The mixing of media was already prevalent among the prewar avant-garde in Japan, and was especially noticeable in the late-1920s journal *Shi to shiron*. Photography, especially, but also painting and other visual art and even filmmaking were subsumed under the concept of *poèsie*.[44]

When interviewed, Katue recalled, "I did not start out as a poet—I was predominantly a painter until part way [through my career]. I painted in relief and numerous other styles. But I didn't get anywhere with painting."[45]

As we have seen in his early poetry experiment "Collection of White Poems" (Chapter 3) and thereafter, poetry for him often meant using words to paint a picture or make a collage. He found possibilities in the indirectness of using one medium to replace another (as had his brother Hashimoto Heihachi in sculpting wood into the shape of a stone). The flexibility that allowed Katue to "paint with words" easily transferred to the equally indirect, and reverse, act of "writing with photography."

The VOU Club had from its inception aimed at gathering avant-gardists from all the arts. Katue accorded poetry a central position, and almost all the members wrote poetry, even those who were primarily musicians, painters, architects, or photographers. In 1958 Katue reiterated his long-held position: "Poetry is the passport to all the arts. Anyone who wants to do something in the art world must grasp his own 'poesy.' All the arts are nothing but a variation of poetry; in that sense it is meaningless to call photography easier than poetry or the novel more difficult than poetry."[46]

In 1961, when introducing VOU member Takahashi Shōhachirō's (1933–) first one-man exhibit, Katue applied his often-repeated comment about avant-garde poetry—namely, that what is important is to break down the current concept of the genre and point in a new direction—to photography. Here we can discover the essential link to his plastic poetry.

Modern photography can be divided into the four categories of news, documentary, commercial, and *zōkei* ["plastic"; literally: "create" + "form"]. Needless to say, our object is plastic photography. The word "plastic" is used in contradistinction to the term "experimental photography" bantered about by young photographers and photo-journalists. Experimental photography concerns itself primarily with displaying technical discoveries and applies to the genres of news, documentary, and commercial photography.

Plastic photography destroys the general concept of what a photograph is and attempts to reconceptualize photography. Therefore, it objectively includes many anti-photography characteristics. Also, being at an extreme, plastic photos are filled with a desire to expand the possibilities of photography.[47]

Some comments in *VOU* no. 100, four issues before Katue's "Note on plastic poetry," hint at the direction in which his thoughts were heading. In the essay "Geijutsu no atarashii jigen" (Art's new dimension), after quoting a New York writer who claimed that in the previous two years the division between painting and sculpture had gradually been eroded, Katue once again displayed enthusiasm for breaking down the conventional borders between the arts:

The new plastic arts (*zōkei geijutsu*), different from painting and sculpture of the past, are shaping the newest dimension of modern art, along with arrivals from the separate paths of kinetic art and concrete poetry. For us the distinction made in a previous age between poet, painter, and sculptor will disappear, and only the word artist (*geijutsuka*) or "art operator" will remain.[48]

Katue then introduces the Parisian kineticists, Groupe des recherches de l'art visuel.

Extending from a dynamic concept of architecture, they are typical of visual groups in making efforts to unify all the arts. Their doctrine is "image = movement = time," and they try to combine the three elements in harmony. Their works are referred to as "kinetic art." In this new art there is a visual function with two tendencies: first, to use the laws of physics with their measurement potential to attain a synthesis of time and space, and second, to use the element of indeterminacy to impart a high specific gravity. *In their complete ignoring of art genres can be found the sharpest avant-gardism.* And, seen from our dimension of poetry, the participation of words or sounds in this kind of new art is inconsequential.[49] (Italics added)

To make the intermedia leap and label photography "poetry" was to Katue the most avant-garde option of the day. He was explicit that the new poems need not have "words or sounds." For him, much of the poetry lay in their defiance of the traditional borders between the arts. The intermedia phenomenon—exemplified in visual poetry, sound poetry, readings with jazz, and the like—is now regarded as one characteristic of the larger, amorphous category "postmodernism." Unlike the intermedia experimentation of the prewar period, the frenzied postwar activity was unprecedented in global scope, in part a reaction to changes brought by wars and technology.

Over the years, experimental photos appeared in VOU's table of contents under such different headings as "photos," "photo poèmes," "poèmes visuels," "graphics," "poésie en noire et blanche." Significantly, Katue never grouped the VOU photos generically as "plastic poems"; he reserved that title for his own compositions.[50] Other VOU photographers named their intermedia works in their own fashion, and we find in English, "block poem" (Takahashi Shōhachirō), "letter picture" (Shimizu Toshihiko, 1929–), "capsule poem" (Itō Motoyuki, 1935–), and "poemgraphy" (Okazaki Katsuhiko, 1929–).[51]

Katue never elaborated on why he called his photographs "plastic poems," and we can only conjecture. As with "ideoplasty" (Chapter 5), it seems he used "plastic" in the sense of "moldable, shapeless," and not with the pejorative meaning of the ubiquitous, non-biodegradable material that has come to symbolize the unnaturalness of modern life.

Plastic poetry was not only the product of Katue's views on poetry and the arts, which had developed over decades of activity, but also his specific response to the concrete poetry movement, in which he was regarded as a leading figure. The blank page for concrete poets had at first been a field of force radiating new possibilities for language, but the euphoria faded as conceptual problems arose. Katue was by no means the first or only concrete poet to find the word-centered movement restrictive. The concretists faced the paradoxical situation that although having successfully created an international movement, they still had not overcome the necessity of translation. Designers, for their part, were finding concrete poetry a fertile ground for displaying their talents, and they used the latest technology to contribute dazzling works that further pulled the visual movement closer toward the pictorial arts and away from word poetry.

Plastic poetry had ample precedent on the theoretical side in mixed media experiments and on the practical side with wordless poems by a number of concrete poets, including the Noigandres group. In 1964 Noigandres poet Décio Pignatari teamed up with Luiz Angelo Pinto and issued a manifesto proclaiming "semiotic poetry," which was an extension of concrete poetry. They credited the Noigandres Pilot Plan for having created a new syntax, but faulted the concrete movement for confining itself to "signs issued from a spoken language, whose form is fit to a linear writing process."[52] Their semiotic poems were arrangements of non-verbal symbols; a "key" was provided at the bottom of the page for deciphering the code. One poem, for example, has clusters of small triangles, some white, some black, some connected, and others floating independently, with the explanatory key: "white triangle = woman" and "black triangle = man." Katue's plastic poems are a further step into semiotics, but he supplied no key to interpreting the images. In a similar vein, Noigandres member Augusto de Campos published a wordless collage of eyes formed into a pyramid, and titled it "Popcrete Poem."

By the time Katue received the letter from Haroldo de Campos, one and a half years had passed since the first VOU photography exhibit in February 1956, and photos by Katue, Kansuke, and other club members were appearing in almost every issue of VOU.[53] Photography, along with words, was considered a parallel channel for poetic expression, but the idea that it should replace word poetry was not yet commonplace.

By 1966, the year Katue issued his manifesto on plastic poetry, he had already published over fifty of his photos in VOU, displayed numerous works in VOU exhibits, and been working in the medium for a full decade.[54] Within those years, his style underwent several transformations.[55] At first he took outdoor photos of walls and shadows of buildings, accenting the two-dimensional geometric patterns that he was also fond of drawing. Later he experimented with blurring, double-exposure, and the superimposing of word poetry on black-and-white images. Soon after his one and only visit to the United States and Europe in 1964, Katue settled on a style that would become the trademark of his plastic poetry: everyday objects arranged into simple designs surrounded by blank space.[56] There are variations of design and material—black or white background, two- or three-dimensional objects, newspaper cutouts or found materials, worded or unworded images—but almost all share certain common traits; namely, they are indoor shots, the objects are relatively small, and blank space is used generously.[57] Specialists refer to photographs of small objects composed with an eye to design such as Katue's plastic poems as "table photographs." Michael Brand, who curated the first exhibition of plastic poems in the United States, noted that

Katue's "plastic poems, though frequently featuring three-dimensional objects, were always intended to be seen in a two-dimensional format."[58]

Critics who consider photography the art of capturing a moment of reality may fault designed photos for the artificiality of their construction. For those who do not reject the subgenre of table photography outright, however, plastic poems offer fresh imagery. Unlike photographs packed with stimulation from corner to corner, plastic poems feature the delicate interplay of a few fragments of quotidian objects—newspaper, wire, Styrofoam, string, a rock, French bread—with the bold use of background space to cast the objects into relief. The materials Katue chose are trivial in themselves and would normally go unnoticed. By isolating and spotlighting them, Katue reveals how their shapes take on a special life of their own. A few examples will illustrate his techniques.

Esthetic Imagery

"Extreme" (Fig. 33), in which written signs are dispensed with altogether, predates his manifesto by one year. On a black background appear two images: the first, in the upper half of the photo, is of a loaf of French bread with wire implanted in it; and the other, in the lower half of the photo, is of a lone black rectangle outlined by a thin white line. The space of the black rectangle, just large enough to contain the loaf of bread, represents absence, nothingness, and the void; in other words, what the upper image potentially was, will be, or could be. The sharp white outline of the black rectangle contrasts with the dull curve outlining the oval bread in black, creating a surface tension that rivets the images. Without the black rectangle, the loaf of bread would float unanchored. More visually compelling than the two balanced halves of the photo, however, is the tiny piece of coiled wire inside the French bread.

The plastic poem's content is enhanced by the design, especially the symmetry of the three rectangles (the black background of the full photo, the black rectangle in the lower half, and the light-colored rectangle within the French bread) and in the way the viewer's eyes are directed to the tiny coil of wire—the most pronounced circularity in the primarily angular photo—painted black for contrast and placed conspicuously in the top center of the photo. Katue has created a surreal image, at once humorous and grotesque, with more precision than if he had described it in words. Besides

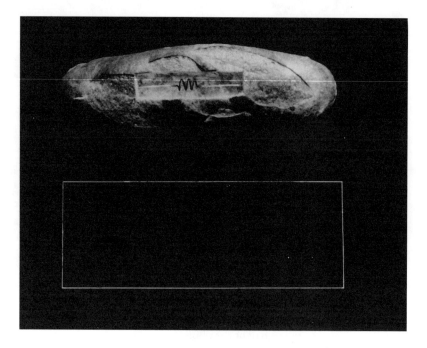

Fig. 33   Katue, "Extreme, 1965. Bread and Wire. Exhibition VOU, Tokio,"
VOU, no. 100 (June-July 1965): 27.

the experience of encountering the image and its resonating associations, the
viewer is also urged to come to terms with the tripodal relationship of the
image, the title ("Extreme"), and the genre (plastic poetry).

Narrative Potential

One of the most narrative plastic poems is an untitled photograph (see Fig.
34) in which two human-like figures appear seated (without chairs) and
facing each other, while a round object resembling the sun or moon hovers
above them. The viewer may interpret the figure on the right as a woman
because of the long hair curling over the shoulder and the bust protrusion.
This plastic poem is a good example of why Katue defined the genre as "a
device for poetry": the three pieces of crumpled newspaper are like theater
props that come to life when assembled before the camera lens. The rela-
tionship between the two figures can be interpreted as romantic tranquillity,
confrontational aggression, or in any number of ways, but the image's evoca-

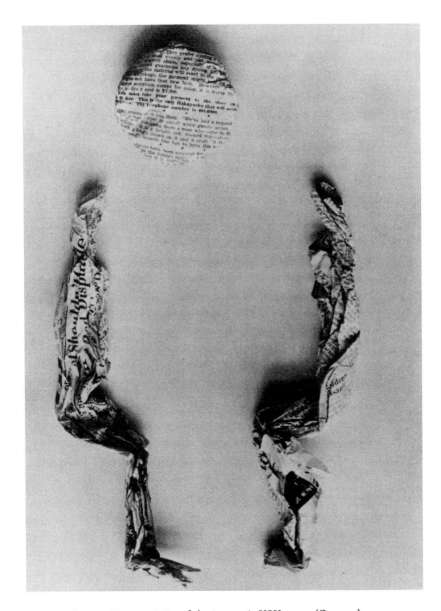

Fig. 34 Katue, variation of plastic poem in *VOU*, no, 133 (Oct. 1972): 22.

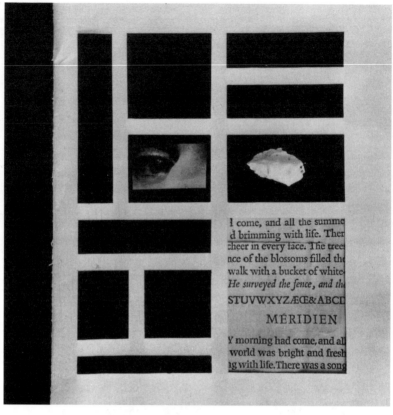

I come, and all the summ
d brimming with life. Ther
cheer in every face. The tree
nce of the blossoms filled th
walk with a bucket of white
He surveyed the fence, and th
STUVWXYZÆŒ&ABCD

MÉRIDIEN

Y morning had come, and all
world was bright and fresh
ig with life. There was a song

Fig. 35   Katue, "Composition B, 1967," *VOU*, no. 110 (June 1967): 19.

tive power lies in the tension generated by the characters facing one another. The photo, like much of Katue's word poetry, does not tell a complete story; rather, it acts as a catalyst that requires the viewer to fill in the gaps in perception. Other of his plastic poems also resemble miniature, three-dimensional sculptures whose materials were chosen and arranged with an intent to stir kinetic activity in the viewer's imagination. Sculpture in movement was an integral aspect of the plasticity (*zōkei*) of plastic poetry.

Among Katue's most anthologized plastic poems is "Composition B" (see Fig. 35). In it a woman's eye gazes out toward the viewer, creating an imaginary horizontal line from eye to eye that is intersected vertically by the black and white partition surrounding her eye. A piece of Styrofoam whimsically stands in as replacement for her other eye. The content of the type sample at the bottom right corner is ebullient: "summer," "brimming with life," "blossoms filled," "morning had come," "world was bright and fresh," "there was a song." The upbeat lyricism in the pastiche passage is reminiscent of Katue's second book of poems, *Wakai koronii* (1932). As we have seen elsewhere, he was fond of using the word *shiro* (white) often and abstractly, as in the title of his first book, *Shiro no arubamu* (Album of whiteness), and in the concrete poem "Monotonous Space." Therefore, it is possible that he cut the type sample in "Composition B" along the right-hand margin to eliminate the noun following the hyphen after "white" so that he could preserve the unusual phrase "a bucket of white."

Eros

More overtly sensual than the eye peering at the viewer in "Composition B" are the buttocks of the woman in the chocolate container of "Both side[s]" (see Fig. 31) and the naked woman sliding toward the viewer in "Plastic poem, 1976" (see Fig. 36).

Even though it was and is illegal in Japan to publish photos showing pubic hair, Katue boldly published "Plastic poem, 1976" along with several other illegal works by VOU photographers. The risk was slight in light of the magazine's limited circulation, yet he was taking a stand by defying the law.

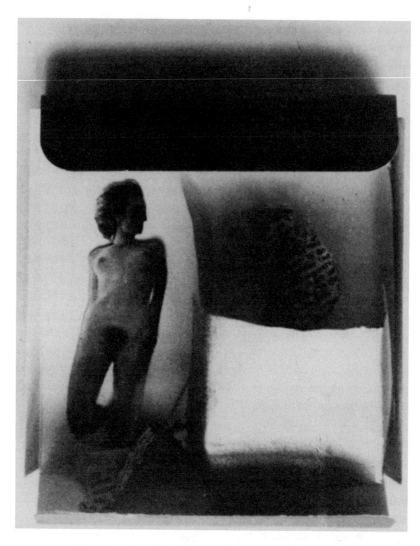

Fig. 36   Katue, "Plastic poem, 1976," *VOU*, no. 153 (Nov. 1976): 26.

Process

The plastic poems fall roughly into two categories: those whose meticulous designs give a sense of completion and those whose intentional haphazardness emphasizes the process of creation. An example of the latter is the crinkled newspaper in no recognizable shape titled "Plastic poem, 1970" (see Fig. 37), which gives the impression of a trial-and-error experiment in a certain direction rather than a fully-composed, finished product. The way the process calls attention to the medium of photography is reminiscent of Katue's use of fragmentary words and phrases in *Kuroi hi* to call attention to the nature of language. We have seen that Kuroda Iri described Katue's postwar language experimentation in terms of Roland Barthes's concept of "writing degree zero" (Chapter 7). French critic Max Chaleil claims that Katue's plastic poetry "goes beyond what Barthes has called 'writing degree zero'":

> We could also cite other ideogramic poets, but there is another current in Japanese concrete poetry which is no less important, namely "plastic poetry," coined by Kitasono Katue, whom I have previously mentioned. In fact, the majority of Japanese visual poems are photographic montages. However, they differ from those found in the West in that they are not intended to be completed works. On the contrary, they attempt to represent a state of reflection that goes beyond what Barthes has called "writing degree zero." To achieve this, a greater value is placed on accenting the process of communication than on the message.[59]

Katue's word poetry weaves back and forth between continuity and discontinuity, and, similarly his photos alternate between the orderly composition of images and a more chaotic, spontaneous presentation. "Plastic poem, 1970" may have been inspired by Man Ray's paper mobile, "Lampshade" (1919), which was to be exhibited for the prestigious Société anonyme but was discarded by the janitor on the night before the opening because he thought it was waste paper.[60] In Katue's displaying a squashed newspaper as a "plastic poem," we can also detect the avant-gardist's disregard for the audience. There is added humor in the context of the concrete poetry movement, as if Katue were taunting them: "Concretists, if you need words with meaning, find them here on this newspaper!" His use of newspaper letters with a tongue-in-cheek message is in line with his assertion that a photo is a "plastic poem."

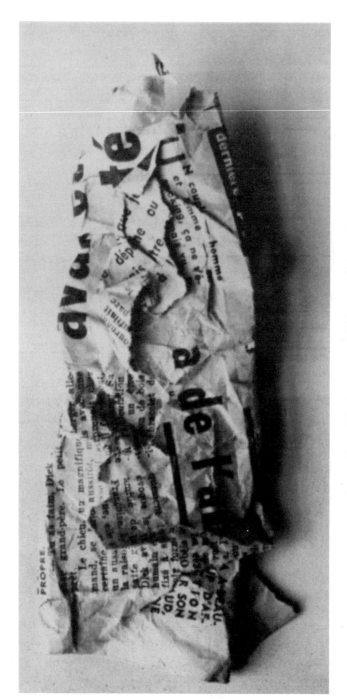

Fig. 37 Katue, "Plastic poem, 1970," *VOU*, no. 123 (May 1970): 18.

Humor

Katue's poetry and theorizing over a half-century show that he took his avant-garde activity extremely seriously; yet, paradoxically, a great deal of the charm of his creations lies in their wit. The plastic poems abundantly display Katue's subtle sophistication and sense of humor, whether the woman in a chocolate box, the coiled wire in French bread, or the crumpled piece of newspaper. His meticulous attention to design exaggerates the importance of the everyday objects in the photos, thus turning them into caricatures. Because Katue was known as a poet and not as a photographer, his plastic poetry represented a playful release from the confines of his stature.

Design

Although Katue gave up his ambition to become a painter early in his career, he stayed closely involved in visual creation by designing almost 500 magazines and books in the half century after his initial involvement with *Ge.Gjmgjgam.Prrr.Gjmgem* (1925). He could choose to present images that appear to be incomplete or as finely composed art products because of his sharp design sense. Besides his main job as head librarian at Japan Dental College, he was also a professional designer.[61] Four of his most lucrative postwar jobs were editing the magazine *Tsukue* (Desk) for the Kinokuniya bookstore chain and designing for the Hayakawa publishing company their "H" logo, the cover of their best-selling *Heminguuei kessakusen* (Selected Hemingway masterpieces; 1957), and the covers for seventeen books in their Ellery Queen Mysteries series. Katue completed the Ellery Queen project from his hospital bed.[62]

Covers for books and magazines had to include the necessary written information (date, title, and volume number) along with the cut-out photographs and a suitable framing device. Occasionally Katue incorporated the typographical information directly onto the central image of the cover design, for example, for the cover of issue no. 85 of *VOU* (see Fig. 29) he filled four of sixteen pigeonholes with the months and year of the issue (Avril, Mai, Juin, 1962). As he had been doing for years, Katue was taking photos and designing, but he was not yet calling these designed photographs "plastic poems." It was indeed a small step from his daily, hands-on work with table photography such as the cover design of *VOU* no. 85 to "plastic poetry," in

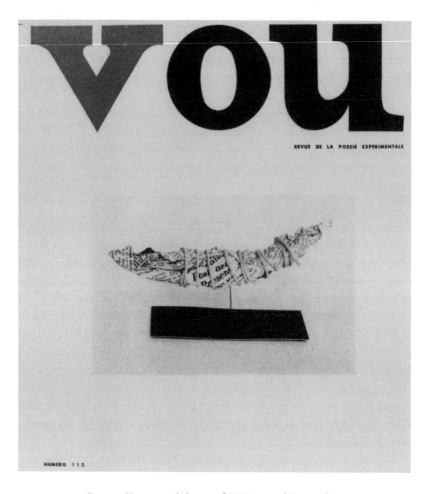

Fig. 38   Katue, untitled cover of *VOU*, no. 112 (Oct. 1967).

which he arranged objects and photographed them without regard to supplying required information. In this sense, designing covers—a part of the world of advertisement—and exhibiting only the central image as "plastic poetry" without the peripheral verbal information are two sides of the same coin.

The cover of *VOU* no. 112 (Fig. 38) is one of many examples of a plastic poem serving as the centerpiece for a magazine or book cover. Katue's plastic poems found their way onto the covers and inside the pages of literary publications in a dozen countries.[63] From the viewpoint of his book design work, the apparent leap of genre from word poetry to plastic poetry was no more than a change in label for a development that had been occurring within his photography over the course of a decade of sustained activity.

Image and Ideoplasty

Katue's fondness for geometric shapes and his belief in the effect of crisp imagery shows in his word poems, plastic poems, short stories, paintings, drawings, book and magazine covers, and three surviving 8mm short films.[64] For him, belief in the image implied disbelief in straightforward logic, especially direct expression of personal thoughts and feelings.

In Katue's most important prewar essay on poetics, he explained that language is collected, arranged, and combined to create imagery, which in turn evokes in the reader a vague poetic effect he called "ideoplasty." His central concern was imagery; language was the vehicle to form it, and ideoplasty results from having formed it. Because his concept of poetry was impersonal, his reliance on the image for poetic effect was satisfied just as well, if not better, by substituting arranged objects for words and the photo image for the verbally described image. Although the media of words and photos are unquestionably distinct, Katue used them for the similar purpose of eliciting poetic effect. His two routes to visually oriented ideoplasty can be formulated as follows:

> *word poetry:*   language + image = ideoplasty
> *plastic poetry:*   design + photo image = ideoplasty[65]

Zen

Katue's manifesto on plastic poetry explicitly criticizes Zen, yet his attention to everyday objects, his creative use of blank space, and the elegant simplicity of his designs resonate with the esthetic principles underlying such Zen-influenced arts as flower arrangement, the tea ceremony, and calligraphy. He

may have been put off by Zen meditation because the Japanese Navy appro-
priated it during World War II to keep sailors alert in order to enhance one-
pointed concentration for efficient killing.

French and English Newspapers

One intriguing aspect of the plastic poems is that Katue invariably used
French and English newspapers and not Japanese ones. Likewise, cutouts of
people are always of whites and blacks and not of Asians. By neglecting
Japanese magazines and newspapers as a source, what statement was Katue
making? Perhaps he found the alphabet more poetic than Japanese and Chi-
nese characters, the flip side of the "awe of the ideogram" experienced by
Pound, Laughlin, de Campos, and other Western poets. If so, the implied
homage to the West was related in part to the healing that took place after
World War II between formerly bellicose nations in which artists took an
active role in creative intercultural exchanges. Katue's reaching out to the
West by not clinging to Japanese signs and symbols in his art may have rep-
resented an appeal to the West on its own terms, which can be interpreted
either as the fawning subservience of a semi-colonial mentality or as just the
opposite, the refusal to satisfy the Western exoticist hunger for ideograms.
The plastic poems were intended also, if not primarily, for domestic con-
sumption, and Katue's use of Western imagery and the alphabet may have
been meant to appeal to the exoticist desire in his Japanese "Occidentalist"
audience (including himself). He did not, in any case, make two sets of plas-
tic poems, one for home consumption and one for abroad.

Despite Katue's theoretical claims that his designed photographs were
"plastic poetry," there is no denying the practical convenience of not needing
to pass his work through the intermediary of translation to reach a foreign
audience. His plastic poems enjoyed a wide circulation in part because they
did not require translation. And as we have seen, they were not a rupture
with his prior sensibility but a "translation" into photography of the major
concerns of his avant-garde poetry since the 1920s.

The plastic poems Katue sent to the West emphasized the designed im-
age and did not require words. They were his ideograms for a future-
centered poetry, mutations of the old language of squiggles filled with
meaning. After a half-century of absorbing Western literary and art trends,
he was able to spend his last decade, by means of his plastic poetry, to return
the West to itself in his own image.

Fig. 39   Katue, untitled plastic poem, ca. 1968.

In a case of art imitating art, Katue once made a plastic poem (Fig. 39) based on an image in one of his word poems:

> newspaper is clipped in the shape of a poet holding
> a yellow umbrella and passing through space[66]

With plastic poetry Katue came out forcefully on the side of non-verbal poetry against the old guard—including concretists—who still were attached to words. Visual poetry gave new life to the concrete poetry movement at a time when it had reached a theoretical dead end, but it also stretched the definition of the word "poetry" beyond what many readers and viewers were willing to tolerate. For this reason and because of the political and literary conservatism of the 1980s and 1990s, the movement lost momentum and eventually died out, although individual poets continue to exhibit and publish visual works (some even under the rubric "plastic poetry"). The vestiges of the concrete, visual, and plastic poetry movements no longer catch the attention of the mass media, but the fruitful results of those two decades of experimentation have been absorbed by other arts—and especially by advertising—to such an extent that they have become a common part of our visual landscape.

Katue's foresight in proclaiming concrete poetry's demise while it was still in its heyday resulted from a lifetime (except during the Pacific War) of honing his intuitions at the forefront of the avant-garde. Now that two decades have passed since his death, we can see that he was indeed ahead of his time, or, as avant-gardists like to point out, he was of his time, but the world lagged behind.

APPENDIXES

A INFORMATION RECORDED
in KATUE'S
1944–1945 DESK DIARY

Food Received During the Last 20 Months of World War II

(* = food ration; + = food purchases)

1944

month   received

1   5 eggs, *mochi* (rice cake), *hoshigaki* (dried persimmons), 10 *katsuobushi* (dried bonita), liver, beef*, *kashi* (candy), cheese, *mochi*, ham, tea+

2   *mikan* (tangerines), *kakimochi* (sliced and dried rice cake), sugar, meat, spinach

3   miso, powdered milk, *shiitake* (mushrooms)

4   *karei* (flatfish), eggs, peanuts

5   azuki beans, wheat, strawberries

6   *konago* (fish), *wakame* (seaweed), peanut butter, asparagus, *himono* (dried fish)

7   various small fish, 10 bonita

8   chocolate, beef

9   —

10   —

11   ham, beef, *imo* (potatoes: 43.6 lbs.), 5 *konoshiro* (gizzard shads)

12   sugar

1945

1   *sushi, mikan, mochi*, rice

2   rice, *bancha* (tea), *macha* (tea), *misozuke* (pickles), *mochi*

3   beer, rice*, tomato catsup

4   beef+, sugar*
5   1 *yamaimo* (potato), rice*, *tororo konbu* (tangle flakes), *furikake* (fish flour), sake*, vegetables*, *migaki nishin* (dried herring)*
6   *sora mame* (fava beans)
7   *bareisho* (Irish potatoes), *kōcha* (Chinese tea)
8   —

Financial Situation During the Last 20 Months of World War II

(Note: Numerous transactions are recorded in the diary, but the following list includes only those in which a specific figure is given.)

Receipts	*Expenditures*
Amount (¥) Date	*Amount (¥) Date*

1944

Receipts	Expenditures
50 book design 2/19	40 receive package 2/3
80 salary bonus 3/28	20 sliding-door repairs 3/30
60 ms. for *Gendai shi* 4/13	50 to revive *Shin shiron* 4/25
20 ms. for Bureau of Weights and Measurements 5/10	
50 from publisher (Shōshinsha) 5/15	
90 unspecified 5/16	
10 ms. for Hōkokukai 5/16	18 Noh flute 5/16
	90 *chūgen* summer gifts 6/21
	24 rucksack for Akio 7/19
	203 binoculars 7/29
150 for work on journal of Japan Dental College 8/21	
50 unspecified 8/24	5.66 butter 8/31
	5 one-way tickets for 3 to Sanjō, Niigata 10/3
	5 baggage to Sanjō 10/3
	2.80 Japanese-English dictionary sent to friend 10/21
	20 farewell gift to friend relocating in Kyoto 10/22
	17.50 straw mats 10/25

555.30 salary for 3 months—
  (¥185.10 per month) 11/6
130 salary year-end bonus 12/27

49.67 *Mugi tsūshin* printing 11/13
8.50 lady's compact—gift for
  friend's wedding 11/28

1945

50 ms. for Taisei-Yokusankai
  (-¥6 tax) 1/12
30 *Mugi tsūshin* dues from 3
  people 1/25
100 donation for *Mugi tsūshin* 2/14
10 *Mugi tsūshin* dues 2/14
38 unspecified part-time work
  at ¥2.3 per day 2/20

1.79 rice ration bought 3/29

100 salary bonus 4/6
30 publisher (Tōhōsha) 4/6

40 beef bought—200 momme
  (760 grams) 4/6

15 books sold 4/8
500 song fee for Tokyo Industrial
  College 4/11

200 sent to Eiko in Sanjō 5/21
10 for funeral of friend's wife 5/22
7.50 sake ration bought 5/22
15 for 5 books 5/23
30.50 fire insurance premium
  (¥5,000 coverage) 5/23
16.87 life insurance 5/28

50 unspecified 5/29

800 sent to Eiko (received) 5/31
120.20 *Mugi tsūshin* printing
  —2 issues 6/26

References to "Mugi tsūshin" and "Kindai shien"

1944
month/day

2/10	I drafted a letter for Mugi no Kai
6/16	I finished mailing out *Mugi tsūshin*, no. 1 [pp. 1–4]
9/17	Edited *Mugi tsūshin*, no. 3
10/14	*Mugi tsūshin*, no. 2 [pp. 5–8] came out

11/13   Paid ¥49.67 to Shōwa Printing for *Mugi tsūshin*
11/20   Received *Mugi tsūshin*, no. 3 [from printer]
11/21   *Mugi tsūshin* [no. 3, pp. 9–12] mailed out
12/27   Paid [printer] for *Mugi tsūshin*, no. 3
12/30   Finished proofreading *Mugi tsūshin*, no. 4 [pp.13–16]

1945 (wartime)

1/11   *Mugi tsūshin* ready
1/25   Received *Mugi tsūshin* dues from 3 people, ¥30 [total]
2/14   Donation received for *Mugi tsūshin*, ¥100
2/14   Received *Mugi tsūshin* dues from 1 person, ¥10
2/23   1st proofs of *Mugi tsūshin*
3/6   Edited *Mugi tsūshin*, no. 2
6/4   *Mugi tsūshin* 2, no. 1 [= no. 5, pp. 17–20] printed
6/26   *Mugi tsūshin*, no. 2 [= no. 6, pp. 21–24] ready. Paid ¥120.20 to
          printer for nos. 1 and 2

1945 (postwar)

10/3   Paid printer ¥97.50 for *Mugi tsūshin* [no. 7, pp. 25–28; no. 8, pp. 29–
          32] printing
11/18   Iwasa [Tō'ichirō] visited; held a meeting about *Kindai shien*
11/29   *Mugi tsūshin* [no. 9, pp. 33–36] came out
12/8   I edited *Kindai shien*
12/9   Finished editing *Kindai shien*
12/18   *Kindai shien* proofs ready

A total of 9 issues of *Mugi tsūshin* appeared: four in 1944; two during the
wartime months of 1945, and three during the postwar months of 1945. It is
difficult to know exactly when the issues of *Mugi tsūshin* appeared, because
they are undated. They are, however, paginated, and each issue is one sheet
of paper folded into four pages. From internal evidence on page 32, we know
that no. 8 was published after the war. We can infer from the diary that no.
7 was also published after the war, although the issue seems to have been ed-
ited by Katue before the end of the hostilities, perhaps at his evacuation
quarters in Sanjō, Niigata. (I thank Chiba Sen'ichi for sending me a copy of
pp. 25–32, and Sakuramoto Tomio for telling me of the existence of pp. 33–
36 in his possession.) There is a possibility that the 10/3/1945 entry refers to

only one issue (no. 7 or no. 8) and that the other was left unrecorded. In any case, Katue's diary helps date *Mugi tsūshin* more precisely than was previously possible. *Kindai shien*, no. 1, published by Iwasa Tō'ichirō and edited by Kitasono Katue, appeared in January 1946. One of the first postwar poetry magazines, it folded with issue no. 3 (April 1946) due to the high rate of inflation.

B PHOTOGRAPHS by KATUE PUBLISHED in VOU, 1956–1978

no.	date	VOU. no.	page no(s).	no. of photos	title(s)*
1	1956.12	53	18–19	2	*sakuhin* (composition, *tō* (tower)
2	1957.4	55	22	1	*le temps perdu*
3	1957.6	56	22	1	*sakuhin*
4	1957.9	57	19	1	*shiroi kūkan* (white space)
5	1958.1	59	21	3	(series) *shiro no chūshō* (abstract of whiteness)
6	1958.5	61	17	1	*sakuhin*
7	1958.7	62	19	1	*sakuhin*
8	1958.9	63	26	1	*machi* (city)
9	1958.12	64	26	1	*tamago ni yoru zōkei* (egg's plasticity)
10	1959.1	65	24	1	*yomarete iru shishū* (poetry book being read)
11	1959.3	66	18	2	mannequin
12	1959.9	71	21	1	*kuroi higaa* (black figure)
13	1959.11	72	17	1	*chapeau hiver*
14	1960.1	73	21	1	*tamago ni yoru zōkei*
15	1960.3	74	26–27	2	*kūkan 1, 2* (space)
16	1960.5/6	75	cover	1	
17	1960.7/8	76	cover	1	Hasebe Yukio;
			17	1	*la disparition d'honore subrac*
18	1960.9/10	77	cover	1	Shimizu Toshihiko
			28	1	the phone did not ring in her room

no.	date	VOU. no.	page no(s).	no. of photos	title(s)*
19	1960.11/12	78	cover	1	Motoki Kazuo
20	1961.1/2	79	cover	1	Shimizu Masato
21	1961.3/4	80	cover	1	
			25	1	passers-by in the wall
22	1961.5–7	81	cover	1	
23	1961.8/9	82	cover	1	
24	1961.10–12	83	cover	1	
25	1962.1–3	84	cover	1	
26	1962.4–6	85	cover	1	
			28–29	2	figure; figure
27	1962.7–9	86	cover	1	
28	1962.10–				
	1963.1	87	17	1	*de vénus*
29	1963.2–4	88	cover	1	
			28	1	op. 6828
30	1963.5/6	89	cover	1	
			26	1	op. 772
31	1963.7/8	90	cover	1	
32	1964.2	92	27	1	avenue
33	1964.2/3	93	22–23	2	figure 1; figure 2
34	1964.4/5	94	cover	1	
			17, 28	2	i am her[e]; i am her[e]
35	1964.6/7	95	cover	1	
			25, 28	2	high noon; figuration
36	1964.11–				
	1965.1	97	cover	1	
			25, 28	2	i passed the west; i passed the west
37	1965.2/3	98	cover	1	
			17	1	an angle
38	1965.4/5	99	cover	1	
			27	1	plastic poem**
39	1965.6/7	100	cover***	1	
			27–28	4	extreme; statics; plastic poem a; plastic poem b
40	1965.8/9	101	21	1	brainchild
41	1965.10/11	102	26–27	2	plastic poem; plastic poem

no.	date	VOU. no.	page no(s).	no. of photos	title(s)*
42	1965.12/				
	1966.1	103	20–21	2	plastic poem; plastic poem
43	1966.2/3	104	24–25	2	plastic poem; plastic poem
————"A Note on Plastic Poem" [manifesto]————————					
44	1966.4/5	105	27	1	plastic poem
45	1966.7	106	cover	1	
			19	1	plastic poem
46	1966.10	107	cover	1	
			24–25	2	a portrait of a poet 1; a portrait of a poet 2
47	1967.1	108	cover	1	
			20	1	*une femme*
48	1967.4	109	cover	1	
			21	1	*une femme*
49	1967.6	110	cover	1	
			18–19	2	composition A; composition B
50	1967.8	111	cover	1	
			20–21	2	plastic poem; plastic poem
51	1967.10	112	cover	1	
			20	1	plastic poem
52	1968.1	113	cover	1	
			20	1	*hommage à j. f. bory*
53	1968.3	114	cover	1	
			20–21	2	plastic poem; plastic poem
54	1968.6	115	cover	1	
			24–25	2	plastic poem; plastic poem
55	1968.9	116	cover	1	
			24–25	2	plastic poem; plastic poem
56	1968.12	117	cover	1	
			24	1	plastic poem
57	1969.3	118	cover	1	
			18	1	strollers
58	1969.9	120	cover	1	
			17	1	both side[s]
59	1969.12	121	22–23	2	plastic poem; both side[s]

| 60 | 1970.2 | 122 | 17 | I | plastic poem |

no.	date	VOU. no.	page no(s).	no. of photos	title(s)*
61	1970.5	123	18	I	plastic poem
62	1970.9	124	22	I	plastic poem
63	1970.12	125	20–21	2	L'homme triste; L'homme triste
64	1971.11	129	19	I	plastic poem
65	1972.10	133	22	I	plastic poem
66	1973.1	134	26	I	plastic poem
67	1973.3	135	26	I	plastic poem
68	1973.5	136	26–27	2	plastic poem; plastic poem
69	1973.8	137	20–21	2	plastic poem; plastic poem
70	1973.10	138	20–21	2	anthropologie A; anthropologie B
71	1974.1	139	22	I	plastic poem
72	1974.3	140	19	I	anthropologie c
73	1974.6	141	22	I	anthropologie d
74	1974.8	142	26	I	prospérité solitaire
75	1974.10	143	28	I	Fig. A
76	1975.3	145	25	I	op. 6
77	1975.12	148	19	I	night of figure
78	1976.2	149	17	I	Plastic poem: Forgotten man
79	1976.4	150	21	I	plastic poem
80	1976.7	151	27	I	plastic poem
81	1976.11	153	26	I	plastic poem
82	1977.2	154	26–27	2	plastic poem; plastic poem
83	1977.11	158	28	I	plastic poem
84	1978.6	160	17	I	plastic poem

* Cover photographs are untitled except for *VOU*, nos. 76–79.
** This is the first photograph labeled "plastic poem" (1965.4/5).
*** The same photograph is repeated on the cover of *VOU*, nos. 100–105, but here it is counted as one item.

Total no. of photographs: 138; 58 of these appeared before and 80 appeared after Katue adopted the label "plastic poem"; 42 of them are explicitly entitled "plastic poem."

C JAPANESE
PERSONAL NAMES
and DATES

Aida Kenzō 相田謙三 (1916–)

Akai Ki'ichi 赤井喜一 (1915–)

Akutagawa Ryūnosuke
芥川龍之介 (1892–1927)

Andō Kazuo 安藤一男 (1929–)

Anzai Fuyue 安西冬衛 (1898–
1965)

Arima Akihiko 有馬秋彦 (1920–
96)

Asahara Kiyotaka 浅原清隆
(dates unknown)

Asaka Kenkichi 亜坂健吉
(alternative pen name of
Hashimoto Kenkichi, or
Kitasono Katue)

Ema Shōko 江間章子 (1913–)

Engo Kokugon 園悟克勤 (1063–
1135)

Fuji Takeshi 富士武 (dates
unknown)

Fujitomi Yasuo 藤富保男
(1928–)

Fujiwara Sei'ichi 富士原清一
(1908–died WWII)

Fukuzawa Ichirō 福沢一郎
(1898–1992)

Gyō Shōtarō 暁正太郎 (dates
unknown)

Hagiwara Kyōjirō 萩原恭次郎
(1899–1938)

Hagiwara Sakutarō 萩原朔太郎
(1886–1942)

Hara Sekitei 原石鼎 (1886–1951)

Haruyama Yukio 春山行夫
(1902–94)

Hashimoto Akio 橋本明夫
(1934–)

Hashimoto Ei 橋本ゑい (1874–
1928; Kitasono's mother)

Hashimoto Ei 橋本栄 (1910–87;
Kitasono's wife, Eiko)

Hashimoto Fumi 橋本婦み
(1891–?)

Hashimoto Heihachi 橋本平八
(1897–1935)

Hashimoto Kenkichi 橋本健吉
(1902–78; real name of Kitasono
Katue)

Hashimoto Shōji 橋本正二 (1907–64)

Hashimoto Yasukichi 橋本安吉 (1865–1932)

Hashimoto Yuki 橋本ゆき (1910–?)

Hattori Shinroku 服部伸六 (1913–98)

Hinatsu Kōnosuke 日夏耿之介 (1890–1971)

Hiraiwa Konji 平岩混児 (dates unknown)

Hirata Atsutane 平田篤胤 (1776–1843)

Hirato Renkichi 平戸廉吉 (1893–1922)

Hiroe Michi 宏江ミチ (dates unknown)

Hirotsu Takashi 弘津隆 (dates unknown)

Horiguchi Daigaku 堀口大学 (1892–1981)

Ihara Saikaku 井原西鶴 (1642–93)

Ikuta Shungetsu 生田春月 (1892–1930)

Inagaki Taruho 稲垣足穂 (1900–1977)

Iokibe Kin'ichi 五百旗頭欣一 (1913–78)

Itō Masako 伊東昌子 (dates unknown)

Itō Michio 伊藤道郎 (1893–1961; known as Miscio Ito in the West)

Itō Motoyuki 伊藤元之 (1935–)

Itō Noe 伊藤野枝 (1895–1923)

Iwamoto Shūzō 岩本修蔵 (1908–79)

Iwanari Tatsuya 岩成達也 (1933–)

Iwasa Tō'ichirō 岩佐東一郎 (1905–74)

Iwasaki Ryōzō 岩崎良三 (1908–76)

Jō Naoe 城尚衛 (1915– ; pen name of Hirata Naoe 平田尚衛)

Jō Samon 城左門 (1904–76)

Kambara Tai 神原泰 (1898–1997)

Kamijō Takejirō 上条竹次郎 (1932–)

Kaneko Mitsuharu 金子光晴 (1895–1975)

Kasuga Shinkurō 春日新九郎 (alternative pen name of Hashimoto Kenkichi, or Kitasono Katue)

Katō Hajime 加藤一 (1900–1968)

Katō Takeo 加藤武雄 (1888–1956)

Katsu Yoshio 勝承夫 (1902–81)

Katsushika Hokusai 葛飾北斎 (1760–1849)

Kawabata Yasunari 川端康成 (1899–1972)

Kawamura Yōichi 川村洋一 (1932–95)

Kihara Kōichi 木原孝一 (1922–79)

Kikushima Tsuneji (real name) 菊島恒二; (pen name) 菊島常二; (1916–89)

Kinoshita Tsunetarō 木下常太郎
(1907–86)

Kitagawa Fuyuhiko 北川冬彦
(1900–1990)

Kitahara Hakushū 北原白秋
(1885–1942)

Kitasono Katue 北園克衛
(1902–78; pen name of
Hashimoto Kenkichi; also
romanized Kitazono Katué or
Katsue)

Kobayashi Ei 小林栄 (see
Hashimoto Ei; maiden name of
Kitasono's wife)

Kobayashi Hideo 小林秀雄
(1902–83)

Kobayashi Takiji 小林多喜二
(1903–33)

Kobayashi Yoshio 小林善雄
(1912–)

Koga Harue 古賀春江 (1895–
1933; also romanized Harué)

Koike Takeshi 小池驤 (dates
unknown)

Komori Teruo 小森輝夫 (dates
unknown)

Kondō Azuma 近藤東 (1904–88;
also romanized Kondoh)

Kondō Masaji 近藤正治 (dates
unknown)

Kunitomo Chie 国友千枝 (dates
unknown)

Kuroda Iri 黒田維理 (1929– ;
pen name of Hirosawa Kiyoshi
広沢清)

Kuroda Saburō 黒田三郎 (1919–
80)

Kuwakado Tsutako 桑門つた子
(dates unknown)

Matsuo Bashō 松尾芭蕉 (1644–
94)

Miki Rofū 三木露風 (1889–1964)

Miki Tei 三木偵 (dates unknown;
pen name of Kanazawa
Fukucho 金沢福緒)

Miura Kōnosuke 三浦孝之助
(1903–64)

Miyakoda Ryū 宮古田龍 (dates
unknown)

Miyamoto Kenji 宮本顕治
(1908–)

Miyamoto Yuriko 宮本百合子
(1899–1951)

Miyazaki Tomoo 宮崎友雄
(1901–?; Don Zakki; Zacky?)

Miyoshi Tatsuji 三好達治 (1900–
1964)

Miyoshi Toyo'ichirō 三好豊一郎
(1920–92)

Momota Sōji 百田宗治 (1893–
1955)

Mori Ōgai 森鴎外 (1862–1922)

Moriya Hitoshi 森谷均 (1897–
1969)

Motoori Norinaga 本居宣長
(1730–1801)

Motoyama Shigenari 本山茂也
(dates unknown)

Murano Shirō 村野四郎 (1901–
75)

Murayama Tomoyoshi 村山知義
(1901–77)

Murō Saisei 室生犀星 (1889–
1962)

Nagai Kafū 永井荷風 (1879–1959)

Nagashima Miyoshi 長島三芳 (1917–)

Nagayasu Shūichi 長安周一 (1909–90)

Nakada Sadanosuke 仲田定之助 (1888–1970)

Nakada Yoshie 仲田好江 (1902–95)

Nakagiri Masao 中桐雅夫 (1919–83; pen name of Shiragami Kōichi 白神鉱一)

Nakahara Minoru 中原実 (1893–1990)

Nakahara Sen 中原泉 (1929–)

Nakamura Chio 中村千尾 (1913–82)

Nakamura Kikuo 中村喜久夫 (dates unknown)

Nakano Ka'ichi 中野嘉一 (1907–98)

Nakano Shigeharu 中野重治 (1902–79)

Natsume Sōseki 夏目漱石 (1867–1916)

Niikuni Sei'ichi 新国誠一 (1925–77)

Nishiwaki Junzaburō 西脇順三郎 (1894–1982; occasionally used the pen name Jacobus Phillipus before WWII)

Nogawa Hajime 野川孟 (dates unknown)

Nogawa Takashi/Ryū 野川隆 (1901–44)

Noguchi Yonejirō 野口米次郎 (1875–1947; known as Yone Noguchi in the West)

Oda Masahiko 小田雅彦 (dates unknown)

Ogihara Toshitsugu 荻原利次 (1910–92; pen name of Tanaka Toshitsugu 田中利次)

Oguri Sen'ichirō 小栗馬一郎 (also Oguri Sen; alternative pen name of Hashimoto Kenkichi, or Kitasono Katue)

Okada Yoshihiko 岡田芳彦 (dates unknown)

Okazaki Katsuhiko 岡崎克彦 (1929–)

Okazaki Sei'ichirō 岡崎清一郎 (1900–1986)

Okunari Tatsu 奥成達 (1942–)

Onchi Kōshirō 恩土孝四郎 (1891–1955)

Ōnuma Jaku 大沼寂 (dates unknown)

Osada Tsuneo 長田恒雄 (1902–77)

Ōsugi Sakae 大杉栄 (1885–1923)

Sagawa Chika 左川ちか (1911–36)

Saijō Yaso 西条八十 (1892–1970)

Saitō Mokichi 斎藤茂吉 (1882–1953)

Sakuramoto Tomio 桜本富雄 (1933–)

Santō Kyōden 山東京伝 (1761–1816)

Sasajima Toshio 佐々島敏夫 (dates unknown)

Sasaki Kikyō 佐々木桔梗
(1922– ; pen name of Sasaki
Kyōjō 佐々木教定)

Sasazawa Yoshiaki 笹沢美明
(1898–1984)

Satō Chōzan 佐藤朝山 (1888–
1963)

Satō Haruo 佐藤春夫 (1892–
1964)

Satō Naohiko 佐藤直彦 (dates
unknown)

Satō Nobuo 佐藤信夫 (dates
unknown)

Satō Saku 佐藤朔 (1905–96;
occasionally used the pen names
Sekimizu Ryū 関水龍 and
Tosu Kō 鳥巣公)

Satō Sōnosuke 佐藤惣之助
(1890–1942)

Sawaki Takako 沢木隆子
(1907–)

Seki Shirō 皙四郎 (dates
unknown; now known as
Tanabe Shin 田名部信)

Senge Motomaro 千家元麿
(1888–1948)

Setsu Chō 雪竇 (980–1052)

Shibahara Hidetsugu
芝原ひでつぐ (dates
unknown)

Shimizu Masato 清水雅人
(1936–)

Shimizu Toshihiko 清水俊彦
(1929–)

Shiraishi Kazuko 白石かずこ
(1931–)

Sō Takahiko 宗孝彦 (1915–96)

Suzuki Masafumi 鈴城雅文
(1947–)

Suzuki Takashi 鈴木崧 (1898–
1998)

Takagi Haruo 高木春夫 (dates
unknown)

Takahashi Shinkichi 高橋新吉
(1901–87)

Takahashi Shōhachirō 高橋
昭八郎 (1933–)

Takai Kōzan 高井鴻山 (1806–83)

Takamura Kōtarō 高村光太郎
(1883–1956)

Takeda Takehiko 武田武彦
(1919–)

Takei Teruo 武井照夫 (1927–)

Takenaka Iku 竹中郁 (1904–82)

Takiguchi Shūzō 滝口修造
(1903–79)

Tamamura Zennosuke 玉村
善之助 (dates unknown; pen
name of Tamamura Hokuto
玉村方久斗)

Tamura Ryūichi 田村隆一 (1923–
98)

Taniguchi Eizō 谷口英三 (dates
unknown)

Tanno Sei 丹野正 (1910–)

Terayama Shūji 寺山修司 (1935–
83)

Tōgō Seiji 東郷青児 (1897–1978)

Tokuda Jōji 徳田戯二 (1898–
1974)

Tokuda Shūsei 徳田秋声 (1871–
1943)

Tomoya Shizue 友谷静栄
(1898–)

Torii Ryōzen 鳥居良禅 (1913–)

Tosaka Jun 戸坂潤 (1900–1945)

Towada Misao 十和田操 (1900–1978)

Tsuboi Shigeji 壷井繁治 (1897–1975)

Tsuji Jun 辻潤 (1884–1944)

Tsuji Setsuko 辻節子 (1927–93)

Tsuruoka Yoshihisa 鶴岡善久 (1936–)

Ueda Osamu 上田修 (1915–96; pen name of Ueno Hideshi 上野秀司)

Ueda Tamotsu 上田保 (1906–73)

Ueda Toshio 上田敏雄 (1900–1982)

Ueno Saburō 上野三郎 (1947–)

Utagawa Kunisada 歌川国貞 (1786–1864)

Utagawa Kuniyoshi 歌川国芳 (1797–1861)

Watanabe Masaya 渡辺正也 (1929–)

Yamada Kazuhiko 山田一彦 (dates unknown)

Yamamoto Kansuke 山本悍右 (1914–87)

Yamamoto Shūgorō 山本周五郎 (1903–67)

Yamanaka Sansei 山中散生 (1905–77; also Chiruu or Tiroux)

Yasoshima Minoru 八十島稔 (1906–83)

Yoshikawa Eiji 吉川英治 (1892–1962)

Yoshimoto Takaaki 吉本隆明 (1924–)

Yoshioka Minoru 吉岡実 (1919–90)

NOTES

Introduction

1. The poet, who translated from French and English, usually chose to romanize his name as "Kitasono Katue" (or "Katué"). Over one hundred published documents exist with this spelling, and Westerners are often familiar with it through numerous references to him in Ezra Pound's essays. In deference to his preference and not to confuse those who already know him into thinking that I am dealing with a different person, I decided not to revise the spelling into the currently standard, modified Hepburn romanization of "Kitazono Katsue."

2. Valuable exceptions include Hosea Hirata, *The Poetry and Poetics of Nishiwaki Junzaburō: Modernism in Translation* (Princeton: Princeton University Press, 1993); Earl Jackson, Jr., "The Heresy of Meaning," in *Harvard Journal of Asiatic Studies* 51, no. 2 (1991): 561–98; Dennis Keene, *Yokomitsu Riichi: Modernist* (New York: Columbia University Press, 1980); Lucy Beth Lower, "Poetry and Poetics: From Modern to Contemporary in Japanese Poetry," (Ph.D. diss., Harvard University, 1987); Ko Won, *Buddhist Elements in Dada: A Comparison of Tristan Tzara, Takahashi Shinkichi, and Their Fellow Poets* (New York: State University of New York Press, 1977); and Vera Linhartova, *Arts du Japon: Dada et surrealisme au Japon* (Paris: Publications Orientalistes de France, 1987).

3. Karatani Kōjin makes a similar point, "The Japanese nineteenth century may have been an impediment to 'modernization,' but it promises to be an accelerating factor for a postmodern society" ("One Spirit, Two Nineteenth Centuries," in Masao Miyoshi and H. D. Harootunian, eds., *Postmodernism and Japan* [Durham, N.C.: Duke University Press, 1989], p. 265).

4. Conversation with the literary historian and poet Nakano Ka'ichi on Nov. 11, 1985.

5. Interview with Takahashi Kei on Nov. 18, 1985. Incidentally, the head curator of the Japanese Modern Literature Library (Nihon Kindai Bungaku Kan) informed me that on several occasions poets had torn out the pages on which their patriotic poems appeared before donating volumes to the library collection, so ashamed were they of their complicity in the war effort.

6. Birth and death dates are provided in the text for Japanese but omitted for Westerners.

7. In his lifetime, only thirty-five of Katue's over five hundred poems were printed in translation in small magazines outside Japan. The meager quantity, although enough to establish Katue's reputation, was insufficient to reveal the breadth of his development. For a volume of Katue's poetry in English translation, see my *Glass Beret* (Milwaukee, Wisc.: Morgan Press, 1995); copies may be ordered directly from the publisher at 2979 S. 13th Street, Milwaukee, WI, 53215.

Chapter 1

1. Told to me by Gonokuchi Reiji, Asama historian and a distant relative of the Hashimotos, Nov. 27, 1985.

2. Gonokuchi Reiji is of this opinion (interview, Nov. 27, 1985). Taniguchi Eizō agrees (interview, Nov. 28, 1985). Hashimoto Chiyo, however, says that her husband (Kitasono's brother Heihachi) told her that the Hashimoto family's ancestors were farmers, not samurai (interview, Nov. 26, 1985).

3. Kitasono Katue, "Watakushi no kokoro no genfūkei to shite no Asama mura," *Geijutsu Mie* (Tsu: Mie-ken geijutsu bunka kaikan), no. 6 (May 1973): 7; also in Nakano Ka'ichi, "Kitasono Katue ron," *Rekishō*, no. 88 (1978), pp. 25–26; and in abbreviated form in Fujitomi Yasuo, *Kindai shijin hyōden: Kitasono Katue* (Critical biographies of modern poets: Kitasono Katue) (Yūseidō, 1983), pp. 8–9. Most of the information about Kitasono's family and childhood is taken from Kitasono's article.

4. Kitasono in *Geijutsu Mie*, no. 6, p. 7. In a conversation I had with Hashimoto Chiyo (Katue's sister-in-law) on Sept. 30, 1985, she recalled that Yasukichi was one of the first to grow tomatoes and potatoes in Asama village. All poetry and prose translations in the book—unless otherwise noted—are by me.

5. Conversation with Hashimoto Chiyo, Sept. 30, 1985.

6. The *Shin-kokinshū* is the eighth imperial anthology of poetry, compiled between 1201 and 1205.

7. Kitasono in *Geijutsu Mie*, no. 6, p. 7. "Hinkōkō" (Chinese: "Binjiao xiang") was written by Du Fu, the great eighth-century Chinese poet.

8. Later in life, Katue may have conceded that surrealism went better with his father's "Rube Goldberg" attitude than with "inventiveness."

9. Conversation with Hashimoto Chiyo, Sept. 30, 1985.

10. Kitasono in *Geijutsu Mie*, no. 6, p. 7.

11. I am unaware what camera the Hashimotos owned, but until the early Shōwa period (1926–1989) the value of a Leica was equal to the cost of building an average house. See Minami Hiroshi, *Nihon modanizumu no kenkyū* (Brain, 1982), p. 211.

12. The names and dates of Katue's siblings are Fumi (1891–?), Heihachi (1897–1935), Shōji (1907–64), and Yuki (1910–?).

13. Kitasono Katue, "Hashimoto Heihachi no koto," *Gendai no me: Kokuritsu kindai bijutsukan nyusu* (Gendai bijutsu kyōkai), no. 11 (Oct. 1955): 2.

14. Mie Prefectural Art Museum held an exhibition, Hashimoto Heihachi and Enkū (Tsu: Mie kenritsu bijutsukan, 1985), 7 Sept.–13 Oct. 1985; the catalogue contains most of the pieces exhibited, some essays, and a chronology of Heihachi's career.

15. See Hashimoto Heihachi, *Junsui chōkoku ron*, ed. Kitasono Katue (Shōshinsha, 1942), pp. 25–27.

16. Hashimoto Chiyo (interview Nov. 26, 1985) said that Katue's aunt, Hashimoto Masa, told her that he had been a mischievous child.

17. Conversation with Atake Yoshio, Katō Kōjirō, and Shimamura Sakutarō on June 9, 1986.

18. No listing is available for Katue's first year, but he ranked 37 out of 57 his second year, and 22 out of 39 his final year.

19. "We all have to work hard if we wish to earn money" is written on the blackboard in a photograph of an English class at Yama-shō in Katue's graduation album, *Sotsugyōsei kinen shashin chō* (Uji-Yamada: Uji-Yamada Shiritsu Shōgyō Gakkō, 1917), n.p. The album contains two photos of Katue, one alone (see Fig. 6, p. 17) and one in a group.

20. Hashimoto Chiyo (interview, Nov. 26, 1985) said Heihachi mentioned to her that Katue used to argue with his father, causing family strife.

21. Conversation with Kitasono's wife, Hashimoto Eiko (1909–87), on Sept. 24, 1985.

22. Conversation with Taniguchi Eizō on Nov. 28, 1985.

23. Fujitomi, p. 9.

24. Conversation with Gonokuchi Reiji, Nov. 27, 1985.

25. Kitasono Katue, "Watakushi no nijūdai," *Wakai hito*, Apr. 1968, p. 22.

26. Kitasono, *Gendai no me*, no. 11: 2.

27. *Kōyū*, no. 11 (Dec. 1922): 13–15.

28. Kitasono, "Watakushi no nijūdai," p. 22.

29. For a typical example of Shungetsu's sentimental verse, see "Aru ojō-san ni" in *Nihon shishū* (Shinchōsha, 1920), pp. 19–21. Shungetsu committed suicide in 1930 by jumping overboard a ship.

30. *Bunshō kurabu*, Sept. 1924, pp. 70–71. There is confusion concerning the number of poems introduced—the table of contents gives the title as "Four New Poems," but the title inside the magazine, "Five New Poems," gets the count correct.

31. Ibid.

32. Japanese of the period typically sat on *zabuton* cushions on *tatami* mats and used *sudare* screens to block the sunlight.

33. For more on the avant-garde and antagonism, see Renato Poggioli, *The Theory of the Avant-garde*, trans. Gerald Fitzgerald (Cambridge: Harvard University Press, 1968), pp. 25ff.

Chapter 2

1. For an English translation of Marinetti's manifesto, see László Moholy-Nagy, *Vision in Motion* (Chicago: Paul Theobald, 1956), p. 302.

2. Mumeishi (anonymous), "Mukudori tsūshin," *Subaru*, May 1909, pp. 102–4; Nakano Ka'ichi, *Zen'ei shi undō shi no kenkyū* (Research on the history of avant-garde poetry movements) (Shinseisha, 1975), p. 88. Without offering any evidence, Nakano credits Mori Ōgai (1862–1922) with having translated it.

3. An important influence on Japanese futurist and avante-garde painting was the Russian David Burliuk, who lived in Tokyo from 1920 to 1922. See Toshiharu Omuka, "David Burliuk and the Japanese Avant-garde," *Canadian-American Slavic Studies* 20, no. 1–/2 (Spring–Summer 1986): 111–25; and Emma Chanlett-Avery, "Pacific Overtures: Exploring Russia's Encounter with Japanese Aesthetics," (unpublished senior thesis, Amherst College, 1996), pp. 57–96.

4. For example, there was the magazine *Shin ryōdo* named by Haruyama Yukio after the English magazine *New Country*, as well as *Arechi*, a group and its journal, named after T. S. Eliot's poem "The Wasteland."

5. Tamura Ryūichi (1923–98), a prominent poet, made this point at the obscenity trial for Nagai Kafū's novel *Yojōhan fusuma no shitabari* (Paper covers for the sliding doors of a four-and-a-half-mat room). According to Tamura, Kafū's nostalgia for the past was a result of his having witnessed the sweeping away of the last remnants of Edo life by the destructive earthquake (Maruya Saiichi, ed., *Sakka no shōgen: "Yojōhan fusuma no shitabari" saiban* [Asahi, 1979], p. 216).

6. Takahashi Shinkichi is an example. His *Dadaisuto Shinkichi no shi*, published seven months before the earthquake, begins, "Dada asserts and negates everything" (p. 29), and contains lines such as "Is Mr. God possible?" (p. 31) and "The universe is foolish, / Limits are also foolish" (p. 125).

7. For a major altercation that presaged the end of dadaism in Europe, see Robert Motherwell and Jack D. Flam, eds., *The Dada Painters and Poets*, 2d ed. (Boston: G. K. Hall, 1981), p. 193.

8. Thomas A. Stanley, *Ōsugi Sakae: Anarchist in Taishō Japan* (Cambridge: Harvard University Council on East Asian Studies, 1982), pp. xvii, 159.

9. *Nihon kindai bungaku dai jiten* (Dictionary of modern Japanese literature) (Kōdansha, 1984), p. 947.

10. Kitasono Katue, "Watakushi no kakawatta shishi" (Journals I have worked on), *Furusawa Iwami Bijutsukan geppō* (Monthly newsletter of the Furusawa Iwami Art Museum), no. 25 (June 1977): 7.

11. Kitasono, *Gendai no me*, no. 11: 2.

12. Kitasono, "Watakushi no nijūdai," p. 23.

13. For the text of "Tokai no koi," see Fujitomi, *Kindai shijin hyōden*, pp. 11–13. The poem is full of punctuation, a characteristic that Kitasono would soon abandon for esthetic reasons.

14. Kitasono Katue interview with Sugiura Kōhei and Matsuoka Seigō in *Yū*, no. 8 (1975): 88. Hereafter cited as "*Yū* interview." Katue refused many requests for interviews, but this one time he consented.

15. Kitasono, "Watakushi no kakawatta shishi," p. 7.

16. Ibid. Kitasono states that he met Nogawa Hajime the second time he visited Tamamura. Previously, he had written that Nogawa Hajime was the one who introduced him to Tamamura; see Kitasono, "GGPG kara *VOU* made" (long version), in *Hon no techō* (Memo on books) (Shōshinsha, 1963), p. 37.

17. Kitasono, "GGPG kara *VOU* made," p. 37.

18. *Epokku* was never revived.

19. Literal translation of a saying from classical Chinese meaning "to be superfluous"; in other words, a snake manages fine without feet. An equivalent English expression is "coals to Newcastle."

20. Nogawa Ryū, *Ge.Gjmgjgam.Prrr.Gjmgem*, 1, no. 1 (June 13, 1924), inside back cover.

21. For one of the earliest soundless poems, see "Fisches Nachtgesang" (Fish's nightsong) by Christian Morgenstern (1871–1914), in Alan Young, *Dada and After* (Manchester: Manchester University Press, 1981), p. 13. Incidentally, "Fisches Nachtgesang" was written for children, but dada does not trace its lineage to nursery rhymes.

22. Sound poems were also written by Tristan Tzara, Kurt Schwitters, and Theo van Doesburg.

23. Hugo Ball, *Flucht aus der Zeit*, published in English with translation by Eugene Jolas in *transition*, no. 25 (Fall 1936); reprinted in Moholy-Nagy, *Vision in Motion*, p. 317.

24. Richard Huelsenback, "Dada Lives," Aug. 1916; trans. Eugene Jolas, *transition*, no. 25; reprinted in Moholy-Nagy, *Vision in Motion*, p. 311.

25. Moholy-Nagy, *Vision in Motion*, p. 315; also reproduced in Motherwell and Flam, *The Dada Painters and Poets*, p. xviii.

26. Motherwell and Flam, *The Dada Painters and Poets*, p. 106.

27. Ibid., p. 117.

28. For his political views, see Aimé Césaire, *Discourse on Colonialism*, trans. Joan Pinkham (New York and London: Monthly Review Press, 1972).

29. Nogawa Ryū, GGPG 1 no. 1: n.p. As far as I know, Nogawa's play was never performed.

30. Kondō Masaji, GGPG 1, no. 1: n.p.

31. Hiraiwa Konji, GGPG 1, no. 1: n.p..

32. Kitasono, "Watakushi no kakawatta shishi," p. 8.

33. Kitasono Katue, "GGPG kara *VOU* made" (short version), *Geppō*, July 1952, p. 8, in pamphlet accompanying *Nihon gendaishi taikei* (Series of contemporary Japanese poetry), 10 (Kawade shobō, 1952).

34. Hashimoto Kenkichi, GGPG, no. 2 (2, no. 1; Jan. 1925): n.p. The title contains the word "Excerpt," but no fuller version was ever printed. This poem and all others published by Kitasono in GGPG were collected by Torii Shōzō and published as *Shikisai toshi, Couleur ville: Kitasono Katue shoki shigun* (Colorful city: the poetry magazines of Kitasono Katue's early career) (Press Bibliomane, 1981).

35. We can recall rebellious youth groups of later times in which fashion played a provocative role—greasers and rockers of the 1950s, mods and hippies of the 1960s, and punks of the 1970s, and on.

36. Tristan Tzara, "Memoirs of Dadaism," in Edmund Wilson, *Axel's Castle* (1931; rpt.—New York: W. W. Norton, 1984), p. 308.

37. GGPG, no. 8 (2, no. 7; July 1925): n.p.

38. Annabelle Melzer, *Latest Rage the Big Drum: Dada and Surrealist Performance* (Ann Arbor, Mich.: UMI Research Press, 1980), p. 41.

39. *Yū* interview, p. 88.

40. Ibid., p. 84.

41. Hirato Renkichi, *Hirato Renkichi shishū* (Hirato Renkichi poems) (Hirato Renkichi shishū kankōkai, 1931), p. 193.

42. An exception is the introduction of the non-revolutionary Bengali poet Rabindranath Tagore by Ezra Pound in the journal *Poetry* in 1912. For concepts of Japan by American poets from Whitman to Ginsberg, see Sanehide Kodama, *American Poetry and Japanese Culture* (Hamden, Conn.: Archon, 1984).

43. Nakano, *Zen'ei shi undō shi no kenkyū*, p. 22.

44. Ibid.

45. Ibid.

46. Nogawa Ryū, "Futatsu no kisoteki kōri" (Two basic axioms), GGPG, no. 4 (2, no. 3; 1925): n.p.

47. Hashimoto Kenkichi, "GGPG no hōkoku," GGPG, no. 3 (2, no. 2; 1925): n.p.

48. Hashimoto Kenkichi, "GGPG no hōkoku," GGPG, no. 4 (2, no. 3; 1925): n.p.

49. Hashimoto Kenkichi, "Underline," GGPG, no. 3 (2, no. 2; 1925): n.p.

50. Nogawa Hajime, GGPG, no. 3 (2, no. 2; 1925): n.p. *Seirisui* (生理水), Hajime's neologism, could also refer to a "physiological saline solution."

51. Hiraiwa Konji, GGPG, no. 8 (2, no. 7; July 1925): n.p.

52. Takagi Haruo, GGPG, no. 8 (2, no. 7; 1925): n.p. According to Catholic doctrine, those who commit suicide are destined for hell.

53. Fujitomi (*Kindai shijin hyōden*, p. 16) claims that Ryū died in a Korean jail; *Nihon kindai bungaku dai jiten* (p. 1141) states that he died in a Manchurian hospital.

54. Hashimoto Kenkichi, "Underline," GGPG, no. 3 (2, no. 2; 1925): n.p.

55. For the names of all the GGPG poets, see Fujitomi, *Kindai shijin hyōden*, p. 20.

56. Conversation with Nakano Ka'ichi on Nov. 11, 1985.

57. For a brief introduction to Murayama, see Yoshida Sei'ichi and Inagaki Tatsurō, eds., *Nihon bungaku no rekishi* (History of Japanese literature), vol. 12 (Kadokawa, 1968), pp. 110–12; and, in English, Toshiharu Omuka, "To Make All of Myself Boil Over: Tomoyoshi Murayama's Con[s]cious Constructionism," in *Dada and Constructivism* (Seibu Museum of Art, 1988), pp. 19–24. Gennifer Weisenfeld's full-length study of Murayama is eagerly awaited.

58. *Yū* interview, p. 84. "Throwing names in the air" was a Dada experiment with chance, prescribed by Tristan Tzara. Here, Kitasono mistakenly thinks that the initial "V" stands for her family name, when it was actually her personal name. On Bubnova Varvara, see *Konnichi no soren pō*, no. 624 (28, no. 3; Feb. 1985): 48–52; and Chanlett-Avery, "Pacific Overtures," pp. 97–115.

59. In 1991 the complete run of *MAVO* was reissued in a replica edition by the Nihon Kindai Bungaku Kan (Japanese library of modern literature) with accompanying articles. For more on *MAVO*, see *Bijutsu hakubutsukan nyūsu* (Tokyo daigaku, Kyōiku gakubu, Bijutsu hakubutsukan i'inkai), no. 20 (June 1984) and the accompanying pamphlet "Dada in Japan, 1920–1970."

60. *Yū* interview, pp. 84–85. In a follow-up question, Katue was asked, "How about Takahashi Shinkichi?" and he replied, "Around the time we were doing GGPG, he was doing Dada in a completely different space." Marcel Duchamp was a seminal artist whose attitude and artwork exerted a great influence on dadaism, surrealism, and later art movements.

61. Zacky?

62. *Neo donachi kometo*, no. 2 (May 1926); reprinted in *Shikisai toshi*, pp. 53–56. For a full translation of the poem, see *Glass Beret*, pp. 67–69.

63. Kitasono Katue, "GGPG kara *VOU* made" (long version), p. 38.

64. Nakahara Minoru, chronology in *Gemälde kaiga* (Bijutsu shuppansha, 1966), n.p. (p. 354).

65. For example, "Ningyō to pistōru to fūsen" (Doll, pistol, and balloon; 1929) and "Mirai no tabako" (Tobacco of the future; 1929); for translations, see *Glass Beret*, pp. 4–5, 44–48.

66. Kitasono Katue, "*Shōbi.Majutsu.Gakusetsu* no kaisō," *Shōbi.Majutsu.Gakusetsu* (1927–28; rpt.—Nishizawa shoten, 1977), p. 1 of pamphlet accompanying reprint.

67. Sasaki Kikyō has tracked down Katue's early work, which appeared in dozens of magazines, and wrote a short and informative monograph, *Kitasono Katue to modanizumu zasshigun* (Press Bibliomane, 1980).

68. Tsuboi Shigeji, ed., *Aka to kuro*, 4 vols. (Aka to kuro sha, Jan.-May 1923; rpt.—Tōji shobō, 1963).

69. Ibid. The manifesto appears on the covers of the first three issues.

70. Hagiwara Kyōjirō, *Shikei senkoku* (Chōryūsha, 1925; rpt.—Meicho kankō kaikan, 1970), pp. 160–61.

Chapter 3

1. Satō Saku makes this point in a roundtable discussion, "Chōgenjitsu shugi to shiteki kūkan" (Surrealism and poetic space), in *Shururearisumu dokuhon 2: shururearisumu no tenkai* (The development of surrealism) (Shichōsha, 1981), p. 35.

2. A preliminary version of this chapter appeared as part of my Ph.D. dissertation, "Shredding the Tapestry of Meaning: The Poetry and Poetics of Kitasono Katue (1902–1978)" (Harvard University, 1989). It was revised and published in *Philological Papers* (West Virginia University; ed. Armand Singer), 39 (1993/94): 27–56. Additional changes have been made since then.

3. Dai'ichi shobō, 1925.

4. Ueda Toshio, *Bungei tanbi* 2, no. 4 (1927): 12–13.

5. A case in point was Salvador Dali's obsession with his wife, Gala (cf. his 1963 painting *Galacidalacideoxyribonucleicacid*). See also André Breton's book, *L'Amour fou* (Paris: NRF, 1937).

6. Ueda Tamotsu, *Bungei tanbi* 2, no. 4 (1927): 16. Ironically, Tamotsu's perspective from distant Japan may better explain the transition from dadaism to surrealism than some local accounts, which center on Breton's upstaging of Tzara in their personal feud.

7. Kitasono Katue, *Kiiroi daen: Essays, Criticism, Scraps* (Hōbunkan, 1953), pp. 112–13, 122.

8. One exception to the superior tension of "Kigō setsu" is the final part of "Hakushoku shishū" (no. 11). Kitasono cut the phrases "wet paint" and "hands off" (which appear in English), thereby sacrificing a provocative counterpoint to the otherwise mild imagery.

9. "Kigō setsu" does have two verbs, but gives the same overall impression of stasis.

10. Although Americans and Europeans would probably first associate "white" with Caucasian, especially in light of Kitasono's francophilism, the racial connotation would be distant if not absent for the Japanese reader.

11. It is common for the first two characters of the magazine's name now to be read as *bara* instead of *shōbi*. However, in an editorial note in 1, no. 2, Ass (a rarely used alternative pen name of Kitasono) twice mentions that it should be read *shōbi*.

12. *Shōbi.Majutsu.Gakusetsu* (1927–28; rpt.—Nishizawa shoten, 1977), pamphlet accompanying rpt.: Kitasono Katue, "*Shōbi.Majutsu.Gakusetsu* no kaisō" (Recollections of *SMG*), no. 3.

13. The Special Higher Police (Tokubetsu kōtō keisatsu, abbreviated Tokkō) had been created in 1911 to suppress left-wing movements, but poets who considered themselves apolitical were not targeted until 1940. The Tokkō, specializing in crimes of thought, were commonly referred to as the "Thought Police." See Chapter 6 for Katue's brush with the law.

14. Kitagawa Fuyuhiko, trans., "Chōgenjitsu shugi sengen sho (1)" (Surrealist Manifesto [1]), *Shi to shiron* (Kōseikaku), 2, no. 4 (June 1929): 23–29; and "Chōgenjitsu shugi sengen sho (2)" (Surrealist Manifesto [2]), *Shi to shiron* 2, no. 5 (Sept. 1929): 66–69.

15. Perhaps an allusion to Rosicrucianism.

16. Kitasono is referring to the meaning of the word and the complexities of these particular Chinese graphs, which consist of thirty-two strokes (薔薇).

17. Ass (Kitasono Katue), *SMG* 1, no. 2 (Dec. 1927): inside back cover.

18. André Breton, Louis Aragon, Pierre Unik, Benjamin Péret, and Paul Eluard.

19. Kitasono remembered the translation as being in English ("*Shōbi.Majutsu. Gakusetsu* no kaisō" [1977], p. 3), but in another article written the same year, he claimed it was in French ("Watakushi no kakawatta shishi," *Furusawa Iwami Bijutsukan geppō*, no. 25; [June 1977], p. 8).

20. Asaka (Kitasono Katue), *SMG* 2, no. 1 (Jan. 1928): inside back cover.

21. "A Note" was drafted by Ueda Toshio and touched up by Katue and Tamotsu; see Kitasono Katue, *Ten no tebukuro* (Shunjū shobō, 1933), p. 44; reiterated in "*Shōbi.Majutsu.Gakusetsu* no kaisō" (1977), p. 3. It is unclear why Kitasono's name appeared first.

22. Substitute *zazen* (Zen sitting) for "poetic operation" and *rōshi* (master) for "poetic scientist," and we can see that the authors' so-called objective attitude is consonant with and probably drawn from Buddhism as much as surrealism.

23. Kitasono, "Watakushi no kakawatta shishi," p. 8.

24. Kitasono Katue, "GGPG kara *VOU* made" (long version), *Hon no techō* (Shōshinsha), 3, no. 3 (May 1963): 39.

25. For the map, see André Breton, *What is Surrealism? Selected Writings*, ed. Franklin Rosemont (New York: Monad/Pathfinder, 1978), p. 42.

26. For a book-length critical treatment of Nishiwaki, see Hirata. For Nishiwaki's poetry in English translation, see Junzaburō Nishiwaki, *Gen'ei: Selected Poems of Nishiwaki Junzaburō, 1894–1982*, trans. Yasuko Claremont, University of Sydney

East Asian Series, 4 (Sydney, Australia: University of Sydney Press and Wild Peony, 1991); James Kirkup, trans., *Modern Japanese Poetry* (Australia: University of Queensland Press, 1978), pp. 45–48; Hiroaki Sato and Burton Watson, trans., *From the Country of Eight Islands* (New York: Anchor, 1981), pp. 507–20; and Geoffrey Bownas and Anthony Thwaite, trans., *The Penguin Book of Japanese Verse* (Middlesex, Eng.: Penguin, 1964), pp. 200–201; for a discussion with translations, see Donald Keene, *Dawn to the West: Poetry, Drama, Criticism* (New York: Holt, Rinehart and Winston, 1984), pp. 323–35.

27. Takenaka Iku (1904–82), who lived in Paris from 1929 to 1931 and befriended Cocteau, was the other.

28. Tsuruoka Yoshihisa, "Ishō no taiyō," in *Nihon no shūrurearisumu: Surrealism in Japan, 1925–1945* (Nagoya: Nagoya shi bijutsukan), p. 24.

29. Ibid.

30. J.N. (Nishiwaki Junzaburō), "Jobun," *Fukuiku taru kafu yo* (Dec. 1927; rpt. with full set of *Ishō no taiyō* [Tamura shoten, 1987]), p. 1. Passage also quoted in Nakano Ka'ichi, "Nōzui no shi to genjitsu" (The brain's poetry and reality), *Rekishō*, no. 67 (1970): 10–11.

31. Statements such as "the event from which each of us is entitled to expect the revelation of his own life's meaning—that event which I may not yet have found, but on whose path I seek myself" and "perhaps life needs to be deciphered like a cryptogram" illustrate that for Breton surrealism was a method of keeping oneself awake to strange signs in external reality that would be instrumental in unlocking the enigma of one's existence. Quotes from André Breton, *Nadja*, trans. Richard Howard (New York: Grove, 1960), pp. 60, 112.

32. For translations of Takiguchi's poems, see Sato and Watson, *From the Country of Eight Islands*.

33. Tsuruoka, *Nihon no shūrurearisumu: Surrealism in Japan, 1925–1945*, p. 24. Also in Satō Saku, "Nihon no shururearisumu: Taishō kara Shōwa e" (Japanese surrealism: from Taishō to Shōwa), "*Ishō no taiyō*": *fukkokuban bessatsu* (*Ishō no taiyō*: reprint supplement) (Tamura shoten, 1987), pp. 1–15. All six issues of *Ishō no taiyō* were reprinted in this limited-edition set of 300 copies.

34. The members were Kitasono Katue, Ueda Toshio, Ueda Tamotsu, Fujiwara Sei'ichi, Yamada Kazuhiko, Nishiwaki Junzaburō, Takiguchi Shūzō, Miura Kōnosuke, and Nakamura Kikuo (dates unknown). Satō Tadashi (dates unknown) joined from issue 4; Tomoya Shizue (1898–?; the only woman in the group and later Ueda Tamotsu's wife) from issue 5; and Satō Naohiko (dates unknown) for the final issue, no. 6. Perhaps for convenience, or perhaps because he funded the magazine, Fujiwara Sei'ichi was credited as editor and publisher for all six issues.

35. *Uta-awase* in the Heian (794–1185), *renga* in the Kamakura (1185–1333), and *haikai* and *senryū* in the Edo (1600–1868) periods are examples. Of course, individu-

ality was also appreciated, but the poem as an anonymous group activity was by no means novel to Japanese culture.

36. *Ishō no taiyō* 1, no. 1 (Nov. 1928): 19–20.

37. *Ishō no taiyō* 2, no. 4 (Feb. 1929): 18–19.

38. "Yōroppa no tsume" (Europe's nails) is the title of another Katue poem (*Ishō no taiyō* 2, no. 1 [Jan. 1929]: 26).

39. The last line of the second poem, "you are all idiots," is a definite throwback to his Dada days and sentiments, indicating that for Kitasono the rejection of dadaism and turn toward surrealism was a gradual process.

40. Kitasono Katue, "Nōzui no ōmu" (The brain's parrot), *Shiro no arubamu* (Kōseikaku, 1929), p. 100; also included in his *Zenshishū* (Chūsekisha, 1983), p. 87.

41. *Shi to shiron* nos. 1–4 were edited by Okamoto Shōichi. On *Shi to shiron*, see Lucy Beth Lower, "Poetry and Poetics: From Modern to Contemporary in Japanese Poetry" (Ph.D. diss., Harvard University, 1987).

42. Circulation figures provided by former editor Haruyama Yukio (via Kikushima Tsuneji) on Feb. 17, 1987.

43. Ueda Toshio was the only regular member from the *Ishō no taiyō* group.

44. According to Kitasono, about one-third of the Japanese contributors were surrealists. See his "*Shi to shiron* to kaiga" (*Shi to shiron* and painting), *Shigaku* (Poetry studies), June 1950, p. 57.

45. In March 1932 the magazine's name was changed to *Bungaku* (Literature), and an additional six issues were published. *Shi to shiron* and *Bungaku* were reprinted as one set (Kyōiku shuppan center, 1979), and now some writers refer to all twenty issues as *Shi to shiron*.

46. Almost every prewar avant-garde poet has written at least a few pages of reminiscences about *Shi to shiron*. For Kitasono's periodization of the movement surrounding the magazine, see his "*Shi to Shiron* to kaiga," *Shigaku*, June 1950, pp. 56–60.

47. Haruyama Yukio, "Zatsugaku are kore: Haruyama Yukio-san ni kiku" (Asking wealth-of-information Haruyama Yukio), *Honoho* (Flame), no. 5 (Winter 1986): 34–35.

48. Haruyama Yukio, "Nihon kindai shōchōshugi shi no shūen" (The death of modern Japanese symbolist poetry), *Shi to shiron*, no. 1 (Sept. 1928): 66–84.

49. Nishiwaki Junzaburō, who was penning poetry in Latin, English, and French, wrote in his native Japanese only after being moved by Hagiwara's *Tsuki ni hoeru* (1917; English trans. by Hiroaki Sato, *Howling at the Moon* [University of Tokyo Press, 1978]).

50. On Hagiwara Sakutarō's poetics, see Makoto Ueda, *Modern Japanese Poets* (Stanford: Stanford University Press, 1983), pp. 137–83.

51. Breton, *What Is Surrealism?*, p. 363.

52. On the same subject, see my short article "Kōmorigasa no shisseki" (The parasol's abscondence) in the special issue on Japanese surrealism, *Bōsho gekkan* 2, no. 9 (Sept. 1986): 13–14.

53. Pierre Reverdy, *Nord-Sur*, 1918. Quoted in English translation in Patrick Waldberg, *Surrealism* (New York: Oxford University Press, 1965; rpt. 1978), p. 22. *Just* is translated as "accurate" by J. H. Matthews, *The Imagery of Surrealism* (Syracuse, N.Y.: Syracuse University Press, 1977), p. 66. Breton's objections aside, Reverdy's definition concisely sums up the new appreciation of discordant imagery.

54. Named after the opening lines of the first experiment, "le cadavre—exquis—boira—le vin—nouveau."

55. Matsuo Bashō, *Oku no hosomichi* (1694), annot. Hagiwara Yasuo (Iwanami shoten, 1979), p. 46.

56. Nishiwaki Junzaburō, "Kamisori to ringo" (The razor blade and the apple), *Shi to wa nani ka: Gendai shi kanshō kōza 1* (What is poetry? lectures on appreciating modern poetry) (Kadokawa shoten, 1969); rpt. in *Nishiwaki Junzaburō zenshū* (The collected works of Nishiwaki Junzaburō) (Chikuma shobō, 1971), pp. 511, 528. Nishiwaki also referred to Joyce's *Finnegans Wake* as "the greatest of all surreal works" (*Hon no techō*, no. 4 [April 1961]; quoted in Chiba Sen'ichi, *Gendai bungaku no hikaku bungakuteki kenkyū* [Comparative literature research on modern literature] [Yagi shoten, 1978], p. 171).

57. Kawanabe Kyōsai (or Gyōsai; 1831–89) is one among many Japanese artists who could be considered a precursor of surrealism (Katsushika Hokusai [1760–1849], Takai Kōzan [1806–83], Utagawa Kunisada [1786–1864], Utagawa Kuniyoshi [1797–1861], and Santō Kyōden [1761–1816] come to mind). On Kyōsai, see Timothy Clark, *Demon of Painting: The Art of Kawanabe Kyōsai* (London: British Museum, 1993).

58. Attributed to Kyōsai in *Nihon no giga* (Japanese cartoons) (Suntory Museum, 1986), p. 45.

59. Ibid., p. 38. Painting by Katsushika Hokusai. Similar works by Itō Jakuchū and others are abundant from the Edo period.

60. The print is dated between 1830 and 1843 and is reproduced in Fukuda Kazuhiko, *Ukiyoe yōroppa korekushon* (European collections of ukiyo-e) (KK Bestsellers, 1989), p. 138.

61. Hukuzawa Itiro [Fukuzawa Ichirō], *Surréalisme* (Atelier, 1937).

62. Fukuzawa's own paintings of this period are quite mysterious and often portray bearded men imbibing strange potions through balloons and glass straws. He, along with Koga Harué, is one of the most acclaimed prewar Japanese surrealist artists. For examples of both of their work, see *Japon des avant-gardes, 1910–1970* (Paris: Editions du Centre Pompidou, 1986).

63. Acknowledged by Takiguchi Shūzō in *Nishiwaki Junzaburō shishū* (Shichōsha, 1979), p. 146.

64. Also used by Apollinaire in a 1917 letter when he coined the term *surrealism*: "As a result of my investigations, I have finally come to believe that, rather than the term I first used, *surnaturalisme*, it is preferable to say *surréalisme.*" My English translation is based on the Japanese translation by Chiba Sen'ichi, "Geijutsuteki kindaiha," in Hasegawa Sen, ed., *Nihon bungaku shinshi: Gendai* (Shibundō, 1986), p. 25.

65. Nishiwaki Junzaburō, *Chōgenjitsu shugi shiron* (Kōseikaku, 1929; for Takiguchi's essay, see pp. 131–68). Takiguchi's essay was replaced with one by Kihara Kōichi, "Surréalisme, 1924–1954," in the first reprinting of Nishiwaki's book, *Chōgenjitsu shugi shiron* (Arechi, 1954). The book was again reprinted in *Nishiwaki Junzaburō zenshū*, 4: 8–88. In this edition, which omits the Takiguchi and Kihara essays, the gap between Nishiwaki's title and the contents becomes readily apparent.

66. *Nishiwaki Junzaburō zenshū*, 4: 83.

67. Originally written in Aug. 1954 and quoted in ibid., 4: 678–79 (Afterword). Nishiwaki stated at a roundtable discussion with Fukuzawa Ichirō and Ebara Jun, "Surreal was a newer title, although the meaning was really surnatural" ("Shi to kaiga no mondai," *Mugen*, no. 4 [May 1960]: 103).

68. This was published along with "Sekai shijin jinmei jiten" (Who's who of foreign poets) as one volume (Momota Sōji, ed., *Gendai shi kōza*, vol. 10 [Kinseidō, 1930]). Momota is credited as sole editor; there is no list of contributing authors in the book.

69. Ibid., p. 149.

70. Kōseikaku, 1931.

71. Ibid., p. 24. Table adapted from the same page.

72. Haruyama Yukio, *Shi no kenkyū*, pp. 22–23.

73. Kōseikaku, 1929. Sales figures provided by Haruyama Yukio (via Kikushima Tsuneji), Feb. 17, 1987.

74. *Tōkyōdō shuppan nenkan* (Tōkyōdō, 1930), pp. 207–11.

75. Kitasono Katue, "Watakushi no shojo shishū," *Hon no techō*, Oct. 1961, pp. 44–45.

76. On the back cover of Ueda Toshio, *Kasetsu no undō* (A hypothetical movement) (Kōseikaku, May 1929).

77. Kitasono Katue, *Kiiroi daen*, pp. 112–13.

78. For a translation by Brian Coffey, see Stéphane Mallarmé, *Selected Poetry and Prose*, ed. Mary Ann Caws (New York: New Directions, 1982), pp. 103–27.

79. For example, the famous calligramme "It's raining" (1916) in which the printed letters look like falling rain; see Guillaume Apollinaire, *Calligrammes*, trans. Anne Hyde Greet (Berkeley: University of California Press, 1980), pp. 100–101.

80. Haruyama Yukio, *Shi to shiron*, no. 4 (June 1929): 102–3.

81. Haruyama Yukio, *Shokubutsu no dammen* (Cross-section of a plant) (Kōsei-kaku, 1929), pp. 64–65; and idem, *Shi no kenkyū*, pp. 97–98.

82. Haruyama Yukio, *Shi no kenkyū*, pp. 98–99.

83. At first reading, Westerners will undoubtedly find racial overtones in Haru-yama's "white girl." However, "white" could also be interpreted as the color of the girls' uniforms, a lightish skin color, or as a metaphor for innocence, purity, virginity, and so on. To specify Caucasian in Japanese, it is necessary to add the graph *hito* (person) and form the compound *hakujin* (white person). The racial overtones, al-though not directly stated in Japanese, are not altogether absent, as is apparent from Anzai Fuyue's statement (quoted in Kikuchi Yasuo, *Gendai shi no taidōki* [The fetal movement period of modern Japanese poetry] [Genbunsha, 1967], p. 434).

84. Ueda Toshio, "Bihatsu kūkan no ningen gakusetsu," *Bungei tanbi*, July 1927, pp. 34–35; Hashimoto Kenkichi (Kitasono), "Jōsō kigō kenchiku," *Bungei tanbi*, Aug. 1927, pp. 21–32 (esp. p. 25). Note that the poem with the title "Shiro no arubamu" is completely different from that given in the book of the same name.

85. For Kitasono's manifesto on plastic poetry and a brief article by me, see *Plastic Poems: Kitasono Katue and the VOU Group* (Providence: Rhode Island School of De-sign, Museum of Art, 1986).

86. Haruyama Yukio, "Preface," in Kitasono, *Shiro no arubamu*, p. 2.

87. Haruyama Yukio, "Poesiologiste Kitasono," *Rekishō*, no. 88 (1978): 13. Haru-yama, in this article written shortly after Kitasono's death, suggests that Katue had also been a specialist at "poesiology and poesiosemantics."

88. Haruyama, "Preface," in Kitasono, *Shiro no arubamu*, p. 3.

89. Ibid., pp. 5–6. Haruyama chose a large selection of the preface to be reprinted as an example of his literary criticism of the late 1920s in *Gendai shi kanshō kōza*, vol. 9 (Kadokawa, 1969), pp. 405–15.

90. "Kigō setsu" and the diagrammatic poems were classified as "poésie," and "umi no umi," embedded in a primarily prose piece, was listed under "poésie en prose." "Poésie graphique" refers to drawings. Cocteau also had three additional categories: "poésie critique," "poésie cinématographique," and "poésie plastique" (sculpture). See Hori Tatsuo, trans., *Cokutō shō* (Kōseikaku, 1929), pp. 178–80; and Francis Steegmuller, *Cocteau: A Biography* (Boston: Godine, 1986), p. 4. Unfortu-nately, Kitasono's categories were not reproduced in the *Zenshishū* edition's table of contents of *Shiro no arubamu*.

91. This attitude is perhaps more prevalent in the contemporary popular music scene than it is among poets.

92. According to Haruyama's recollection in *Rekishō*, no. 88, p. 12. The book seems to have engendered mostly silence among the critics. The only review I have come across is by Kitasono's friend and fellow-poet Ueda Tamotsu, who wrote a

prose-poem praising Kitasono as "an elegant genius" and "magical" (*Shi to shiron*, no. 5 [Sept. 1929]: 208–9).

93. For the French surrealists' roundtable discussions on sex, see *Investigating Sex: Surrealist Discussions, 1928–1932*, ed. José Bierre, trans. Malcolm Imrie (London and New York: Verso, 1992).

94. Ueda Toshio, "Le Gaz de Toshio Ueda et le yacht de Cleopatre," *Ishō no taiyō*, no. 4 (Feb. 1929): 1–3. Takiguchi Shūzō can also be regarded as an exception in that he mentions breasts, pubic hair, and semen in his automatic poems; for a selection in English, see Sato and Watson, pp. 532–38.

95. Satō Saku recalls how the animosity puzzled him: "Even though the surrealists and Cocteau fought like dog and monkey, what they wrote did not seem all that different to me. Breton and Cocteau, in their use of dreams and the subconscious, are equally representative of the 1920s" (discussion with Irisawa Yasuo and Kagiya Yukinobu, "Chōgenjitsu shugi to shiteki kūkan," in *Shururearisumu dokuhon 2*, p. 35).

96. Dawn Ades, "Surrealism," in *Concepts of Modern Art* (London: Thames and Hudson, 1981), p. 124.

Chapter 4

1. Internationally, among proletarian writers, Kobayashi Takiji (1903–33), who was murdered by the police, is ranked second only to B. Traven. Nakano Shigeharu (1902–79) is one of Japan's greatest proletarian poets; see Miriam Silverberg, *Changing Song: The Marxist Manifestos of Nakano Shigeharu* (Princeton: Princeton University Press, 1990).

2. Kitasono Katue, "Shi to shiron to kaiga," *Shigaku*, June 1950, p. 58.

3. The splinter group left after *Shi to shiron*, no. 7 (March 1930); their own magazine lasted for five issues from June 1930 until June 1931.

4. On Hashimoto Kenkichi's pen names, see Sasaki, *Kitasono Katue to modanizumu zasshigun*, pp. 5–6; and Fujitomi, *Kindai shijin hyōden*, pp. 10, 42.

5. According to Sasaki (*Kitasono Katue to modanizumu zasshi gun*, p. 6), the name was first used in the magazine *Bungei toshi*, and later in *Ishō no taiyō*, *Shi to shiron*, *Ciné*, and other journals.

6. Ibid., p. 5. When I asked Katue's wife (interview, Aug. 20, 1986) what the pen name might have meant, she wittily replied, "I never asked him about it—we were always so busy."

7. After the Pacific War and until his death in 1978, all the members of VOU called Kitasono by the affectionate abbreviation "Zono-san" ("Mr. Zono").

8. Shiraishi Kazuko (1931–) told me that she first heard the name Kitasono Katue in her midteens and thought it referred to a woman. When she was taken by

poet Murano Shirō to meet Kitasono, she was shocked to find a man! (interview on May 10, 1985.)

9. Shibuya Ei'ichi, *Shidan jinkokki* (Kōransha, 1933), pp. 77–78.

10. Tanno Sei told me that he had suggested the name "Pan Poésie," although he was not active in the club (interview on June 9, 1987).

11. Conversation with Ueda Osamu, on July 20, 1986. Motoori Norinaga was the classical scholar who brought the Kokugaku (National Learning) movement to fruition. Hirata took Motoori's ideas and put them into practice in reviving Shintoism, an important step leading to the overthrow of the Tokugawa shogunate and the restoration of the emperor.

12. Also reproduced as the frontispiece in *Shururearisumu dokuhon 2*.

13. Kitasono Katue, *Wakai koronii* (Bon shoten, 1932), n.p.

14. The same can be said about *Shin ryōdo* (New country), which was named after a British publication but, like *Wakai koronii*, was easy to mistake as a celebration of Japanese imperialist expansion.

15. The same photo is used for the cover illustration on all three books. Although no one is credited, it looks suspiciously similar to László Moholy-Nagy's photo "Stockholm, 1930" in Andreas Haus, *Moholy-Nagy: Photographs and Photograms*, trans. from German by Frederick Samson (New York: Pantheon Books, 1980), fig. 10.

For more on Bon shoten, see Uchibori Hiroshi, *Bon shoten no maboroshi: modanizumu shuppansha no hikari to kage* (The vision of Bon Books: the light and shadow of modernism publishing) (Hakuchisha, 1992). For his seminal article that grew into the book, see Uchibori Hiroshi, "Kosho to no deai: Bon shoten no koto" (Encountering old rare books: the Bon shoten affair), *iichiko* (Bélier Art Center), no. 7 (Spring 1988): 14–16.

16. "Bluesky" is personified in Japanese because the past-tense verb *ita* of *seiten ga ita* is ordinarily used only for humans and animals. Since the English verb "to be" does not distinguish between the animate and the inanimate, an equivalence was attempted by capitalizing the noun.

17. My translations are based on the original 1932 volume (see note 13 to this chapter). After the war, Kitasono revised the poems, added a few and published them as *Wakai koronii: jōbon* (Young Colony, standard edition; Kokubunsha, 1953). After his death, the poems from *Wakai koronii* were republished in his *Zenshishū* (Collected Poems; 1983); unfortunately, they are presented as the 1932 poems when in fact they are the altered 1953 version. The overall changes are minimal, but line and stanza divisions are reassembled, as well as words dropped or replaced.

18. Kitasono Katue, "Kotoba," *Wakai koronii*; in *Zenshishū*, p. 109.

19. Kitasono Katue, "Umi no nikki," *Wakai koronii*; in *Zenshishū*, p. 115.

20. Kitasono Katue, "Karui tenisu," *Wakai koronii*; in *Zenshishū*, p. 114.

21. Katue nevertheless continued to publish other poems in the same style, for example, in the magazines *Etoile de mer* and *Madame Blanche*. His poem "Wakai koronii" (*Shi to shiron*, no. 13 [1931]: 84), not included in the book *Wakai koronii*, is also in the lyrical mode.

22. I am grateful to Eiko for having given me information regarding their whereabouts during this little-documented time in Kitasono's life (interview on April 14, 1987).

23. Interview on April 14, 1987.

24. Katue's mother had died in 1928 (see Chapter 3).

25. Kondō Tomie, in a study of literary Magome, downplays Katue's role in the scene and erroneously states that "he had no contact with Hagiwara Sakutarō and Murō Saisei" (*Magome bungaku chizu* [Chūō kōronsha, 1984], p. 241). In fact, correspondence from Murō Saisei, novelist Yamamoto Shūgorō (1903–67) and other Magome residents and Kitasono's wartime diaries attest to nearby literary friendships, and so we know that he had his niche in the neighborhood scene of creative artists. Katue translated Hagiwara Sakutarō into English and had him published with his own poems in a New York collection in 1952, and it is quite possible that the two poets met. See Hagiwara Sakutarō, "A Bar at Night," trans. Kitasono Katue, in *A Little Treasury of World Poetry*, ed. Hubert Creekmore (New York: Charles Scribner's Sons, 1952), p. 421. Besides VOU poets and Hagiwara, Kitasono translated Kitahara Hakushū (1885–1942), another Magome resident.

26. For a black-and-white reproduction of the 1940 painting *Shijin Kitasono Katue zō* (Portrait of the poet Kitasono Katue; 80.3 × 65.1 cm), see *Nakada Yoshie gashū* (Paintings by Nakada Yoshie) (Bijutsu shuppan, 1986), p. 98.

27. Kitasono Katue, *Ensui shishū* (Bon shoten, 1933), n.p.

28. Kitasono Katue, *Kiiroi daen* (Hōbunkan, 1953), p. 122.

29. Kitasono Katue, "Miracle," *Ensui shishū*; in *Zenshishū*, p. 132.

30. Kitasono Katue, "Furasuko no naka no shōnen no shi," *Ensui shishū*; in *Zenshishū*, p. 136.

31. Kitasono Katue, "Nul," *Ensui shishū*; in *Zenshishū*, p. 131.

32. Kitasono Katue, "Kinzoku no shima no aru shōnen to shujutsushitsu no kiiroi wa," *Ensui shishū*; in *Zenshishū*, p. 134.

33. Kitasono Katue, "Spherical cone no kajitsu," *Madame Blanche*, no. 12 (Dec. 1933): n.p.

34. Ibid.

35. Ibid.

36. Ibid.

37. Ibid.

38. Poggioli, pp. 65–68, 182–83, 201.

39. Kitasono Katue, "Garasu no ribon o kubi ni maita shōnen no suishō no chi-busa to sono obitadashii kaidan," *Ensui shishū;* in *Zenshishū,* p. 135.

40. Tamura Ryūichi, "Kitasono Katue cho—*Garasu no kuchihige*" (Kitasono Katue author—*Glass Mustache*), *Tsukue* (Kinokuniya), 7, no. 11 (Nov. 1956): 29–30. Yoshioka Minoru, *Ekitai* (Fluid) (1941; rpt.—Yūkawa shobō, 1971). For Yoshioka Minoru on Kitasono, see "Atarashii shi e no mezame—Kitasono Katue: *Ensui shishū*" (Awakening to new poetry: Kitasono Katue's *Conical Poems*), *Eureka,* Sept. 1975, pp. 144–145; and "Danshō mitsu to ippen no shi" (Three literary fragments and one poem) in pamphlet (*shiori*) accompanying *Kitasono Katue zenshishū* (Chūsekisha, 1983), p. 7. For Kitasono on Yoshioka, see "Yoshioka Minoru no shi ni tsuite no kantan na iken" (A simple opinion on Yoshioka Minoru's poetry), *Eureka,* Sept. 1973, pp. 70–71.

41. *Nihon kindai bungaku daijiten,* vol. 5 (newspapers and magazines) (Kōdansha, 1977), does not list *Hakushi;* Katue erroneously recalled that it lasted for ten issues (*Kiiroi daen,* p. 125). I have been able to locate *Hakushi,* no. 14, in a private collection. The vanishing issues and inattention given to the magazine make the title appear a self-fulfilling prophesy.

42. Katue Kitasono, "VOU Club: Notes," *Townsman* (London), 1, no. 1 (Jan. 1938): 4. For Katue's association with *Townsman,* see Chapter 5.

43. The women were Sagawa Chika (1911–36), Sawaki Takako (1907–), and Yamanaka Tomiko (dates unknown).

44. Kitasono did not contribute to *Madame Blanche,* nos. 4 and 5.

45. Kikushima Tsuneji, conversation Dec. 3, 1986.

46. Ema Shōko, *Umoreshi no homura* (The flame of buried poems) (Kōdansha, 1985), p. 134.

47. Ibid.

48. Edited by Momota Sōji.

49. Ema., p. 131. Not all the women poets mentioned by Ema appear on the club lists in *Madame Blanche.* Some were members of the later VOU Club to which she also belonged, and others probably went to meetings without officially joining. In a conversation on Oct. 19, 1987, Ema reiterated that women poets felt comfortable at the Arcueil Club.

50. Conversation with Ueda Osamu, Kikushima Tsuneji, and Jō Naoe on July 20, 1986.

51. *Madame Blanche,* no. 2, n.p.

52. Kitasono Katue, *Kon* (Minzokusha, 1936).

53. My translation based on the edition by Kanaya Osamu, ed., *Sōshi* (Iwanami shoten, 1971), 1: 17–18. For another translation, see Burton Watson, trans., *The Complete Works of Chuang Tzu* (New York: Columbia University Press, 1968), p. 29. Chuang-tzu's point was to stretch the reader's imagination by breaking down cate-

gories of relativity. The Zen saying "The stars in the sky are the insides of the mind" enacts a similar erasure of imagined boundaries.

54. Interview with Ueda Osamu on May 22, 1987. If true, this might account for Kitasono's lack of interest in the Confucianism advocated by Ezra Pound (see Chapter 5).

55. Kitasono Katue, "Kon," *Madame Blanche*, no. 7 (June 1933): n.p.; in *Kon*, p. 9; in *Zenshishū*, p. 143; "Nowaki," *Madame Blanche*, no. 11 (Nov. 1933): n.p.; in *Kon*, p. 13; in *Zenshishū*, p. 144; "Mukashi no ie," *Mita bungaku*, Dec. 1933; in *Kon*, p. 21; in *Zenshishū*, p. 147.

56. Murano Shirō, "Kaisetsu" (Explanation), in idem, ed., *Gendai shijin zenshū* (The collected works of modern poets) (Kadokawa, 1967), p. 307; also referred to by Chiba Sen'ichi, "Kitasono Katsue," in *Nihon kindai bungaku daijiten* (Kōdansha, 1984), p. 476.

57. Kitasono Katue, "*Spherical Cone* no kajitsu" (The fruit of spherical cone), *Madame Blanche*, no. 12 (Dec. 1933): n.p.

58. Kitasono Katue, "Wakaki josei shijin no baai" (The situation of young women poets), in *Ten no tebukuro* (Heaven's glove) (Shunjū shobō, 1933), p. 126. Twenty years later Katue did the book design for Iino Tetsuji, *Bashō nyūmon* (A primer on Bashō) (Kokubunsha, 1956); reviewed by Kihara Kōichi in *Tsukue* (Kinokuniya), 7, no. 7 (July 1956): 29.

59. Kitasono Katue, "Shōden" (Biographical sketch), in Nishiwaki Junzaburō, ed., *Gendai Nihon meishishū taisei 9* (Compendium of famous modern Japanese poetry books) (Sōgensha, 1961), p. 150.

60. Kitasono Katue, untitled preface to *Kon*; in *Zenshishū*, p. 141. In spite of the disclaimer of privacy, the book was advertised in *VOU*, no. 7 (1936): 8.

61. Letter, July 17, 1936; quoted in Kodama Sanehide, ed., *Ezra Pound and Japan* (Redding Ridge, Conn.: Black Swan, 1987), p. 29.

62. Interview with Kobayashi Yoshio on May 29, 1987.

63. Kitasono Katue, *Haiburau no funsui* (Hōbunkan, 1941).

64. Interview with Ueda Osamu on April 20, 1987.

65. Oguri Sen'ichirō, "Yatagan no jōkigen" (Yatagan in high spirits), *Madame Blanche*, no. 9 (Sept. 1933): n.p.

66. Ibid. In present-day Japan, "Madame Blanche" is the name of a high-class line of designer goods, which has existed since 1976. Empress Michiko has been known to wear Madame Blanche outfits.

67. The name "Madame Blanche" is the title of a short story by Fujiwara Sei'ichi published in 1927, and there is also a character named Blanche Derval in Breton's *Nadja* of 1928. See Fujiwara Sei'ichi, "Madame Blanche," *SMG* 1, no. 3 (Dec. 1927): 17–24; and André Breton, *Nadja* (Paris: Librairie Gallimard, 1928); *Nadja*, trans. Richard Howard (New York: Grove, 1960), pp. 47–49.

68. Occasionally Kitasono dropped the "-ichirō" and used the name Oguri Sen.

69. His identity was revealed to me by Kikushima Tsuneji and confirmed by Ueda Osamu and Jō Naoe (1915–), all three of whom were members of the Arcueil Club. Conversation with Kikushima Tsuneji, Ueda Osamu, and Jō Naoe on April 20, 1987.

70. Yoshikawa Eiji, "Kennan jonan" (Death by sword, death by woman), *Kingu* (King), 1, no. 1 (Jan. 1925): 264–77; serialized monthly through 2, no. 9 (Sept. 1926).

71. The heroes, respectively, of *Ise monogatari* (Tales of Ise; mid-tenth century); Murasaki Shikibu, *Genji monogatari* (The tale of Genji; ca. 1,000); and Ihara Saikaku, *Kōshoku ichidai otoko* (The life of an amorous man; 1682).

72. Kasuga Shinkurō, "Shishū no shinpan," *Madame Blanche*, no. 12 (Dec. 1933): n.p.

73. Kasuga Shinkurō, "Watakushi no benkai," *Madame Blanche*, no. 13 (Feb. 1934): 26.

74. Kitasono Katue, "Kanshi," *Madame Blanche*, no. 13 (Feb. 1934): 27; in *Kon*, p. 14; in *Zenshishū*, pp. 144–45. Bashō is a pun, referring to the banana plant and the haiku master.

75. Kasuga Shinkurō, "Shishū no shinpan," *Madame Blanche*, no. 11 (Nov. 1933): n.p. Behind the posturing of Kasuga is the pathos of Katue having to beat his own drum about *Ensui shishū*. In *Kon* (1936) is a list of Katue's books; all six of his pre-1934 books were out-of-print at that point except for *Ensui shishū*. Certainly one of his most innovative experiments, *Ensui shishū* was little appreciated at the time in comparison with his lyrical and traditional styles.

76. Although not explaining much about Katue, there is the fascinating case of the "heteronyms" of Portuguese poet Fernando Pessoa (1888–1935). Pessoa wrote with four different personalities, each in a separate poetic style. His approach superficially resembles multiple-personality disorder (he attributed the phenomenon to neurasthenic hysteria). For an excerpt of his essay "The Genesis of My Heteronyms," see *Selected Poems by Fernando Pessoa*, trans. Edwin Honig (Chicago: Swallow Press, 1971), pp. 163–66.

77. Kasuga Shinkurō, "Shishū no shinpan," *Madame Blanche*, no. 13 (Feb. 1934): 25. Kasuga's criticism is not as sweeping as it may appear: "Sofu no ie" in *Bungei hanron* contains only three poems, and Kasuga commends two of them. The section "Sofu no ie" in *Kon* contains eight poems (approximately half the book).

78. Ibid.

79. Interview with Kikushima Tsuneji on April 20, 1987.

80. *Madame Blanche*, no. 13 (Feb. 1934): 23.

81. Paul Eluard, *Les Petites justes*, trans. Kitasono Katue (Abe shoten, 1933); Stéphane Mallarmé, *Koi no uta: Madrigaux*, trans. Kitasono Katue (Bon shoten, 1934).

82. The tone of self-mockery evades Sasaki Kikyō (*Kitasono Katue to modanizumu zasshigun*, p. 6), who interprets the comment as Katue's serious confession of his lack of training in French.

83. Satō Saku (discussion with Irisawa Yasuo and Kagiya Yukinobu), "Chōgen-jitsu shugi to shiteki kūkan" (Surrealism and poetic space), in *Shururearisumu dokuhon* 2, p. 29. On the same page Kagiya mentions that Ueda Toshio once told him of translating Eluard's "étoile de mer" literally as "sea star" rather than "starfish" for a poem in *Shōbi.Majutsu.Gakusetsu.*

84. In Torii Shōzō's copy of Raymond Radiguet, *Hi no hoho* (Cheeks of Fire), trans. Kitasono Katue (Hakusuisha, 1953). For an English version, see Raymond Radiguet, *Cheeks on Fire: Collected Poems*, trans. Alan Stone (London: John Calder, 1976).

85. Kikushima Tsuneji claimed that *Les Petites justes* is Kitasono's best work, superior to any of his original poetry (interview on Dec. 3, 1986).

86. Yamanaka Sansei, ed., *Hommage à Paul Eluard* (Kobe: Kaihansha, 1934), n.p. Yamanaka and Fujiwara Sei'ichi were the translators; the volume included original poems by, among others, Nishiwaki Junzaburō (one in French, one in English), Yamanaka Sansei (French), and Kitasono (English). Of the 300 copies printed, 50 were distributed in Japan.

87. Kitasono never wrote about *JaNGLE*, even though he is listed as editor. Instead, he credited *Madame Blanche* with two extra issues (nos. 18 and 19), as in the *Townsman* article cited in the next note.

88. Katue Kitasono, "VOU Club: Notes," *Townsman* 1, no. 1 (Jan. 1938): 4.

89. Kitasono Katue, "Watakushi no kakawatta shishi," *Furusawa Iwami Bijutsukan geppō*, no. 25 (June 1977): 9.

90. Kitasono Katue, "GGPG kara VOU made," *Hon no techō*, May 1963, pp. 40–41.

91. Kitasono Katue, *Haiburau no funsui* (Shōshinsha, 1941), inside jacket.

92. Kawamura Yōichi (1932–95) tried to rectify the situation with his series of short articles on *Madame Blanche* in *Sei'en* (Blue flame), nos. 20–32 (Summer 1991–Autumn 1994), except no. 30 (Spring 1994).

Chapter 5

1. For permission to include the Ezra Pound material, I thank The Ezra Pound Literary Property Trust and New Directions Publishing Corp.; the Beinecke Rare Book and Manuscript Library, Yale University; and Mary de Rachewiltz. The entire correspondence has been painstakingly annotated by Sanehide Kodama and included in *Ezra Pound and Japan* (Redding Ridge, Conn.: Black Swan, 1987), hereafter referred to as *EP & Japan*.

2. A few words on the origin of the name "VOU." In one letter Pound punned, "VOUtai and who sings or paints" (*utai* is the sung part of the Nō), and in another

he queried, "What does VOU stand for? telescope word?" Katue responded, "The word VOU has no meaning as the word DADA. only a sign. One day I found myself arranging whimsically these three characters on the table of a cafe. That's all" (*EP & Japan*: Ezra Pound, Nov. 24, 1936, and Feb. 9, 1938, pp. 34, 56; Kitasono Katue, March 16, 1938, p. 57).

After the war Kitasono wrote a more detailed explanation in English in which he credited Iwamoto Shūzō with creating the name: "I can remember the moment in which the strange name VOU was adopted by us. It was on the table of a small coffeehouse on the Ginza street. We had been satisfied with none of the names introduced there, each of them having its own meaning restrictive to our activities, when we hit upon the meaningless spell[ing] which Iwamoto was scribbling automatically on a scrap of paper, and thus we became VOUists." He wrote this explanation for Ezra Pound's friend and biographer, Michael Reck, who was with the American occupation army in Japan after the war (Michael Reck, *Ezra Pound: A Close Up* [New York: McGraw-Hill, 1967], p. 98).

The origin and meaning of "VOU," like those of "DADA," became a bone of contention, taking on more significance as the stature of the club increased. For those who could not pronounce "VOU," the first issue included a *katakana* transcription (ブアウ; bu-a-u), which was subsequently dropped. Then in *VOU*, no. 34, fifteen years later, the following explanation appeared: "Since I am asked about the name VOU from time to time, I will now answer. VOU has no meaning whatsoever. It consists of only three letters used as the sign of our club and magazine. We have some affection for the arrangement of these three letters, as we have for our own names. And there is no more to it than that. Whether VOU is pronounced *bu-a-u* (ブアウ) or *ba-u* (バウ) is the reader's choice. We ourselves even switch back and forth between the two readings" (Anonymous, *VOU*, no. 34 [Jan. 1950]: 48). For additional comments by Kitasono on *VOU*, see "Hitori no VOU poetto no kiroku" (Records of one VOU poet), in *Kiiroi daen*, pp. 179–89; "GGPG kara VOU made," in *Hon no techō* (Shōshinsha, 1963), pp. 165–69; and "Watakushi no kakawatta shishi," *Furusawa Iwami Bijutsukan geppō*, no. 25 (June 1977): 7–10.

3. After the war, Katue worked as curator and started a design bureau within the dental college, which was shut down when he retired in 1978. Recently, fifteen unpublished letters, written in the early 1930s, from Nakahara to Kitasono have been discovered. They shed new light on the relationship between these two up-and-coming artists, often assumed to be the typical pattern whereby a sympathetic patron (Nakahara) supports a poor poet (Kitasono). The documents disclose that Kitasono, on the intervention of his brother Heihachi, helped Nakahara.

4. On Ezra Pound's interwar reputation in Japan and his lack of abilities with the Japanese and Chinese languages, see my "The Hooking of Distant Antennae" in

Richard Taylor and Claus Melchior, eds., *Ezra Pound and Europe* (Amsterdam and Atlanta: Rodopi, 1993), pp. 119–29.

5. Katue must have sent *VOU*, nos. 7 (Mar. 1936) and 8 (Apr. 1936).

6. April 26, 1936, *EP & Japan*, p. 27.

7. Ezra Pound, *Guido Cavalcanti Rime* (Genoa: Edizioni Marsano, 1932).

8. Kitasono Katue, "Veu" [i.e., Vue], *VOU*, no. 11 (Aug. 1, 1936): 42.

9. Ibid.

10. Aug. 12, 1936, *EP & Japan*, p. 30.

11. "Decoupage," *VOU*, no. 13 (Oct. 15, 1936): 36.

12. Ibid., pp. 37–38.

13. Pound's repeated request for Kitasono to send ideograms with the English translations of the VOU poems was ignored (EP letters of Nov. 24, 1936, Mar. 11, 1937 [twice], and Feb. 9, 1938; *EP & Japan*, pp. 34, 41–42, 56). There were, of course, no copy machines in those days; nonetheless, Kitasono's silent refusal is puzzling.

14. Ezra Pound, "VOU Club," *Townsman*, Jan. 1, 1938, p. 4.

15. *Townsman*, Jan. 1, 1938, p. 9. Part I of Katue's poem is a translation of "Garasu no koiru" (Glass coil), in his *Katai tamago* (Hard egg) (Bungei hanronsha, 1941), pp. 10–11. I have been unable to locate the source of Part II; it may be a compilation of lines from several poems.

16. For example, the works of Hagiwara Kyōjirō, Takahashi Shinkichi, Nishiwaki Junzaburō, Takiguchi Shūzō, and other poets introduced in preceding chapters.

17. E. Fuller Torrey, *The Roots of Treason* (San Diego: Harcourt, Brace and Jovanovich, 1984), p. 250.

18. Letter of Jan. 25, 1938, *EP & Japan*, p. 54.

19. Ezra Pound, *Guide to Kulchur* (1938; rpt.—New Directions, 1970), pp. 137–39.

20. James Engell and W. J. Bate, eds., *Biographia Literaria: The Collected Works of Samuel Taylor Coleridge* (1817; rpt.—New Jersey: Princeton University Press, 1983), pp. 168–70.

21. Ibid.

22. Kitasono Katue, "Iwayuru imijirii to ideopurasuti ni kansuru kantan naru shiron" (A brief poetry essay on so-called imagery and ideoplasty), *VOU*, no. 14 (Nov. 1936): 3.

23. Ibid., p. 2.

24. Kitasono Katue, "Shi e no soshikigaku-teki kiyo" (Histology's contribution to poetry), *VOU*, no. 3 (Nov. 1, 1935): 7–8.

25. Fujitomi, *Kindai shijin hyōden*, p. 78.

26. Iwanari Tatsuya, "Kuroi sorera no kuroi sorera: Kitasono Katue shōron" (Black somethings' black somethings: critique of Kitasono Katue), *Gendai shi techō*, Oct. 1986, p. 113.

27. Quoted in ibid.

28. July 17, 1940, *EP & Japan*, pp. 91–92.

29. *EP & Japan*, p. 165.

30. Ibid., p. 94. "Miaco" is Miyako, the ancient capital city.

31. Ibid., p. 108.

32. Ibid., p. 79. As wrongheaded and repulsive as Pound's racist views are, he did have considerable insight into the machinations of what was called the "military-industrial-complex" and is now referred to as TNCs (transnational corporations).

33. Pierre-Simon (Marquis de) Laplace (1749–1827), French mathematician, physicist, and astronomer whose work on the stability of the solar system was the most important advance in physical astronomy since Newton. Because Laplace did not hold strong political views, he was able to escape imprisonment and execution during the French Revolution.

34. *EP & Japan*, pp. 81–82.

35. Pound, *Guide to Kulchur*, p. 148.

36. Ibid., p. 242.

37. Letter, Jan. 1, 1937, *EP & Japan*, p. 35.

38. *Broletto* (Como, Italy), no. 25 (Jan. 1938): 20–21. The introductory paragraphs on Kitasono and the translation were probably by editor Carlo Peroni. Pound is quoted as comparing Katue with Duncan, Zukofsky, and Cummings.

39. Kitasono Katue, "Seven Pastoral Postcards," *Townsman* 2, no. 6 (Apr. 1939): 10–11. The poems are from *Natsu no tegami* (Summer letters) (Aoi shobō, 1937).

40. James Laughlin, "Modern Poets of Japan," *New Directions*, vol. 3 (New York: New Directions Books, 1938), n.p.; hereafter cited as *ND 1938*. Of the fourteen poems, three were reprinted from *Townsman* (1938).

41. James Laughlin, "Editor's Note," in *ND 1938*, pp. 361–79. For more on chain-poems, see below.

42. *ND 1938*.

43. Ibid.

44. Unpublished "Notes" from Kitasono Katue to James Laughlin for *ND 1938* feature. In Katue file at New Directions; kindly sent to me by James Laughlin in June 1985. The following statement by Katue was also not printed, probably because it conflicted with Pound's view of culture subscribed to by Laughlin:

In modern times, Civilizations are flowing back, from the West to the East, towards the near East that was the cradle of them. The contemporary music, painting, architecture, and sculpture have already started there. Poetry of to-day should come back there. Cultures of Japan at the end of the East, and those of the United-States at the end of the West will there get to the perfect comprehension for the first time.

45. James Laughlin, *The Master of Those Who Know: Ezra Pound* (San Francisco: City Lights, 1986), p. 15.

46. Charles Henri Ford et al., "Chainpoems," *New Directions* (New York, 1940), pp. 361–79. The rules of "chainpoems" or "linked verse" vary with the situation, but the main point is that the poets create together. For post–World War II examples, see Octavio Paz, Jacques Roubaud, Eduardo Sanguineti, and Charles Tomlinson, *Renga: A Chain of Poems* (New York: George Braziller, 1971); and Ōoka Makoto and Thomas Fitzsimmons, "Rocking Mirror Daybreak," in *A Play of Mirrors* (Rochester, Mich.: Katydid, 1987), pp. 201–30. Ford also edited the prestigious *View* magazine. For a recent re-edit, see Charles Henri Ford, ed., *Parade of the Avant-Garde: An Anthology of "View," 1940–1947* (New York: Thunder's Mouth Press, 1991).

47. Hugh Gordon Porteus, *Criterion* (ed. T. S. Eliot), 18, no. 71 (Jan. 1939): 397; also quoted in *EP & Japan*, p. 225.

48. Porteus, pp. 397–98.

49. Letter, Mar. 11, 1937, *EP & Japan*, p. 41. Pound wrote: "I shall correct only a few typing errors, or what seem such."

50. For example, in the poem "Passion" by Jun Higashi we have, "Like a dying / Peacock, / In a desperate agony, / Flapping the wings." The editor should have corrected the last line to "Flapping *its* wings." The VOU poets depended on their foreign editors to correct such mistakes.

51. Kitasono Katue, "The Life of a Pencil," *Diogenes* 1, no. 2 (Dec. 1940–Jan. 1941): 53.

52. Kitasono Katue, *Black Rain* (Mallorca, Spain: Divers Press, 1954).

53. Kenneth Rexroth, "Literature" in R. M. Hutchins and M. J. Adler, eds., *The Great Ideas Today* (New York: Praeger, 1970), pp. 169–70.

54. Letter, Apr. 26, 1936, *EP & Japan*, p. 27.

55. Letter, May 24, 1936, *EP & Japan*, p. 28.

56. Letter, July 17, 1936, *EP & Japan*, p. 30.

57. Letter, Mar. 16, 1938, *EP & Japan*, p. 56.

58. Mary Pound, "Gais or the Beauties of the Tyrol," trans. Kitasono Katue as "Utsukushii Chiroru," *Reijokai* (Hōbunkan), 18, no. 1 (Jan. 1, 1939): 98–111.

59. Mary de Rachewiltz, "Postscript: In Place of a Note to Letter 71," in *EP & Japan*, p. 214.

60. Letter, Mar. 20, 1939, *EP & Japan*, p. 74.

61. Letter, Apr. 22, 1940, *EP & Japan*, p. 89. Pound never explained the name to Katue. Spelled "Kit Cat," it refers to the first important club of English poets, the Kit Cat Club of the early eighteenth century. According to one explanation of the name's origin, club meetings were held at a restaurant where the cook, Christopher Cat, specialized in mutton pies called "Kit Cat." See *Memoirs of the Celebrated Persons Composing the Kit-Cat Club* (London: Hurst & Robinson, 1821) wherein Horace Walpole is quoted as saying, "The Kit-Cat Club, generally mentioned as a set of

Wits, were in reality the Patriots that saved Britain." Since the turn of the twentieth century, "kit cat club" has referred to a nightclub specializing in striptease acts.

62. Letter, Nov. 24, 1936, *EP & Japan*, p. 34.

63. *EP & Japan*, p. 151.

64. Torrey, *Roots of Treason*, p. 211.

65. Kitasono Katue, *Saboten tō* (Aoi shobō, 1938), p. 20; in *Zenshishū*, p. 180.

Chapter 6

1. On the applicability of the term "fascism" to Japan, see Olavi K. Fålt, *Fascism, Militarism or Japanism? The Interpretation of the Crisis Years of 1930–1941 in the Japanese English-Language Press*, Studia Historica Septentrionalia 8 (Rovaniemi, Finland: Societas Historica Finlandiae Septentrionalis), 1985; for Richard Mitchell on the subject, see his review of Fålt's book in *Monumenta Nipponica* 40, no. 4 (Winter 1985): 447–49.

2. Sakuramoto Tomio is the most strident among them. He has made a literary career of exposing the wartime verse of poets who had previously advocated internationalist, avant-gardist, proletarian, or communist positions. See, e.g., his *Hi no maru wa mite ita* (I saw the Rising Sun flag) (Marujusha, 1982).

3. Fujitomi, *Kindai shijin hyōden*, pp. 131–32.

4. Besides Sakuramoto Tomio, Yoshimoto Takaaki also takes this approach. For their comments on Kitasono, see Yoshimoto Takaaki, *Jojō no ronri* (The logic of lyricism) (Miraisha, 1963; 1976 ed.), pp. 115–18; and Sakuramoto Tomio, *Kūhaku to sekinin* (Blankness and responsibility) (Kobayashi insatsu kabushiki gaisha shuppanbu, 1983), pp. 248–53.

5. Masao Miyoshi, "Against the Native Grain," in idem and H. D. Harootunian, eds., *Postmodernism and Japan* (Durham, N.C.: Duke University Press, 1989), pp. 152–53.

6. The Proletarian school was an exception, seeing all cultural production as "political."

7. On the Kobe Incident, see Adachi Kenichi, "'Kobe shijin' shoshi" (Bibliography of the "Kobe poets"), *Bungaku* 53 (Jan. 1985): 120–27.

8. Two VOU members, Shimizu Masato (1936– ; interview, Nov. 23, 1987) and Andō Kazuo (1929– ; interview, Nov. 24, 1987), told me that they wanted to ask Katue about his patriotic poetry but were afraid of angering him.

9. Conversation on Nov. 24, 1987.

10. Katue's abstract poems are collected in *Katai tamago* (Bungei hanronsha, 1941).

11. Kitasono Katue, *Natsu no tegami* (Aoi shobō, 1937); *Hi no sumire* (Violet of fire) (Shōshinsha, 1939). For discussions of Katue's particular brand of lyricism— contemporary words combined surrealistically—see Chapters 4 and 7.

12. Kitasono Katue, *Saboten tō* (Aoi shobō, 1938).

13. Kitasono Katue, *Kon* (Minzokusha, 1936). For a discussion of these poems, see Chapter 4.

14. Katue's haiku were collected and posthumously published as Kitasono Katue, *Mura* (Village), ed. Funaki Jin and Fujitomi Yasuo (Garandō, 1980); reissued along with haiku by Natsume Sōseki (1867–1916), Akutagawa Ryūnosuke (1892–1927), and others in *Gendai haiku shūsei bekkan 1: Bunjin haiku shū* (Compilation of modern haiku, supplement 1: collection of haiku by literati) (Kawade shobō shinsha, 1983).

15. See, e.g., Thomas R. H. Havens, *Valley of Darkness: The Japanese People and World War II* (New York: Norton, 1978), p. 22. See also Elise Tipton, *Japanese Police State: Tokkō in Interwar Japan* (Honolulu: University of Hawai'i Press, 1990).

16. VOU members who joined were Osada Tsuneo, Kitasono Katue, Nagayasu Shūichi (1909–90), Yasoshima Minoru (1906–83), Kihara Kōichi (1922–79), and Nakamura Chio (*Shin gijutsu* no. 31, p. 4).

17. Kitasono Katue, "Decoupage," *VOU*, no. 24 (Nov. 20, 1938): 7.

18. Kitahara Hakushū, "Jo" (Preface), in Osada Tsuneo, ed., *Sensō shishū* (War poems) (Shōshinsha, 1939), pp. 1–3.

19. A copy of the special edition of *Hi no sumire* includes an original painting by the famous artist Tōgō Seiji (1897–1978). Among Katue's books, it is the most valuable, selling at an auction in summer 1998 for over $3,000.

20. I thank Chiba Sen'ichi for pointing out that *Sensō shishū* was the first anthology of wartime poetry (interview on Jan. 12, 1988).

21. For a photo of Nagashima Miyoshi on crutches, see *VOU*, no. 28 (Dec. 1, 1939): 6. In the same issue (p. 49) appears a review by Nagayasu Shūichi of Nagashima's book of poems, *Seiei butai* (Elite corps). VOU poet Sasajima Toshio (dates unknown) was also drafted and sent to the front in January 1939.

22. Kihara Kōichi makes the point that traditionalist poets published fewer patriotic poems; see his "Abangyarudo no shūen" (The death of the avant-garde), *Chikyū* (Earth), no. 34 (*bessatsu*) (Feb. 1962), p. 3. In the same issue (p. 10), Isomura Hideki discussed the journals *Shiki* and *Kogito* and concluded that although poets in those groups were not pressured to show loyalty (as were the former avant-gardists), some of them did in fact contribute jingoist verse to anthologies.

23. According to two poets active in the Tokyo Poets Club, Ema Shōko (interview, Feb. 5, 1988) and Kikushima Tsuneji (interview, Feb. 14, 1988).

24. The proverb in Japanese is *Deru kugi wa utareru.*

25. On self-censorship in the Japanese publishing industry, see Jay Rubin, *Injurious to Public Morals* (Seattle: University of Washington Press, 1984), pp. 5, 270–72.

26. Kitasono Katue, "Sensen no aki," in *Sensō shishū*, pp. 102–3.

27. Reprinted in *EP & Japan*, p. 203. For a discussion of Katue's "ideoplasty," see Chapter 5.

28. For example, Yoshimoto Takaaki, *Jōjō no ronri*, p. 117.

29. See, e.g., "Ningyō to pisutōru to fūsen," *Shiro no arubamu*, pp. 23–27; in *Zenshishū*, pp. 29–32; my trans., "Doll, Pistol and Balloon," can be found in *Glass Beret*, pp. 4–5.

30. Kitasono Katue, "Decoupage," *VOU*, no. 26 (Apr. 25, 1939): 43.

31. For a photograph of a poster requesting women with permanents to refrain from entering the town, see Havens, *Valley of Darkness*, p. 19.

32. Kitasono Katue, "Shidan jihyō" (Comments on current poetry), *Bungei hanron* (Bungei hanronsha), Sept. 1939, pp. 24–25; also quoted in Fujitomi, *Kindai shijin hyōden*, pp. 99–100.

33. Kitasono Katue, "Decoupage: VOU kurabu-in e no shingō," (Decoupage: signal to VOU Club members), *VOU*, no. 29 (June 1940): 20.

34. Amar Lahiri, *Japan Talks* (Hokuseidō Press, 1940), p. 135.

35. Interview on July 12, 1986.

36. Yoshikawa Norihiko, ed., *Nihon shidan* (Nihon shidan hakkōsho, 1938).

37. Yamamoto Kansuke, ed., *Yoru no funsui*, nos. 1–4 (Oct. 1938– Oct. 1939).

38. Taped interview with Yamamoto Kansuke on June 7, 1986.

39. Kihara, p. 2.

40. According to a quote by Itagaki Naoko in Sakuramoto Tomio, *Shijin to sensō* (Poets and war) (Kobayashi insatsu kabushiki gaisha shuppanbu, 1978), p. 16.

41. Ibid., p. 44. "Cactus Island" is the translation of *Saboten tō*, Katue's 1938 book of poems.

42. Letter of Apr. 11, 1939; see *EP & Japan*, p. 76.

43. The project was never revived.

44. Havens, *Valley of Darkness*, pp. 30–31.

45. Interview with Ueda Osamu on Feb. 14, 1988.

46. Jay Rubin suggests that Miyamoto Yuriko (1899–1951), proletarian novelist and avowed communist who was arrested several times and spent almost two years in jail during the Pacific War, joined the Hōkokukai (see below in this chapter) because she was afraid of ostracism (*Injurious to Public Morals*, p. 275). He bases this assertion on Donald Keene's synopsis of her I-novel, *Fūchisō* (The weathervane plant) in "The Barren Years: Japanese War Literature," *Monumenta Nipponica* 33, no. 1 (Spring 1978): 102–3.

47. For a detailed explanation of the *tenkō* system, see Richard H. Mitchell, *Thought Control in Prewar Japan* (Ithaca, N.Y.: Cornell University Press, 1976), pp. 127–47: and Tipton, *Japanese Police State*.

48. Nakano, *Zen'ei shi undō shi no kenkyū*, p. 452; Tsuruoka Yoshihisa, "Nihon

kaigai shururearisumu nenpyō" (Chronological table of Japanese and foreign surrealism), in *Shururearisumu dokuhon 2*, p. 259.

49. Telephone conversation with Torii Ryōzen on January 28, 1988. Arima Akihiko (1920–96), another VOU member at that time, confirmed Torii's account (interview on Mar. 22, 1988).

50. Kitasono Katue, "The VOU Club," *Nine* (London), 3, no. 4 (Summer/Autumn 1952): 314. Katue's assertion aside, there is no proof of his having specifically helped anyone avoid arrest.

51. *VOU*, no. 30, pp. 1–2.

52. Amar Lahiri, *Japanese Modernism* (Hokuseidō Press, 1939); *Mikado's Mission* (Japan Times Press, 1940); *Japan Talks* (Hokuseidō Press, 1940).

53. Lahiri, *Japanese Modernism*, p. 223.

54. Ibid., p. 209.

55. Lahiri, *Japan Talks*, p. 129.

56. Letter of Dec. 30, 1940; *EP & Japan*, pp. 105–6.

57. Letter of July 17, 1936; *EP & Japan*, p. 29.

58. Lahiri, *Japan Talks*, p. 135.

59. "VOU kurabu genkō kinki jikō" (Taboo styles for VOU manuscripts), *Shin gijutsu*, no. 31 (Dec. 25, 1940): 3–4; repeated in *Shin gijutsu*, no. 32 (Mar. 20, 1941): 5.

60. In *VOU*, no. 11 (Aug. 1, 1936): 28, he had printed a "List of Style Taboos" which proscribed *furigana*, subtitles, lines after *kana*, roman letters horizontally aligned on the page [they had to be vertical], and gothic and other special type forms. Conspicuously absent from the earlier list are prohibitions against foreign words, old Chinese words, and dialectal usages. An almost identical list was printed in *VOU*, no. 14 (Nov. 15, 1936): 25.

61. Torii Ryōzen, "Fukusō ni okeru shin gijutsu" (New dress techniques), *Shin gijutsu*, no. 31 (Dec. 1940): 4.

62. Kitasono Katue, "Katai kyokusen" (Hard, curved line), *Shin gijutsu*, no. 32 (Mar. 20, 1941): 34–35.

63. Nagayasu Shūichi, "Kyōshū" (Longing for hometown), *Shin gijutsu*, no. 32 (Mar. 20, 1941): unnumbered page between pp. 16 and 17.

64. Osada Tsuneo, "Sakyū no danpen" (A dune's fragment), *Shin gijutsu*, no. 32 (Mar. 20, 1941): 7. Perhaps because Katue also found the younger generation more accessible, or because of his desire to mold poets, we find a note for prospective members in the same issue (p. 4) stating that applicants must be graduates of junior high school but under twenty-five years old. In *Shin gijutsu*, no. 35 (Feb. 10, 1942): 18, the maximum age is dropped to twenty. Katue was thirty-seven years old at the time.

65. *Shin gijutsu*, no. 32 (Mar. 20, 1941): 3. The international anthology was never published (interview with Charles Henri Ford on Mar. 12, 1996).

66. Ibid., p. 34.

67. Ibid., p. 36.

68. Kitasono Katue, *Katai tamago* (Bungei hanronsha, 1941); and *Haiburau no funsui* (Shōshinsha, 1941).

69. *Gendai Nihon nenkan shishū* (Sangabō, 1941), pp. 98–99.

70. Kitasono Katue, "Shin shiron" (New poetics), *Gendai shi*, May 30, 1941, pp. 231–46.

71. A brief anthology of Nazi poetry translated into Japanese by Sasazawa Yoshiaki (1898–1984) appears in the third issue of *Gendai shi*, June 27, 1942, pp. 279–95.

72. Kitasono Katue, "Shin shiron," p. 233.

73. Kinoshita's book, *Bungaku seishin no gensen* (The source of the literary spirit) (Kinseidō, 1933), contained the Pound essays *How to Read* and "James Joyce: At Last the Novel Appears."

74. The last letter Katue received from Pound before the Pacific War is dated Apr. 12, 1941, and the last one he sent Pound is dated May 28, 1941; *EP & Japan*, pp. 113–14.

75. Kinoshita Tsunetarō, "Shidan jihyō" (Comments on current poetry), *Mita bungaku*, Aug. 1941, pp. 208–10.

76. On the Chinese continent, 185,000 Japanese had died before the strike on Pearl Harbor widened hostilities to the east and south. Over three million Japanese out of a population of seventy million died before the war ended on August 15, 1945. No official figures exist for how many people Japanese soldiers killed from 1937 to 1945. I asked Sakuramoto Tomio what his research would lead him to believe, and he estimated the number at well over six million (interview on Mar. 17, 1988).

77. Kitasono Katue, *Shin gijutsu*, no. 33 (Aug. 25, 1941): 1–2.

78. Kitasono Katue, "Tonkōsan ki" (Chronicle of Mt. Tonkō), *Shin gijutsu*, no. 34 (Nov. 25, 1941): 17.

79. Katue knew Takiguchi quite well because they had worked together on the surrealist magazine, *Ishō no taiyō* (1928–29). For more on Takiguchi and Fukuzawa, see Chapter 3.

80. See Takiguchi Shūzō, "Jihitsu nenpu" (An autobiographical chronology), in *Takiguchi Shūzō* (Shichōsha, 1985), p. 244; and Nakamura Gi'ichi, *Nihon no zen'ei kaiga* (Japan's avant-garde painting) (Shichōsha, 1968; rpt. 1977), pp. 155–56, 173. According to Tsuruoka Yoshihisa, police records state that the two men were arrested on April 5 (one month later). Tsuruoka confronted Takiguchi with the disparity, but the aged poet wryly retorted, "So you trust the Thought Police more than my memory" (telephone interview with Tsuruoka Yoshihisa on Apr. 10, 1988).

81. Havens, *Valley of Darkness*, p. 90.

82. Kitasono Katue, "Yoru" (Night), *Shin gijutsu*, no. 34 (Nov. 25, 1941): 16; reprinted in *Fūdo* (Shōshinsha, 1943), pp. 53–55; and in *Zenshishū*, pp. 303–4.

83. "Mugi" (Wheat), in *Fūdo*, p. 66; in *Zenshishū*, p. 309.

84. Kitasono Katue, "Shōkan" (Almost midwinter), *Gendai shi* (Kawade shobō), Spring 1942, pp. 178–79; reprinted in *Fūdo*, pp. 59–61; and in *Zenshishū*, pp. 307–8.

85. In the poem "Ie" (House), the protagonist asserts, "Time [lit., the years and months] is already / close to eternity" (*Fūdo*, pp. 41–43; *Zenshishū*, pp. 295–96).

86. Kitasono Katue, *Kyōdo shiron* (Shōshinsha, 1944), p. 83.

87. Kitasono Katue, "Yoru," in *Fūdo*, pp. 34–37; in *Zenshishū*, pp. 291–92.

88. Kitasono Katue, "Mizu" (Water), in *Fūdo*, pp. 16–17; in *Zenshishū*, pp. 277–78.

89. Kitasono Katue, untitled essay, *Shin shiron*, no. 57 (Feb. 1, 1942): 2; reprinted as "Shin shiron," *Gendai shi*, no. 3 (Spring 1942; (June 27, 1942): 309.

90. Ezra Pound, *Guide to Kulchur*, p. 138.

91. Kitasono Katue, untitled essay, *Shin shiron*, no. 59 (Apr. 1, 1942): 1; also in *Gendai shi*, no. 3 (Spring 1942): 310.

92. Although Katue is not known to have practiced *zazen* (zen sitting), he dabbled in the native arts of haiku, tea ceremony, sword appreciation, and held a rank in *kendō*. VOU member and close friend Nagayasu Shūichi, also skillful at *kendō*, described a match he once had with Katue in which the two poets raised their sticks and glared intently at one another, but each wanted to let the other win, and, unable to strike, they finally gave up, calling it a draw (Nagayasu Shūichi, "Kitasono Katue to watashi" [Kitasono Katue and me], *Dorobune*, no. 6 [July 10, 1986]: 12–13).

93. Kitasono Katue, untitled essay, *Shin shiron*, no. 60 (May 1, 1942): 2; also in *Gendai shi*, no. 3 (Spring 1942): 315.

94. Kitasono Katue, untitled essay, *Shin shiron*, no. 62 (July 1, 1942): 1; also in *Gendai shi*, no. 4 (Autumn 1942; Dec. 20, 1942): 273.

95. Kitasono Katue, "Fue" (Flute), in *Fūdo*, pp. 44–46; in *Zenshishū*, pp. 297–98. Originally published without stanza breaks in *Shin gijutsu*, no. 33 (Aug. 25, 1941): 23.

96. Kitasono Katue, "Kōki" ([Editorial] Postscript), *Shin shiron* (Aoi shobō), no. 57 (Feb. 1, 1942): 16.

97. Ibid., p. 16.

98. Ibid. The original wording of the italicized portion is "Kono ippen ni jibun no Dai Tōa sensō ni tai suru subete no kangeki o asshuku shita tsumori de aru."

99. Kitasono Katue, "Zōhoin sono hoka" (Book collecting seal, etc.), in *Kyōdo shiron* (Shōshinsha, 1944), p. 87. I checked the *Yomiuri shinbun* issues of Dec. 8, 1941—June 1942 at the Kokkai Toshokan (National Diet Library, Tokyo).

100. Kitasono Katue, "Seiki no hi," in Satō Sōnosuke and Katsu Yoshi, eds., *Kuni o kozorite* (Kashisha shobō, 1942), pp. 209–12. Three thousand copies were printed. I am grateful to Sakuramoto Tomio for bringing this book to my attention (Oct. 13, 1988) and sending me a copy of Katue's poem.

101. Ibid., p. 222.

102. Ibid., pp. 209–12.

103. Kitasono Katue, "Fuyu" (Winter), in *Fūdo*, pp. 62–64. The poem is dated Jan. 4, 1942 (p. 79).

104. Kitasono Katue, *Gendai Nihon shijin zenshū 13* (The complete poems of modern Japanese poets, vol. 13) (Sōgensha, 1955), pp. 141–236. "Fuyu" is listed in the table of contents (p. 148) with an unexplained asterisk instead of a page number and the poem does not appear in the body of the text. Fujitomi Yasuo, the editor of Katue's *Zenshishū*, also omitted "Fuyu," because, in his words, "I thought Katue would have preferred it that way" (conversation on Feb. 16, 1988). Fujitomi's awareness of "Fuyu" contradicts the view expressed in his biography that "he [Katue] did not write so-called patriotic poetry" (Fujitomi, *Kindai shijin hyōden*, p. 131).

105. A special edition of sixty copies, with an original painting by Katue, was issued in 1944. Sasaki Kikyō, an authority on poetry publishing in the twentieth century, told me that he doubts that all 1,500 copies of the regular edition of *Fūdo* were actually printed, even though that is the figure appearing in the colophon. According to Sasaki, it was common for publishers to inflate figures on government-approved books to stock paper for other projects, and he speculates that publisher Moriya Hitoshi would have done so with Katue's consent (interview on Nov. 29, 1987).

106. *Shin gijutsu*, no. 35 (Feb. 10, 1942); no. 36 (June 10, 1942); and no. 37 (Sept. 15, 1942).

107. Issue no. 37 appeared on September 15 with a mysteriously improbable September 20 deadline for manuscripts for the next issue; *Shin gijutsu* folded uneventfully.

108. Shimori Tarō of Aoi shobō published *Shin shiron*. He had previously published two of Katue's most glamorous books, *Natsu no tegami* (1937) and *Saboten tō* (1938), both designed by Onchi Kōshirō (1891–1955), one of the first abstract painters in Japan and a leader of the Sōsaku Hanga (New-style prints) movement. Murano Shirō was an avant-garde poet; Katue had designed his popular book of poems, *Taisō shishū* (Gymnastic poems; 1939).

109. Not to be confused with the magazine of the same name published by Atorie (Atelier) from 1932 to 1933.

110. Kitasono Katue, "Kōki," *Shin shiron* (Aoi shobō), no. 63 (Aug. 1, 1942): 16.

111. According to Sakuramoto Tomio, candidates to fill these positions volunteered their services and were not appointed (interview on Mar. 17, 1988).

112. In the early 1920s, Katue had taken his poems to Ikuta Shungetsu, and the older poet wrote a letter of introduction for him to Saijō Yaso. Saijō praised Katue and thereafter helped him to get published (see Chapter 1).

113. Nihon Bungaku Hōkokukai, ed., *Bungei nenkan* (Literary arts annual) (Tōkei shobō, 1943), pp. 132–33.

114. Saijō Yaso, "Shi bukai no seikaku to dōkō" (Character and trends of the Poetry Section [of the Patriotic Association for Japanese Literature]), in ibid., p. 10.

115. On the existence of a three-tier writers' blacklist with the worst offenders targeted for army service, see Sakuramoto, *Shijin to sensō*, pp. 21–22. When I asked Sakuramoto whether he thought Katue might have been on the blacklist, he grinned, shook his head, and declared, "Oh no, no way. I'm certain he never was" (interview on Mar. 17, 1988).

116. Katue also joined the patriotic literary group, the Kuroganekai (Black iron association). The particulars of his activity there are unknown, but, to judge from the name, we can conjecture that the members raised funds for battleships. Katue and Osada also organized a series of poetry and sculpture exhibitions, one of the non-publishing activities of the Poetry Section of the Hōkokukai.

117. Kitasono Katue, "Kōki," *Shin shiron*, no. 74 (July 1, 1943): 112.

118. Kitasono Katue, "Hata," *Bungei hanron* (Bungei hanronsha), April 1, 1942, pp. 6–7; quoted in Sakuramoto, *Kūhaku to sekinin*, pp. 249–52.

119. "Bankokuki wa sabishii ne." Author's collection.

120. Murano Shirō, "Kōki," *Shin shiron*, no. 66 (Nov. 1, 1942): 16. To keep the mission secret, Murano's brother left the enemy unnamed.

121. Murano Shirō, "Kōki," *Shin shiron*, no. 63 (Aug. 1, 1942): 16.

122. Kitasono Katue, "Kōki," *Shin shiron*, no. 67 (December 1, 1942): 16. The issue number is misprinted as 66 both on the cover and the colophon.

123. I am grateful to poet-doctor Kuroda Iri (1929–) for answering my questions related to Katue's physical condition (telephone interview on Mar. 20, 1988).

124. Unsigned and untitled note, *Shin shiron*, no. 69 (Feb. 1, 1943): 21.

125. Murano Shirō, "Kōki," *Shin shiron*, no. 76 (Sept. 1, 1943): 144.

126. *Bungei hanron* (July 1, 1943): 6–10. Takiguchi Shūzō also contributed an essay on hometown poetry (pp. 23–27). Katue claimed to have coined the term *kyōdo shi* (see "Hatsu" [Epilogue], in idem, *Kyōdo shiron* [Shōshinsha, 1944], p. 95).

127. Kitasono Katue, *Kyōdo shiron*. See, however, note 105 to this chapter.

128. Murano Shirō, untitled essay, *Shin shiron*, no. 58 (Mar. 8, 1942): 1–2. Murano's comments were directed more to strident patriotic verse than to hometown poetry, but he also penned nationalistic verse. Apparently, his qualms were directed not at the genre of patriotic poetry but at the poor quality of what was being produced.

129. Ueda Tamotsu, "Nihon to seiyō" (Japan and the West), *Shin shiron*, no. 65 (Oct. 1, 1942): 12–13.

130. Miyakoda Ryū, "Tairiku shijin kesshū no tame no riron" (Theory for poets amassed on the continent), *Shin shiron*, no. 69 (Feb. 1, 1943): 25.

131. Kuroda Saburō, "Shijin o chūshin to suru yotsu no sankakukei" (Four triangles centering on poets), *Shin shiron*, no. 61 (June 1, 1942): 6.

132. Kihara Kōichi, "Abangyarudo no shūen," p. 4. It is difficult to ascertain if Kihara is referring to hometown poetry in *Shin gijutsu* (when the VOU Club was still active) or to the abstract poetry of the VOU Club before the police crackdown, or to both of them. All of Katue's poetry—except the patriotic poems—are free of overt social and political commentary. In that sense, the expression "pure poetry" covers both the hometown and the abstract modes.

133. Katue's poems in the hometown mode written after the publication of *Fūdo* are included in *Ie* (House; 1959).

134. Kitasono Katue, "Jibun no shi" (My own poetry), *Bungei hanron* (April 1943): 10; reprinted in idem, *Kyōdo shiron*, p. 60.

135. Kitasono Katue, "Haiku," *Shin shiron*, no. 73 (June 1, 1943): 90.

136. Stephen Spender, "Two Armies," in Jon Stallworthy, ed., *The Oxford Book of War Poetry* (Oxford: Oxford University Press, 1984), p. 240.

137. Kitasono Katue, "Haiku," p. 91.

138. I thank Torii Fusako for assisting me in reading difficult passages. This section about the desk diary will appear in Marlene Mayo and J. Thomas Rimer, eds., *War, Occupation, and Creativity: Japan and East Asia, 1920–1960* (Honolulu: University of Hawai'i Press, forthcoming).

139. Katue kept a diary three times in his life: 1917–18, 1944–45, and 1948.

140. Akio was first relocated to Izu-taga, located near Atami, about sixty miles from their Magome home. The newsreel films were, of course, government propaganda.

141. The banker's starting salary is noted in Shūkan Asahi, ed., *Nedan (Meiji, Taishō, Shōwa) fūzoku shi* (A history of customs: prices in [Meiji, Taishō, Shōwa]) (Asahi Shinbun, 1987), 1: 601. The two volumes of this book record everything from the prime minister's salary to the price of pachinko balls. Statistics for the war years, however, are often scanty or unavailable. Other approximate salaries of the time (according to Hattori Shinroku, interviewed on June 26, 1988): a beginning employee in the Foreign Ministry, ¥65; a section head of a company (*kachō*), ¥120; company president (*shachō*), ¥500.

142. For a list, see the Appendix.

143. Interview with Hashimoto Akio on May 20, 1988. It is recorded in Katue's diary that Eiko paid a visit to Akio because he had fallen sick one week after being relocated to Atami. Akio told me, "I was not really sick, only hungry." He also related the following anecdote: "Since outgoing mail was censored, my parents suggested that if I was lonely and wanted to be visited, I should draw a picture of a cow as a sign to them. I hated the school and drew a cow on each letter I sent home. The school authorities grew puzzled—I kept drawing cows, even though there were none in Atami."

144. Kitasono Katue, "Furusato e no tegami" (Letter to my hometown), *Rekishō*, no. 10 (Feb. 1954): 15. Katue wryly added: "But my poems and paintings are so overly simple that only specialists seem to understand them."

145. Every soldier was given a Japanese flag on which it was customary to have family and friends sign their names.

146. Jan. 18, Feb. 12, Mar. 10, May 8, Aug. 8.

147. *Tsuji shishū* (Intersection poetry anthology) and *Tsuji shōsetsu shū* (Intersection short-story anthology) were published by the Hōkokukai to raise money for battleships. Citizens would stand at intersections and read a poem or brief prose piece, exhorting passersby to donate. The nature of the relationship between the Hōkokukai and the Kuroganekai is unclear, but the organizations were apparently working along parallel lines.

148. Kitasono Katue, "Natsu," *Shi kenkyū*, no. 1 (June 1, 1944): 25–26.

149. Kihara Kōichi informs us that besides Katue, Miyoshi Toyo'ichirō (1920–92) and other poets also used the newsletter format to circumvent the ban on publishing; see "Teikō to zasetsu no shi: kaisetsu" (Commenting on poems of resistance and collapse), *Gendai shi techō* 15, no. 11 (Sept. 1, 1972): 98. Miyoshi Toyo'ichirō said he was unaware of Kitasono's *Mugi tsūshin* until after the war and did not know of any other private newsletters, but he imagined that a few existed. Miyoshi added, "There were four or five of us contributing to my nameless newsletter. The first three issues were printed, but after our printer's small shop was shut down, I had someone at my workplace type it for us" (telephone conversation on May 29, 1988).

150. See the Appendix for a list of references to *Mugi tsūshin* culled from the diary.

151. On the upper right-hand side of pages 25 and 29, inside a rectangular box, appears the only information about the newsletter: "*Mugi tsūshin*, Mugi no Kai, Ōmori, Magome, Nishi, 1–1649 [Katue's address]." The fifteen authors whose work appears in these two issues are Okada Yoshihiko (dates unknown), Satō Nobuo (dates unknown), Hirotsu Takashi (dates unknown), Komori Teruo (dates unknown), Takeda Takehiko (1919–), Kihara Kōichi, Akai Ki'ichi (1915–), Kitasono Katue, Iwasa Tō'ichirō (1905–74), Sasazawa Yoshiaki, Jō Samon (1904–76), Oda Masahiko (dates unknown), Iokibe Kin'ichi (1913–78), Aida Kenzō (1916–), and Osada Tsuneo. I thank Chiba Sen'ichi for showing me these rare issues of *Mugi tsūshin*.

152. Although the issue number is not stated in the diary, from other statements in the diary we can assume that it was the issue whose printing bill Katue paid on Oct. 3, 1945.

153. The final issue, pp. 33–36, came out on Nov. 29, 1945. I thank Sakuramoto Tomio for calling it to my attention.

154. *Mugi tsūshin*, p. 26. Many of Katue's hometown poems from this time were collected in the book *Ie* (1959), but the poem "Ie" was not included.

155. For example, *Mugi tsūshin* is unlisted in Watanabe Kazuo, "Kindai shien," in *Nihon gendai shi jiten* (Japanese modern poetry dictionary) (Ōfūsha, 1986), p. 156. *Shi kenkyū*, the government-sanctioned poetry journal, also bridged the war and postwar periods, ceasing publication with the Nov. 1945 issue.

156. There are various ways of scoring haiku; from the information provided, we cannot determine which system was used.

157. Jan. 14, Feb. 4, Mar. 18, May 13, June 24.

158. The Battle for Guam took place between July 21 and Aug. 10. Of the 23,000 Japanese troops on the island, 20,000 were killed and another 1,000 were captured.

159. June 10, June 11, and June 14, 1944.

160. For an eyewitness account of the 1942 raid, see John Morris, *Traveller from Tokyo* (London: Book Club, 1945), pp. 116–20.

161. Kitasono Katue, "Furusato e no tegami," *Rekishō*, no. 10 (Feb. 1954): 13.

162. He recorded 52 air raids in the diaries, but six entries are notes about news reports. We can assume all the others occurred in the greater Tokyo area (including Yokohama).

163. For a photograph of people evacuating while the imperial army band un-flinchingly marches on, see Havens, *Valley of Darkness*, p. 178.

164. Interview with Sō Takahiko on July 14, 1987.

165. Joseph C. Grew, *Report from Tokyo* (London: Hammond, Hammond, 1943); quoted in Morris, *Traveller from Tokyo*, p. 148.

166. Morris, *Traveller from Tokyo*, p. 148.

167. Taped interview with Kobayashi Yoshio on May 29, 1987. In 1948 Katue helped Kobayashi Yoshio obtain a teaching post at Japan Dental College.

168. Katue uses the literary phrase *yūshū iwankata nashi*.

169. FDR died on April 12 (American time), the same day reported by Katue. Notice how quickly news traveled when it benefited Japanese morale.

170. They are (1) "Sensen no aki" (1939); (2) "Hawai kaisen senbotsu yūshi ni okuru shi" / "Seiki no hi" (1942); (3) "Fuyu" (1942); and (4) "Hata" (1942).

171. (5) "Fune o omou" (1943); (6) "Sōshun no sakyū ni" (1944); and (7) "Kigen setsu" (1945). I do not count his haiku (*tekki aru*), because it was not published.

172. *Tsuji shōsetsu shū*, ed. Kume Masao for Nihon Bungaku Hōkokukai (Hak-kōsha Sugiyama shoten, 1943); *Tsuji shishū*, ed. Kume Masao for Nihon Bungaku Hōkokukai (Sugiyama shoten, 1943). There are 208 poets represented in the latter.

173. Hashimoto Akio told me that he and his father used bamboo gramophone needles during the war. "The sound quality was fine, but one needle lasted for only about ten minutes" (interview on May 20, 1988).

174. Kitasono Katue, "Fune o omou," in *Tsuji shishū*, pp. 124–25. To the side of the characters *gunkan* (battleship) in the title, Katue gives the reading *fune* (boat).

175. Incidentally, Katue's first use of the word "enemy" in the desk diary appears after the second air raid (Dec. 3, 1944).

176. Kitasono Katue, "Sōshun no sakyū ni," in *Dai Tōa*, ed. Nihon Bungaku Hōkokukai (Kawade shobō, 1944), pp. 66–67.

177. *Shin shiron*, no. 68 (Jan. 1, 1943): 1–2.

178. In 660 B.C.E. a different calendar was in use, and written records first appeared in Japan only a millennium later, making it historically impossible to pinpoint a particular day.

179. Kitasono Katue, "Kigen setsu," *Shūkan shōkokumin* (Young citizens weekly), Feb. 4, 1945; quoted in Sakuramoto Tomio, *Shijin to sekinin* (Poets and responsibility) (Kobayashi insatsu kabushiki gaisha shuppanbu, 1978), pp. 525–26.

180. Quoted in John Dower, *War Without Mercy* (New York: Pantheon, 1986), p. 89. Dower notes that in the mindset of the Americans, "it was almost a favor to kill the Japanese."

181. Kitasono Katue, "Shijin no ninmu: kakumei no senkusha tare," *Yomiuri shinbun*, Dec. 20, 1945, p. 4; also quoted in part by Sakuramoto, *Shijin to sekinin*, pp. 547–48.

182. Ibid.

183. Kitasono Katue, "Futtōteki shiron," in *Kiiroi daen*, pp. 34–38; reprinted in Kitasono Katue, *Nikakkei shiron* (Bi-angular poetics) (Libroport, 1987), pp. 57–62.

184. In 1946 the Shin Nihon Bungakukai (New Japan literature association) was formed, and the organization took up the issue of wartime responsibility. Saitō Mokichi (1882–1953), Kobayashi Hideo (1902–83), Takamura Kōtarō, and twenty-two others were initially named as culpable, but after much debate ensued and time passed, further finger-pointing was stopped (Sakuramoto, *Kūhaku to sekinin*, p. 267).

185. Interview with Hashimoto Eiko on July 12, 1986.

186. Kitasono Katue, "Jibun no shi" (My own poetry), *Bungei hanron* (Apr. 1, 1943), p. 11; reprinted in Kitasono Katue, *Kyōdō shiron* (Shōshinsha, 1944), p. 63.

187. Sakuramoto has made a career out of exposing the wartime production of poets. Yoshimoto has also written about it frequently but has branched out and dealt with other topics. See notes 2 and 4 to this chapter.

188. Sakuramoto, *Kūhaku to sekinin*, p. 248.

189. Andō Kazuo, interview on Dec. 17, 1986; Sakuramoto Tomio, interview on Mar. 17, 1988.

190. Takei Teruo, *Geijutsu undō no miraizō* (The future shape of artistic movements) (Gendai shichōsha, 1960), p. 120.

191. Yoshimoto Takaaki, *Takamura Kōtarō*, enl. ed. (Shunjūsha, 1977).

192. Ibid., pp. 148–49.

193. For more on *Kon*, see Chapter 4.

194. Kitasono Katue, "Jibun no shi," in *Kyōdo shiron*, pp. 62–63. Katue explained in an editorial note in *Shin shiron*, no. 58 (Mar. 8, 1942): "My friends may say that my poetry of late has a haiku quality, but, as I have already pointed out, it originates from the world of Zen and the tea ceremony. I just say this in passing and not as self-justification." Murano Shirō's book review of *Fūdo* can be found in *Shin shiron*, no. 70 (Mar. 1, 1943): 40. Murano offered high praise: "*Fūdo* is probably the most memorable of Katue's ten poetry books."

195. As stated previously, Katue never published any self-criticism related to patriotic poetry and the war. The extent of his public remorse can be found in a statement made about surrealism near the end of his life: "In the way we took in surrealism there was a tendency to undervalue the Japanese social ideology and philosophy lurking in the background. We laid more emphasis on estheticism and the art itself, and that can be seen as a weakness" (*Yū* interview, 1975).

Chapter 7

1. Kitasono Katue, "Ushinawareta machi ni te," *Ten no mayu* (Heaven's cocoon) (Tenmeisha, 1946), pp. 2–4.

2. For a discussion of Katue's anarchism, see Andō Ichirō et al., "Zadankai: Kitasono Katue o bunseki suru" (Panel discussion: analyzing Kitasono Katue), *Shigaku* 6, no. 6 (July 1951): 78. Katue made the remark that he was an anarchist to Kuroda Iri in 1953 or 1954, who related it to me on Sept. 21, 1985. Whether or not his poems were intended to be anarchistic, they can be read as such.

3. Kitasono Katue, "Yoru no yōso," *VOU*, no. 34 (Jan. 1950): 58–59; in *Kuroi hi* (Shōshinsha, 1951), pp. 46–53; in *Zenshishū*, pp. 362–64. For another translation of the poem, see Ichirō Kōno and Rikutarō Fukuda, *An Anthology of Modern Japanese Poetry* (Kenkyūsha, 1967 [1957]), pp. 59–62.

4. Murano Shirō, "Kitasono Katue," in Kaneko Mitsuharu et al., eds., *Gendai shi kōza: shi no kanshō* (Course on appreciating modern [Japanese] poetry) (Sōgensha, 1950), 3: 140.

5. Yamanaka Sansei (Tiroux), "Kitasono Katue hen" (Kitasono Katue volume), in Kitagawa Fuyuhiko et al., eds., *Gendai shi kanshō: Shōwa ki* (Appreciations of modern [Japanese] poetry: Shōwa period) (Daini shobō, 1951), pp. 105–6.

6. Itō Shinkichi, commentary, in Murano Shirō, ed., *Gendai Nihon shijin zenshū* (Collected poems of modern Japanese poets) (Sōgensha, 1955), 13: 398.

7. Among the many poets who have adopted this usage of Katue's (although with varied contents) are Ōha Shintarō (dates unknown), Andō Kazuo, Okunari Tatsu (1942–), and Tsuji Setsuko (1927–93).

8. Tsuboi Shigeji, in "Zadankai: Kitasono Katue o bunseki suru," *Shigaku*, July 1951, p. 87.

9. Okunari Tatsu, "Shi wa kijutsu no gaku dewa nai" (Poetry is not the study of description), *GUI* 8, no. 19 (Jan. 31, 1986): 82.

10. See the first nineteen installments of Okunari's book-length manuscript "Kitasono Katue *Kyōdo shiron* o yomu" (Reading Kitasono Katue's *Hometown Poetics* [1943]), *GUI* 14–20, nos. 37–55 (Dec. 1992– Dec. 1998).

11. The poems are (1) "Black Mirror" ("Kuroi kagami"), *Right Angle* (Washington, D.C.: The American University,), 3, no. 1 (May 1949): n.p.; (2) "Monotonous Solid" ("Tanchō na rittai"), *New Directions* (New York), no. 11 (1949): 297–99; (3) "Poem of Death and Umbrella" ("Shi to kōmorigasa no shi"), *Imagi* (Philadelphia), 5, no. 3 (1951): n.p.; (4–7) "A une dame qui me donna une chigarette, quand j'etais fatigue, triste, revant du cheval vert" (the original has the same title), "Dark April" ("Kurai shigatsu"), "Dark Room" ("Kurai shitsunai"), and "Black Portrait" ("Kuroi shōzō"), *New Directions*, no. 14 (1953): 105–8. Katue's translations are usually reliable, and skillful considering he was not a native speaker, but he changes words, reverses the word order in most stanzas, and tends to choose one dominant image in English where the original is more ambiguous. Therefore, in this book I use my own, somewhat more literal, translations for textual analysis.

12. Charles Olson, ed., *Right Angle* (Washington, D.C.: The American University), 3, no. 1 (May 1949): n.p. For Pound, Duncan, and Laughlin on Katue, see Chapter 5; for Rexroth and the de Campos brothers, see Chapter 8.

13. Kitasono Katue, *Black Rain* (Mallorca, Spain: Divers Press, 1954). At Creeley's request, Katue did the cover drawing for the first four issues of *The Black Mountain Review* (Black Mountain College, N.C.: Spring, Summer, Fall, Winter 1954) and for Douglas Woolf's *Hypocritic Days* (Divers Press, 1955).

14. Quoted by Katue in "*Gala* no techō" (Notebook on *Gala*), *Gala*, no. 11 (5, no. 1; Apr. 15, 1955).

15. Kitasono Katue, "Shōden" (Brief autobiography), in *Gendai Nihon meishishū taisei* (Sōgensha, 1961–62), 9: 150.

16. Fujitomi Yasuo, "Kitasono Katue no shi o fukan suru" (A bird's-eye view of Kitasono Katue's poetry), in *Zenshishū*, pp. 833–53.

17. Kuroda Iri, "How to Read: Kit Kat" (text in Japanese), *Will* (Keel Press), no. 1 (Winter 1981): 22, 32.

18. The drawback to Kuroda's classification is that he places classic and modern lyricism together, thereby implying by his third category that Katue wrote poems synthesizing experimental verse and classic lyricism in the postwar period, which is not the case. After the war, Katue did not write poems with classic vocabulary (although he published the collection *Ie* in 1959 that contained poems written during the war). In 1961 Katue expressed an interest in combining his three styles, but he acknowledged he had not yet found "that ideal style" (Kitasono Katue, "Shōden," 9: 150).

19. Katue championed *shuchishugi* (intellectualism) in the 1930s. For translations of his lyrical poems, see the discussion of *Wakai koronii* (1932) in Chapter 4; for *Natsu no tegami* (1937), see *Glass Beret*.

20. Including *Moonlight Night in a Bag* (title in English; 1966) which is a collection of photographs, but Katue issued it as a book of "plastic" poems.

21. During the war Katue wrote, "Half of the fate of poetry's future rests on how poets elevate the technical value of 'the line' and 'the stanza'" (*Kyōdo shiron*, p. 54).

22. Quoted in Itō Shinkichi, commentary, 13: 399.

23. Kōno and Fukuda, *An Anthology of Modern Japanese Poetry*, p. 164.

24. When the book was reprinted in Katue's *Zenshishū* without the special design features, the overall impact was greatly diminished. In Katue's works, the design is an intricate part of the poem's impact.

25. Katue himself used the phrase "continuity of discontinuity" (*Yū* interview).

26. Katue said, "Metamorphosis is similar to the automatism of surrealism and does not impress me." *Yū* interview.

27. Michael Riffaterre, *Text Production*, trans. Terese Lyons (New York: Columbia University Press, 1983), pp. 221–22.

28. Kitasono Katue, *Mahiru no remon* (Shōshinsha, 1954).

29. "Tanchō na rittai" (Monotonous solid), in *Kuroi hi*, p. 16; in *Zenshishū*, p. 351.

30. "Natsu no kokoro" (Summer's heart), in *Wakai koronii*, n.p.; in *Zenshishū*, p. 120.

31. *fuyu wa / kibō ni nurete / doro no machi o aruku.* "Kuroi ame" (Black rain), in *Kuroi hi*, p. 23; in *Zenshishū*, p. 356.

32. *shigatsu / wa viridian / no ame / ni kurete.* "Kurai shigatsu" (Dark April), in *Kuroi hi*, p. 27; in *Zenshishū*, p. 358.

33. *hoshi / wa namida shite suwaru.* "Ou une solitude," in *Kuroi hi*, p. 58; in *Zenshishū*, p. 377.

34. For examples, see the section "The plurisignation of the particle *no* in Katue's poetry" below.

35. *kage no tamago.* "Kuroi shōzō" (Black portrait), in *Kuroi hi*, p. 33; in *Zenshishū*, p. 362.

36. *shi / no / kame.* "Kuroi shōzō," in *Kuroi hi*, pp. 33–34; in *Zenshishū*, p. 363.

37. Inversion can also be generated by simply reversing common phrases, but the result is perhaps too easy. For example, Katue does this with *hi no mori* "fire's forest" (instead of "forest['s] fire") and *shinju no umi* "pearl's ocean" (instead of "ocean['s] pearl"). Both examples are from "Chishitsugaku-teki aregorii" (A geological allegory), in *Mahiru no remon*, p. 53; in *Zenshishū*, p. 447.

38. *nurete iru oushi / no naka / no shindai.* "Kurai shitsunai" (Dark room), in *Kuroi hi*, p. 6; in *Zenshishū*, p. 345.

39. "Kakuzato no naka no pantomaimu," in *Mahiru no remon*, p. 8; in *Zenshishū*, p. 411.

40. From his 1925 poem "Concept 999" (see Chapter 2).

41. *namari no hata.* "Tanchō na rittai," in *Kuroi hi*, p. 20; in *Zenshishū*, p. 354; *namari no yuri.* "A une dame," in *Kuroi hi*, p. 37; in *Zenshishū*, p. 365; *namari no taiyō.* "Kuroi kyori" (Black distance), in *Kuroi hi*, p. 43; in *Zenshishū*, pp. 368–69.

42. *garasu no hata.* "Sorushikosu-teki yoru" (A Zorcicos-like night), in *Mahiru no remon*, p. 15; in *Zenshishū*, p. 417; *garasu no makaronii.* "Shinkū no naka no sukyandaru mata wa kimagure na yūshoku" (Scandal in a vacuum, or the capricious supper), in *Mahiru no remon*, p. 17; in *Zenshishū*, p. 419.

43. *hone no tsubasa.* "Kuroi kagami" (Black mirror), in *Kuroi hi*, p. 30; in *Zenshishū*, p. 360; *hone / no bara.* "Shi to kōmorigasa no shi" (Poem of death and umbrella), in *Kuroi hi*, p. 10; in *Zenshishū*, p. 348.

44. *garasu no kaze.* "Kiiroi retorikku" (Yellow rhetoric), in *Mahiru no remon*, p. 12; in *Zenshishū*, p. 414.

45. *rikyūru no hoshi.* "Kaban no naka no tsukiyo" (Moonlight night in a bag), in *Mahiru no remon*, p. 20; in *Zenshishū*, p. 421.

46. *gomu no yō / ni domorinagara.* "Kiiroi retorikku," in *Mahiru no remon*, p. 13; in *Zenshishū*, p. 414.

47. *hitotaba no oto.* "Sorushikosu teki yoru," in *Mahiru no remon*, p. 16; in *Zenshishū*, p. 417.

48. Katue himself never used the term.

49. Kitasono Katue, *Kūki no hako* (Editions VOU, 1966).

50. *kūki no [haite iru] hako.*

51. *kūki no [naka no] hako* [= *kūchū no hako*; *kūkichū no hako*].

52. *kūki no hako* = [*kūki de dekite iru hako*]. Incidentally, "air in the shape of a box" is also an example of "Conversion of Categories 2," in this case a gas (air) taking the shape of a solid (box).

53. "Kuroi shōzō," in *Kuroi hi*, p. 33; in *Zenshishū*, p. 362.

54. *hone no kago* = [*hone de dekite iru kago*].

55. *hone no [naka no] kago.* This reading, far-fetched but not implausible, implies *no* in the dual roles of possessive and locative, so that the cage is construed as existing within the bone, as in a carved sculpture. Another example of this common usage of *no* is "*hako no [naka no] o-mamori*" ("the box's talisman"; i.e., "the talisman [located in] the box").

56. *hone no [tame no] kago.*

57. The paradoxical nature of the weighty perception-apparatus created by Katue with his surreal meta-images hints at an ironic view of life reminiscent of that of his father who constructed Rube Goldberg–like contraptions (see Chapter 1).

58. Katue would have rewritten Lautreamont's image "operating table / that umbrella / 's sewing machine." With Lautreamont the three objects converge as if on a single point, and none is in a dominant or subordinate relation to another.

59. *isu / sono hari no ue no / niji.* "Kurai shitsunai," in *Kuroi hi*, p. 6; in *Zenshishū*, p. 345.

60. *hoshi / sono kuroi yūshū / no hone / no bara.* "Shi to kōmorigasa no shi," in *Kuroi hi*, p. 10; in *Zenshishū*, p. 348.

61. *higeki no ato no higeki / no nagare / sono hone / no kage.* "Aki no rittai" (Autumn's solid), in *Kuroi hi*, p. 13; in *Zenshishū*, p. 350.

62. *yume / sono / namari / no / yuri.* "A une dame," in *Kuroi hi*, p. 37; in *Zenshishū*, p. 365.

63. *hone / sono zetsubō / no / suna / no / totte.* "Yoru no yōso," in *Kuroi hi*, p. 46; in *Zenshishū*, p. 370.

64. Michael Riffaterre, *Semiotics of Poetry* (Bloomington: Indiana University Press, 1978), p. 5.

65. The poem is "umi no umi no umi no . . . ," in *Shiro no arubamu*, p. 59; in *Zenshishū*, p. 57.

66. Alex Preminger, ed., *Princeton Encyclopedia of Poetry and Poetics* (Princeton: Princeton University Press, 1974 [1965]), p. 760.

67. Ōno Susumu et al., *Kogo jiten* (Iwanami, 1974), p. 1443.

68. Ibid.

69. *hi/no/mayu.* "Yoru no yōso," in *Kuroi hi*, pp. 51–52; in *Zenshishū*, p. 373.

70. *inmō/no/yoru.* "Yoru no yōso," in *Kuroi hi*, p. 51; in *Zenshishū*, p. 372.

71. "Kurai shitsunai," in *Kuroi hi*, p. 7; in *Zenshishū*, p. 345.

72. "A une dame," in *Kuroi hi*, p. 39; in *Zenshishū*, p. 366.

73. "Kurai shitsunai," in *Kuroi hi*, p. 7; in *Zenshishū*, p. 345.

74. "Kurai shitsunai," in *Kuroi hi*, p. 8; in *Zenshishū*, p. 346.

75. "Kuroi kagami," in *Kuroi hi*, p. 29; in *Zenshishū*, p. 360.

76. "Kuroi kyori," in *Kuroi hi*, p. 44; in *Zenshishū*, p. 368.

77. "Kuroi kagami," in *Kuroi hi*, p. 30; in *Zenshishū*, p. 360.

78. "Kuroi ame," in *Kuroi hi*, p. 24; in *Zenshishū*, p. 356.

79. "Kuroi shōzō," in *Kuroi hi*, p. 32; in *Zenshishū*, p. 362. Incidentally, Katue "mistranslated" "vodka" as "brandy"; see Kitasono Katue, "Black Portrait," *New Directions*, no. 14 (1953): 108.

80. I use the word "dynamic" because the reader, in trying to figure out how the grammar fits, makes a series of instantaneous choices in the process of decoding the text. This is unlike stationary plurisignation in which the grammatical apparatus itself is clear (e.g., a possessive) although the content generated can be full of possible interpretations. At times, as we shall see, the two types of plurisignation occur simultaneously.

81. "Kuroi shōzō," in *Kuroi hi*, pp. 33–34; in *Zenshishū*, p. 363.

82. "Tanchō na rittai," *Kuroi hi*, pp. 20–21; *Zenshishū*, p. 354. Katue translated the above as "dream's/butterfly's/burst/heated arms / that still smell / coquettishly/on / a smashed plate. *New Directions* 11 (New York, 1949), p. 298.

83. Kitasono Katue, *Yū*, no. 8 (1975).

84. "Aki no rittai," in *Kuroi hi*, p. 14; in *Zenshishū*, p. 350; "Tanchō na rittai," in *Kuroi hi*, p. 15; in *Zenshishū*, p. 351; "Ou un solitude," in *Kuroi hi*, p. 54; in *Zenshishū*, p. 375.

85. "Kuroi shōzō," in *Kuroi hi*, pp. 32–36; in *Zenshishū*, p. 362.

86. "Kaban no naka no tsukiyo" (Moonlight night in a bag) in *Mahiru no remon*, p. 23; in *Zenshishū*, p. 423. Only a fragment from a stanza is cited here, and meaning perhaps could be squeezed out of the text if one were to force connections between other parts of the poem.

87. Kitasono Katue, *Yū*, no. 8 (1975): 86.

88. "Shiroi retorikku," in *Mahiru no remon*, p. 34; in *Zenshishū*, p. 432.

89. Kitasono Katue, *Garasu no kuchihige* (Kokubunsha, 1956).

90. "Kihaku na tenkai" (A diluted development), in ibid., pp. 10–11; in *Zenshishū*, p. 501.

91. Respectively, *nanika kage no yō na mono; sono kage;* and *kage no naka ni.*

92. "Kihaku na buaiorin" (The diluted violin), *Gala*, no. 11 (1955): 4; in *Garasu no kuchihige*, p. 65; in *Zenshishū*, p. 536. See *Glass Beret* for a full translation of this and other poems quoted.

93. "Kiete iku poésie" (Vanishing poetry), in *Garasu no kuchihige*, pp. 14–15; in *Zenshishū*, p. 504.

94. "Mitsu no aru shunkan" (Three distinct moments), in *Garasu no kuchihige*, p. 23; in *Zenshishū*, p. 510.

95. "Itsusu no kihaku na tenkai" (Five diluted developments), in *Garasu no kuchihige*, p. 18; in *Zenshishū*, p. 507.

96. "Meshian no tabako," in *Garasu no kuchihige*, pp. 75–82; in *Zenshishū*, pp. 543–47. Olivier Méssiaen (1908–92) was an influential French composer.

97. For example, the *no* opening Part 2 of the poem.

98. Keene, *Dawn to the West*, p. 363.

99. Kuroda Iri also makes this point in "How to Read: Kit-Kat," p. 35.

100. Roland Barthes, *Writing Degree Zero*, trans. Annette Lavers and Colin Smith (New York: Hill and Wang, 1968; 1979), pp. 47–48.

101. Quoted in Marjorie Perloff, *The Poetics of Indeterminacy* (Princeton: Princeton University Press, 1981).

102. Ōha Shintarō was the first of many to copy Katue's pattern of short lines and repetition of the particle *no*, but his poetry is less effective, in part because there are

no limits on the imagery. See Ōha Shintarō, "Yoru to hiru VI" (Night and day VI), *Tengai*, no. 4 (Sept. 1, 1951): 4–5.

103. Perloff, p. 13.

104. Ibid., pp. 9–11, 15.

105. Ibid., blurb on dust jacket.

106. Kuroda Iri takes Norman N. Holland's analysis of the three stages of modernism (early modern, high modern, postmodern) and applies it to Katue, claiming that he was the first Japanese postmodernist. See Norman N. Holland, "Postmodern Psychoanalysis," in Ihab Hassan et al., eds., *Innovation/Renovation* (Madison: University of Wisconsin Press, 1983), pp. 291–309; and Kuroda Iri, "Modanizumu kara posutomodanizumu e" (From modernism to postmodernism), *Shiro* (White), 24, no. 5 (Jan. 1987): 14–19.

107. Riffaterre, *Semiotics of Poetry*, pp. 4, 6.

108. David Lodge, *The Modes of Modern Writing*, p. 226; quoted in Perloff, p. 51.

109. Riffaterre, *Semiotics of Poetry*, pp. 13–14.

110. Conversation with Suzuki Masafumi, on Jan. 17, 1996; augmented on Sept. 10, 1997.

Chapter 8

1. Shimizu Toshihiko et al., eds., *Kitasono Katue and VOU* ("Kitasono Katue and VOU" kankōkai, 1988).

2. James Laughlin letter to Shimizu Toshihiko, dated Mar. 23, 1979. I quote from the unpublished original letter; for a Japanese translation, see ibid., p. 251.

3. Eugen Gomringer letter to Shimizu Toshihiko, dated Mar. 19, 1979. Original unpublished; translation in ibid., p. 237.

4. For an explanation of concrete poetry and examples, see Emmett Williams, ed., *An Anthology of Concrete Poetry* (New York: Something Else Press, 1967); Mary Ellen Solt, ed., *Concrete Poetry: A World View* (Bloomington: Indiana University Press, 1968). For a study of concrete poetry's roots in the distant past, see Dick Higgins, *Pattern Poetry: Guide to an Unknown Literature* (Albany: State University of New York Press, 1987).

5. Kenneth Rexroth letter to Shimizu Toshihiko, undated. Original unpublished; translation in Shimizu et al., *Kitasono Katue and VOU*, p. 258.

6. Ibid.

7. In Japanese magazines, Katue occasionally listed himself as a member (*dōnin*) of New Directions, somewhat misleadingly suggesting to readers that the New York publishing enterprise is structured like a Japanese poetry club in which members pay dues to support publication. Katue was a member in the loose sense that New Directions published a number of writers regularly, including him, and many of them were friends.

8. Although the founders and prime movers of the concrete poetry movement (Eugen Gomringer and the de Campos brothers) had published before, none was well established; rather, they represented a new generation with a new vision.

9. Haroldo de Campos quoted in Williams, *An Anthology of Concrete Poetry*, p. 337.

10. In 1958 Japanese avant-garde poets from VOU, Pan Poesie, and other groups formed the Zen'ei shijin kyōkai (Avant-garde poets' association); Katue was selected as the leader. The group published *Eikaku.Kuro.Botan* (Acute angle. black. button) in 1958, 1959, and 1961. Katue did the layout for all three issues, as well as the covers for the first two, and also contributed poems and photos. He was regarded as a veteran avant-garde leader in Japan, but was unable to win unequivocal praise at home, because of his wartime poetry and because a number of other important avant-garde poets, such as Yoshioka Minoru, Tamura Ryūichi, Terayama Shūji (1935–83), and Shiraishi Kazuko, were establishing themselves on the scene.

11. Katue continued to publish word poems in Japanese, and even translated some for publication abroad, but never in concrete anthologies.

12. Kitasono Katue, *VOU*, no. 58 (Nov. 1957): 39; in *Kemuri no chokusen* (Smoke's straight line) (Kokubunsha, 1959), pp. 54–59; in *Zenshishū*, pp. 579–582. In the original word order, consonant with Japanese grammar, the objects and colors are conceptualized from larger to smaller (the first white square containing the next white square, which then contains the black square, and so on). I have rendered the poem into English literally, but the explanatory intrusion of "it" takes away much of the poetic effect. Another possibility is "white square / enclosing / white square / enclosing / black square . . . ," but *no naka no* generates its charge without a verb. For the smoothest flow of English syntax, the order of the imagery needs to be reversed, as in Haroldo de Campos's translation, "Monotony of Void Space," in Williams, *An Anthology of Concrete Poetry*, n.p.

13. Katue was no doubt influenced by painter Josef Albers's series entitled *Homage to the Square*.

14. Haroldo de Campos in his translation changed "tobacco" to "smoke" and "handkerchief" to "scarf," images he must have considered more poetic. How to translate words that have more poetic connotations in the original language is a difficult problem for any translator.

15. Haroldo de Campos, unpublished letter of Mar. 18, 1979, to Shimizu Toshihiko. A Japanese translation appears in Shimizu et al., *Kitasono Katue and VOU*, pp. 234–36. Elsewhere, de Campos was even more specific about his initial letter to Katue, "On July 9, 1957, we wrote to Kitasono, sending him verses of concrete poetry in English and French, together with an exposition of the theoretical fundamentals of concrete poetry and of certain points that corresponded between the movement's postulations and [Katue's] theory of ideoplasty / William Carlos Wil-

liams / Pound-ideogram" (Haroldo de Campos, "Poesia concreta no Japão: Kitasono Katue," *Suplemento Literário de O Estado de São Paulo*, May 10, 1958, p. 9; translated from the Portuguese).

16. Interview with L. C. Vinholes, Apr. 15, 1988.

17. Katue, *Yū*, no. 8, pp. 84–97. The line of contact was probably Pound–de Campos–Katue, because there is no mention of the de Campos brothers in the extant letters from Pound to Katue in *Ezra Pound & Japan*.

18. *Noigandres* (São Paulo), no. 4 (March 1958); for a discussion and partial translation, see Mary Ellen Solt, *Concrete Poetry: A World View*, pp. 13–16.

19. In Canto XX the "I" of the poem asks "old Lévy," an expert on Provençal culture, about the word "noigandres" in a poem by the troubadour Arnaut Daniel. Perplexed, old Lévy answers, "'Noigandres! NOIgandres! / 'You know for seex mon's of my life / 'Effery night when I go to bett, I say to myself: / 'Noigandres, eh, noigandres, / 'Now what the DEFFIL can that mean!'" (Ezra Pound, *The Cantos of Ezra Pound* [New York: New Directions, 1972], pp. 89–90).

20. *Noigandres*, no. 4 (Mar. 1958) also includes concrete poems by Ronaldo Azeredo.

21. Katue owned the 1952 Gallimard (Paris) edition in which he scribbled in pencil his Japanese translations of the first half of the book (author's collection). In 1934 Bon shoten had published Katue's translation of Mallarmé's love songs, *Koi no uta*.

22. Strictly speaking, Noigandres was also concerned with the aural aspect of concrete poetry, and their works were occasionally performed audiovisually. The concrete poetry movement is remembered now mostly for its visual contributions.

23. Augusto de Campos, Décio Pignatari, and Haroldo de Campos, "Pilot Plan for Concrete Poetry," *Noigandres*, no. 4 (Mar. 1958): n.p.

24. For Pound and Laughlin on the ideogram, see Chapter 5.

25. Haroldo de Campos, unpublished letter of Mar. 18, 1979 to Shimizu Toshihiko.

26. Augusto de Campos, Décio Pignatari, and Haroldo de Campos, "Pilot Plan for Concrete Poetry," n.p.

27. Décio Pignatari's concrete poem in Portuguese from 1957, "An Anti-advertisement," is an example of a Noigandres poem mixing esthetics and politics. The opening line "beba coca cola" (drink Coca-Cola) transforms letter by letter into new words that finally spell out "cloaca" (cesspool).

28. Haroldo de Campos, "Poesia concreta no Japão," p. 9.

29. Haroldo de Campos, "Monotony of Void Space," in Williams, *An Anthology of Concrete Poetry*, n.p.

30. Eugen Gomringer, ed., *Spirale* (Bern), no. 8 (Oct. 1960): 43.

31. Kitasono Katue, "Geijutsu to shite no shi," in Nishiwaki Junzaburō and Ka-

neko Mitsuharu, eds., *Shi no hon*, vol. 2, *Shi no gihō* (Book on poetry, vol. 2, poetic techniques) (Chikuma shobō, 1967), pp. 187–89.

32. Ibid., p. 189. Katue's *Kūki no hako* (VOU Club, 1966) was printed in an edition of 200 copies. Katue's concept of the "antipoem" may have been influenced by Nicanor Parra's *Anti-poems* (trans. Jorge Elliott; San Francisco, Calif.: City Lights, 1960).

33. Niikuni Sei'ichi, untitled poem, in Mary Ellen Solt, *Concrete Poetry: A World View*, p. 161.

34. Kitasono Katue, "A note on plastic poem," *VOU*, no. 104 (Feb./Mar. 1966): 23; reprinted as "a note on visual poem," in *Moonlight Night in a Bag* (Editions VOU, 1966), n.p. Only 100 copies of *Moonlight Night in a Bag* were printed; all of the plastic poems were originally published in *VOU*.

35. This version, with a few grammatical corrections, appeared in the exhibition pamphlet *Plastic Poems: Kitasono Katue and the VOU Group* (Providence: Rhode Island School of Design, Museum of Art, 1986), n.p.

36. The prewar VOU members, including Katue, had put great energy into their surrealistic drawings, perhaps because photography was prohibitively expensive (until the late 1920s a Leica camera cost the same as a house!). On the covers of nos. 28 and 30 of *VOU*, however, we do find abstract photographs by club members Asahara Kiyotaka (dates unknown) and Yamamoto Kansuke.

37. A total of thirty-one VOU exhibitions were held from 1956 to 1976; one took place in Milan, Italy, the rest throughout Japan.

38. See, e.g., *VOU*, no. 53 (Dec. 1957): 17–20. Included in this issue are photographs by Torii Ryōzen, Kamijō Takejirō (1932–), Shimizu Toshihiko (1929–), and Katue. Ryōzen's blurry photo, "Taiyō to tori" (Sun and bird) of a dead chicken on the sand with sun shining, was later used on a record jacket.

39. One of Kansuke's techniques was to cut up negatives, arrange them, and then print a single copy per image, unlike most collage artists who cut and paste prints.

40. Kansuke actually debuted in *VOU*, no. 29 (June 1940).

41. The photographs are reproduced in *VOU*, no. 58 (Nov. 1957): 24–25.

42. Kitasono Katue, "Reflet diffus," *VOU*, no. 53 (Dec. 1956): 34.

43. *Yū* interview.

44. See Chapter 3.

45. *Yū* interview. Katue was being modest. He was accepted into the Nika group of avant-garde painters in 1932 and contributed regularly to their exhibits; after the war, he was one of three painters in their Theory Division (Suzuki Takashi [1898–1998], a VOU member, was another). Katue's success as a poet coupled with lack of funds to rent studio space and purchase art supplies eventually caused him to curtail his painting career in favor of writing and book designing. Throughout his life, he dabbled in painting and, after the war, made a minor career as an art critic.

46. Kitasono Katue, "Mélange," *VOU*, no. 61 (May 1958): 27.

47. Kitasono Katue, "Takahashi Shōhachirō no shashin sakuhin ni tsuite" (About the photographic works of Takahashi Shōhachirō), in "Takahashi Shōhachirō dai ikkai sakuhin ten" (First exhibition of works by Takahashi Shōhachirō), Aug. 1–8, 1961, Yamagoya Gallery, Kitakami, unpaginated exhibit pamphlet. I do not use the word "experiment" in the narrow sense suggested by Katue but prefer to categorize his *zōkei* (plastic) as a variation of experimental photography.

48. Kitasono Katue, "Geijutsu no atarashii jigen," *VOU*, no. 100 (June/July 1965): 3.

49. Ibid. "Inconsequential" is literally "no more than one stride" (*hon no hitomatagi ni suginai*).

50. VOU members, taking a cue from Katue, occasionally titled their own photos "plastic poems"; for example, Itō Motoyuki (1935– ; *VOU*, no. 115) and Seki Shirō (dates unknown; *VOU*, no. 157). For the latter's brief article on the subject, see Seki Shirō, "Plastic poem ni tsuite" (About plastic poems), *O*, no. 2 (March 1979): 5–6.

51. Brief comments by VOU members on their "photo poetry" are excerpted from the catalogue of their twenty-seventh exhibit and reprinted in "Shashin shi ni tsuite no iken" (Opinions on photo poems), *VOU*, no. 119 (Apr.–June 1969): 29–30; included are Itō Motoyuki, Kitasono Katue, Koike Takeshi (dates unknown), Okazaki Katsuhiko, Shimizu Masato, Shimizu Toshihiko, Takahashi Shōhachirō, and Tsuji Setsuko.

52. Quoted in Mary Ellen Solt, *Concrete Poetry: A World View*, p. 15.

53. Refer to the "List of Kitasono Katue Photographs in *VOU*" in the Appendix for publishing dates, titles, and number of photos.

54. Katue's first photo titled "plastic poem" appeared in *VOU*, no. 99 (April/May 1965); his manifesto is in *VOU*, no. 104 (Feb./Mar. 1966).

55. For an informative article on Katue's photography and the cameras he used, see Sasaki Kikyō, "Kitasono Katue to Kontakkusu" (Kitasono Katue and the Contax [camera]), *Trap* (Itō), no. 8 (Jan. 1988): 7–26.

56. Katue used the term "plastic poem" in two ways: generically to stand for the new intermedia art, and as the title of many of the individual works. Katue traveled abroad with a group of librarians from various colleges but did not visit his literary friends.

57. The only book of plastic poems Katue published in his lifetime, *Moonlight Night in a Bag* (1966), includes his VOU photos from as far back as March 1959; some of these photos were taken outside, but his subsequent plastic poems were all taken indoors. Katue's second book of plastic poems, *Study of Man by Man* (1979), was published posthumously by the Italian poet Sarenco. Katue sent the plastic poems and titled the work, but he died before it came out. All of the plastic poems included are newspaper cut-ups crumpled into the shape of people.

58. Michael Brand, "Introduction," in *Plastic Poems: Kitasono Katue and the VOU Group*, n.p.

59. Max Chaleil, "La Poésie après le verbe" (Poetry after the Verb), in *La Créativité en noir et blanc* (Paris: Nouvelles Editions Polaires, 1973), p. 75.

60. Jean-Luc Daval, *Avant-garde Art, 1914–1939* (New York: Rizzoli, 1980), p. 24.

61. Katue persuaded the Japan Dental College to set up a Design Department with a private office and make him head designer. He shuffled between the library and the Design Department, where he worked with his administrative assistant, Tsuji Setsuko, who was also a VOU poet and photographer. Tsuji relates (interview, July 20, 1989) that Nakahara Minoru, the college president who was an avant-garde painter and ex-VOU member, grew impatient with Katue for doing outside work on college time, and once stormed into the design office shouting, "Not *VOU* again! When are you going to *work* for your salary?" Fortunately for Katue, his forty-year service at the school afforded him ample job security. He took advantage of the facilities and made the best of the situation, apparently content in his semi-isolation. After Katue died, the Japan Dental College immediately disbanded with the Design Department.

When Katue, upon reaching the age of seventy, was to be decorated by the Japanese government for his long service at the library, he notified Nakahara Minoru's son, Sen, that he would reject the award and requested that the college not apply for it on his behalf; it complied (interview with Nakahara Sen on April 3, 1987).

62. As editor of *Tsukue* (Desk), Katue was able to commission VOU members to write poems and pay them from the budget; for many it was the only money they ever made from poetry.

63. See the Bibliography for "A Partial List of the Plastic Poems of Kitasono Katue in Publications Outside Japan."

64. For 8mm films by Katue and Yamamoto Kansuke, see the video *Glass Wind* (Hollywood, Calif.: highmoonoon, 1998).

65. Katue, it should be mentioned, never discussed his plastic poems in terms of ideoplasty, but the concept is as appropriate to the photos as to the poems.

66. *Shijin no katachi ni kirinukareta shinbunshi ga kiiroi yōgasa o sashite kūkan o . . . yogitte iku.* Kitasono Katue, "Haibooru teki kūkan" (A highballish space), in *Kūki no hako* (VOU, 1966), p. 27.

SELECTED
BIBLIOGRAPHY

Note: All titles are published in Tokyo unless otherwise noted. An "*" indicates that the original title was given in romanization rather than in *kanji* or *kana*. Works by Kitasono Katue are listed chronologically in the first section.

Works by Kitasono Katue

Books of Poetry

Shiro no arubamu (Album of whiteness). Kōseikaku, 1929.
Wakai koronii (Young colony). Bon shoten, 1932.
*Ma Petite Maison (My small house). Shiba shoten, 1933.
Ensui shishū (Conical poems). Bon shoten, 1933.
Kon (The leviathan). Minzokusha, 1936.
Natsu no tegami (Summer letters). Aoi shobō, 1937.
Saboten tō (Cactus island). Aoi shobō, 1938.
Hi no sumire (Violet of fire). Shōshinsha, 1939.
Katai tamago (Hard egg). Bungei hanronsha, 1941.
Fūdo (Climate). Shōshinsha, 1943.
Suna no uguisu (Sand warbler). Kyōritsu shoten, 1951.
Kuroi hi (Black fire). Shōshinsha, 1951.
Wakai koronii (Young colony). Rev. ed. Kokubunsha, 1953.
Mahiru no remon (Lemon at high noon). Shōshinsha, 1954.
*Black Rain. Mallorca, Spain: Divers Press, 1954 (poems in English; trans. Kitasono Katue).
Vinasu no kaigara (Venus's seashell). Kokubunsha, 1955.
Garasu no kuchihige (Glass mustache). Kokubunsha, 1956.
Aoi kyori (Blue distance). Papyrus Press, 1958.
Kemuri no chokusen (Smoke's straight line). Kokubunsha, 1959.
Ie (House). Shōshinsha, 1959.
Megane no naka no yūrei (Ghost in eyeglasses). Press Bibliomane, 1965.

Kūki no hako (Airbox). VOU, 1966.

Shiro no dampen (White fragments). VOU, 1973.

*Blue. Ed. Fujitomi Yasuo. VOU, 1979.

*Shikisai toshi, Couleur ville: Kitasono Katue shoki shigun (Colorful city: the early poems of Kitasono Katue). Ed. Torii Shōzō. Press Bibliomane, 1981.

Kitasono Katue shishū. (Selected poems of Kitasono Katue). Ed. Fujitomi Yasuo. Gendaishi bunko, 1023. Shichōsha, 1981.

Kitasono Katue zenshishū (The collected poems of Kitasono Katue). Ed. Fujitomi Yasuo. Chūsekisha, 1983.

Omoi kasetsu (Heavy hypothesis). Ed. Torii Shōzō. Itō: Kaijinsha, 1985.

*Glass Beret: The Selected Poems of Kitasono Katue. Trans. John Solt. Milwaukee, Wisc.: Morgan Press, 1995.

Books of Plastic Poetry (Photographs)

*Moonlight Night in a Bag. VOU, 1966.

Kitasono Katue: Study of Man by Man. Ed. Sarenco. Verona, Italy: Factotum-Art, 1979.

Kitasono Katue zenshashinshū (The complete photographs of Kitasono Katue). Chūsekisha, 1992.

Book of Short Stories

Kuroi shōtaiken (Black invitation card). Mira Center, 1964.

Books of Essays

Ten no tebukuro (Heaven's glove). Shunjū shobō, 1933.

Kukyō (Haiku sutras). Fūryūjin hakkōsha, 1939.

Haiburau no funsui (Highbrow fountain). Shōshinsha, 1941.

Kyōdo shiron (Hometown poetics). Shōshinsha, 1944.

Kiiroi daen: *essays, criticism, scraps (Yellow oval). Hōbunkan, 1953.

Kagiya Yukinobu, Shimizu Toshihiko, Fujitomi Yasuo (eds.). *Nikakkei shiron* (Bi-angular poetics). Libroport, 1987.

Kitasono Katue zenhyōronshū (The collected essays of Kitasono Katue). Ed. Tsuruoka Yoshihisa. Chūsekisha, 1988.

Haiku

Mura: Kitasono Katue kushū (Village: Collected haiku of Kitasono Katue). Ed. Funaki Jin. Garandō, 1980.

Gendai haiku shūsei bekkan 1: Bunjin haiku shū (Modern haiku compilation, supplement 1: collection of haiku by literati). Kawade shobū shinsha, 1983 (a reissue of the preceding item along with haiku by Natsume Sōseki, Akutagawa Ryūnosuke, and others).

Translations

*Eluard, Paul. *Les Petites justes* (Little justices). Abe shoten, 1933.
Mallarmé, Stéphane. *Koi no uta: madrigaux* (Love songs). Bon shoten, 1934.
Radiguet, Raymond. *Hi no hoho:* (Les Joues en feu; Cheeks of fire). Hakusuisha, 1953.

Main Literary Journals Edited

*Ge.Gjmgjgam.Prrr.Gjmgem. Nos. 2–10. 1925–27.
Shōbi.Majutsu.Gakusetsu (Rose.magic.theory). Nos. 1–4. 1927–28.
Hakushi (White paper). Nos. 1–14(?). 1930(?)–31.
*Madame Blanche. Nos. 1–17. 1932–34.
*VOU. Nos. 1–160. 1935–40, 1946–47, 1949–78.
Shin gijutsu (New techniques). Nos. 31–37. 1940–42.
Shin shiron (New poetics). Nos. 57–77. 1942–43.
Mugi tsūshin (Wheat dispatch). Nos. 1–9. 1944–45.
*Cendre (Ashes). Nos. 1–7. 1948.
Ao garasu (Blue glass). Nos. 1–5. 1953.

Interview

Matsuoka Seigō and Sugiura Kōhei, *Yū* (Play), no. 8 (Aug. 1975): 84–97; rpt. in Shimizu Toshihiko, Shimizu Masato, Fukuda Kazuhiko, Kiyohara Etsushi, eds., *Kitasono Katue and VOU.* "Kitasono Katue and VOU" kankōkai, 1988.

Correspondence with Ezra Pound

D. D. Paige, ed. *The Letters of Ezra Pound, 1907–1941.* New York: Harcourt, Brace, Jovanovitch, 1950; rpt. as *The Selected Letters of Ezra Pound, 1907–1941.* New York: New Directions, 1971, pp. 281–82, 292–93, 297, 319, 335–36, 345–48.
Sanehide Kodama, ed. *Ezra Pound and Japan.* Redding Ridge, Conn.: Black Swan Books, 1987, pp. 25–128.

Kitasono Katue Poems (non-plastic) and Essays in Foreign Journals (translations by Kitasono unless otherwise noted)

Townsman (London), no. 1 (Jan. 1938): 4–9.
"Modern Poets of Japan." *New Directions* (New York), 1938, n.p.

"La mano d'estate scrive" ["The hand of summer wrote" is Ezra Pound's mistranslation of the title of Katue's book of poetry *Summer Letters*]. *Broletto* (Genoa), no. 25 (1938): 20–21.

"Seven Pastoral Postcards." *Townsman* (London), 2, no. 6 (Apr. 1939): 10–11.

"White Doctrine." In Charles Henri Ford et al., "Chainpoems." *New Directions* (New York), no. 3 (1940): 199–200.

"The Life of a Pencil." *Diogenes* (Madison, Wisc.), 1, no. 2 (Dec. 1940–Jan. 1941): 53.

"A Shadow." *Four Pages* (Galveston, Tex.), no. 6 (June 1948): 3.

"Black Mirror." *Right Angle* (Washington, D.C.: The American University), 3, no. 1 (May 1949): n.p.

"Monotonous Solid." *New Directions* (New York), no. 11 (1949): 297–99.

"Dirty Town," "Poem." *Quarterly Review of Literature* (Annandale-on-Hudson, N.Y.), 4, no. 4 (1949): 343–45.

"Poem of Death and Umbrella." *Imagi* (Philadelphia), 5, no. 2 (1951): n.p.

"The VOU Club" (essay). *Nine* (London), 3, no. 4 (Summer/Autumn, 1952): 313–14.

"Green Sunday." In Hubert Creekmore, ed., *A Little Treasury of World Poetry*, pp. 422–23. New York: Charles Scribner's Sons, 1952.

"Monotonous Rhetoric," "A une dame qui me donna une chigarette, quand j'etais fatigue, triste, revant du cheval vert," "Dark April," "Dark Room," "Black Portrait." *New Directions* (New York), no. 14 (1953): 104–8.

"Yellow Rhetoric." *Four Winds* (Gloucester, Mass.), no. 4 (Winter, 1953): n.p.

"Eight Contemporary Japanese Poets" (essay); "Moonlight Night in a Bag." In Arabel J. Porter et al., eds., *New World Writing: 6th Mentor Selection*, pp. 57–58, 63. New York: New American Library, 1954.

"Poetry Going Out." In *Perspective of Japan* (An *Atlantic Monthly* Supplement). New York: Intercultural Publications, 1954; rpt. in *The Atlantic*, Jan. 1955, p. 151.

Donald Keene. *Japanese Literature: An Introduction for Western Readers*. New York: Grove Press, 1955, p. 19. English trans. by Donald Keene of part of "Kigō setsu."

"The Elements of a Night," "Night a la Zorzicos." In Ichirō Kōno and Rikutarō Fukuda, eds., *An Anthology of Modern Japanese Poetry*, pp. 59–63. Kenkyūsha, Tokyo, 1957. English trans. by Kōno and Fukuda.

"Blue Fragments," "A Humming to Be out Of," "A Rarefied Violin," "Poetry Going Out," "White Rhetoric," "Moonlight Night in a Bag," "Pantomine in a Sugar Cube." *Olivant* (Fitzgerald, Ga.), no. 1 (1957): 145–50.

"Monotonia do espaço vazio." In the literary supplement of *O Estado de São Paulo*, May 10, 1958, pp. 1–2; rpt. in *Invençao* (Brazil), May 21, 1960, p. 3. Portuguese trans. by Haroldo de Campos.

"Home." *Galley Sail Review* (San Francisco), no. 5 (Winter 1959–60): 16.

"Tanchō na kūkan" (Monotonous space). *Spirale* (Bern, Switz.), no. 8 (Oct. 1960), p. 43. German trans. by Eugen Gomringer.

"Poeme." In the literary supplement of *O Estado de São Paulo*, July 25, 1964, p. 3. Portuguese trans. by Haroldo de Campos.

"Monotony of Void Space." In Emmett Williams, ed., *An Anthology of Concrete Poetry*, n.p. New York: Something Else Press, 1967. English trans. by Haroldo de Campos.

"Some 3 Moments," "Aspirin Pigeon." *Literature East & West* (Austin: University of Texas), 12, nos. 2–4 (Dec. 1968): 249–53. English trans. by Sam Grolmes.

Kenneth Rexroth. "Literature." In R. M. Hutchins and M. J. Adler, eds., *The Great Ideas Today*. New York: Praeger, 1970, p. 170. Uncredited English trans. of part of "Monotony of Void Space."

"Passage," "Pré-histoire," "L'ombre," "Noble biere." *Les Cahiers de l'Oronte* (Beirut), no. 11 (1973): 63–64. French trans. by Hiroe Kimura and Samia Toutounji.

"Flowers." *Third Rail* (Los Angeles), no. 6 (1984): 23. English trans. by John Solt.

"Morning Letter." *Nostoc* (Newton, Mass.: Arts End Books), no. 16. English trans. by John Solt.

"Summer's Esplanade," "Words," "Sur Un Paroissien," "Casual Tennis," "In a Mourning City," "Blue." *Third Rail* (Los Angeles), no. 7 (1985–86): 45–49. English trans. by John Solt.

"Doll, Pistol and Balloon," "Dessin du Poete." *GUI* 9, no. 22 (Mar. 1987): 97–94 (reverse order). English trans. by John Solt.

"The Diluted Violin." *Third Rail* (Los Angeles), no. 9 (1988): 24. English trans. by John Solt.

"Ocean's Ocean's Ocean's . . . ," "Mustache," "Song of Acetes," "A Mi Querida," "Blue Square," "Dark Caricature." In Bob Moore, ed., *Nexus* (Dayton, Ohio: Wright State University), 25, no. 2 (1990): 40–51 (special section titled "Nihilist in the Eraser: A Kitasono Retrospective"). Intro. and English trans. by John Solt.

"Blue Background," "Blue Square." In Lawrence Ferlinghetti and Nancy Peters, eds., *City Lights Review* (San Francisco: City Lights), no. 4 (1990): 174–76. English trans. by John Solt.

"Ashes of a Sorceress." *Printed Matter* (Tokyo), 16, no. 1 (Spring 1992): 28–29. English trans. by John Solt.

"Drama in a Blue-Striped Box." In Hilda Raz, ed., *Prairie Schooner* (Lincoln: University of Nebraska), 70, no. 2 (Summer 1996): 53. English trans. by John Solt.

A Partial List of the Plastic Poems of Kitasono Katue
in Publications Outside Japan

2 plastic poems, titled "Plastic Poem 1" and "Plastic Poem 2." *Chicago Review* (Chicago), 19, no. 4 (Sept. 1967): 110–11.

1 plastic poem, untitled. In Julien Blaine and Jean Clay, eds. *Robho* (Paris), no. 2 (Nov.–Dec. 1967): 2.

3 plastic poems, untitled. In Jean-François Bory, comp. *Once Again*. New York: New Directions, 1968, pp. 59–61.

1 plastic poem, untitled. In Pierre Garnier, *Spatialisme et poésie concréte*. Paris: Gallimard, 1968, p. 90.

1 plastic poem titled "Portrait of a Poet, 1966"; 1 concrete poem titled "White." In Mary Ellen Solt, ed., *Concrete Poetry: A World View*. Bloomington: Indiana University, 1968, pp. 159–60 (text comments on Kitasono and concrete poetry in Japan, pp. 7, 13, 31–32).

2 plastic poems, titled "Plastic Poem A '67" and "Plastic Poem '67." In Jean-François Bory and Julien Blaine, eds., *Approches*, no. 3. Paris: Approches, 1968, pp. 20–21.

Agentzia (Paris), no. 11/12 (1969).

3 plastic poems, titled "Hag's Nook," "Both Sides," and "Poem, 1966"; also includes two brief essays by Kitasono, "A Note on Visual Poem, 1966" and "A Note on My Work, 1969." *Stereo Headphones* (Suffolk, Eng.), no. 5 (Winter 1972): 10–12, 27.

Exposición exhaustiva de la nueva poesía. Montevideo, Uruguay, 1972 (museum catalogue).

1 plastic poem titled "Poéme plastique"; 1 concrete poem titled "Blanc." In Marc Hallain et al., eds., *Le Créativité en noir et blanc*. Paris: Nouvelle Editions Polaires, 1973, pp. 72, 76.

1966 cutouts titled "Four Portraits of a Poet" and "Plastic Poem II, 1973"; also includes Feb. 15, 1974, note on plastic poetry. *Stereo Headphones* (Suffolk, Eng.), no. 6 (Summer 1974): 30–31.

1 plastic poem, untitled. In Fernando Millan and Jesús García Sánchez, eds., *La Escritura en libertad: antología de poesía experimental*. Madrid: Alianza Editorial, 1975, p. 198.

2 plastic poems, both titled "Poeme plastique." In G. J. Rook, ed., *Visual Poetry Anthology: 133 Poets from 25 Countries*. Utrecht: Uitgoverij Bert Bakker, 1975, n.p.

"Plastic Poem 1976" used as cover artwork since 1967 for Vladimir Nabokov's *The Real Life of Sebastian Knight*. New York: New Directions [1959].

3 plastic poems—1 untitled on cover, 1 titled "Strollers, 1969," and 1 in color titled "Forgotten Man, 1975," which was included as an insert in a special edition of 15 copies. *Stereo Headphones* (Suffolk, Eng.), no. 7 (Spring 1976): cover, p. 25, and insert.

6 plastic poems, titled "Plastic Poem 1966," "Plastic Poem 1966," "Plastic Poem 1973," "Plastic Poem 1975," "Plastic Poem 1975," "Plastic Poem 1969," respectively; Kitasono credited also as a contributing editor. In Julien Blaine, ed., *Doc(k)s* (Marseille), no. 7 (July 1977): 116–21.

4 plastic poems, titled "Op. 1969," "Komposition B 1967," "Plastikpoesie 1971," "Strollers [Wandertruppe] 1969"; also contains a concrete poem by L. C. Vinholes about Kitasono. In Uwe Obier, ed., *Japanische konkrete und visuelle Poesie* (museum catalogue). Recklinghausen, West Germany: Kunstverein Gelsenkirchen, 1978, n.p.

1 titled "Plastic Poem 1973." In James Laughlin, ed., *New Directions*, no. 34. New York: New Directions, 1977, p. 37.

2 plastic poems, titled "I am here" and "Moonlight Night in a Bag." *Delo* (Belgrade), 28, no. 4 (April 1982): 38–39.

3 plastic poems by Kitasono. *Aktuelle konkrete und visuelle Poesie aus Japan.* Siegen, West Germany: n.p., 1986, pp. 3–5 (exhibition catalogue).

7 plastic poems by Katue. *Plastic Poems: Kitasono Katue and the VOU Group.* Providence: Rhode Island School of Design, Museum of Art, 1986, n.p. (exhibition pamphlet).

1 plastic poem, untitled. In Uri Hertz, ed., *Third Rail* (Los Angeles), no. 9 (1988): 25.

5 plastic poems, 4 drawings, 1 diagrammatic poem. In Bob Moore, ed., *Nexus* (Dayton, Ohio: Wright State University), 25, no. 2 (Winter 1990): 46–49.

"Night of Figure," 1975. In Darin Cain, ed., *Nexus* (Dayton, Ohio: Wright State University), 25, no. 3 (Spring 1990): 63.

Papercut and drawing, "Four Portraits of a Poet." In Lawrence Ferlinghetti and Nancy Peters, eds., *City Lights Review*, no. 4. San Francisco: City Lights, 1990, p. 176.

Other Sources

Andō Ichirō, Tsuboi Shigeji, and Kihara Kōichi. "Zadankai: Kitasono Katue o bunseki suru" (Panel discussion: analyzing Kitasono Katue). *Shigaku* 6, no. 6 (July 1951): 76–95.

Balakian, Anna. *Surrealism: The Road to the Absolute.* New York: Noonday, 1959.

Barnhart, Michael A. *Japan Prepares for Total War: The Search for Economic Security, 1919–1941.* Ithaca, N.Y.: Cornell, 1987.

Barthes, Roland. *Writing Degree Zero.* Trans. Annette Lavers and Colin Smith. New York: Hill and Wang, 1968.

Brand, Michael. "Introduction." In exhibition pamphlet "Plastic Poems: Kitasono Katue and the VOU Group," Providence: Rhode Island School of Design, Museum of Art, 1986.

Breton, André. *What is Surealism? Selected Writings.* Ed. Franklin Rosemont. New York. Monad/Pathfinder, 1978.

Brotchie, Alastair, comp. *Surrealist Games.* Boston: Shambhala, 1993.

Burger, Peter. *Theory of the Avant-garde.* Minneapolis: University of Minnesota Press, 1984.

Chaleil, Max. "La Poésia apres le verbe." In *La Créativité en noir et blanc*. Paris: Nouvelles Editions Polaires, 1973.

Chiba Sen'ichi. *Gendai bungaku no hikaku bungaku-teki kenkyū* (Comparative literature research on modern literature). Yagi shoten, 1978.

―――. "Kitasono Katue." In *Nihon kindai bungaku daijiten* (Great dictionary of modern Japanese literature). Kōdansha, 1984, pp. 475–76.

Clüver, Claus. "Augusto de Campos' 'terremoto': Cosmogony as Ideogram." *Contemporary Poetry* 3, no. 1 (Winter 1978): 38–55.

―――. "Brazilian Concrete: Painting, Poetry, Time, and Space." In Zoran Konstantinovic, Ulrich Weisstein, and Steven Paul Scher, eds., *Proceedings of the IX Congress of the International Comparative Literature Association*, vol. 3, *Literature and the Other Arts*. Innsbrucker Beiträge zur Kulturwissenschaft. Innsbruck: Innsbrucker Gesellschaft zur Pflege der Geisteswissenschaften, 1981, pp. 207–13.

―――. "Languages of the Concrete Poem." In K. David Jackson, ed., *Transformations of Literary Language in Latin American Literature: From Machado de Assis to the Vanguards*. Austin: University of Texas, Department of Spanish and Portuguese, 1987, pp. 32–43.

de Campos, Haroldo, "Poesia concreta no Japão: Kitasono Katue." In literary supplement to *O Estado de São Paulo*, May 10, 1958.

Dimanche, André, ed. "Le Jeu de Marseille," Marseille: n.p., 1983. Reproduction of surrealist playing cards.

Dower, John. *War Without Mercy*. New York: Pantheon, 1986.

Drake, Chris. *Japanese Poetry as Universal Poetry: Nishiwaki Junzaburō, Translation, and* [review of Hirata's book] *"The Poetry and Poetics of Nishiwaki Junzaburō: Modernism in Translation."* Atomi English Studies 10. Saitama: Atomi College, 1997.

Ema Shōko. *Umoreshi no homura* (The flame of buried poems). Kōdansha, 1985.

Eysteinsson, Astradur. *The Concept of Modernism*. Ithaca, N.Y.: Cornell University Press, 1990.

Fenollosa, Ernest. *The Chinese Written Character as a Medium for Poetry*; 1920 in *Instigations*; 1936 with Ezra Pound's notes; bilingual edition, trans. Takata Tomi'ichi. Tokyo bijutsu, 1982.

Fujitomi Yasuo. *Kindai shijin hyōden: Kitasono Katue* (Critical biographies of modern poets: Kitasono Katue). Yūseidō, 1983.

―――. "Kitasono Katue no shi" (Kitasono Katue's poetry). In *Pantsu no kamisama* (God's underpants). TB Design kenkyūjo, 1979, pp. 123–38.

Fukuda Kazuya, *Nippon no kakyō* (Japan's ancestral home). Shinchōsha, 1993.

Hamana Yoshiharu. "Kitasono Katue ron" (On Kitasono Katue). In *Shironshū: gendaishi ni kansuru nanatsu no teoria* (Selection of poetry essays: seven theories on modern poetry). Shōshinsha, 1939.

Harada Osamu. "Kitasono Katue." In *Boku no bijutsu techō* (My art notebook). Parco, 1982.

Haruyama Yukio. "Poesiologiste Kitasono." *Rekishō*, no. 88 (1978): 12–14.

Havens, Thomas R. H. *Valley of Darkness: The Japanese People and World War II.* New York: Norton, 1978.

Higgins, Dick. *Pattern Poetry: Guide to an Unknown Literature.* Albany: State University of New York Press, 1987.

Hirata, Hosea. *The Poetry and Poetics of Nishiwaki Junzaburō.* Princeton: Princeton University Press, 1993.

Ise kyōdo kai, ed. "Kitasono Katue shihi konryū o kinen shite" (Commemorating the erection of a monument to Kitasono Katue). Pamphlet. Ise: Ise kyōdo kai, 1980.

Itō Shinkichi. Commentary. In Murano Shirō, ed., *Gendai Nihon shijin zenshū* (Collected poems of modern Japanese poets), vol. 13. Sōgensha, 1955.

Iwanari Tatsuya. "'Kuroi sorera no kuroi sorera': Kitasono Katue shōron" ("Black somethings' black somethings . . . ": critique of Kitasono Katue). *Gendai shi techō*, Oct. 1986, pp. 112–17.

Kagiya Yukinobu. "Kitasono Katue." In *Shijin Nishiwaki Junzaburō* (Poet Nishiwaki Junzaburō). Chikuma shobō, 1983.

Kambayashi Michio. "Zono-san no bishō" (Zono's smile). In *Kotoba to shijin* (Words and poets). Sunakoya shobō, 1989 (cover features an oil painting by Kitasono Katue).

Kamiya Tadataka. *Nihon no dada* (Japanese Dada). Kyōbunsha, 1987.

Karatani Kōjin. *Origins of Modern Japanese Literature.* Trans. Brett de Bary. Durham, N.C.: Duke University Press, 1993.

Kato, Shuichi. *A History of Japanese Literature*, vol. 3, *The Modern Years.* Trans. Don Sanderson. Tokyo, New York, and San Francisco: Kodansha, 1983.

Keene, Dennis. *Yokomitsu Riichi: Modernist.* Columbia University Press, 1980.

Keene, Donald. *Dawn to the West: Poetry, Drama, Criticism.* New York: Holt, Rinehart and Winston, 1984.

———. *Japanese Literature: An Introduction for Western Readers.* New York: Grove Press, 1955.

Kihara Kōichi. "Abangyarudo no shūen" (The death of the avant-garde). *Chikyū*, no. 34 (*bessatsu*) (Feb. 1962): 1–4.

Kinoshita Tsunetarō. "Shidan jihyō" (Comments on current poetry). *Mita bungaku*, Aug. 1941: 208–10.

Kitagawa Fuyuhiko, ed. and comm. *Gendaishi* (Modern poetry). 3 vols. Kadokawa shinsho, nos. 34–36. Kadokawa shoten, 1957.

Kodama, Sanehide, *American Poetry and Japanese Culture.* Redding Ridge, Conn.: Archon, 1984.

———. "Ezura Paundo" (Ezra Pound). In Fukuda Mitsuharu et al., eds., *Hikaku bungaku shiriizu: Ōbei sakka to Nihon kindai bungaku* (Comparative literature series: European and American writers and modern Japanese literature), vol. 5, *Eibei hen II* (Britain and America volume). Kyōiku Shuppan Center, 1975.

Kume Masao, ed., for Nihon Bungaku Hōkokukai. *Tsuji shishū* (Intersection poetry anthology). Hakkōsha Sugiyama shoten, 1943.

Kuroda Iri. *"How to Read: Kit Kat" (text in Japanese). *Will* (Keel Press), no. 1 (1981): 21–36.

———. "Modanizumu kara posutomodanizumu e" (From modernism to postmodernism). *Shiro* 24, no. 5 (Jan. 1987): 14–19.

———. "*Object kara *subject e mukau shi: Kitasono Katue" (Poems that face from object to subject: Kitasono Katue). *Gendaishi techō*, 1983.

Kuroda Saburō. "Kitasono Katue." In Itō Shinkichi et al., eds., *Gendai kanshō kōza* (Course on appreciating the modern), no. 9, *Modanizumu no kishu tachi* (The standard bearers of modernism). Kadokawa shoten, 1969.

Lahiri, Amar. *Japanese Modernism*. Hokuseidō Press, 1939.

———. *Japan Talks*. Hokuseidō Press, 1940.

———. *Mikado's Mission*. Japan Times, 1940.

Laughlin, James. "Editor's Note." *New Directions*, vol. 3. New York, 1938.

Linhartova, Vera. *Arts du Japon: Dada et Surréalisme au Japon*. Paris: Publications Orientalistes de France, 1987.

Matthews, J. H. *Toward the Poetics of Surrealism*. Syracuse, N.Y.: Syracuse University Press, 1976.

Mizusawa Tsutomu. "Japanese Dada and Constructivism: Aspects of the Early 1920s." In *Dada and Constructivism* (exhibition catalogue), pp. 25–32. Tokyo Shinbun, 1988.

Munroe, Alexandra. *Japanese Art After 1945: Scream Against the Sky*. New York: Harry Abrams, 1994.

Murano Shirō. "Kaisetsu" (Explanation). In Murano Shirō, ed., *Gendai shijin zenshū* (Collected poems of modern Japanese poets). Kadokawa, 1967, 13: 301–15.

———. "Kitasono Katue." In Kaneko Mitsuharu et al., eds., *Gendai shi kōza: Shi no kanshō* (Course on appreciating modern [Japanese] poetry). Sōgensha, 1950, pp. 133–41.

Myers, Ramon H., and Peattie, Mark R., eds. *The Japanese Colonial Empire, 1895–1945*. Princeton: Princeton University Press, 1984.

Nagayasu Shūichi. "Kitasono Katue to watashi" (Kitasono Katue and me). *Dorobune*, no. 6 (July 1986).

Nakano Ka'ichi. "Kitasono Katue ron" (Essay on Kitasono Katue). *Rekishō*, no. 88 (1978): 23–27.

————. *Modanizumu shi no jidai* (The age of modernist poetry). Hōbunkan, 1986.

————. *Zen'ei shi undō shi no kenkyū* (Research on the history of avant-garde poetry movements). Shinseisha, 1975.

Nihon Bungaku Hōkokukai, ed. *Bungei nenkan* (Literary arts annual). Tōkei shobō, 1943.

————. *Dai Tōa* (Greater East Asia). Kawade shobō, 1944.

Nihon kindai shika bungakukan. "Gendai shi no furontia—modanizumu no keifu ten" (The frontier of modern poetry: exhibit of modernism's genealogy). Archives of Japanese Modern Poetry, Morioka City, Iwate Prefecture, 1994 (pamphlet from exhibit on Kitasono Katue, Nishiwaki Junzaburō, and Takiguchi Shūzō).

Nishiwaki, Junzaburō. *Gen'ei: Selected Poems of Nishiwaki Junzaburō, 1894–1982*. Trans. Yasuko Claremont. University of Sydney East Asian series, 4. Sydney, Australia: University of Sydney Press and Wild Peony, 1991.

Noigandres (São Paulo; ed. Haroldo and Augusto de Campos et al.), no. 4 (Mar. 1958).

Okunari Tatsu. "Kitasono Katue *Kyōdo shiron* o yomu" (Reading Kitasono Katue's *Hometown Poetics* [1943]). Parts 1–19 of book-length ms. *GUI* 14, no. 37—20, no. 55 (Dec. 1992–Dec. 1998, ongoing).

————. "Kitasono Katue to Satie, 'no' no shikō ni tsuite" (Kitasono Katue and Satie, regarding the experiment with "no"). *GUI* 8, no. 20 (May 1986).

————. "Shi wa kijutsu no gaku dewa nai" (Poetry is not the study of description). *GUI* 8, no. 19 (Jan. 31, 1986): 82 ff.

Olson, Charles, ed. *Right Angle* (Washington, D.C.: The American University), 3. no. 1 (May 1949).

Omuka, Toshiharu. "David Burliuk and the Japanese Avant-garde." *Canadian-American Slavic Studies* 20, no. 1/2 (Spring–Summer 1986): 111–25.

————. "To Make All of Myself Boil Over: Tomoyoshi Murayama's Cons[c]ious Constructivism." In *Dada and Constructivism* (exhibition catalogue), pp. 19–24. Tokyo Shinbun, 1988.

Perloff, Marjorie. *The Poetics of Indeterminacy*. Princeton: Princeton University Press, 1981.

Pierre, José, ed. *Investigating Sex: Surrealist Research, 1928– 1932*. Trans. Malcolm Imrie. London and New York: Verso, 1992.

Poggioli, Renato. *The Theory of the Avant-garde*. Cambridge, Mass.: Harvard University Press, 1968.

Porteus, Hugh Gordon. *Criterion* (London), 18, no. 71 (Jan. 1939): 395–403.

Pound, Ezra. *Guide to Kulchur*. New York: New Directions, 1938.

————. "The VOU Club." *Townsman* (London), no. 1 (Jan. 1938): 4–9.

Rachewiltz, Mary de. "Postscript: In Place of a Note to Letter 71." In Sanehide Kodama, ed., *Ezra Pound and Japan*. Redding Ridge, Conn.: Black Swan, 1987, pp. 214–15.

Reck, Michael, *Ezra Pound: A Close Up*. New York: McGraw-Hill, 1967.

———. "Memoirs of a Parody Perry." In Sanehide Kodama, ed., *Ezra Pound and Japan*. Redding Ridge, Conn.: Black Swan, 1987.

Rexroth, Kenneth. "Literature." In R. M. Hutchins and M. J. Adler, eds., *The Great Ideas Today*. New York: Praeger, 1970, pp. 139–77.

———. "On Kitasono Katue." In Uri Hertz, ed., *Third Rail* (Los Angeles), no. 7 (1985–86).

Riffaterre, Michael. *Semiotics of Poetry*. Bloomington: Indiana University Press, 1978.

———. *Text Production*. Trans. Terese Lyons. New York: Columbia University Press, 1983.

Sakuramoto Tomio. *Hi no maru wa mite ita* (I saw the Rising Sun flag). Marujusha, 1982.

———. *Kūhaku to sekinin* (Blankness and responsibility). Kobayashi insatsu kabushiki gaisha shuppanbu, 1983.

———. *Shijin to sekinin* (Poets and responsibility). Kobayashi insatsu kabushiki gaisha shuppanbu, 1978.

———. *Shijin to sensō* (Poets and war). Kobayashi insatsu kabushiki gaisha shuppanbu, 1978.

Sasaki Kikyō. "Kitasono Katue to Kontakkusu [Contax]" (Kitasono Katue and the Contax [camera]). In Torii Shōzō, ed., *Trap* (Itō), no. 8 (Jan. 1988).

———. *Kitasono Katue to modanizumu zasshigun* (Kitasono Katue and modernism journals). Press Bibliomane, 1980.

Sawa Masahiro et al., eds. *Sakuhin de yomu gendai shi* (Reading modern poetry works). Hakuchisha, 1993.

Shimizu Toshihiko, Shimizu Masato, Fukuda Kazuhiko, and Kiyohara Etsushi, eds. *Kitasono Katue and VOU*. "Kitasono Katue and VOU" kankōkai, 1988.

Shiraishi Kazuko. "Kitasono Katue, yuku: keimō to bigaku" (Kitasono Katue: enlightenment and esthetics). *Shigeijutsu*, 1978.

———. *Kuroi hitsuji no monogatari: *personal poetry history* (Black Sheep Tale: personal poetry history). Jinbun shoin, 1996.

Shururearisumu dokuhon 2: shururearisumu no tenkai (Surrealism reader 2: the development of surrealism). Shichōsha, 1981.

Silverberg, Miriam. "The Modern Girl as Militant." In Gail Lee Bernstein, ed., *Recreating Japanese Women, 1600–1945*. Berkeley: University of California Press, 1991, pp. 239–66.

———. "Remembering Pearl Harbor, Forgetting Charlie Chaplin, and the Case of the Disappearing Western Woman: A Picture Story." *positions* 1, no. 1 (Spring 1993): 24–76.

Solt, John. "Forged Passports for a Borderless World: The Plastic Poems of Kitasono Katue" (with partial Japanese trans.: "Pasupo—to no renkinjutsu: bo—daresu no sekai e no purasutikku poemu"). In Tsuruoka Yoshihisa, ed., *Kitasono Katue zenshashinshū* (The complete photographs of Kitasono Katue). Tokyo: Chūsekisha, 1992, insert.

———. "Kitasono: East Asian Avant-gardist." In Uri Hertz, ed., *Third Rail* (Los Angeles), no. 7 (1985–86): 45–49.

———. "Kitasono Katue and the VOU Poets." In Uri Hertz, ed., *Third Rail* (Los Angeles), no. 9 (1988): 20–24.

———. "Mudai no mudai no mudai no mu" (Untitled's Untitled's Untitled's Un). *Gendai shi techō*, special issue: "Kitasono Katue: Kigō to forumu" (Kitasono Katue: sign and form), Nov. 1990.

———. "Nihilist in the Eraser: A Kitasono Retrospective." In Bob Moore, ed., *Nexus* (Dayton, Ohio: Wright State University), 25, no. 2 (Winter 1990).

———. "The Plastic Poems of Kitasono Katue." In exhibition pamphlet "Plastic Poems: Kitasono Katue and the VOU Group." Providence: Rhode Island School of Design, Museum of Art, 1986.

Stallworthy, Jon, ed. *The Oxford Book of War Poetry*. Oxford: Oxford University Press, 1984.

Suwa Yū. "Kitasono Katue ten: Purasutikku na mono" (Kitasono Katue exhibit: plastic things). *Bijutsu techō* (Bijutsu shuppansha), 36, no. 530 (Aug. 1984).

Takahashi Yōji, ed. *Kindai shijin hyakunin* (One hundred modern poets). *Taiyō* bessatsu. Heibonsha, 1978.

Tamura Ryūichi. "Kitasono Katue cho—*Garasu no kuchibige*" (Kitasono Katue author: *Glass Mustache*). *Tsukue* (Kinokuniya), 7, no. 11 (Nov. 1956): 29–30.

Tanaka, Stefan, *Japan's Orient: Rendering Pasts into History*. Berkeley: University of California Press, 1993.

Tatehata Seki. "Nihon no shikaku shi no undō ni tsuite: *VOU* to *ASA* o chūshin ni" (On the Japanese visual poetry movement: focusing on *VOU* and *ASA*). *Kokuritsu kokusai bijutsukan kiyō* 1 (1983).

Teitelbaum, Matthew, ed. *Montage and Modern Life, 1919–1942*. Cambridge, Mass.: MIT Press, 1992.

Tipton, Elise. *Japanese Police State: Tokkō in Interwar Japan*. Honolulu: University of Hawai'i Press, 1990.

Tokyo Metropolitan Museum of Photography. *The Age of Modernism* (photography exhibition bilingual catalogue). 1995–96.

Trumbull, Randolph. "The Shanghai Modernists." Ph.D. diss., Stanford University, 1989.

Tsurumi Shunsuke. *An Intellectual History of Wartime Japan, 1931–1945.* London and New York: KPI, 1986.

Uchibori Hiroshi. *Bon shoten no maboroshi: modanizumu shuppansha no hikari to kage* (The vision of Bon Books: the light and shadow of modernism publishing). Hakuchisha, 1992.

Vinholes, L. C. "Intercâmbio, Presença e Influência da Poesia Concreta Brasileira no Japão." *Anais* (Tokyo), no. 9 (1975).

Watanabe Masaya. "Furusato ni tatta Kitasono Katue shihi" (The Kitasono Katue poem monument erected in his hometown). In Nakano Ka'ichi, ed., *Rekishō,* no. 95 (1981).

Wescher, Herta. *Collage.* New York: Abrams, 1971.

Won, Ko. *Buddhist Elements in Dada: A Comparison of Tristan Tzara, Takahashi Shinkichi, and Their Fellow Poets.* Albany: State University of New York Press, 1977.

Yamanaka Sansei (Tiroux). "Kitasono Katue hen" (Kitasono Katue volume). In Kitagawa Fuyuhiko et al., eds., *Gendai shi kanshō: Shōwa ki* (Appreciations of modern [Japanese] poetry: Shōwa period). Daini shobō, 1951, pp. 91–107.

Yoshimoto Takaaki. *Jojō no ronri* (The logic of lyricism). Miraisha, 1963.

———. *Sengoshi shiron* (Postwar poetics). Yamato shobō, 1983.

Yoshioka Minoru. "Atarashii shi e no mezame—Kitasono Katue: Ensui shishū" (Awakening to new poetry—Kitasono Katue's "Conical Poems"). *Eureka,* Sept. 1975, pp. 144–45.

———. "Danshō mitsu to ippen no shi" (Three literary fragments and one poem). In pamphlet (*shiori*) accompanying *Kitasono Katue zenshishū.* Chūsekisha, 1983.

INDEX

HARVARD EAST ASIAN MONOGRAPHS

(* out-of-print)